BREAK
POINT

BREAK POINT

A NOVEL BY

ILIE NASTASE

ST. MARTIN'S PRESS • NEW YORK

This novel is a work of fiction. The events depicted herein have
never occurred. Names, characters, places, and incidents either are
the product of the author's imagination or are used fictitiously.

Design by Victoria Hartman

Library of Congress Cataloging in Publication Data

Nastase, Illie, 1946–
    Break point.

    I. Title.
PR9170.R63N37   1986   823   86-3673
ISBN 0-312-09514-7

First Edition

10   9   8   7   6   5   4   3   2   1

CONTENTS

PART I

THE
FRENCH
OPEN

"Field of the Cloth of Green"

ONE

He drove with his left hand, pivoting the big car smoothly southwest, through the streets of Paris, while the other wandered languorously over the girl's thigh. The white Rolls Royce "Silver Streak" progressed almost silently away from the Seine and along the Rue La Fontaine. Light drops of late May rain fell sporadically on the windscreen as the wipers smoothed them systematically away. They had just passed the Orphelins and he could see the intersection with the Avenue Mozart up ahead.

"You aren't listening to me." There was a cautious pout in the girl's voice.

Isolated behind his sunglasses, the man admitted to himself that she was right. He had pulled up the collar of his raincoat and adjusted the felt hat over his forehead to shut himself off more completely from the world of streets, trees, the clamor of Paris—and beautiful women. He had a tough tennis match coming up, a blinding need to concentrate. He felt sorry for the girl, so pretty, so earnest, trying so hard.

"The Rue Fontaine," she said, leaning close, "is a virtual Guimard museum. There on the right, you'll find the Castle Béranger, which won first prize as the best façade in the city of Paris in 1900. Guimard was our French Gaudí . . . he produced wonderful erotico-vegetal architecture."

The man smiled to himself. Her mentioning Gaudí, the turn-of-the-century Spanish architect, made him think of Barcelona in early October, a court surface that was too dry, returning balls that came too fast. Gaudí . . . and this girl with the fiery red hair sitting next to him, her voice hoarser now from his

caresses, trying to repeat the lesson in architecture recently
learned at the Camondo School, her alma mater, which specialized in educating young debutantes without specialty.

"That's number eighty-five over there," she said. "The house
Guimard built for himself."

She looked at him from the corner of her eye, tracing his
angular features, the slightly hawk-like nose and high cheekbones that revealed his Slavic origins. Despite the seven-day
growth of blond beard, the skin stretched over the hard set of
his jaws looked almost translucent. She wanted so much to
touch it again . . .

"What are you thinking about?" she asked.

He didn't answer. Only his tanned hand stroked the girl's
thigh. It was always like that, an hour before a match; looking
vaguely pleasant was the best he could do—he was far away and
the girl beside him was fading into one of his "ghosts from the
night before." She was a beauty, not easy to forget, and all he
had to do was close his eyes to remember last night, the curves
of her body under his hand, her firmness and her softness, her
lovely willingness to please. Now he had to detach.

The road to failure was paved with beautiful distractions. He
had seen it happen to player after player—Milo Tigrid, Armando Reyes, Mikhail Polak, Will Channer. It would not happen to him.

The girl leaned forward to switch on the radio, and an old
Beatles song burst forth, grating on his nerves, jolting him from
his half sleep. He reached forward, abruptly turned off the
music. The girl tried to hide her confusion by resettling herself
on the seat, showing a flash of pretty knees. She had lost him;
she didn't know why. Less happily now, her voice tense with
resignation, she went on:

"On the right is one of the few Métro exits designed by
Guimard that have managed to survive modernization. Most of
the others were destroyed by the city's administrators—those
arrogant Philistines. It's a real masterpiece, don't you think?
One day the whole thing will be in the Louvre."

"Porte d'Auteuil," he said finally. "We're nearly there."

Up ahead, on a billboard, there appeared a giant photo reproduction of the face of Terry Laville, advertising Ryker tennis equipment. Laville wore his famous Indian headband. His teeth looked huge, and his steel-gray eyes seemed faintly crossed. Laville was his opponent today, at Stade Roland-Garros.

"Isn't that the man you fought with? Last night?"

"Yes."

"Why won't you tell me what it was about?"

"Laville's bigger than I am. He likes to drag our rivalry off the court."

"You're not taking me seriously!" She was pouting again.

He smiled sadly to himself, because she was so young.

She tried to keep the conversation light, cheery. "It must be exciting to travel to so many places, playing tennis. Where do you play next?"

"Only my manager knows."

"Will you play in Monte Carlo? I was there last summer, for a holiday. I would love to meet the Prince, or the Princess. Did you ever meet Princess Grace?"

"Yes."

"What was she like?"

"She was very beautiful. Like you."

The girl bit her lip. "Am I going to see you again?"

He turned to face her at last, but his eyes were far away from the pretty girl in the passenger seat. "I would like that."

She was thrilled. "When?"

But the man was watching a Peugeot that was parked at the curb. He had no answer for her.

Evelyne Dumont was sitting at the wheel of the idling Peugeot 604, an elegant slate-colored limousine. The coach work had just been meticulously polished after a brief rain shower two hours before, over Clignancourt.

In the rearview mirror, she watched the Rolls arriving. Nervously, she swept back a strand of blonde hair from her forehead and bit her lips to make them fuller and redder. Today the man had to notice her. It was time that she became more to him than the driver who provided him with the same, eternally renewed Peugeot every day. But none of that was in the contract he had signed with the car manufacturers; it specified only that he would arrive and leave Roland-Garros at the wheel of their 604. So she would have to amend things a little, write her own contract, to take care of "the extras."

Evelyne had plotted and schemed for weeks to get this job, pulling as many strings as she could in the marketing company that had organized the endorsement deal. She had even slept with the manager in charge of the project. When Evelyne confessed her motives, he was stunned. "You did this so you could drive that sonofabitch around for two weeks?"

What could a man of fifty, with a paunch, two cars, two children, and a dog, understand about Evelyne's obsession? At least the manager had not, eventually, been without a sense of humor. He let her keep her job; he gave her what she wanted.

Now she was waiting again for the man in the Rolls to see her. She knew that she was beautiful and men had very willingly proved this to her—gifts, favors, even money—but she had driven this man twice a day for over a week and he seemed to be blind to any of her obvious attractions.

The Rolls pulled up several yards behind the 604. Evelyne had twisted the rearview mirror so that she could follow the approach of the car. She saw him step out and walk toward her. He wore scuffed white tennis shoes, white tennis socks with red stripes, and his legs were bare beneath the Bogart trench coat. As he approached the Peugeot, he took off his soft hat, freeing the striking blond mane which had become a part of his myth —King Koras, the Samson of the Courts. He opened the door, climbed into the front seat next to her. As he adjusted the wheel, he removed his sunglasses.

"Hello, young lady."

"Hello."

"It's turning out to be a nice day, after all."

"Yes. It's lovely."

It was always difficult to place his accent exactly. He was fluent in six languages, and could make himself understood in five others. He seemed to change the accent as he pleased.

His name was Pantakoras Belynkas—Koras, for short—as the Rolls heralded on its orange-and-white number plates: KORAS

ONE, NEW YORK CITY. He placed the Ray-Bans gently on the tip
of his nose, and sighed.

"Now I have to remember how to start this thing."

He had asked them to give him an automatic transmission—
more practical for driving in the city.

Evelyne lounged back in her seat, leaning against the door,
watching his clumsy attempts at starting the car. The Peugeot
gave a start and glided forward. As they turned into the Avenue
de la Porte d'Auteuil, Evelyne had time to notice the silhouette
of a young woman leaving the Rolls, walking quickly, holding
a white handkerchief to her face as if she were upset, heading
toward a taxi stand.

The crowds grew thicker as they approached Roland-Garros.
People pointed to the car and its driver. For Evelyne, the ritual
of arriving at the stadium was fabulous. For the space of several
hundred yards, she could savor the illusion that she had always
been there, accompanying someone who embodied the living
glory of the grand prix tournaments, one of the gods of professional tennis. No one had to know she was his companion only
by contract. She had already had the thrill of seeing photos of
herself in *Paris Match,* captioned as "the mysterious blonde
who accompanies Koras to victory." And as he fought his way
up the ladder and toward the finals at Roland-Garros, an event
full of prestige, she had hopes of getting even closer.

They were only about a hundred yards away from the stadium now, and the crowd was almost solid. Koras tooted his
horn. When the people on the sidewalk recognized the impatient driver, the enthusiasts among them greeted him with
shouts of encouragement: "Koras, you are the greatest! Hey,
King Koras!" He smiled at them behind the safety of the closed
windows. The blonde girl smiled too, letting herself forget that
she was merely a gadget that came with the car, courtesy of
Peugeot.

Seeing a few photographers among the crowd, Koras slowed
to a strolling pace and rolled down his window, to keep the sun
from reflecting on their camera lenses. Koras knew this part of
the pageant well. He and Evelyne played their parts nicely:

himself at the wheel, mysterious behind dark sunglasses; and she beside him, looking beautiful and elegant.

He pulled up beside the Suzanne Lenglen Gate and parked the car in front of the locker rooms. "Thank you, Mademoiselle Dumont," he said, getting out.

"You are welcome, m'sieu." She got out, too, to stand beside him. "Good luck today."

"Thank you." He seemed very formal, very gentlemanly. "I'm going to need luck."

"Your match is against Terry Laville, right?"

"Correct." He smiled, but his eyes seemed distant. "In a week, you have become a tennis specialist."

Evelyne found herself blushing. "It is an exciting game."

He stood looking down at her. "Each year, the crowds wait."

"For what?"

"For younger and younger magicians."

"But you, Monsieur Koras, you're not old."

That made him smile. He said a formal goodbye, and they arranged to meet after the match, again a part of his contract with her company. Standing beside the car, she watched him walk off, looking lonely, his bare legs vulnerable beneath the hem of the coat. He was full of surprises. She had no idea he would think himself old.

Koras stepped inside the gate to find Jack Di Rocca waiting. Di Rocca was sturdy and powerful, with a thick chest and burly arms. His black beard was neatly trimmed, to hide a single streak of gray, and his dark hair was cut short. When he didn't dress in tennis clothes, Di Rocca always wore a coat and tie. He owned three warm-up suits, all dark blue, piped in red-and-white stripes, to display the fact that he was an American star.

Koras, born in New York, felt like a gypsy, a jet-setting citizen of the world. If he was at home anywhere, it was in Paris. Di Rocca, also a native of New York, liked to advertise that he was an American. He was thirty-two, two years younger than Koras.

Koras noted the warm-up suit. "You must have won."

Di Rocca grinned. "Yeah. On to the quarters, like they say. If you have a minute, I'd like to talk."

"What's on your mind, Jack?"

Di Rocca walked a couple of steps with Koras, keeping pace, before answering. "Sally Vicenti."

Sally Vicenti was a name from Koras's past, those dangerous immigrant streets, the start of the sixties, a time of ducktail haircuts, Saturdays at Yankee Stadium or at Aqueduct, grinning Italian teenagers in their flashy fishtail cars, the beautiful flickering legs of the girls, and himself, a lonely Lithuanian kid with a trick knee, a laughable name that no one could pronounce, and a magical talent for stickball.

"Is Sally out of jail?"

Di Rocca laughed. "That was a long time ago, Koras. He's out, and he's sitting pretty. Sally wants to make contact with you."

"What for?"

Di Rocca stepped closer. "He thought it would be a good way to start. Three New York boys, immigrant kids with something in common, talking a little business." Koras looked around at a pretty girl passing. She wore a yellow dress, lifted up by the breeze. The girl smiled at him, and Koras smiled back. "You make it sound poetic, Jackie."

"Hey." Di Rocca grinned.

"The last time I saw Sally, it was in front of the Sherry Netherland. He was so fat he couldn't squeeze into a limo. There was a call girl with him. He was so out of shape, waving at me made him break into a wheeze."

"He recognized you, didn't he?"

"Sure. He yelled at me and called me Panties, just like the old days."

"Sally, he never forgets a face. His mind is like a video camera."

Koras stopped. They were near the locker room. He could hear the murmur of the crowd out for some sun, an afternoon's diversion. Diversion, that was the story of his career. "So, what's up?"

"Sally had a heart attack, maybe you heard, so he decided to take up sports for his health. He wound up on a tennis court, staring up girls' dresses. He wasn't as bad at tennis as he was at golf, so he got himself a membership at the Oyster Bay Club. He met some hackers from Long Island, Saturday-morning players from Wall Street, and he was able to exchange favors, place a couple bets, you know."

Koras nodded. "I should have seen it coming, Jackie. Sally's setting up a bucket shop in big-time tennis."

Di Rocca grinned. "Could be a real money-maker."

"Don't tell me," Koras said. "In the fall, right after the U.S. Open, we'll have 'Monday Night Tennis.' We'll have bettors in side streets all across America, putting their hard-earned wages on the point spread in the third set between Laville and Davey Cooper."

"It's no joke, Koras. There's big money coming on board. A ton."

"And Sally wants to get control, is that it?"

"Something like that."

"What does he want with me?"

"To build an organization. He knew you. From the old days. He likes people he can count on."

"I used to hit the stickball right through Sally's brother, until he learned not to call my mother names. Is he still around?"

"Joey, he got killed."

"He was bound to." Koras glanced over his shoulder as a security guard passed. "What do they want?"

"Information. Talk. A trade here and there."

"What kind?"

"Winners. Losers. Predictions."

Koras shook his head. Sally Vicenti was a hood, with the morals of a pack rat. There would be real money in the pool. "How much?"

"Sal's coming in conservative right now. Half a million, as a test merely."

"What kind of a test?"

"Well, you remember Sally. He hates to lose. He'll play safe, quiet, cards close to the chest. This will be very secure, for everyone connected."

"I don't have the handle on handicapping. You know that. I picked Armando to win at Monte Carlo. He lost in straight sets."

"Sally still values your opinion. He knows you need time to think it over, and he wants to have a sit-down when you get to New York."

Koras grinned. "The money's against him if he waits until the finals."

"Hey, you understand the game from the inside, King. He trusts you, from the street and all. With you on the team, ranked number one, he's got to come in a winner."

Koras knew what Sally really wanted, which was control of the game, so he could place bets and make sure his people won money. Two years ago, a Miami syndicate had raised a quarter of a million dollars to bet on Wimbledon. As a result, two bookmakers had died, and the newspapers had raised hell. It said a lot about how big tennis had become, if Sally Vicenti was moving in. "Sally wants me to call the final here, that's what you're saying?"

Di Rocca nodded. "He'd make it worth your while. He's been asking around, the word is that you're a little short of cash, because of the debt service on that fancy real estate."

Koras felt a momentary twinge of panic, a memory of running through a dirty street, looking back, pale green streetlights, harsh breathing, the boyhood terror of being pursued. "Tell Sally I think Davey Cooper will win. That's free."

"Come on. Cooper's a hard-court player!"

"He's playing better, and his mother's back in the States."

"I can't tell Sally that. He'd think I was crazy."

"Then we'd better not work together."

Di Rocca grabbed his arm. "Maybe Laville will get lucky this week and win the French."

"He'll have to drop something in my beer first."

Di Rocca gave Koras a shrewd look. He remembered the time in Houston when Laville had dropped something into his own beer before the quarters at River Oaks. He was surprised Koras knew about that. He tried to get back on track. "At the Round of Sixteen, twenty grand. At the quarters, ten. Cash. To keep the tax guys in the dark."

"No thanks." Koras turned away again and started toward the locker room. The time was growing closer for his match, and he needed to focus on how he would play Terry Laville.

"Is that no for an answer?"

"Yes. It's no for an answer."

"Hey, then good luck out there."

Di Rocca walked away, arms swinging, burly shoulders hunched. Koras opened the heavy door and went inside.

For the thousandth time, Koras immersed himself in the empty sonority, the disinfected smell common to locker rooms the world over. He thought back to the first time he had played in the French Nationals—just out of the army, barely twenty years old, he had gone no further than the fourth round. In those days, the stadium still retained some of the faded charm of an old and venerable country club, with all its discomforts. But now everything at Roland-Garros had been remodeled, reorganized, re-equipped. The locker rooms looked like a cross between an Icelandic sauna and an operating room. The scene was functional, but devoid of the anachronistic appeal that had once surrounded the sport.

Across the room, Terry Laville was deep in conversation with his manager, Archer Bell, a round-faced energetic man who owned a basketball team in Chicago. Bell, who had meaty shoulders and a pronounced stomach, exuded the power of an entire conglomerate. His picture had twice been on the cover of national magazines, once when his team won the NBA title, a second time during the huge drug scandal that had swept basketball three years ago. In both cover portraits, Archer Bell had been smiling. He was a winner, and he had brought Terry Laville up from number 73 on the Association of Tennis Professionals computer to number 7. As Bell always said during press interviews, they weren't finished just yet.

As he passed his opponent, Koras greeted Laville, who answered with a forced smile that barely concealed his anger and frustration.

"Sorry about the mix-up last night," Koras said.

Laville's face tightened, bringing the high Indian cheekbones into prominence. "Get lost, and don't try any of this psych-out shit on me right before a match, okay?"

"Okay." Koras wanted to ask about Nora, Laville's wife, but now was not the time. The Lavilles' marriage was a well-known battleground, and Nora Laville was constantly flying home, then reappearing. She drank too much, and the circuit gossips wondered how long the marriage would last.

Koras turned to go, but Laville got up from the bench and took him aside. His eyes were crazy. He spoke in a harsh whisper. "Isn't my wife a little young for you?"

"I won't dignify that with a reply, Terry. There's nothing between Nora and me."

"If you say so, pal." Laville started to walk off. "But you better watch your step in dark alleys, even with all the Paris cops around."

Angry now, Koras broke away from a grinning Laville and walked over to his coach, the great Australian player Will Channer, who was sitting on a bench in front of a TV mounted on wall brackets. Channer was six feet tall, with wavy hair, solid legs, and the wide shoulders of a distance runner. For the last ten years, his craggy Australian face had looked the same. As Koras came up, Channer flipped the channel changer from the Peter Abraham match.

"I see Terry's in his usual restrained and cheerful mood."

Koras grinned. Channer had a great sense of humor, and was always pulling Koras back to a stable reality. "Just a few friendly words between guys who really dislike each other. How's Pete doing?"

"It's the best he's played," Channer said. "But he keeps see-sawing."

Peter Abraham was the President of the Association of Tennis Professionals. He was ranked number 20 on the ATP computer, and he was now winning his match in the Round of Sixteen. There had been a rain delay yesterday, so Abraham was finishing up today, as the quarterfinals got under way. As Channer changed channels, the handsome face of Armando Reyes came into view. Reyes was on the Court Central, playing the French hopeful, Ivan Leroy.

"That's Pete's style. When he's on, the see-saw can drive you crazy."

"It's better to put the ball away," Channer said.

The two men watched the screen for a moment, before Will pulled out his notebook for a last-minute strategy session.

"How's the knee?"

Koras flexed his right knee, which had been giving him trouble since he was fifteen. "It's better."

"Laville looked mad enough to chew nails."

"Yes."

"Someday he'll take a run for you in a dark street."

"Funny. That's what he just said."

Channer flipped the channel back to the Abraham match. Abraham was toying with his opponent. "We've got to avoid the Abraham Syndrome today."

"Yes." Koras nodded.

"It's a sign of age. You think you're losing power, so you hold off. It happened to me."

"Pete's only twenty-eight."

"Didn't Tony Roche have his elbow problem about then?"

"Don't think about elbow problems. Or knee problems."

"Okay."

Koras knew what Channer was talking about. In the late fifties and early sixties, Channer had dominated the men's professional game. Writers compared his power to that of Vines, Budge, and Sedgman. He had been raised in the Australian Outback on a sheep station, and had entered the game right after the Hoad-Rosewall heyday. His chief weapons had been a serve that cracked like a whip and a forehand that was flat and punishing. Because of a ready smile for the cameras, tennis fans had taken to the friendly Australian. His third year as a professional, Channer had won Wimbledon. His fifth year, he had won the Australian, the British, and the U.S. titles. His loss of the French, to fellow Australian Roy Emerson, had prevented him from taking the Grand Slam.

A nagging shoulder injury had forced Will Channer into three operations. He had come back after the first two, but the third operation had convinced him to retire. He ran a tennis camp for a while in Texas, then another one in New Hampshire. Four years ago, Channer had returned to the circuit to coach Koras. They had been perfecting Koras's serve ever since.

Earlier this morning, they had worked out at the Polo, but the sudden showers had cut them off before they had finished. Now, because of that, Channer was exasperated. All winter, they had worked on Koras's serve, which was still erratic under pressure because of some minute changes in the grip, from Continental to Backhand, then back to Continental. One grip allowed more control, the other more power. Koras wanted to serve like Tilden. Channer thought he should follow the style of Jack Kramer. The ideal, of course, was a controlled serve that was packed with power, a real stinger of a weapon, but so far the two men had not found the right combination. Koras remembered icy days at his home on Long Island, the winter wind howling outside, while he and Will struggled with the serve on Koras's specially constructed indoor court. Two weeks ago, Koras had lost to Laville in Rome, at the Foro Italico. Channer thought the loss had been due to the serve, so they had continued to experiment once they got to Paris. Today, as a test, Koras would play Laville in the quarterfinals. Because the French title was the second step to the Grand Slam, both Koras and his coach felt the pressure.

Will flipped the pages in his notebook, going over strategies.

"All right, we'll play our Mister Laville down the middle. Hit deep, and then come to the net behind the shot. Try some lobs when he's facing the sun, and try them early in the match, to jolt his confidence. The same goes for the drop shot. And try coming in on the high balls to his backhand. Laville hates high balls."

"All right." Koras had heard the advice before, but he made mental notes. That was what a coach was for—to remind you about the basics.

"Hit the slice deep, with more pace than you used in Rome. It set the ball up there."

"The Italian clay is slower."

Channer nodded. "Okay." He slapped Koras on the arm, in a comradely way. "How's your mental health?"

"The lady departed," Koras said.

Channer smiled. "Where do you find them?"

"They find me."

Channer grinned, and turned back to the television. The coaching session was over, and Koras needed some time to himself. As he removed the raincoat and threw it onto a chair, Koras wished that Channer hadn't reminded him he was thirty-four. Was this his last real shot at the Grand Slam?

Koras sat down on a bench and leaned against the wall. Taking some deep breaths, he let his arms and legs dangle. With his eyes closed, he began to concentrate on his breathing, counting slowly from zero to five, inhaling through his nose; then to ten, keeping the air in his lungs; and then to twenty, exhaling through his mouth. He had learned to control his respiration in this way since he had discovered yoga, during the Italian championships two years before, with an Italian countess as deep as the dead of a Roman night. After the games, she would take him back to her palace, a block off the Via Veneto, and in a sitting room as large as the Foro Italico she had taught him the "Scorpio in Lotus" position beneath the disapproving stares of her endless ancestors, emerging from their portraits on her walls.

At first, that scene had amused Koras. But eventually the beautiful black eyes of the Countess had become too demanding, and he had been forced to make his exit from her life and the endless distractions it offered. But he had used her techniques ever since to increase his self-control.

The next year, he remembered, he had chosen to play in the Bavarian championships, which took place at the same time as those in Rome. Bavaria was less strenuous on his preparation for the important internationals which followed—Paris, Wimbledon, New York—but, as usual, material considerations had also weighed. His manager, Frank Fenwick, had been negotiating an important contract with a German construction company, so Koras's presence in Munich had been an important diplomatic move. They had offered him $600,000 over a period of four years, on condition that he abandon his Rolls for some prestigious German auto during his rounds in the States. He had thought of the lovely Countess, waiting eagerly for him in her sitting room, and the thought had made him sad. She had read about his Bavarian tournament in the papers and had sent him a telegram that said simply, "I wait."

This year, Koras had returned to Rome, but her gate had been locked and she had not appeared at the tournament. He had asked about the Countess, and someone had said she was away, refreshing herself in some mountain fastness of India or Tibet.

Her smile had been maddening, and she possessed a truly wicked body . . .

Koras opened his eyes. Will Channer had stopped twisting the dial and was now engrossed in the match on the first court, where Armando Reyes, nicknamed the Peruvian Playboy, was beating the young Frenchman Ivan Leroy. Even though Leroy was a finalist at last year's Roland-Garros, there was little hope for him this year. Injuries were part of the problem. At the beginning of the season, he had sprained his right shoulder, which slowed down the pace of his shots. Unwilling to disappoint his public, the popular French player had fought bravely for every ball, plunging for the most desperate ones, only to miss the easiest.

"Leroy is giving it everything," Channer said.

"He's always had a great heart," Koras said.

"If he keeps pushing, it means another injury. Then he won't play Wimbledon."

"He hates the grass, anyway."

Koras stared at the screen, where Armando Reyes was amassing points with an ease that was staggering. So far, in Paris, Reyes was playing in the Zone, a nickname borrowed from the TV series "The Twilight Zone." Playing in the Zone, or "zoning," meant a player was in a no-miss state beyond hypnotism, where his racket could do no wrong. Armando Reyes was a devout Catholic, so he referred to his own personal Zone as "a state of grace." Now, as Koras watched, Leroy saved a match point, then one more. A television close-up of his face showed he was white with pain. The score was deuce, but the Frenchman's energy was spent. Although his honor was intact, it was clear that he had lost all hope of victory.

Watching Leroy's struggle, Koras rubbed his right knee and again remembered how elbow problems had driven Tony Roche, the great Australian, out of professional tennis. He wanted Armando to win, but he felt great sympathy for the Frenchman.

Behind him, a loud voice called: "Watch out! Today's the day of the Paris freak show!"

Koras saw Milovan Tigrid, the Mad Montenegrin, approaching from the showers. Milo was wrapped in one bright red towel and carried another, which he used to scrub himself vigorously. Water drops glistened on his hairy back and shoulders. "Scarlet," he bellowed. "To mask my blushing cheeks if a girl were to find her way by chance into the little boys' locker room. . . ."

Milovan Tigrid, whom everyone on the circuit called Milo, was an enormous Yugoslavian who had descended from the mountains of Montenegro, had crossed national frontiers, and was now living in less rugged countries off a combination of his immense charm and his immense strength.

Other globe-trotting Yugoslavs with similar talents had become wrestlers or football players or mercenaries. But Milo, who was quicker of foot and brighter of mind, chose to try his hand at a more elegant, less strenuous sport. Ten years before, he had been the reigning tennis champion for two straight years, and he was still considered to be one of the most brilliant players of all time. Although ranked twenty-eighth in the world, he continued to do the circuit rounds imperturbably, having transformed his will to win and his legendary talent into a one-man tennis show, perfected, or so it seemed, for his amusement alone. When he played, the crowds and officials could always be sure that some extracurricular event would interrupt the placidity of the games. At White City, back in January, Milo had come onto the court accompanied by a tame orangutan, dressed in top hat and tails, and had tried to seat the animal in the umpire's stand.

Milo's fans were overjoyed with his antics. The officials, more often than not, reacted with heavy penalties. So far this year, Milo's fines totaled more than six thousand dollars.

People who had known Milo at his peak were divided about his decision to continue playing professionally. On good days, he demonstrated flashes of the artistry and genius that had made him a member of the Top Ten for almost a decade. On bad days, he resorted to being a clown. And tennis aficionados knew that beneath the agile clown there lurked a desperate man.

He knew what Milo felt—the madness, the whirlwind of the circuit, endless flights in the dead of night, finishing a tournament on Sunday and flying a thousand miles to another tournament that started at noon on Monday. It was Australia in January, then Japan, Hawaii, Florida, while all the time one thought of Rome, changing from American hard courts to slow European clay, and the preparation for Paris. And then Paris rolled around, and while one suffered on the slow clay there were thoughts of Wimbledon, and changing to the erratic grass surface, and then, lurking behind everything, the U.S. Open in New York, the gaudiest and richest tournament of them all. The madness of the circuit pressured you to keep going. It was addictive.

"Well, are you ready for Davey?" Koras asked.

"Aha!" Milo took a karate fighter's stance. "Bring on the Stupid One!"

Koras smiled. He knew there was no chance that his old friend could beat Davey Cooper, who was ranked number 4 on the ATP computer. And yet, miracles still happened. "Well, best of luck." He shook Milo's hand.

"Tigrid plays for the hearts of the women."

"That's your big secret, Milo."

Milo turned to stare at Koras. "What do you think of our glorious Princess taking up with an Arab?"

Koras knew his friend was talking about Abdul Saadi, the latest conquest of Princess Athena von Heidelberg. Koras had seen Saadi around, but they had not yet been introduced. "How long has it been now?"

"Weeks. Perhaps even months. They met in Los Angeles, while I was winning my exhibition at Pauley Pavilion. In Honolulu, she was alone, seeking companionship, which I tried to provide. In Rome, she was with Saadi. Her choice cannot be explained with logic."

Koras grinned. "Because you were available?"

Milo thumped his chest, and then leaned down closer to Koras's ear. "A pox on wealthy Arabs. I hear he is doing a capitalist maneuver on Sport City, what you profiteers call a leveraged buyout."

Koras laughed out loud. Milo's perspective on economics was a mixture of opportunism, Karl Marx, and J. Pierpont Morgan. He paid lip service to communism, but only went back home for special holidays, or when his mother was ill and called for her son. "What circus treats have you planned for today?"

Milo stood up to stare again in the mirror, grinning. "They will have to wait and see, until mighty Tigrid takes the court."

"Keep them in suspense, right?"

"Precisely. As the great Jaroslav Drobny before me." Drobny, a brilliant player from Prague, Czechoslovakia, had begun his career in 1938 on the slow courts of Roland-Garros, and had finally won Wimbledon in 1954 by beating Ken Rosewall in four sets. Drobny was Milo's hero against the onslaught of capitalism. Now he pranced in front of the mirror, flexing and making faces like a Zulu witch doctor. He heard his name on the intercom, calling him out to the courts. He winked at Koras, who was watching Milo in the mirror, and then he secured the towel about his middle and ran screaming from the room.

"Mad," Will Channer said.

"One of us," Koras said.

The girl on the closed-circuit television screen spent eleven minutes and thirty-one seconds under the shower spray, the time clocked in infinite precision by the solid-gold timepiece of Abdul Saadi's grandfather. The watch and its chain had been given to the grandfather, a Bedouin sheik, by Sir Walter Drummond, a petroleum geologist whose skill made the Saadi family rich beyond their wildest dreams. The watch had been passed down from father to son, until it came to rest in the hands of its present owner, Abdul Saadi, at thirty-one the head of Sahara Sports, Ltd.

Waiting made Abdul restless.

The television picture was in color. The system was Japanese. It had excellent resolution, sound that was crystal-clear, and a special tint control that brought out the magical luster of a young girl's skin. Saadi was a busy man. Technology helped him get through the day.

In each of his hotels, in the major cities of the world, the same system had been installed.

When the girl came out, dripping, reaching for a thick yellow towel while she pushed back the wet hair from her face, Saadi was reminded of the Botticelli portrait of Venus rising from the shell. Steam rose from the shower, gray clouds, filmy and soft, tinged with silver. Water droplets beaded on the camera lens, slightly distorting the image of the naked girl. Saadi shifted in his swivel chair and licked his lips.

Pressing a control button for a series of close-ups, he scanned her naked body. Trim legs, long for a French girl, swelling subtly into strong thighs and slim waist and tight buttocks, the sudden exciting flair of rib cage, the tremulous thrust of high breasts with erect nipples, the tufts of hair beneath her arms, no suggestion of fat anywhere, the smooth throat he longed to kiss, severe lips, eyes slightly slanted, a face like a Modigliani.

The face was not beautiful, Saadi thought, as the girl wrapped the towel around her waist, sarong style, and strolled into the bedroom. A better word would be "arresting." He felt arrested by those eyes, grayish blue, which could handcuff your very breath.

Standing at the French doors opening out onto the balcony, looking pensively out at Paris, one hand on the door frame, the pensive girl made Saadi sweat.

Her name was Laure Puget. She was a distant cousin of his current mistress and traveling companion, the Princess Athena von Heidelberg. This was Mademoiselle Puget's third visit. She had her own room in the penthouse of the Hôtel Paladin, on the Right Bank of the Seine.

She turned away from the window, unwrapping the towel. The simple action made him remember Clothilde, his father's Parisian mistress, now dead. In 1973, at the age of eighteen, Abdul Saadi had seduced Clothilde in her flat on the Rue Bienfaisance, near the Gare St.-Lazare, while his father had been busy, buying up gold in London. Saadi had been in love for the first, and only, time in his life. Like Laure Puget, Clothilde had been in her mid-twenties, slender and dark, with gray-green eyes and a face that radiated sensuality.

The seduction had been all the more exciting because it had taken place in his father's bed. Saadi had known pure joy because he was replacing his father between her legs.

When Clothilde had died in a motoring accident three years ago in Monaco, Saadi wanted to commit suicide. His religion kept him from it.

Saadi adjusted the controls. Laure Puget sat naked on a rumpled coverlet, right knee raised, foot on the edge of the bed, toes curled upward as she trimmed her toenails. The position allowed visual access to her most secret parts. His mouth was dry. He wet his lips with his tongue and mopped his face with a silk handkerchief.

For two months, an arm of Saadi's vast Sahara conglomerate had been providing financing for the girl's archaeological project, an excavation of the fortress of Alesia in northeastern France, where Caesar's army had vanquished the Gauls under Vercingetorix. The money was a minor sum—three million U.S. dollars so far—and Saadi, who was interested in history, had been waiting for the girl to demonstrate the degree of her gratefulness.

So far, Laure Puget had been polite but distant. Saadi sighed, thinking of Clothilde and her willing sensuality.

The girl turned her back and Saadi turned his mind to business. He was here in Paris to discuss endorsement contracts with tennis players on their way up. He wanted the right names to launch his Sahara line of rackets, shoes, and clothing. The date for the launch was August. The event was the U.S. Open. Already, Saadi had rejected Koras, the number 1, because of his past intimacies with the Princess. Saadi was a jealous man, and just hearing the old stories about Koras and Athena made him sick to his stomach. With Koras eliminated, that left three players on the rise—Davey Cooper, Terry Laville, and Mikhail Polak. At the moment, Saadi wanted Polak, the Archangel of Gdansk. He was a star from the Eastern Bloc. He was ranked number 2 in the world. Best of all, Polak seemed innocent, untouched by the jaded jet-set world of the tennis groupies.

Saadi's family owned thirteen hotels, in major cities across the world. London. Tokyo. Singapore. Hong Kong. Honolulu. Acapulco. Los Angeles. Dallas. Chicago. New York. Vienna. Berlin. Cairo. The New York Paladin was being refurbished, but the work had been delayed by slowdowns. Next month, he would open Casino Paladin in Atlantic City. It would boast 2,500 rooms, and accommodate 4,100 gamblers at once, on one gigantic floor. A party was already planned. In his mind, Saadi thought of it as the Polak Party.

The girl on the screen began dressing for the matches. Underwear first. Then a bra, a half slip, a pretty dress. What was her price? In Saadi's view, everyone was a whore—only his sister and mother were excluded—and all whores had a price.

A red button winked on the console. The maid. Saadi pressed the button. "Oui, Suzette?"

The maid told him the Princess had phoned from the Rue St. Honoré. She was finished with her shopping. They would leave for Roland-Garros within the hour.

Saadi did not like taking orders from the imperious Princess. "Oui, Suzette."

On the screen, Laure Puget stood in front of the mirror. She was dressed now. His pleasures were, for the moment, at an end.

Milo's sudden exit had left a strange silence in the dressing room. Koras went back to his deep breathing. Laville talked to Archer Bell, while he jogged in place to keep warm. Laville was still angry from last night, and his eyes registered blank hatred. Before a match, Laville allowed his anger for his opponent to build in an irrational and uncontrolled way; he felt it helped him get pumped up for victory. This kind of behavior, in Koras's view, was demented. You should save your emotion and feed it into the the magic of the match. So far, Laville's anger build-up hadn't worked against Koras, who had twenty matches to seven, over Laville. Someday, the anger would wash over the court, drowning the players and the crowd.

Now Koras's only urge was to be out on the court, into the game, confronting his opponent at last. Koras also knew that Laville, a few feet away, was summoning all his energy to win, to beat him. And his usual anger was even greater, because of last night . . .

Koras winced as he remembered. The night before, Régine had thrown a party for him at the club. It was still too early for the place to be really crowded, but the dining room had been full, and Koras, tired by the day's training, had been absent-mindedly reviewing the unattached women, listening to the talk around him.

"You'll probably want to leave early," someone said.

"I beg your pardon?"

"You're playing tomorrow, aren't you?"

"Yes."

Koras didn't know this man with the soft, featureless face. Where had he seen him before? Paris? New York? He hated to be counseled, especially by strangers. Advice always came from bogus sports enthusiasts, the tennis player's equivalent of the Monday-morning quarterback, who could tell you where you went wrong in the last match you lost.

Koras turned away just as a lovely strawberry-blonde girl came by, returning from the powder room. She wore high heels, which gave her a swaying walk, like an island maiden. Passing Koras's table, the girl gave him a long look and smiled. She wore dark green, to enhance her coloring. She sat down three tables away. Her companions were three men, two in their early thirties, a third who was fifty-five or so. The older man wore a business suit of expensive make and he was trying to monopolize her. As he spoke, gesturing, candlelight winked off a gold ring and a gold watch. The two younger men watched, awaiting their chance for an opening.

Through all this, the girl stared right at Koras, with a faint smile of amusement on her face.

With considerable fanfare and nearly a dozen waiters in tuxedos, the maître d'hôtel brought in the desserts. Koras, bored by the predatory atmosphere and the endless meal, had the urge to be far from this room, maybe alone with the lovely Titianesque girl. Koras had a reputation for leaving social occasions early, especially when he was playing a tournament. As his eyes met the girl's clear gaze, she smiled and he smiled back.

"Tell me," his neighbor said. "Are you going to give us the Grand Slam this year?"

"First, I must win the French."

People were desperate to become familiar with him. Strangely, his fame seemed to work against him, trivializing his talent, making him feel like a waning star.

"Is that the way one does it, one step at a time?"

"It's the way I do it. One stroke at a time. Otherwise, you forget why you're out there."

"Why are you out there?"

"To give my best."

The man smiled at Koras with a shrewd gleam in his eyes. He was about to go on with his interrogation when a terrible clamor came from the bar next door. In the next instant, Nora Laville, Terry's wife, hurried in, looking haggard. She wore no makeup, and her rich brown hair was disheveled. When she saw Koras, she ran up to him, threw herself into his arms.

"Nora. What's wrong?"

Waking from her trance, Nora realized people were staring at them. She stared at Koras, her face a mask of anguish. "Terry. He . . ." She was breathless, her bosom heaving, and two spots of color showed in her pale cheeks.

"Nora, will you tell me what's happened?"

Koras led Nora to an adjoining room. Trembling, she pressed herself against him, wetting his neck with her tears.

"You must think I'm crazy. I just can't stand it anymore. Terry's insane. He—"

She began to cry again.

"It was horrible. We had a fight. He's always bringing up my past. A few harmless photographs in a magazine and he makes me feel like the worst whore. Tonight, he even slapped me."

Koras looked into her eyes. He knew she had posed in two different women's magazines, for lingerie ads. Her husband had not thought them to be risqué until after the marriage. He smelled alcohol on Nora's breath.

Just then, a murmur rose from the people in the main room, and he heard Terry Laville calling for his wife. "Nora!"

Someone must have sent the Canadian after them, because in seconds he was standing in the doorway, glowering at Koras and his wife. Involuntarily, Nora huddled close to Koras. Terry wore jeans and a jacket thrown carelessly over his red-and-white-striped pajama top. His feet were bare inside tennis shoes; his ankles looked huge.

"Koras, you sonofabitch!"

"Terry," Nora said. "Go away!"

Agitated faces appeared in the doorway behind Laville, who advanced on Koras and Nora, clenching his huge fists. Koras moved Nora aside just as Laville took a swing. Koras danced away from the blow, which went wild. At the same time, Terry let out a "whoofing" sound, and Koras caught the rank smell of alcohol. It had been a bad night for both Lavilles, and while he felt sorry for them in their marriage, he didn't want to stop one of Laville's roundhouse punches. One hammer blow would put a fit man in the hospital for a week.

Nora grabbed Terry's left hand, but he threw her aside. He took another wild and drunken swing, but Koras grabbed his arm and swung him with a thump into the wall. Laville hit his left shoulder, spun around, and crashed into a table. The maître d' rushed in with three waiters to put a stop to the fight. Nora was sitting on the edge of a chair, crying. The fight solved nothing. Koras would have liked to take her with him, keep her in a safe place until Terry cooled down. But he had to stand there, doing nothing, while Terry marched out with Nora.

Back at his table, Koras thought of going after them. Then the polite table talk started up again, and the foolhardy impulse passed. Koras ordered a beer, which tasted bitter. When Régine came up to talk for a moment, he realized the muscles in his back and shoulders were tight as violin strings. He had a match tomorrow. It was time to go.

"Régine, I'm sorry for the trouble. It was a super party."

"Well, you see why Terry wasn't invited. The man's an absolute boor. I don't see why she stays with him."

Koras did not answer. Instead, he kissed Régine on both cheeks, waved a general goodbye to the other guests. Waiting for the elevator, he stretched, testing those tight muscles. When the elevator door opened, the strawberry-blonde stood inside, leaning casually against the back wall. One strand of her brilliant hair had come loose and dangled down the right side of her head. The rich green dress clung to her body. Her eyes were shining and the faint smile still lurked at the corners of her mouth.

"Mademoiselle?" He made way for her to exit.

The girl did not move. "I'm coming with you."

His car was waiting in front of the club. As if nothing could be more natural, the pretty girl slipped in beside Koras and curled up on the seat, facing him.

As the loudspeakers announced that the court was free, Koras gave a start and came out of his reverie. Jean Hoffman, the fussy tournament umpire, came to collect the two players in person.

It would begin again, the same motions, the same battle. Koras took the time to pull on his lucky black Laval warm-up suit. He was thinking about saving it for the final, but something about last night, and the way Laville had acted, made him bring the suit along for the quarters.

He walked out behind Laville, who advanced with his slow, bearlike step. Both men stayed silent, and Koras knew Laville was thinking about last night at Régine's. They left the locker room and walked through the labyrinthine passages under the stands, until they came out onto the Court Central, flooded in sunlight, crushed under the applause of fifteen thousand spectators. For once, the weather forecast had been right: the sky was cloudless.

Koras squinted, raising his eyes to the scoreboard, which still showed the score from the preceding match. He heard the announcer giving results of other matches: "Armando Reyes beats Ivan Leroy, 6–2, 6–4, 6–7, 6–1; on the second court, Milovan Tigrid is leading David Cooper, 5–4, in the second set. Mr. Tigrid took the first set, 7–5."

T W O

The loudspeaker made the announcement, and Koras was, as always, surprised to hear his name—it meant the dream had come true. He was really here, about to play for a huge crowd: "The quarterfinals of the French Inter-Nationals. Pantakoras Belynkas, of the United States, versus Terry Laville, of Canada."

Before walking to the end of the court, Koras put on the forest-green headband that kept his hair out of his eyes. He felt especially sensitive to vibrations today, so he took extra care not to step on the white lines as he walked to his end of the court for the warm-up. Once the ball was in flight, the lines lost their uncanny superstitious qualities. He could not explain it, and he seldom spoke to anyone about how he felt. All he knew was that the lines vibrated, as if charged with magnets.

During the warm-up, slamming the ball at Laville, Koras felt his fears subside, to be replaced by the familiar yogic detachment. Now there was only the ball crossing the net, touching down, the red earth below, the feel of the rubber sphere as it met the sweet spot in the center of his racket. Above all, there was Laville, his grinning opponent.

It was unbelievable. Milo was leading Davey. Davey Cooper, a young player from New York well known for his irascibility on court, was never beaten until the last ball. The tenacious power player punctuated each shot with a strange guttural incantation to pagan gods known only to himself. If Milo won today, he would be all smiles and would spend the season buying drinks for everyone.

Koras tore his thoughts away from Davey and concentrated on his match against Laville. He sat down in his chair and looked at the stands. Athena von Heidelberg had not yet arrived, and Saadi's private box was empty. Koras brought out three rackets, all Belynkas Autographs, made by his major equipment sponsor, Laval Sportif. He checked the tension on each one, pressing his fingertips against the strings, and then tapping the strings on the edge of a second racket. He chose the middle one to start the match.

The let cord judge, standing by his chair beside the next post, flipped a coin. Koras won and chose to serve. Laville took the side that put his back to the sun. Staring at Laville, Koras felt a flutter of dread. The tournament in Paris would mark the second leg of the Grand Slam. He had won Australia in January, he was thirty-four, and this might be his last chance.

What if he lost here today, to a man as out-of-control as Terry Laville?

Laville, the Calgary Woodcutter . . . Calgary, the railway crossing where he had been born, a pioneer town famous for a rodeo and a collection of refineries, with not much else to place it on the map until Terry's ascension in the world of tennis.

At twenty-five, Terry Laville still had the intense aggressiveness that had marked his first appearance on the tennis circuit a half dozen years ago. Indeed, with his height, his incredible power, and his heavy, lumbering game, Laville was like some natural force sprung from his natal forests. The Laville myth, promoted in the media by his clever manager, Archer Bell, had him training by felling trees by lamplight in the darkness and gloom of the Canadian Northwest with his brothers.

There was some truth to the myth. Felling huge trees had taught Laville the secrets of balance, and using a chain saw had given him a sense of leverage as he gained a certain elemental sway over nature. But the real benefit of Laville's life in the woods had been the accuracy he had learned swinging an ax. This exercise, which built up the muscles in his shoulders, back, and upper arms, had given him the most powerful serve in tennis, and there were stop-action photographs of the Laville serve, taken last summer at Hilton Head Island, which showed the ball in flight being compressed into a fluffy wafer. The caption beneath the photos had read: "How would you like to be a tennis ball served at 148 m.p.h. by Terry Laville, the Canadian Woodcutter?" Tennis writers compared the power of Laville's serve to Roscoe Tanner's and its easy, deceptive motion to Pancho Gonzales's.

Terry was always complaining to the press that tennis kept him away from his homeland. These days, he spent what little time he had in Canada jogging in the woods around the house he had bought near Vancouver.

Laville's ascent had begun the day he won the Alberta championships. Given a scholarship by the University of Winnipeg, he had rapidly risen to the summit of the game at home, to become Canada's long-awaited tennis hope. Unfortunately, Laville had come onto the circuit at the same time Koras had been playing his best tennis. Milovan Tigrid had started to fade, and his place at the top had been assumed by Koras. Three years ago, on the verge of winning at Roland-Garros, Laville was eliminated by Koras in the semifinals. Since then, they had met seventeen times, and Koras had won fourteen of the seventeen matches.

It was just one more grudge Laville held against Koras.

The sun came out just as they finished warming-up serves. From the other end of the court, Koras watched Terry Laville shake his astonishing white hair, his face screwed against the glare. That face, accented by its sharp planes, narrow-lidded eyes, and long aquiline nose, reminded Koras of an Indian warrior preparing for battle. He could sense the violent hatred emanating from Laville, like a huge force, vibrating toward him in waves. The referee gave the signal to play. Koras held up the ball in the time-honored opening gesture, and then he served. The ball kicked high on the soft clay, going to Laville's backhand. Laville hit a short return. Koras intercepted the ball just in front of the service line, hit a forcing volley that pinned Laville to a spot deep in the court, behind the baseline, and won the first point with his knifing second volley. The stands responded with a round of applause.

He won three games in a row before Laville got a point.

At the changeover at 4–1, Koras surveyed the stands, packed to the top of the steep stadium, very full for a Wednesday of quarterfinal play. In the private boxes near courtside, he recognized all the partially notorious faces, people of the jet set who flocked to premieres and openings to compete with whatever spectacle there was.

These were the stars, the luminaries. They came from the world of film and theater, from music and art and politics. He saw Gerald Duncan, a best-selling writer, and next to him was Charles St. Etienne, the movie star. He recognized Harrison Cabot, the wealthy President of the United States Tennis Association. Cabot was not one of Koras's favorite people. The man had never worked in his life, existing in splendor on an income earned by his great-grandfather, a banker in Connecticut. Cabot had gone to Yale to study English and the classics. He had crewed, of course, had played varsity tennis, and then, back in the forties, had represented the United States for the Davis Cup. Koras was angry that American tennis had been controlled for almost a century by men like Cabot.

In the players' box, Koras spotted Armando Reyes, smiling and making jokes with his latest inamorata, an attractive redhead. The woman wore a fashionable jump-suit and kept turning away from Reyes to snap pictures of people in the crowd with an expensive-looking camera. He had heard the woman was married, but that had never fazed Armando.

All of wealthy Paris had turned out for the matches and had

set up camp in the Main Stand, certain in the knowledge that they would be a focus of attention of both the public and publicity-seeking cameras.

As Koras watched, Princess Athena von Heidelberg made her entrance. Saadi was not with her, but she had her maid and a chauffeur in livery and a young girl with dark glasses and a large leather shoulder bag. The girl looked familiar, but Koras could not place her.

The Princess's title made him smile. No one could say whether she actually had a right to it, but this did not matter to Athena, because in the circles which she frequented, discretion was the keynote for behavior. Athena was a fountain of gossip, and if any one of her countless acquaintances had dared to question her right to be called "Princess," she would have fought them with every subtle weapon at her disposal. The Princess was a formidable foe, as Koras had found.

It was almost time. On the other side of the umpire's chair, Terry Laville was mumbling to himself as he rewrapped the yellow gauze around his racket handle. Was he on the verge of a temper tantrum?

Koras took some water to rinse his mouth.

Today Princess Athena was resplendent in a gorgeous tomato red dress, of a soft velour material that clung to her breasts and outlined her figure. The dress was tied on with two spaghetti straps. Whenever Athena twisted in her seat to wave at someone, people turned to watch. She was a beautiful woman, sensual, wealthy, magnificently regal.

As he stood up, Koras looked again at the pretty young girl with Athena. Who was she?

"Mr. Belynkas?" said the umpire. "Shall we resume?"

Laure Puget, wearing a dress of raw silk, eggshell color, and a cerulean-blue jacket, watched with amusement as her cousin Athena directed the maid where to put the picnic hamper. The chauffeur followed, carrying a cooler filled with ice, beer, wine, and Dom Perignon. Athena was tanned and very beautiful.

All across Europe and the major cities of America, Athena was famous for neither wearing a brassiere nor needing one. Her breasts—high, full, and insolent—were legendary. At sporting events, carnivals, the opera, photographers were constantly turning away from their subjects to capture a few pictures of Athena's spectacular figure. Now, at Roland-Garros, spectators craned their necks for a look at the rich aristocrat who dressed like a high-fashion poster girl. The Princess obliged. She was there to be admired, and strangers were always waving, pointing, asking for her autograph. Because her photo appeared in newspapers every week, people felt they knew Athena. Wherever she went, people waited for Athena to lean over, bend, laugh, move.

Everyone loved her.

She had a ready laugh, a saucy walk, a beautiful winning smile. The smile, when combined with her money and impelling confidence, had gotten her a screen test with a major Hollywood studio. But the Princess refused to get up before dawn to go to work on the movie set. Still, she was the consummate entertainer, bringing light into a dark world.

Athena was the daughter of Helga von Heidelberg, a Belgian beauty who was as spectacularly endowed as her daughter. Helga had married Count Osten of Augsburg before World War II. Count Osten, a great hunter and a manufacturer of military weapons, made huge sums of money, which he smuggled out to secret accounts in the Zurich banks. But in staking so much on the new rulers of Germany, the Count had been as shortsighted as he was ambitious. In May 1945 he had put a bullet through his head rather than face the humiliation of defeat.

His young and beautiful widow had grieved properly and circumspectly. Her problem was not money, but rather how to find a replacement who would allow her the same noble station to which she claimed to belong. True, her reputation was slightly tainted in the eyes of a few aristocrats by her late husband's politics, but as national economies blossomed and the world again enjoyed relative peace, Helga was able to survive, and quite nicely. Forced into the ranks of the plebeians, Helga married a wealthy and politically ambitious U.S. Army colonel named Riker, who had his eye on a Senate seat in Virginia. He never became a senator, but he did amass millions. When the colonel died, in 1962, Helga became an even richer widow.

Athena was only six when her mother found herself alone,

again. Helga secured both their livelihoods by placing her massive inheritance with a Wall Street broker who became her financial adviser and her lover. She and her daughter kept her maiden name, von Heidelberg, which had a more impressive ring than Riker.

Athena had gone to school at Montesano, in Gstaad, where she gained an education equal to her ambitions. At Montesano, she studied French, German, English, mathematics, art, history, and classical literature. She mixed with girls of her own social class, and saw her mother only twice a year, at a summer house in the Bahamas, and at St. Moritz, where they spent a lavish Christmas.

At Montesano, Athena played her first tennis, and proved to have a natural talent for the game. On the court, she was flashy, bold, adventurous. Like many of the players from France, Athena lacked discipline, or she would have become a champion. Instead, she drifted into the role of tennis groupie, and by the age of eighteen had slept with most of the Top Ten. For Athena, that was a good enough ranking.

Athena handed the chauffeur a bottle of champagne. "Here, Edouard. Be a good boy. Put this between your powerful legs and pop it open."

Laure laughed as the chauffeur blushed and then opened the champagne. As the champagne cork exploded, a handsome man arrived, wearing a warm-up suit of bright yellow. He had strong legs, a deep tan, and a booming voice that carried in the steep confines of the stadium. Athena introduced him as the player Armando Reyes, from Peru. Reyes, who had just won his quarterfinal match, bent over to kiss Laure's hand. "Ah, Mademoiselle Laure. So nice to have you here. Do you know tennis?"

"Not very well, I'm afraid."

"Laure is an archaeologist, Armando. She digs in the dirt of France."

"Amazing," Reyes said. "What do you dig for?"

"Artifacts," she said. "Connections."

"Connections leading where?"

"Between past and present." Laure crossed her tanned legs. She got another admiring look from Reyes, and Athena noticed. "Here, Armando. Have some champagne. Take your mind off the tennis." She handed Reyes a glass.

"Are you here for the tournament, Mademoiselle Laure?" Reyes asked.

"Laure finds tennis decadent," Athena cut in.

"Let her speak, cherie." Reyes turned back to Laure, who stopped reading.

"Actually, I've been in Mexico, on a dig. I came back to France in early spring for another dig, down near Dijon." She said nothing about the financing that came from Saadi's business.

"Ah, how interesting." The Peruvian leaned closer. Even though he was trying his best to be charming, he wasn't really interested in her work. "Near Dijon?"

"Um, yes. At Alesia. It's just north. Near Montbard."

"I know Dijon. In 1978, I had a wine there to curl the toes."

"Armando, you have a favorite wine everywhere." Athena spoke to Laure. "Once, after the tournament finished up here, Armando had his pilot fly us around France. There was a car waiting. We sampled every winery from Bordeaux to Dijon. Truly."

"That was in the old days," Reyes said. "We stayed *borracho* until Wimbledon."

"The pilot was mad, a daredevil. Whatever happened to him, Armando?"

"He is in Peru. He works for my brother."

"Give him my best, will you."

Reyes spoke to Athena over his shoulder. "Only you can do that, cherie."

When Reyes spoke to Athena, he was making love. It was an automatic gesture, and Laure wondered if Saadi was alert enough to notice. Laure did not care for Saadi, and had been surprised when he agreed to finance her excavation at Alesia. Saadi fancied himself a scholar with an interest in history. Still, Laure felt uneasy around him. Down on the court, Belynkas won a long point from the huge Canadian.

"Poor Laville," Reyes said.

"Why do you say that?" Laure asked.

"He plays so hard. Yet he can never win against Koras."

Athena cut in, with her opinion. "They say Pantakoras has the 'Indian sign' on Monsieur Laville."

"I know what that means," Laure said. "An American expression, having to do with a hold on someone."

"Bravo," Reyes said, and smiled out at the players. "I admire Koras immensely, you know?"

"You do? Why?"

"He is always giving his time, for clinics, for charity exhibitions. He calls it paying his dues."

"To whom?" Laure asked.

"To the world. The world helped him when he was starting out by sending along a man named Al Moscowitz. Now Koras wants to pay it back."

"I find that awfully abstract," Athena yawned.

But Reyes went on. "He even helped Terry Laville, at first."

"But not anymore?"

"No. Not anymore."

Laure understood. She liked helping people. When she was finished with her studies, and had turned the material into a substantive little book, she wanted to become a teacher. She was thinking of this when another man, Jean-François Colombier, entered the box. Before introducing him to Laure, Athena gave him a huge hug. The conversation swirled around her— rich people in Dallas, Paris, Singapore. A fur coat Athena had just bought in Rome, a bargain at $97,000.

Laure read for a while, a treatise on Alesia by Wallensborough. When she looked up to watch Koras, she had the feeling he had changed since their tennis lesson on the shady court at Innsbruck, so many years ago. Through Athena's opera glasses, Laure studied Koras's face, strong, with wide-set eyes and an expressive mouth. The man she remembered had been younger, less experienced, more spiritual. This man, playing so surgically, made her edgy.

Beside her, Armando Reyes was acting as tennis tutor.

"That's a cross-court volley. He's too far from the net to do any good. Close in, Señor Koras, close! Excellent." He looked at Laure, to see if she understood.

She smiled back. "You like him, don't you?"

"Like him? To me, Koras is next to God and Jack Kramer."

Laure changed the subject. "Has he never married?"

"Almost." Armando cut his eyes at Athena, who had her back turned as she spoke to someone in the next box. "A Swedish lady, some artist type he met in Paris."

"What happened?"

Armando shrugged. "I don't know. He refuses to talk about it much."

At that moment, they were joined by a dazzling redhead carrying a camera. She wore a white jump-suit. Armando introduced her as Madame Muriel Broussard-Gauthier. Shaking the woman's hand, Athena was all smiles, but Laure sensed an electric jealousy.

"Are you photographing for business, madame? Or for pleasure?"

The redhead smiled. "It began as pleasure." She glanced at Armando. "But now I think I shall make a book."

Armando Reyes stood up to leave the box. "I shall leave you now. It is time to rest before the next round."

"Good luck, Armando."

As Reyes left the box, Athena turned to the redhead, who snapped her photo before turning the camera on Laure.

Koras took the first set of his quarterfinal, 6–1, with an ace. Laville seemed to be chasing a phantom ball. Leading 2–1 in the second set, Koras looked at the brunette, who was still reading. Armando's redhead had left the players' box and was chatting away with Athena. Time for some fun, so he tossed the ball very high in the air and put his hands on his hips, watching it come down.

The ball hit him squarely between the eyes. Laughter, from the stands. The girl looked up.

Across the net, Laville thought Koras was making fun of him, and began to play better tennis. He won three games.

Koras realized he was losing his hold on the match. He quickened the pace of the game, sending explosive passing shots that barely touched the ground, devouring the ball with his eyes, taking the ball on the rise with wicked half volleys. He crunched away the shots at the net. He wanted a lot of applause, to distract the brunette from her damned book. He hoped it was fascinating.

"Mr. Belynkas takes the second set, 6–4."

In the middle of the third set, Terry Laville threw a tantrum over a line call. He spent several moments berating the line judge, a portly man wearing dark glasses and a beret. Then he turned his venom on the umpire, who was forced to call the crowd to order. "Please serve, Mr. Laville." Laville prepared to serve. The first shot went wild, out of court. The second slapped against the tape of the net.

He threw his racket to the ground in a rage.

The crowd jeered. In the boxes, people turned around disapprovingly. The whistles and catcalls continued. It was more like a football game in the European Cup than a staid tennis match at Roland-Garros. If the Federation did nothing to control this type of behavior from the spectators, the day might come when they would be throwing firecrackers and smoke bombs, and perhaps worse, onto the courts.

"Match point."

The Canadian survived two match points, but succumbed in the third, to the applause of a crowd that would surely have fed him to the lions. Three straight sets, a massacre. Koras walked to the net to shake hands, but Laville, piqued about last night at Regine's, only brushed his fingers against Koras's hand.

Laville was now eliminated from the French Open, but Koras would advance to the semifinals, where he would play the winner of the Polak-Colombier match.

For almost two weeks, the stadium of Roland-Garros is transformed into a "Field of the Cloth of Green," where the sovereigns of tennis defy each other on the courts. On the grounds adjacent to the play, the green-and-white tents of the commercial enterprises set up a rival spectacle, displaying their famous trademarks like coats-of-arms.

In this fast-track world of marketing and high-tech promotions, almost anything that sells can be made acceptable, and although the law prohibits cigarette manufacturers from advertising in stadiums, they sidestep the problem by becoming sports clothes manufacturers.

The stands resembled an entrenched camp, Gauls *vs.* Intruders. It is known as the Village, and that afternoon, after the matches were finished, Laval Sportif sponsored a cocktail party to celebrate the signing of its new contract with Pantakoras Belynkas, and to inaugurate their new line of sportswear.

At the party, lost in a swirl of faces, Koras found Frank Fenwick, his manager, who had arrived from South Africa only an hour before the matches. Fenwick wore his usual costume—twill jacket, twill trousers, Stetson hat, boots. His pockets bulged with notebooks and slips of paper. Fenwick was due in Hamburg, Germany, that evening, for dinner. He would return to Paris on Friday for the semifinals. Koras liked Fenwick, but he wondered what the man was chasing. F.F. was worth millions. Athena, making a wry observations, said that Fenwick's watch was five minutes fast, and that he was circling the globe trying to catch that tiny unit of unattainable time.

Once, at Narita Airport, in Tokyo, Koras and Fenwick had been about to board a flight for California when the porter from the hotel where they had been staying caught up to them, breathlessly. He wanted the room key, no doubt taken by mistake.

"No," Fenwick said. "It's not a mistake." And he'd insisted on keeping the key, and had written out a check to pay for installing a new lock. Koras had watched the scene, bewildered.

"I collect keys," F.F. said. "In New York, I have an entire room full of hotel keys. I have these dreams that if I keep all the keys to all the rooms I've ever slept in, death will never be able to find me. But if that time does come, I'll be able to choose when and where it happens."

Fenwick had his quirks, and one of the strongest was that he did not like surprises. Even if he was in Borneo, Fenwick liked to know where Koras was and how he was playing. Fenwick was a superb manager, professional, solid, with a genuine gift for foresight. Koras and Fenwick had no written contract; instead, a strong bond of friendship had substantiated the business they did in the vast and changing world of big-time tennis.

"Great news!" Fenwick boomed in his Texas accent.

Koras smiled. "Give a guy a break, F.F. No contract talk yet. I just finished working."

Fenwick took Koras by the arm. "You don't understand. I made two holes in one, in six days." Fenwick waved his arm, indicating the hubbub at the Village. "Now when you have to give all this up, you can play golf with me. Arnie'll give you lessons."

Despite the veiled reference to his age, Koras smiled as he pictured playing golf with Arnie Palmer as his mentor. This year, he guessed Palmer might make four million dollars. He was probably sitting on fifty million more, and still he continued to teach, making the game accessible to others. Arnold Palmer was a man to admire.

"Koras. I need a favor."

"What?"

"After Paris, I need you to play Palermo."

"Why Palermo?" Koras looked around, hoping to catch sight of the brunette who had been with Athena.

"We need the money." Fenwick's voice was suddenly serious.

"You're kidding."

Fenwick shook his head. "It's an easy $125,000. And there's this contract with a fruit-juice outfit. They want your beaming face on their label, and they'll pay $75,000 more."

"If we're making all this money, F.F., why don't I feel rich?"

Fenwick grinned at his number-one client. "You spend it real fast, son. Two new cars this year, and we'll be paying for the refurbishing of Court's Court for the next three years."

"I thought it was a tax shelter."

"Yeah. But they cost money, too." Fenwick dug into his pockets and pulled out a crumpled envelope, covered with numbers. "You only need $337,000 to hit the four-million mark."

"That's why I don't understand about Palermo."

Fenwick pointed to a column of neatly printed figures. "See that? Two million of this is the Grand Slam bonus. But you haven't won it yet. *That's* a cash-flow problem, to the tune of thirty-nine thousand a month. That's what goes out."

Koras shook his head. He was playing his heart out, pleasing the fans, taking home trophies, signing checks. There was a studio apartment in Paris on the île St. Louis he'd had his eye on for three years, but Fenwick said they couldn't afford it. Koras didn't like to worry about money. He'd spent his first twenty-five years scrimping pennies. When you became a household name, you shouldn't have to sweat money. "If I go to Palermo, I'll have to play Jackie Di Rocca in the finals. They throw salami at the outsider."

Fenwick grinned. Di Rocca had cousins in Sicily, and they would control the atmosphere of the matches with their cat-calls. "Just think of the money."

"I was counting on a week in Nice."

"That reminds me we need to unload that villa."

Koras stared at his manager. "Are you telling me everything, F.F.?"

"Just play Palermo. We'll make it."

Just then, a marketing vice president from Laval Sportif came up to take Koras away, to meet some important people.

"In a minute," Fenwick said.

The vice president backed off, chastened. Both men watched him go. At that moment, the Princess Athena entered the tent. Armando Reyes was with her, and also the girl with the book, removing her dark glasses to survey the room. She had a long face, with deep-set eyes and skin that seemed translucent despite her early summer tan. She was tall, Athena's height, but more slender. As he watched, she turned to Athena and whispered something. Athena laughed, and both women turned to look in Koras's direction. Koras excused himself and started for the girl, but was intercepted by the vice president.

"You simply have to meet these people."

While Koras chatted and shook hands with smiling buyers who congratulated him on the brilliance of his passing shots, the girl stood aside from the crowd, by the buffet, drinking champagne. Athena had been joined by Saadi, who wore a white suit and a flaming red tie. Jean-Alain, the reigning French movie star, sidled up to Koras, his eyes narrowed, his eyebrows arched, to make a wild prediction: "You want to hear something?"

"From the mouths of the oracles?"

Jean-Alain was notorious for his interest in the Tarot, the ouija board, clairvoyance, and other tools of the occult. He had a long, sad face that women found irresistible. His latest movie had been a French version of the H. Rider Haggard novel *She*, whose central character gets burnt up in a tongue of living fire. "They tell me that you will play the Yugoslav, Milovan Tigrid, in the final."

"Who are 'they'?"

The actor smiled enigmatically and fluttered his eyes. Perhaps, at this very moment, he was communicating with an unseen spirit world. "My guardians, who else?"

"What will the score be?"

The eyes fluttered again. "They also say someone will die."

"Can they get more specific?"

"Someone close." The eyes were really going now, the lids fluttering faster. His face was contorted. "Someone who . . ." He paused, opened his eyes. "No. They have gone."

Koras handed him a glass of champagne. "Here."

The actor drank, stared at Koras. "Well, how are you playing?" He seemed suddenly back to reality.

"Judson Garwood called it 'surgical.' "

"Ah, that one." The actor moved close again. "He has the Evil Eye."

They were discussing the tennis writer Garwood when Princess Athena found him. She wanted to introduce Koras to her cousin.

Walking across the pavilion, the Princess held his arm. "You played brilliantly today."

"And you, my love, are as sensual as ever."

She squeezed his arm. "Money does seem to agree with me."

"Tell me you don't make love with him."

She turned to look at Koras, smiling. "How well you understand me, Pantakoras."

The brunette was waiting, and as they were introduced, Koras had time to study her. She did not smile. Her blue-gray eyes were curious, cool, distant. Her look, a sweeping glance at the false gaiety of the pavilion, seemed disapproving. Perhaps she was a revolutionary.

"Pantakoras, this is my cousin, Laure Puget. Laure, this is Pantakoras Belynkas."

"Hello." They shook hands. Her hand was feminine, but rougher than he had expected.

"What is the book?"

A half smile flickered across her features, then faded. "Wallensborough. On Roman ruins."

He didn't recognize the name.

"Laure is an archaeologist," Athena said.

"You dig things up?"

"Yes."

The conversation wasn't going well and Koras thought of the pretty girl from last night. She had been willing, and her willingness had allowed him to stay cool and detached. He had fought hard to become famous, and now that he'd grown famous, he was accustomed to gushing admiration from pretty young women, if not outright hero worship. Nothing like that was coming from this one. Watching Laure Puget, her erect back, the line of her tanned throat, he tried to remember where he had seen her before. Athena stepped away to talk to some people from Dallas.

"Have we met, mademoiselle?"

"Perhaps. I don't remember."

The smile was gone altogether now. She spoke English with a husky French accent that gave her added sex appeal. As she stood there with her leather bag over her shoulder, the off-white dress making a pleasant contrast to the blue of her jacket, he knew he was taking her distance as a challenge. With her long face and strange eyes, she was not as beautiful as Athena, but she seemed deeper, more mysterious, perhaps more enduring.

"Your English is excellent."

"Thank you. I studied in the States."

"Oh? Where?"

"Los Angeles. At UCLA."

He was about to ask her about Los Angeles when Athena rejoined them. For a moment, he listened to a story about the Dollmers from Dallas. The girl said nothing. Was that a chill he felt coming from her?

"Athena, I really must go," the girl said. "I have work to do."

"Laure thinks we are very decadent, traipsing around the circuit."

"She's got a point."

The girl looked at him as she held out her hand. "Goodbye."

Athena invited him to a party later in the evening. If he went, he might see Laure Puget again. "I'll try." Koras said goodbye and then watched the two women walk away. Nice hips on the girl, and sweet long legs. A waiter passed with a tray of drinks and Koras asked him for a beer. Behind the waiter, a security guard carrying a sub-machine gun was surveying the guests. Times were changing at Roland-Garros.

Someone came up behind him. "Mr. Belynkas. There's someone you have to meet."

As he turned to shake hands and give a weary smile, Koras thought—well, if she wasn't available, there was always the willing Mademoiselle Dumont, the Lady of the Peugeot.

But he admitted to himself Laure was far more intriguing.

Armando Reyes, ranked number 12 on the ATP computer, was about to fly through the roof. He'd climaxed three times, the last one bringing forth a scream, and was now winding toward a fourth. The woman was tireless. She rolled over on top of him, bringing him with her, still connected. He felt smothered, enveloped, enclosed by her flesh, her royal lust. She was a tall woman, statuesque, solid, regal, with a sweet smell that reminded him of springtime in Peru.

"Aiyee, Princess!"

"What is it?"

"Prepare yourself."

They spoke in German, her language, or in Spanish, his language, or in English, which they had both learned in private schools in their respective countries. Sometimes they spoke in French, the language of love.

The Princess laughed, a sound of triumph, a passion goddess in the garden of love. She rose above him, a pulsing shadow, a pure Valkyrie out of a Wagnerian opera. He closed his eyes, feeling the power surge, drive, reach. She was whimpering now, begging, on the verge of release. What *was* in those red pills? He had watched Athena take two, then one more. How many could a person take?

"Ah. Ah. Ah."

"Yes. Holy mother! Si!"

"Ja. Ja. Jaaa!"

They soared together toward the sun, toward a bright light inside their minds. He was Icarus, heading out, powerful wings pumping, eyes strong against the sun. The pills had brought his youth back. She was Aphrodite, Venus, Helen of Troy, Athena.

She came down before he did, sighing, snuggling into him like a peasant girl, not a princess. Armando loved these moments, so tender, when she seemed vulnerable. Clothes made the woman, but then again . . .

It was well after midnight at the Hôtel Sofitel. Outside the hotel, traffic whirred through the Paris streets, toward the Seine, the Heliport, the Eiffel Tower. He had beaten Leroy, the French hope. Tomorrow afternoon, he had a semifinal match against Tigrid. Tigrid had beaten him on the slow clay in Rome, so there was reason to worry. If he took another pill, and then added a blue—what his brother's physician back in Peru prescribed for anxiety and stage fright—what would happen? Could he outlast his friend Milo? Could he go all the way to the top? What a surprise for the fans . . . the Sublime Peruvian triumphs in Paris.

"Was it good, my darling?" The Princess stirred.

"Maravilloso." Reyes squeezed her shoulder. "What are the contents of those pills?"

"I am not a chemist."

"And you got them from Saadi?"

"From his desk, as I said."

"Where did he get them?"

"He uses them when he sees his mistress. Sometimes with the maid."

Reyes laughed. He was an educated man, sophisticated, world-weary. Life was full of ironies. "Where can we obtain more?"

"From his desk. I counted over a dozen bottles. But we must be careful. I take three from each bottle."

"It is too late in my life for being careful."

"No." She snuggled closer to him. "Don't say that."

Reyes was thirty-six that year, next to Tigrid the oldest player on the circuit. The family fortunes, which had once seemed to provide an endless flow of money, were dwindling. The OPEC ministers were to blame for the falling oil prices. The Americans and the Argentinians and the chicken marketeers of Latin America were to blame for the glut of beef on the market. In April, wholesale beef had fallen 8 cents in

America. One could buy a sirloin for $2.55 a pound, prices from twenty years ago. The thought made Reyes ill. For twenty years, he had lived the high life, playing tennis, flying around the world in his private jet, falling in and out of love with women like the Princess. Now the Reyes jet had been sold. And reports from his brother spoke of belt-tightening in the family business, of trimming the fat.

There was money enough for one more season on the circuit, May through the first week in September. After that, Reyes would have to return home, to Lima. There would be no more tennis, no more late nights in hotels across the world, no more high life.

"What time is it?"

He checked the travel alarm with the luminous dial. "Just after one."

"What time is your match?"

"Twoish. Unless almightly Clavier chooses to shift the times around. He has a soft heart for the women."

"You should talk." The Princess rolled away from him, stood up and walked to the chair where she had folded her clothes neatly, like a professional. She began to dress.

"Must you go?"

She spoke without looking at him. "I must, dearest. Saadi will be returning."

"I like waking up with you."

"Yes. That is sweet."

"When will this business be over with Saadi?"

She continued dressing. "I am not certain. He gives me what I want."

"You want to marry the bugger, don't you?"

"Not want to, dearest. Need to." She walked into the bathroom and turned on the light.

Reyes sat up against the pillows. The dizziness that had plagued him for most of last year had gone away, perhaps because of Saadi's pills. He felt maravilloso. It was going to be a magnificent summer season. He wondered what the day would bring. After a few moments, he walked naked to the bathroom, to stand in the doorway, where the Princess was putting the finishing touches on her makeup. She wore the blue cocktail dress from her dinner party. He wondered where she got her awesome energy.

The Princess turned from the mirror, to see that Saadi's pills were working. Armando was ready for love.

"Has Saadi signed Polak yet?"

"No. They spoke twice today. Saadi was very persuasive."

"Does anyone else know?"

"No. It is an industry secret."

Armando stepped into the bathroom and stroked Athena's buttock. "I heard rumors that Saadi was working with some Albanians. Perhaps that's where the drug came from."

Athena looked at Reyes in the mirror. "Saadi is the son of a sheik. He has connections with anyone you want." She finished, turned her head for a profile check. She was thirty that year, and more beautiful than ever, or so said the tabloid newspapers. Athena's mother, Helga von Heidelberg, had elected cosmetic surgery at the age of forty-two, shortly after she married her fifth husband.

Even in this horrid hotel light, her rich blonde hair looked magnificent. She was a beautiful woman, with the confidence of a top fashion model. The abundant hair was one of her best features.

"I must go, darling. Do have good luck against Milo."

"You sound as if you want us both to win."

"Milo is a dear friend."

"And I? What am I?"

She kissed him on the mouth, pressing her lips down on his. "You are my dearest friend."

"That's what Muriel calls me. Her dearest friend."

Athena grabbed his arm. "Be careful of little Muriel."

Armando smiled. He loved making women jealous. "Now who's acting possessive?"

"A woman has more reason than a man."

"Ho. Spoken like a Princess."

"Is Muriel French?"

"Belgian. From Brussels."

Athena clucked him under the chin, stepped away. Playtime was over. "Good luck against Tigrid. Really."

"Thank you, my dear." He held out the pills. "You have given me all the luck I need."

THREE

The fans arrived early for the first match of the women's semifinals, which had all the appearances of an American national tournament. Three of the players were from the States. Tania Pikeste, the little Rumanian player who had stolen the hearts of spectators in Paris, stood alone against the North Atlantic onslaught. The French newspapers had nicknamed her "the Fairy of the Courts" and "the Comaneci of Tennis," titles which had been unanimously accepted by the international press covering the tournament.

Evelyne Dumont parked the Peugeot 604 in the lot reserved for players and officials. Early that morning, she had picked Koras up at his hotel and had driven him to Bagatelle, where she had watched him training.

For an hour, Koras had warmed up with his coach, Will Channer. They worked the hardest on his serve, pounding ball after ball, aiming at tennis ball cans placed strategically in one corner or the other of the service court, forcing ballboys to replenish the bucket without respite. As their legs pumped tirelessly around the court, Koras never stopped, never hesitated. He served to the right court, then to the left, varying the angles, alternating the spin, shaving the net. He perfected his stroke by replacing the empty cans with a small circle of white pasteboard, five inches in diameter. Evelyne was amazed that the ball made contact with the targets so frequently. The coach, a lean man in a white jogging suit, drove Koras mercilessly. Near the end of the workout, Channer made his pupil serve blindfolded. As Koras served, Channer would call out where the ball had landed: "Three inches to the left, two inches behind." "That one was five inches to the right, and level with the target." And then, when Koras adjusted, the coach would grin and say "Bingo!" And Evelyne would applaud.

After an hour, Koras ripped off the blindfold. "Finished!" he said. "And time for breakfast." He looked up at Evelyne and she nodded.

"You need another ten," Channer insisted.

"No. I am finished."

Koras walked off the court, to where his charming chauffeur waited. With the light playing on her blonde hair, she suddenly seemed very attractive. He formalized his invitation for brunch.

Delighted, Evelyne slid behind the wheel, taking advantage of the movement to reveal a lovely expanse of bronze thigh. Bending forward to start the engine, Koras caught a glimpse of her breasts through her gaping shirt, her nipples hardened by the excitement of being seen and allowing herself to be seen. Koras looked at her steadily. She was pretty, but she seemed a little desperate. He flicked on the radio, Evelyne watching him. He stopped the dial at France Musique, the classical music station. For some reason, the music made him think of Laure Puget.

"A lot of men would envy me," he said.

"For the ride in the car?"

"For the ride with the chauffeur."

She liked that. "Where shall we breakfast?"

"That I leave to the expert."

She smiled. "I know just the place."

The Peugeot slid smoothly along the tree-lined street. Koras sat back against the seat, letting the music fill his ears, to think about his next match, a semifinal against Mikhail Polak.

On the day of the most important semifinal in his long career, Armando Reyes woke at midmorning, the scent of Athena still with him. He could still sense the shape of her body, the maddening pressures, the sheen of her long blonde hair. Years ago, he had fallen in love with Athena, when she was younger and wilder and on the rebound from Koras. This time, they were both older, and his feelings for her were far more intense, far more real. Why did one have to become older to feel with such depth? It seemed unfair, and last night, with the new strength from the pills, he had been on the verge of asking her to marry him, a sure sign that he was experiencing a new vulnerability. It would have been a wasted question. If she married anyone, she would marry Saadi, who had endless petro-dollars stored away in vaults in London, Zurich, New York, Tokyo, Hong Kong, and Singapore.

What could they do about Saadi?

Armando phoned down for coffee, noting that service the world over seemed slower, servants more surly, when one ran short of money. Hotel employees had a built-in radar detector that told them who was tipping lavishly and who was not. While he waited for the coffee, Armando took a long hot shower. He would take the pills an hour before his match. He had the mix figured out by now. Four of the reds, for energy. Two of the blues, for stability and a temporary end to stage fright.

He finished his shower. The coffee had not yet arrived. Staring at the small suite, he phoned down again. Oui, monsieur, the coffee was on its way. Compared to last year's huge suite, his present room at the Sofitel seemed confining. He wondered how many people noticed.

Coffee arrived while he was reading the account of yesterday's matches by the London columnist David Kollmore. Kollmore's writing was typically English, not a spare adjective anywhere. Among the sports writers, Armando preferred the work of Judson Garwood, the American who called Armando "the Dark Horse of Lima." Now that phrase, *el Caballo de Lima,* had a particularly nice ring to it.

The surprise visitor arrived while Armando was drinking his second cup of coffee. There was a knock on the door, and he thought perhaps it was Athena, coming back to console him for leaving last night. Muriel wasn't due until noontime. They were driving to Roland-Garros in her BMW Alpina. When he squinted through the security peephole, Armando was surprised to see Jack Di Rocca standing there. Di Rocca, who had lost in the quarters, wore a coat and tie.

Di Rocca was the black sheep of professional tennis. Born in a New York slum, he had grown up hitting balls against the side of a derelict building next to the one he lived in with his mother and two sisters. Di Rocca's father had abandoned the family the year Jack was born and had not been heard from since.

Di Rocca's obsession with the tennis racket had begun the day he stole one from a department store. Di Rocca knew baseball, soccer, basketball. Tennis was mystery turf, a country club world.

While teaching himself the rudiments of tennis on a cracked

concrete court with a neighborhood parish priest, Di Rocca was also a member of the Devil's Rebels, a fearsome Bronx gang noted for hot-wiring late-model cars, which they sold to a middleman, who sold them in turn to a strip shop, where they were cannibalized for parts. At sixteen, he had been arrested for armed robbery of a gas station in Brooklyn. The cash drawer had held only twenty-four dollars, but the station attendant had given evidence, in revenge for the beating he had suffered during the holdup. Di Rocca ended up in prison, with a three-year sentence.

When Di Rocca entered prison in January, he took with him all his possessions—two tennis rackets and a sports bag containing odds and ends of tennis gear. He stayed sane by hitting balls against a concrete wall.

He got his chance when a tournament was organized between the prisoners from different penitentiaries. The trophy was to be presented by Walter Tray, the first American black player to reach world class. Tray would play an exhibition against the winner.

Di Rocca.

In the exhibition, Tray managed to win only after three grueling sets, two hours and twenty-one minutes.

From the stands reserved for relatives and friends, a moon-faced man with narrow Aztec eyes studied Di Rocca's moves. After the match, he introduced himself to Di Rocca as Paco Ortega. Ortega, who had been a circuit player himself, was in the prison visiting a cousin. His business was managing professional tennis players. He liked what he saw in Di Rocca—hunger, ambition, a killer instinct that kept him going—so the next day he obtained a permit to visit. He and Di Rocca talked for a long time.

"In four years, if you work, you'll make the Top Ten."

"In another month, I'll rot in this hole."

"Not if you follow my advice."

"What's that?"

"Keep hitting." Ortega stood, ready to leave. "My lawyer will contact you. We'll start working on parole, right now."

Six months later, Di Rocca was out on parole. Ortega wisely started him out in the minor leagues, playing local tournaments in Texas, Arizona, New Mexico, California, Florida. In four years, he had not yet made the Top Ten, but he was ready for Europe, where he discovered his game was meant for clay. His first big win came at the age of twenty-eight, in Monte Carlo, on a blustery day in November. His best day was the day he handed a check for a thousand dollars in damages to the owner of the gas station. That was a triumph. Di Rocca had never been great. This year, he was number 9 on the ATP computer and he had lost in the quarters to Mikhail Polak.

Now he stood in the hotel room of Armando Reyes. Di Rocca had a deal for the Peruvian.

Armando checked the time. Half-past eleven. His match began at two. He knew Di Rocca was aware of the schedule.

Di Rocca walked to the window, stared out toward the Bois de Boulogne. "You alone?"

"Sí. Would you like coffee?"

Di Rocca sat. "This won't take long."

"Too bad you lost in the quarters."

"I played okay. Polak was in the Zone again." Di Rocca crossed his legs. "You're playing tough yourself. You thinking of going all the way?"

"It has been a long time between wins." Armando poured fresh coffee, added warm milk, two cubes of sugar. "I need a win. So does my brother."

Di Rocca leaned closer. "Armando. I got friends in New York would like to see you lose."

Armando smiled. "Really? I have friends in Lima who would like to see me win. The President of Peru, he would like it, for example."

Di Rocca nodded, but he was not impressed. "These friends in New York, they're willing to pay you quite a bit. To lose, I mean."

Armando took another look at Di Rocca, and then used an American expression. "Get serious."

Di Rocca nodded. His thick eyebrows made him look like a forest creature. "I am. And they are."

"Who are these people?"

"Just . . . friends. Acquaintances. Guys I grew up with, did business with. You wouldn't recognize any names, if I told you."

Armando set the coffee cup down. He felt the raw edge of fear. "Why me, Jack?"

Di Rocca shrugged. "They want Tigrid to get through. He's a long shot, longer than you."

"What about the final?"

Di Rocca grinned. "That's our business. What we want from you is to lose today."

"I might lose anyway, against Tigrid."

"Call this insurance. Armando. Clay's your surface. You're playing over your head. There's a boatload of money coming in from South America and Mexico. Before your Round of Sixteen win, you were 35 to 1. Now you're 6 to 1."

Armando understood. "Your people in New York, they bet against Armando?"

"That's right. And for Tigrid."

Armando set the coffee cup down. It was unbelievable. "They are willing to pay?"

"Fifty grand, to go under in the fourth set." Di Rocca's face told Armando they knew he was having money problems. Fifty thousand would keep him on the circuit another three or four months. He could continue his life-style. If he stretched the money, and made another semifinal or two, he would have another year in bed with the Princess.

"The fourth set?" Armando's mind was spinning. He was playing the best tennis of his career, and some small-minded criminals from New York City wanted him to throw the match.

"Yeah."

The room was quiet. Armando stood up, trembling. "Tell your friends . . ." He stopped, furious. The blood rushing to his face had made his cheeks red beneath the tan. He felt a tiny pain, deep in his chest, disturbing. "How do I contact them?"

"Through me. They'll want to know before the match begins."

"I have time?"

"Until ninety minutes before the match starts."

Armando walked to the door, opened it for Di Rocca. "They are the same people who bet on the baseball? The football?"

Di Rocca nodded.

"And now the tennis?"

"This is a trial run, to see how it goes."

"If they can buy me, you mean?"

"Part of the test."

"And others?"

"Just let me know, amigo."

Armando nodded, but said nothing. Di Rocca walked into the corridor. He left without shaking hands.

Armando stood in the doorway, watching him move down the corridor. Fifty thousand dollars would not stretch far enough. They were pikers, coming to him with so little. And why was he standing here, considering the offer? The pain in his chest came again, a tiny pinprick. He tried to think. What would happen next year? No one knew. If the cattle herds dwindled, beef might soar, OPEC might collapse. He could use the money to buy himself some time. He loved this life, the traveling, the women.

But a stinking fifty thousand!

Did he have a real chance at the title? Or was he only shouting in the wind? He had a chance of beating Tigrid, but probably not Koras, in the final.

Of one thing he was certain. He was not afraid of these faceless men in New York, Di Rocca's friends. As he closed the door, his beautiful morning seemed ugly.

Armando walked into his bedroom closet and took down a black leather bag. Inside were seven vials of pills. Two . . . no, three of the blues. Four of the reds. He walked into the bathroom, stared at his face in the mirror. Another chest pain came, sharp, more bothersome than the last. He swallowed a blue pill, for his anxiety. He followed the blue with three calciums, to calm the nerves, and two large Vitamin C's, for the adrenals, and then a Vitamin E, for oxygen in the blood. Gradually, the chest pain eased, making him think it was a case of nerves. He realized why he was thinking of marriage. Where was Athena now that he needed her?

On the sunny terrace above the courts, Princess Athena introduced Koras to Saadi, her lover. Koras wore a green track suit, new from Laval Sportif. Saadi, as usual, was dressed in white, with a bright red necktie. Koras had heard of Saadi, but this was the first time they had been introduced. As they shook hands, it was clear from Saadi's demeanor that he was jealous of all Athena's old lovers.

"Mr. Belynkas, I still remember your first title, in Rome, back in 1975, wasn't it?"

"Paris, a year earlier."

"Oh?"

Koras looked directly at the Princes. "My win in Paris bought me an invitation to Monte Carlo. And that's where I met your beautiful companion."

"Pantakoras," she said. "You love the past far too much."

Saadi's smile tightened across his dark face. He was tall for an Arab, but he looked soft, out of shape. "Singles is far more important. No one remembers who won the doubles."

"You do, dear," Athena said. "Abdul is a walking tennis encyclopedia."

"Amazing," Koras said.

The Princess looked away from the men and her eyes swept the terrace, to see whom she knew. Her dress was white, a creation from Yves St. Laurent, with a manageable neckline and long sleeves that called attention to her hands, which were lovely. "Would you get me a champagne, darling."

"I think," Saadi said, "that it is time to return to the matches. Coming?"

"In a moment, dear."

Saadi left them and walked hurriedly out of the pavilion. Athena took Koras by the arm. "Well, what do you think?"

"A jealous man. He's King Farouk. He wants you to play Rita Hayworth to his Aly Khan."

Athena laughed. "There is small chance of that."

"I was wondering, just how does all that money smell?"

The Princess put a hand on his arm. Her eyes were slightly sunken today, and a wisp of golden hair had come undone and now trailed down her left ear, toward her mouth. "Oh, Pantakoras. What good times we had, you and I . . ."

Koras remembered the good times, but he did not think they outweighed the bad. He remembered the first time he had seen her, stepping out of a Mercedes limousine in front of the Casino, all sun-rinsed hair and bronzed skin and a figure at the absolute peak of nubility. He'd stared at her, and she had brushed by him, letting her eyes slide away, like a princess looking past the stable boy. Koras was a poor kid from Brooklyn, out to carve a name for himself in the world of professional tennis. That goal had seemed a long way off. But he and Milo had just made two hundred dollars apiece, plus expenses, for winning the French National Doubles title. If they won here, at Monte Carlo, they'd each make five hundred. In those days, tennis was dominated by "shamateurism," an outworn system that hurt the players. In shamateurism, if you were lucky, and if you had crowd appeal, you got paid under the table.

How could that compete with the Princess and her diamonds?

She had been unattainable, unreachable. At a cocktail party in the Royal Palace, Koras managed a dance with Athena. She mocked him with her eyes, tantalized him with her smile. Her body next to his trembling hand was sensual, firm yet yielding. He knew some French, but he didn't know how to talk to a princess. Her hip beneath his hand had a mind of its own. She wore a low-cut dress, yet he was afraid to look down, for fear that she would vanish in a puff of smoke. She was eighteen, ripe. Koras was twenty-two, and broke.

He had decided to take a chance, follow his instincts, try telling the truth. "You know what you smell like?"

"No." Sardonic eyes, smoky and smirky. "Tell me, Mr. Pantakoras."

"You smell like . . . fresh baked bread. In the morning. While they are washing the streets."

Her sky-blue eyes had narrowed. "Summer or winter?"

"Summer."

She had laughed, throwing her head back, aristocracy on wanton display. Koras had been surprised. They danced into the shadow of a potted palm, beyond the eyes of the other guests. She moved close, put her mouth up against his ear, and sank her teeth into his earlobe. Her teeth were sharp, and for a mad moment he thought of the chipmunks in the movie *Cinderella*.

"Cinderella," he said.

"I beg your pardon." She spoke while still biting his ear.

"Chipmunks. In the movie. I don't remember their names."

This made her laugh even more, made her body shake. They were reaching out now, touching in more than just a physical sense. He couldn't believe she would be so friendly. That night, she came to his room. "And you not even in the Top Ten," she said.

"But I will be."

"I know."

Naked, she had slid between the sheets.

They made good copy, the Lithuanian athlete and the Austrian princess. Athena taught him about sex, spending money, art, novels, poetry, Vivaldi, Mozart, the best champagne, how to live in the moment, a life beyond the edge of worry.

He had tried to teach her about honor and pride and tenacity. Athena didn't mind sweating, but she hated to practice. If she couldn't learn it easily, or didn't already know it, she'd drift off, or call to someone to bring her a drink. She'd played tennis at her girls' school in Switzerland and even amazed the fans at the Foro Italico when she was fifteen, by defeating Adrianna Pardona, an Italian champion. When urged, the Princess would sometimes still take the court for a celebrity exhibition.

So Koras and Athena were together for part of a season, an item for the newspapers, and then they drifted apart. The Princess spent money with abandon, while Koras had to pinch pennies. For the next year, he saw her around the circuit, while she traveled with Armando Reyes, a Peruvian who kept cars in every major city on the tennis circuit. Koras decided having lots of cars was an idea with merit.

When Koras won his first major singles title, the Wimbledon singles, Athena reappeared in Koras's life, as if by magic, looking wiser, more beautiful, more mature. She seemed to thrive on love affairs. After Armando, there had been an Italian duke, an Austrian baron, an English country squire named Teddy, and a short-lived marriage to a manufacturer of munitions from Milano.

Athena convinced Koras to buy a villa in Nice. A down payment of $750,000, cash, payments of $33,000 a month, the deal made with a banker she knew, in Zurich. Today, according to

Fenwick, they were still losing money on the Nice villa. Athena had helped him pick out the cars, so he could follow in Armando's footsteps—two Mercedes, two Rolls Royces, one DeLorean, one Jaguar, one BMW, one vintage Volvo—stashed in eight different cities across the world. Only two were left now. KORAS ONE: NEW YORK, which he kept in Paris. And KORAS TWO: NEW YORK, which he kept in the garage at Westhampton.

"Will you marry this one?" Koras asked now.

She smiled. "What do you care?"

"I am jealous of every man you look at."

She laughed, throwing her head back to show her lovely throat. "Pantakoras, you are always a devil."

He asked her what he really wanted to know. "Tell me about Laure Puget."

"Why?" Athena's eyes twinkled.

"I knew you had lots of cousins. I didn't know you had any who could read."

"Awful man!" She pummeled his chest.

Koras waited. Athena looked around at the Parisian crowd. Mikhail Polak was at the bar with his new wife, the American girl from Chicago. "First," she said, "and this is important, she is young." The Princess sighed with recollections of her own wild youth. "That means she can eat whatever she wishes, and does not get fat. She wears sensible clothes. She prefers not to dance, yet she can dance all night. She has one tiny laugh line, here, at the corner of her mouth. Otherwise, her skin is perfection itself. Her greatest expense is books, pencils, papers, subscriptions to dry scholarly journals. She reads constantly, probing books for the secrets of life. Her greatest desire is a computer, from America."

"From what I know of the von Heidelbergs, she sounds like a very distant cousin."

"Mummy adores Laure. She feels Laure will help me contain myself."

Koras laughed. "She'll need some magic for that."

"She studies some magic."

"Oh?"

"Um. She searches for a connection between the Holy Grail and Vercingetorix."

"The Hero of Gaul?" Koras had not attended college, but he knew a smattering of this and that about Roman history.

"Um, yes." Athena swiveled to speak to a French tennis official, Alain Clavier, head of the Federation. The white dress swirled about her legs, and Koras watched, enjoying the show. The Princess possessed perfect balance, and he had always regretted that she had not continued playing tournament tennis. It would have given her more reality. Now flirting was her sport.

"See you later."

Athena broke off talking with Clavier to pluck Koras by the sleeve. "Where are you going?"

"I feel restless. Thought I'd do a quick jog, just to stay loose."

"Where?"

"In the Fleuriste Municipal. The air there is so healthy."

"You are a fanatic."

Koras said goodbye to Athena and Clavier and walked out of the pavilion.

When Saadi arrived at his box, followed by a waiter carrying a magnum of iced Chardonnay, Laure was sitting alone, enjoying the sun. The women's semifinal was dead even, one set each, three games apiece. Princess Athena was nowhere to be seen. Laure was reading when Saadi joined her.

"Ah, Mademoiselle Laure. I was hoping to find you here."

He sat down, pulled his chair close. Laure adjusted the hem of her dress. "Where is Athena?"

"I left her in the pavilion, with some admirers. Would you like some wine?"

It was her favorite. "Yes. Please."

They concentrated on the match while the waiter opened the wine. When the cork was out, Saadi sampled it, then nodded to the waiter, who filled both glasses. Saadi touched his glass to Laure's. "To the project."

"Yes. To the project."

Saadi was sitting close and Laure could feel the heat from his body. She smelled sweat mixed with expensive cologne. She wondered how Athena felt, making love to him.

"I should like to invite you to our yacht," he said. "When the matches are finished."

"Thank you. But I must go along to Dijon. They are expecting me."

He put a hand on her shoulder. "I would consider it a special favor if you were to accompany us." The hand felt like a claw. "There will be people—your own age, of course. Jean-François. The Polaks. Perhaps the young American Davey Cooper."

"Thank you." She moved away from his hand, leaning until his arm was straight and he was forced to let go. "Perhaps another time."

Saadi moved his chair closer. He was acting strangely. "Tomorrow I must drive to Le Havre. Perhaps you would like to accompany me."

"No."

She felt trapped. Why was he doing this?

"We could make a day of it. A picnic lunch. A walk by the river."

Laure stood up quickly. "Pardon me. I must go."

He blocked her way. At the same time, spectators higher up hissed at her, whispered for her to sit down.

"They are playing a point," Saadi scolded. "You should wait until the changeover between sets."

Laure sat down. The trapped feeling would not go away. Saadi patted her hand.

"How is the project going?" he asked.

"Fine. They appreciate the money you've provided."

She felt his fingers close on her hand. "And do you?"

"I? Of course."

"You have a strange way of communicating your appreciation."

His eyes bored into hers. Where was Athena?

"What would you want of me, m'sieu?"

"Have I told you about Clothilde?"

"Clothilde who?"

"Clothilde le Gros. She was my father's mistress. You remind me of her. In the most remarkable way."

Enough. Laure tore her hand free and jumped up. Her sudden, awkward exit spoiled a point for the spectators. More hisses rained down, but she didn't care. A spectator swore at her; someone told her to sit down. A security guard with a severe look blocked her way. Laure stopped, trembling, to wait until the point was over, then hurried out of the stadium. She was breathing hard. The leather shoulder bag flopped against her hip and she was not aware that she clutched her book in one hand until her fingers began to hurt. She knew that Saadi could stop the flow of money at any time. It would be her fault, and now she started to cry.

Laure waited for a break in the traffic and then she trotted across the street to the cool green sanctuary of the Fleuriste Municipal, a timeless vegetal world. Except for a few old gentlemen escaping the exhaust fumes from the streets, the vast public greenhouse was deserted.

Breathing the sweet air, Laure walked to the largest greenhouse. Still trembling, she sat down on an iron chair, grateful to be alone. In here, it felt like a peaceful womb, green and shadowy. She opened her book, but the words blurred. It was time to leave Paris, to get away from Saadi somehow and return to Alesia, where she had her work. If her instincts were right about him, the money would dry up soon enough. It was clear that he had compromised her terribly, and she felt like a fool for not having seen the signals sooner.

What would she tell her colleague, Jean-Luc, at the excavation?

Laure opened her book and forced herself to read. She was deep into a chapter on the speech of Critognatus, a noble Avernian who advised the entrapped Gauls at Alesia to feed on the flesh of the weak and the infirm. Winter was approaching, Critognatus reasoned. If only the Gauls could hold out, snow would drive the Romans away. She had read the speech before, but today the vision of cannibalization brought tears to her eyes. She did not hear the footsteps until they stopped, in front of her.

Laure looked up from her book. Mr. Belynkas stood there. He wore a forest-green track suit with three white stripes along the sleeves, and matching stripes along the trousers. His blue eyes danced sardonically. His blond hair was wet around the forehead, as if he had been running.

She was surprised to see him. His green suit matched the green of the plants inside the Fleuriste Municipal. "Ah, Miss Puget."

His smile, suggestive of vast experience in the fast-paced world of the jet set, made her uncomfortable. Where was the young man with the innocent face who had given her that tennis lesson so long ago? "Hello. Where did you come from?"

He sat down, but changed the subject. "What are you reading?"

"A monograph on Critognatus."

Koras was studying her face. Had the tears made her eyes red? "It must be a very moving book."

She brushed the tears away from her cheeks. "Yes."

"Have you been at the matches?"

She thought of Saadi's advances. "For a while."

"Who was winning?"

She shook her head. "I didn't even know who was playing."

Koras laughed. "I like that. Come and have a coffee."

"I cannot."

"Why?"

"I am leaving Paris."

"Really? When?"

"Today."

"It's a little sudden, isn't it?"

"Yes. But it's important that I get back."

"The lure of the past."

"Yes."

His voice was full of playful confidence. She was sure he had used the same argument, the same tone of voice, with many women.

"How can I persuade you to stay? You must watch me play in the semifinals."

"I watched you play against Terry Laville."

"What did you think?"

She looked into Koras's blue eyes. "Does he get angry often?"

"Only when I beat him in front of fifteen thousand fans."

Laure sensed there was more. "You seem so confident here. And out there. Don't you ever have bad moments, Mr. Belynkas?"

"Oh, yes, many. Before the match, I am nervous about my knee. During the match, I worry whether it will carry me or not. After the match, the knee hurts."

He was smiling, but the seriousness in his eyes told her he had an enemy within his body. Suddenly, in that moment, he seemed less a golden gladiator and a little more vulnerable. "You make it sound painful."

"I'm trying to get your sympathy."

His offhand comment spoiled the moment. Laure snapped her book closed and stood up. "Goodbye, Mr. Belynkas."

She started out of the Fleuriste Municipal and Koras walked along with her. "Let me buy you a drink."

"Sorry." She thought of where she would go, of having to explain why there would be no more money for the excavation. For a moment, she thought of going back to Saadi, begging. Or to Athena—but it was too humiliating. So many people depended on that money to continue their work. And it was valuable work, full of promise. The man walking beside her only reminded her of the frivolity of these idle rich.

"Did I say something wrong?"

"No. Not at all."

They had reached the sidewalk. A cruising taxi passed. Laure waved at it, then watched it continue on up the street. She looked around for another.

"Something is wrong." He put a hand on her arm and she looked up, seeing again the sadness in his eyes.

"I'm sorry. It's got nothing to do with you."

"Let me see you again."

A taxi had spotted her and was drifting to the curb. A shiver went through her and for some reason she wanted to taunt this famous man. Or test him, perhaps. "All right. One drink."

His face brightened. "When and where?"

The taxi had stopped, purring impatiently. "Next week. At our excavation site."

"Where's that?"

"Alesia. Near Dijon."

He laughed shortly. "That's a long way to go for a drink."

She opened the door and got into the taxi. Her skirt rode up and Mr. Belynkas looked at her legs.

"How will I find you?"

"From Dijon, you go north, toward Alise Sainte Reine."

"You are a complete mystery, Mademoiselle Puget."

Leaning forward, Laure told the driver to take her to the Hôtel Paladin. Koras stepped away from the taxi as it pulled away. He was still standing there on the curb when the taxi turned a corner. She wondered how many women he had known. Perhaps, one day, she would ask Athena.

FOUR

The telephone rang.

A young man in white trousers and a red Lacoste shirt picked up the receiver and listened calmly. "I'll get him for you." Placing his hand over the mouthpiece, he called:

"It's Matignon on the line."

Alain Clavier, President of the French and also of the International Tennis Federation, tightened the knot of his navy-blue tie. It was decorated with many little elephants. When he had been elected for the first time to the Presidency, he had declared in his inaugural speech: "The International Federation is much like a horde of elephants; slow to get going but once it is started, impossible to stop." The elephant had become his mascot, the emblem on his tie, and the principal decorative symbol in the President's office.

His desk was a battlefield. On it, Clavier had lined up a hundred elephants of all shapes and sizes. Unavoidably, he had been nicknamed Hannibal, by virtue perhaps of his strategic talents. Clavier was flattered by the analogy. After all, Hannibal was surely the greatest general in history, and in order to win this tennis war, he had to be both soldier and politician.

"Matignon," repeated the young secretary.

"The Prime Minister?"

"I don't know, sir, they didn't make it clear."

Clavier smiled. For fifteen days every year during the spring, he became one of the most sought-after notables in France. Public officials and people in power hung on his telephone lines, throwing their rank to the winds as they pleaded for seats in the

Main Stand, or for boxes, or for just a modest seat, high in the bleachers of the Court Central. Clavier could not please everyone. He was indifferent to political conflict. His only concern was for the protection and perpetuation of the sport. When he gave away a seat at Roland-Garros, he made a date with a man, or a pact. He always achieved some bit of influence that would one day serve the game of tennis.

Clavier took the telephone.

"There are other calls coming through—"

"Let them wait."

Clavier spoke into the instrument. "Clavier here."

"This is Durand," the voice said. "How are things going at the tennis?" Durand was head of the Prime Minister's cabinet, one of the most important posts in France.

"Fine. Everything goes well, thank you." Clavier waited. There was always this nominal show of interest in the sport.

"The Prime Minister asked me to convey his regrets, but he is unable to attend the finals on Sunday."

"How disappointing."

"He asked me to inform you, he'll be in London for the Summit. His agenda is more crowded than we had thought."

"I am sorry. But then the interests of the country come first."

"Naturally, I'm accompanying the Prime Minister." A pause. The request was about to come. "My daughter, you know, is mad about tennis. She spends her days in front of the television when she should be preparing for her exams. She has an autograph from the Canadian, Laville. And from Armando Reyes, the South American. And I was thinking, wondering, if perhaps you might see your way clear to . . ."

"Of course," Clavier said. "But not in the Main Stand."

"Anything. That will be fine."

"I'll have three tickets sent to you."

"They'll be delighted, thank you."

"Yes. I must ring off now. Someone is waiting on the other line." He hung up. "Who is next?" he asked his secretary.

It was the Minister of Sport, a friend of Clavier's from the early days at the Ecole. The two men talked for a while, evoking memories of former tournaments, champions long gone. Clavier was promising places for five of the Minister's friends in boxes booked by advertisers, when there was a knock at the door.

Archer Bell, full of furious energy, barged uninvited into the room. Clavier rang off and looked up from his work. Bell managed Terry Laville and Davey Cooper. His chief rival was Frank Fenwick, the Texan who managed Koras, Tigrid, and Polak. Mercenary and impulsive, Bell had been labeled "Green Thumb" by the tennis writers, mainly for his cultivation of the most ruthless financial tactics to enrich the careers of his players. "Alain, I need a minute."

"All right." Clavier knew Archer Bell would take more than a minute.

"I'll get to the point, Alain. I think Tigrid should be disqualified, before he screws up another tournament. He's an embarrassment to the whole circuit. At this stage in the competition, you can't keep letting him pull that crap and still play."

Clavier had heard these arguments before, but he preferred to stay above them, in his Olympian post of command. There were people to handle such matters.

"He was fined," Clavier said. "After that he calmed down, so the umpire ruled that the match was in order."

"You need to intervene personally, Alain. The man's a goddamned menace to the game."

Clavier knew that Bell wanted to give his own players every advantage. "I have confidence in my staff, Archer."

Bell took out a cigar, which he lit with a gas lighter shaped in the form of a storage tank, bearing the logo of an oil company that sponsored his basketball team, the Chicago Crocodiles.

"He still shouldn't be out there, in that semi."

Clavier stood. "Aren't you being just a little prejudicial, because your man lost? There is no question that a computerized version would have had Davey Cooper besting Tigrid. But the clay beat your man, and Tigrid, like most Europeans, is a past master at clay."

Bell sighed. "Jesus. Where's Mama Lorraine when we need her?"

Lorraine was Davey's mother. She had a habit of traveling with her son around the circuit, and letting her influence be felt. Circuit gossipers said that Lorraine had kept her twenty-four-year-old son at the same age—thirteen and a half—for the last decade.

"I spoke with Mrs. Cooper before she left Paris. There is some vast financial scheme in New York, real estate, I think, that demanded her attention."

"I don't know why I even mentioned her. I never trust a woman with money."

"Yes. But Davey does."

"Poor Davey."

Bell laughed and Clavier joined in, dissipating the flickers of annoyance between the two tennis impresarios. Clavier poured two glasses of Bordeaux, one of which he offered to Archer Bell. The two men toasted.

"To the game."

"Yes. To the lovely, beautiful game."

Armando Reyes rode to Roland-Garros with Muriel in her red BMW Alpina. Today she looked very beautiful in a white dress that displayed her figure to perfection. As she drove, Armando admired her hands, with their long, tapering fingers.

Their conversation was friendly without being intimate. Armando was distracted. He could not keep his mind off the visit from Di Rocca.

It was just before one o'clock when Muriel parked the Alpina in the reserved zone, near the Suzanne Lenglen Gate. She held Armando's arm as they walked past the security guards into the stadium. Di Rocca, wearing a blue summer suit, was waiting outside the door to the dressing room. Armando introduced Muriel and then asked to be left alone, so he could speak to Di Rocca for a moment. When she was out of earshot, he turned to Di Rocca. He had a painful headache. This was the worst moment of his life.

"All right," he said, his voice choked. "I shall do as you say."

Di Rocca answered with a knowing smile. "Hey." He grabbed Armando's hand. "You won't be sorry."

"I am already sorry. Where is the money?"

Di Rocca took his arm and pulled him around a corner, then

handed him an envelope, which Armando dropped into his tennis bag. "Half now. Half when the match is over."

"You are the incarnation of Satan," Armando said, and walked off, carrying twenty-five thousand dollars.

As she left the two men, Muriel knew something was terribly wrong. During the ride from the Sofitel to the stadium, Armando's face had been pale and he seemed to be short of breath. He was distracted, and his conversation, usually so witty and brilliant, was dull. When she had commented on it, his reply had been curt. "I didn't get much sleep."

Now, at the corner of the stadium, Muriel paused to look back. Di Rocca was talking earnestly to Armando, who seemed to be leaning against the wall for support. Without really thinking about it, Muriel chose the mini-camera over the Hasselblad. She brought the mini out of her purse and pressed the red release button. The two men stood in shadow and she could have used the built-in flash. But something told her this particular picture would be better if she left her subjects unawares.

The phone kept ringing. As they were calls from important people, Clavier had to answer. Archer Bell flipped through some copies of *Racquet World,* while he waited for the matches to start. At two o'clock, Milo Tigrid and Armando Reyes walked onto center court for their semifinal. Because Clavier was still on the phone, Bell watched the screen with the volume off.

Reyes came onto the court first, tall, lean, handsome, a perfect example of classic Greek beauty. His features were finely drawn, set off by sculpted lips which betokened his Indian heritage. His deep black eyes explained his enormous success with women.

Bell knew that Armando Reyes was an uneven player, capable of the best and the worst. His greatest success in a Grand Slam tournament had been to reach the final at Wimbledon, four years ago. He lived the life of a jet-setter, on the outer edge of the circuit. At home, the family business interests were managed by Reyes's brother.

The Reyes family owned fifty thousand acres of good land,

along the ocean on the coast of Peru. There was oil there, and huge mountain meadows for grazing cattle. The tennis writers thought of Reyes as the last of the gifted amateurs. If Open Tennis had not come along, he would have whiled away his life at cocktail parties.

Wearing a headband with strings of multicolored pearls hanging down, Milo Tigrid walked a few yards behind Reyes. With each step, an enormous sports bag banged against his hip. Applause greeted both players. Tigrid walked with a weary step.

Clavier put the phone down and turned to the screen. On the court, the umpire had called Milo over. Clavier turned up the volume.

"Mr. Tigrid, your headband is distracting. I'm afraid it will inconvenience your opponent."

Milo's face on the screen twisted in mock outrage. "This? It's a traditional headband from my country."

The umpire's face betrayed his opinion of such traditions. "I don't doubt that. I still must ask you to remove it."

Milo obeyed. Rummaging in his sports bag, he took out a series of objects, which he placed in front of him. A packet of sliced bread, a pot of jam, a Thermos flask, a cup and saucer, and a black frame containing a yellowing photograph of an old lady.

The referee was angry. "Mr. Tigrid, this behavior will not be tolerated." He was shouting, and he had not thought to turn off the network microphone. All the world heard, via satellite.

"See what I mean, Alain," Bell said. "It's not a semifinal. It's a goddamned circus."

On the screen, Milo was brandishing the bread. "Are you asking me to hide the face of my mother? Her noble face brings me luck. And where is the regulation which refuses a player the right to eat or drink during short breaks?"

"Please, Mr. Tigrid."

"I prefer hot tea to the cold drinks you provide. They are bad for the heart." Tigrid thumped his huge barrel chest. "Ask Armando."

"Please." The umpire was livid.

"Furthermore, I'll hand over these to your medical people, so that they can be tested for drugs. Nothing I use is contaminated."

* * *

In Clavier's office, Bell stood. "I can watch this farce better from the stands. If he does it again, I'm throwing the first tomato."

Bell walked out. Clavier returned to his desk, to work on the enormous time chart that laid out the tournaments for the season. The entire game of tennis still wrestled with a series of tournaments started several years ago by G. H. Houston, a wealthy Texan who had tried to grab the best players for himself. It was a freebooting tradition that talent sharks like Bell and Fenwick were still carrying on.

The semifinal match got under way.

At 4–3 in the second set, Armando was sorry he'd taken Di Rocca's offer. He was beginning to wonder what would happen if he just beat the hell out of Tigrid and gave the money back. His game had never been better. He was seeing the ball in slow motion. The power came in long surges, moving him to the ball, giving him time for the setup before his opponent was back in position.

Then, suddenly, as he prepared to serve out the second set, leading 5–3, 40–15, the pills stopped working and a chest pain competed for his attention. He lost two games in a row before rallying to win the second set at 7–6. He had to admit Milo was playing beautifully. At the changeover, Armando was grateful for a minute to rest.

In the stands, he saw Muriel sitting between Di Rocca and his brother, Leonardo, in the players' box. She held a camera to her eye and shot his picture. He thought she was smiling and for a moment wondered what it would be like not to play the circuit. Leonardo had said, again and again, that this was the last year of tennis. The money had been used up. In a way, it was Leonardo who had forced Armando into taking Di Rocca's offer.

A few rows away, he saw Athena and Saadi in Saadi's private box. And Armando wondered what it would be like to be married to Athena. A quiet life in the suburbs. A pleasant home. Children. The only problem was that Athena was a groupie, married to the eternal round of the circuit. There was no sign of the cousin, Mademoiselle Laure Puget.

Taking a glass of water from the ballboy, Reyes gulped down a vitamin C, two E's, three potassium pills, and a red HBO-10.

Muriel shot him through her camera lens.

He felt the pill lift him immediately. Now he would show the world what a player he was. Armando stood, walked to the baseline. Applause boosted him. His mind was sharp and clear. He felt wonderful. He would win. A Peruvian could still grasp the concept of honor. Damn Di Rocca and his New York contacts.

In the players' box, Muriel spoke to Di Rocca while she loaded the camera with fresh film. "Have you known Armando long?"

"Four years. Maybe five. When I came on the circuit, he was one of the big players."

"He is playing well today, no?"

Di Rocca looked at his watch. "He's on a tear."

"An American expression, isn't it? What does it mean?"

Leonardo Reyes grinned at her. He was not as handsome as his younger brother. "It means he's playing well."

She finished loading the camera and went back to work, shooting photos of people in the stands.

"You burn up a lot of film."

"I have decided to make the book. One summer of tennis. Paris, London, New York." She turned to face Di Rocca with the camera ready and shot his picture. At the changeover, she left Di Rocca and Leonardo and moved down closer to the umpire's chair for her photos.

Milo served, and the ball slid away from Reyes.

"Fault," shouted the linesman.

"Are you crazy?" Milo stared at the linesman, then walked to the umpire's chair to protest. "That was an ace, sir. Not a fault. The chalk clearly flew. The man needs a Seeing Eye dog."

The linesman left his chair, bent down, pointed to a spot in the orange clay where the ball had landed. Milo trotted over, showed the linesman another spot, nearer the center of the line. "This is it, blind man." Milo raised his arms, appealing to the crowd. A few people applauded. At last, the umpire got Milo back to his side of the court. Play resumed. With the momentum shifted for the moment, Milo won the next two games to lead 3–4.

At the changeover, Milo poured a cup of tea, which he drank like an old maid at the Ritz in London.

Trailing 3–4 in the third set, Armando took two reds, for energy. His anxiety was building and the lines were starting to blur, so he took another blue, the drug for stage fright.

The effect was instantaneous. Inside his mind, the ball came slower now, meaning he had control again. He hit a drop shot, sucking the Montenegrin to the net, then lobbed over him for a clean winner.

Applause, raining down.

From the sidelines, near the umpire's stand, Muriel shot his picture. He wondered what she was like in bed. The fact that he had not tried to seduce her showed how much he was enamored of the Princess.

He walked to the baseline, feeling slightly dizzy. As he readied himself to serve, he felt the anxiety leave him, like great dark wings receding into the sun, and he knew he was feeling the pills.

Applause came faintly from one of the field courts and for a moment Armando wanted to be there, under the shade of an ancient tree. Those trees had been planted in the twenties, before Armando had been born. He remembered his first sight of them, as a boy of eighteen, on his first visit to Paris. The women had been . . .

He heard the umpire speak to him. "Monsieur Reyes?" And he realized he had been daydreaming. It was his serve. Across the net, a thousand miles away, Milo Tigrid was waiting. Milo was his old friend, the only person besides Athena who knew about the glorious pills. Not even Leonardo knew.

Armando checked the scoreboard, which seemed to waver in the soft afternoon sunlight. The score was 40–30, Armando trailing 3–4. Preparing to serve, he saw the toss clearly, the ball barely rotating against the bright Paris sun, and then his arm cranked, the racket picking up speed as it made the loop and he darted forward to make contact with the ball.

He felt himself falling, thought it was his weight driving forward into the ball.

And crashed into the orange clay of Stade Roland-Garros.

When she saw Reyes falter and fall in her power-zoon lens, Muriel's finger froze, but only for a second; then it contracted, taking pictures from reflex. Hearing the buzz of the crowd, she acted professionally, keeping the camera to her face, pressing hard against her eye socket. The tears started as she continued shooting, and when she took the camera away, it gleamed with wetness. "Oh, no," Muriel moaned.

At that moment, two men brushed past her, Leonardo and Di Rocca, on their way down to the Court Central, where Armando lay face down in the dirt, unmoving.

"Get up, Peruvian!" Milo called. "They know you're faking."

Nervous laughter, from the stands.

But the Peruvian lay still.

Muriel watched, horrified, as Leonardo Reyes pressed his mouth to his brother's and began to pump the rib cage with both hands. A security guard stepped up to stand guard. In a moment, men in blue uniforms trotted out onto the court, carrying a stretcher. A doctor with a black bag knelt down in the orange dust beside the body and used a stethoscope to listen to Armando's chest. Behind the doctor stood Leonardo Reyes and a stricken Milo Tigrid. Off to the right, Jack Di Rocca stood, watching Reyes's Laval tennis bag for him.

At last, the doctor said something to the uniformed men, who lifted Armando onto the stretcher. They carried him off, followed by Leonardo and Di Rocca, who brought the tennis bag. As they walked off, President Clavier arrived on the scene. Still crying, Muriel shot the President, hoping to capture his agitation and forget her own.

Running down the stairs from his office, Clavier had tried to reorganize the tournament in his mind. Two days to go, a second semifinal, a women's final, a men's final. The doubles had to be played, men's, women's, the mixed. If the doctors declared Reyes unable to continue today, play would have to begin immediately in the next semifinal. Perhaps there was a

chance that Reyes and Tigrid could continue their match tomorrow, before the women's final. If Reyes could not continue
at all, that would put Tigrid the clown into the final.

By the time Clavier had reached ground level, the men were
loading the stretcher into an ambulance. Clavier had to get to
the stands, to make an announcement, so he snapped at the
doctor. He needed a prompt diagnosis. He guessed it would be
heat prostration. "Well, how is he, doctor?"

The doctor shook his head. "The man is dead."

"What?" Clavier was horrified. "You can't be sure of that
here. Let's get him to the hospital."

"He's dead. It will do no good."

"Take him to my office."

"Sorry, Monsieur le Président. We must inform the police."

"The *police?*"

The doctor nodded and turned to watch Reyes's brother get
into the ambulance. The men closed the doors behind him. Milo
Tigrid stood off to one side, alone, tennis bag in hand. His face
was covered in tears, as if he were responsible for his friend's
death. Thinking of what he must say to the spectators, Clavier
walked out onto the Court Central. His legs trembled.

President Clavier took the microphone from the umpire and
cleared his throat.

From a phone booth on the Boulevard Murat, two blocks
from Roland-Garros, Jack Di Rocca used a special credit card to
call long distance from Paris to New York. As he listened to the
phone ringing on the other end, his palms grew wet with sweat.
Armando Reyes had been dead less than twenty minutes.

"Yeah."

"This is Di Rocca. Get Sally on the line."

"It's early, pal."

"I don't care if he's in his pajamas. Get Sally."

He waited three minutes, then four. At last, Sally Vicenti
came on the line. "Hey, Jackie."

"Reyes died. Right on the court."

There was a pause while Sally digested the information. Di
Rocca imagined he could hear the numbers ticking through
Sally's mental computer. "Tough. What was the score?"

"Reyes was losing in the fourth set."

"Going to make it a photo finish, was he?"

"Just what we planned." Di Rocca didn't voice his suspicion that Reyes had changed his mind, had died while trying to win.

"Where's the green?" Sally asked.

"Returned." The money had been in Reyes's tennis bag, along with two bottles of pills. Di Rocca had handed the bag to Milo.

"Perfect." Sally made Di Rocca wait while he talked to someone at the other end of the line. When he came back on, his voice sounded happy. "We stay with Panties Koras for the Paris final. For Wimbledon, let's put the squeeze on this Polak, the commie. The plan is that Laville wins in London."

Di Rocca didn't like it. Polak was a good sport, right down to his toenails. He had a little weakness for vodka. There were rumors around the circuit Polak had been a virgin until he married this Gail Hofstedter. A few circuit wags like Laville claimed Polak stayed a virgin after the wedding. "All right. I'll start watching him."

Sally chuckled. "How did Reyes leave us?"

"He was on something, so it looks like an overdose. Maybe heart failure."

"Are we clean?"

Di Rocca thought of Muriel, walking away as he was about to hand over the money to Reyes. She wouldn't have seen the transfer. "Yeah. We're clean." He knew the cops would come sniffing around him first, because of his prison record. You could be the number-one in the world, and if you had a sheet, the cops would roust you first.

"How's the weather over there?" Sally asked.

"A beautiful day for tennis. Sunshine. Birds chirping in the trees. A shitty day to die."

"Well, let me hear from you," Sally said, and hung up.

On Friday evening, the Médecin Légiste—the Chief Coroner —had refused to sign the burial permit after examining the body of Armando Reyes in the morgue. The state prosecutor had intervened, asking for a speedy autopsy, and on Saturday morning the inquest had been handed over to the police, Criminal Division.

Clavier had been called to the morgue, along with Peter Abraham, Leonardo Reyes, and a man from the Peruvian Embassy. Outside the lab, the waiting room was like a sterile chamber, vacant except for an oppressive atmosphere of formaldehyde and human sorrow. Leonardo Reyes sat slumped in a hard wooden chair, staring blindly at the white floor. Next to the grieving Leonardo, in chairs along the wall, were Clavier and Abraham and the embassy man, a dry, scholarly fellow who conveyed all the discomfort of a military officer out of uniform. The scene was depressing, and the men did not talk.

Inside the autopsy room, Louis D'Argent, the lab technician, threw soapy water from his gray bucket onto the thick metal table. The water flooded the surface, mixing with the bloody refuse from the post-mortem, and ran off. Louis grabbed a huge broom and began pushing it along the messy concrete floor, toward the drain. He was angry. He hated working nights, and if things kept up, he would be here on Sunday, when they were running at Longchamps. Louis was good with a knife. He could cut up corpses as well as his boss and he had good intuition, backed up by years of observation on the job, about what killed people. In this case it was drugs. He had made the mistake of broaching his opinion to the Médecin Légiste, who was late for dinner at the house of the Minister of the Interior. An argument had ensued. The chief coroner had left, ordering Louis to write up the report, and not to mention drugs until he had the go-ahead. The coroner's rubber gloves and large brown apron were still hanging over the washbasin. To smother the smell of the dead, the Médecin Légiste smoked constantly. Now Louis had the usual post-autopsy headache, and the leftover smoke from the coroner's pipe was making him sick.

Clavier had made the mistake of wearing a thick gabardine, too heavy for this late in the spring. As he sat there, he was trying to clarify events in his mind. The players had been shocked by the death of Reyes, but even more shocked when his body had been remanded to the police morgue for autopsy. Clavier hoped an inquest by the office of the Chief Coroner would clear the allegations that were being made about drugs on the tennis scene. Gossip ran rampant—stories of cyclists dropping dead during their races, the monstrously mutated muscles of Eastern Bloc athletes. The tennis authorities knew they had to counterattack to stop the rumors from spreading.

Footsteps approached down the hall. Clavier looked up to see two men. One was lean and spare, and reminded him of his wife's cousin Jacquimard, who was a schoolmaster in Toulouse. The other man was shorter, and carried more authority. Well over fifty, he was somberly dressed in a plain gray suit, a white shirt with a starched collar, and a tie that did nothing to enliven his appearance. His hair was gray, untidy, and in need of cutting. The short man stopped in front of Clavier, and produced some identification. He was Inspector Pierre-Aimé Maréchal, of the Préfecture.

Maréchal turned to his assistant. "Stay here, Demetz, and get some statements from these good people." The Inspector stopped halfway in the doorway, to speak in passable English to the men on the bench. "Oh, I forgot to tender my regrets, about the dead man."

And then he swung the door open and vanished into the autopsy room.

Clavier and the others answered routine questions for several moments. The tall officer, Demetz, wrote down their answers in a notebook. After a quarter of an hour, the swinging doors opened and a small man dressed in a high-necked white jacket beckoned them. "If you'll follow me, please?"

He led them into a large room, the walls painted a sickly green, which was separated in two by a thick pane of glass. Behind the glass lay the body of Armando Reyes, resting on a table. Except for his face, Reyes's body was covered by a white sheet.

The small man spoke. "Our autopsy shows that Armando Reyes died of a drug overdose. His bloodstream and viscera were flooded with two drugs which conflicted in his body. The strain, added to a weak heart, was too much for him. When compounded by vigorous physical exercise, the drugs killed him." The man turned to Maréchal. "Inspector?"

Maréchal stepped forward to address the group. "We have two distinct possibilities here. On the one hand, Reyes overdosed himself, while trying to improve his performance on the court. On the other, someone chose to induce the drugs into Reyes." Maréchal smiled. "As you might imagine, I and my department prefer the second hypothesis."

"Murder?" Reyes's brother gasped. "But who would want to murder Armando?"

"That, Señor Reyes, is what we hope to find out. And quickly." He turned to President Clavier. "A team of my detectives will be working with your organization to discover the activities of all the tennis players. We are hoping you will be cooperative."

"But the finals at Roland-Garros, they are scheduled for this afternoon and tomorrow! Surely, you could wait a few hours. This is a premier tournament, an event of national and international importance."

Maréchal smiled. "We shall be discreet, Monsieur Le Président. But we do have our job."

"This is terrible!" Clavier said to Abraham. "It could ruin the entire game!"

"We don't need any more disruptions," Abraham challenged. "Paris is the start of the summer circuit. We need to finish up here and get on to Gstaad and Munich and London."

Maréchal stared at Abraham, then swung to confront Clavier. "Let me be clear about this. If a crime has been committed, we shall detain anyone connected with the case, by house arrest if necessary. To avert the possibility of terrorism, I have already alerted my counterpart in London. If it becomes clear that a conspiracy is involved, we shall widen this investigation to include everything." The Inspector paused while he swept the men with his eyes, indicating the breadth of his power, and then intoned, "We shall investigate here, in Gstaad, in Munich, in London, in all the world."

Clavier and Abraham said nothing.

Maréchal let the words hang there, in the morgue, and then he turned on his heel and stalked out, followed by Demetz.

"Crap," said Abraham.

Reyes had died on Friday. By Saturday at midday, the rumors were flying about the cause of his death. Early Sunday morning, Sven Skaar, the great Scandinavian player, attempted to discuss the situation in a live interview before a television camera. Before his retirement half a dozen years ago, Skaar had had a brilliant career. Three French titles, two Australian, three U.S. Opens. The only title that eluded him was the Wimbledon. Now he was seen as the conscience of professional tennis. On the screen, Skaar looked shrewd, experienced, wily, a veteran of years on the circuit who had come within a few strokes of winning the Grand Slam. The interviewer, Judson Garwood, was trying to probe the death of Armando Reyes.

Q: I'd like to talk about the pressures athletes are under these days. Can you describe that?

A: Well, it varies, of course. I used to feel the most pressure about two hours before a match. It would start then, and it would continue until the first point was over. Then it would go away, just like that.

Q: Didn't you make your fortune in tennis?

A: Yes. What's wrong with making money in a job one loves?

Q: What about the players who don't make a lot of money? What kind of pressures are on them?

A: If you are speaking of Armando Reyes, he came from a wealthy family. He didn't need to make lots of money.

Q: What kind of pressure *was* on Reyes?

A: Obviously, the pressure of time. Armando and Tigrid are the oldest on the tour. Armando had to keep in very good shape.

Q: Otherwise, he's not marketable. Is that right?

A: There is a pressure to remain at an optimum level. We try to preserve the best possible form. That's only natural.

Q: A lot of people say that tennis players are like race-horses—

A: Absurd. Not even a point to discuss.

Q: Are you aware that Armando Reyes is suspected of having used drugs?

A: I knew he took vitamins. Are those the drugs you refer to?

Q: I think the report will tell us he was using something harder.

A: Then I prefer to wait for the report.

Q: Do you know of other players who have used drugs?

A: What sort of drugs? In France, you have sent veal to court for using antibiotics. When I have an infection, I use antibiotics.

Q: Let's get specific, Sven. Do tennis players use anabolics?

A: Impossible, especially now that we know that artificially grown muscles are easily ripped.

Q: What about cortisone?

A: No. No. There is too much risk of stomach ulcers.

Q: What about stimulants, for the actual match?

A: Some sportsmen, or sportswomen, might use stimulants if they knew when precisely they would have to run, to jump, to play ball. A tennis player never knows exactly when he's going onto the court. He can sit in a room and wait two hours, three, four, while other matches go on, or while it rains.

Q: All right. What about hard drugs?

A: Such as?

Q: Cocaine.

A: There is some confusion in your mind between a tennis player and a rock star. We are both professionals. We must entertain, from time to time. There, the resemblance ceases.

Q: All right, Sven. When you were winning out there, what did you do to sustain the desire to win?

A: I did two things. First, I thought about the money. Second, I thought about hatred.

Q: You mean you have to hate your opponent?

A: A player who wishes to reach the top can't afford to feel nice. He must want to kill.

Q: Could we have some more on that?

A: It is common knowledge. On the court, we are enemies. As soon as the match has ended, my opponents become my friends again. Personal ties fall back into place.

Q: Are all players like that, Sven?

A: No. Only the ones who win.

Sunday afternoon at Roland-Garros, the men's final of the French Open. The sky was overcast and gloomy. The fans were restless and there were more security guards evident in the stadium.

Down two sets to one, Koras knew he was going to lose. This was his thirteenth year at Roland-Garros, his seventh time in the final. He'd won here twice. This year, he was seeded number one, but Milo Tigrid, his opponent, was playing out of his mind.

During the changeover, Koras kept looking at Saadi's box, hoping to see Laure Puget, but only Athena sat there, with her entourage. No Saadi. No Laure Puget.

His eyes swept the stands, the faces of the fans. In a box directly ahead of him, a man wearing a straw hat filled delicate balloon glasses with red wine, a metaphor for the good life at Roland-Garros. In the players' box, Jack Di Rocca sat with Terry Laville and the Polaks and Shirley the starlet. If Laville was with a woman, that meant poor Nora was out of town.

On court again, Milo seemed fresher than a man half his age, as if he hadn't run three miles of stop and start across the clay. He was booming the ball, probing Koras's fatigue. Koras narrowed his concentration, tried to slow the pace of the game.

He aimed for the lines, managed to hit a couple of winners, and all the time he kept thinking the crowd hadn't come out today to see tennis. They were here to see someone die.

At 3–4 in the third set, Milo leading, Koras felt his right knee buckle beneath him. He was on his way to a forehand, running wide, and as he pushed off to hit the ball, the knee gave out from under him. The next thing he knew he was in pain, lying on his back smelling the dust of the orange clay while a loud murmur came from the crowd.

Across the net, Milo Tigrid hit the ball long, losing the point.

Koras's fall had distracted him. In the next minute, he was at Koras's side. Milo's face showed fear.

"Pantakoras! Damn you! Get up!"

From where he lay, Koras saw Milo, and beyond him the figure of a Paris policeman, the newest accoutrement of big-time tennis. Koras sat up, shook his head. Milo helped him to his feet. "What happened?"

"It's the knee again." Koras rubbed the offending joint. From the edge of the court, officials wearing jackets and ties hurried toward him. The crowd buzzed as a doctor arrived.

Koras took his three minutes and the pain ebbed as he walked slowly around the baseline. Worried officials asked him if he could continue playing. Finally, he said okay.

He was shaky at the start, but then he found his rhythm. On the first wide forehand, he ran slowly, moving to his right with the utmost caution, waiting for the pain. When it came, a sharp knife in his knee, he was ready. He gritted his teeth and made the winning shot. Across the net, Milo applauded.

But the wily Montenegrin kept playing the forehand, hitting to Koras's weakness. Koras bore Milo no grudge. Tennis was a man's sport. And if you suited up and stepped onto the court, you came to play.

The injury had made Koras aware of time limits. He stopped thinking about Laure Puget and Armando Reyes and began stroking the ball. He forgot the score, Milo, Athena, the voice of the umpire, the buzz of the crowd. He focused on the ball as it flew through the air, slipping across the net, touching down.

At the changeover between odd games, Koras drank some water and closed his eyes. He did his deep breathing. He played a game in slow motion on the magical court inside his mind. In his trance, he was young again, with two perfectly good knees.

At 5–4 in the fifth and final set, Koras brought loud gasps from the crowd when he lost his footing again as he went into the air for an overhead. This time, he caught himself before he fell, and staggered a couple of steps.

"Are you all right for play, Monsieur Belynkas?"

Koras answered in French. "Oui. It is okay."

But it was his serve now, at 40–15, and as he tossed the last ball in the air he knew it would pull Milo off court. The ball went spinning through the air and Milo was already moving. The return came as if shot from a cannon, but Koras was there, covering the alley. He volleyed deeply cross-court. Milo answered with a backhand dipper. Koras closed on the net and volleyed again, a scoop shot just over the net. Milo raced for the shot, but he was too late for a winner, and when he lobbed, Koras had anticipated him and cracked away the last point of the men's final with a booming overhead.

That one, he knew, was for Armando.

"Ahhh!" the girl moaned, writhing. "Ohh, darling!"

The girl in the bed at the Hôtel Sofitel was named Shirley Nash-Winters. She was half English and half American. She'd grown up in England, but attended high school in Winnetka. Shirley had been discovered in a Miss Illinois runoff by Nicky Fortunato, the Hollywood producer.

Three months ago, her flawless face with its peaches-and-cream complexion had been on the cover of *Cosmopolitan*. A month before, on the cover of *Mademoiselle*. A month before that, on the cover of *Elan*. Shirley was pretty, but the feature that set her apart was a set of sleepy gray eyes that in real life projected a come-hither look. On camera, the eyes deepened, making her look intelligent and sophisticated. Inside *Mademoiselle*, Shirley had modeled eight pages of spring clothes for the readers, and suburban girls between the ages of sixteen and twenty-one envied the saucy look and the lithe form that had helped make Shirley a starlet.

After the *Mademoiselle* layout, her agent had come up with a deal from Marvon, the giant cosmetics conglomerate. In the autumn, just in time for school, Shirley would go on television and tell everyone how terrific Marvon products were.

Lots of money kept rolling in. Money was exciting, but it didn't make her happy, did not fulfill her the way Terry Laville did.

When she wasn't squirming on her knees and elbows in Room 405 in the Hôtel Sofitel in Paris, Shirley Nash-Winters lived in Bel Air, California, in an eighteen-room house belonging to Nicky Fortunato, the latest boy genius who was tearing up the track making silly sexploitation films for teenagers. In eleven months, Shirley had made three of them.

In addition, she had just finished filming a remake, in Morocco, of a Hitchcock classic, *The Man Who Knew Too Much.* The leads in Nicky's remake, earlier played by James Stewart and Doris Day, had been Bruce Warner, twenty-four, and herself.

On location in North Africa, Shirley had fought with Nicky, the director and executive producer of the film. The fight was about money. Shirley knew what she was worth these days. She had the Marvon deal, three magazine covers. She had three scripts to read, sitting in her suitcase this very minute, amidst the stockings and the expensive underwear. NBC wanted her for a fall special. Agents called her long distance, to ask was she unhappy with Lolo Darling, her present representative.

To spite Nicky, to make him a little jumpy about the future of his newest property, she had flown to Rome, where she connected with the man who was making her moan and twist that steamy May evening in Paris. That man was huge Terry Laville.

He stood six three, weighed 205 pounds. He had arms like Conan the Barbarian, legs like a linebacker for the Dallas Cowboys. Terry was one-eighth Iroquois Indian, two parts French Canadian, and one part North Woods timber wolf. He could lift Shirley by the waist, grin at her, white teeth against his dark face, mold and shape her like limp putty, hold her high, set her down in any position he chose, and then make her moan for hours, literally.

The Indian part excited Shirley, especially the way his tawniness contrasted with his hair, which was almost white.

With other men before Terry, Shirley had faked sexual pleasure. She was twenty-two, a name in Hollywood, and she had been faking it simply forever, knowing that's what they expected—producers, directors, stars, baseball players, beach hunks on the make, bankers, stockbrokers with houses in Malibu.

They wanted a scene from the camera, and Shirley obliged. They got a scene from the camera.

At an early age, Shirley learned that a loud moan from her

meant her lover was a big man, while a small moan meant disappointment, or worse. For Shirley, volume was no problem.

The faking stopped the minute she met him. He'd been playing a pro-celeb thing at the L.A. Tennis Club, bounding around the court, slamming the ball. One look, and Shirley had started to vibrate, her special way of communicating sexual attraction.

A boy back in Winnetka had called her Shirley the Hummer. She'd simply shake, and her lips would tremble, and she'd feel the energy starting all the way down—stomach, pelvis, thighs, knees, toes, toenails even. It hadn't happened since high school, this special feeling. When it did, Shirley tried to act on it. Life was short, and a girl could burn out in Hollywood in a year, maybe less. That's why she'd flown to Rome. That's why she was in Paris, in Terry's bed, because life, ah, was, ah, short.

"Ahhh!" she cried, squirming.

"You like it, don't you, baby? You like it!"

As her knees twisted into the sheets, Shirley remembered their first meeting, his eyes lighting up when he saw her. She'd been with Nicky and some friends from the studio and Terry had grinned and whispered in her ear that he'd like to lick her all over. From anyone else, it would have been just a bad line.

"Are you—?" she asked, quivering. "Are you gonna—?"

"Shut up, goddammit. Don't talk."

Shirley closed her eyes and tried to visualize Terry on the tennis court, rushing to the net for the kill, but all she could see was Terry naked, in the shower, soaping himself, grinning. One grin made her feel like Jell-O.

The phone by the bedside rang, pulling her mind away from pleasure and back to the world. Behind her, Terry didn't pause. She started counting after a while. Three rings. Or four. Missed one. Six. Seven. She counted to ten before twisting her neck around.

"Terry. The phone."

"Did you tell anyone you were here? That's probably your pal, Ivan Leroy. Or that fag of a producer."

The phone stopped. In her mind, lost in a whirlpool of pleasure, Shirley reconnected, tears in her eyes.

"Ahhh—" she said.

The phone started again. This time, Terry Laville broke rhythm to curse at the caller.

"Sonofabitch! Shut up!"

He had been angry ever since he'd lost to Koras Belynkas in the quarterfinals. He'd quarreled with his wife and sent her back to the States. That was probably who was calling. The only time Terry talked about his wife was when he was drinking. Why didn't he answer? Shirley had a superstition about phones, probably from living in Hollywood, where everyone was waiting for a call from their agent about a part. When a phone rang, Shirley felt compelled to answer.

Thirteen rings, she counted. Fourteen. Missed a beat. Sixteen, ah, seventeen. How long would she let a phone ring before forgetting it? Eighteen was too much. Shirley reached for the phone and felt Terry grab her wrist. The phone clattered to the floor.

"Ouch. You're hurting me!"

Terry let her go. She felt him move away and turned her face to watch. Naked, Terry walked around the foot of the bed, grabbed the phone, and ripped it from the wall connection. In Paris, that was likely to get you thrown in jail. One powerful motion, and it was over.

"There!" Terry grunted.

She held her left wrist and pouted. "You hurt me!"

"Fucking phone."

He stood there above her, holding the phone in both hands. Who was calling Terry Laville?

Inspector Maréchal knew nothing of tennis, except that two years ago a French tennis player named Claude Benoît had been caught at a party on the Right Bank using cocaine. Maréchal remembered the scene when he and three uniformed officers had broken down the door—the smell of marijuana smoke, a movie projector flashing pornography, the heavy sound of American punk rock, the unmistakable reek of sex, and a man in the corner, using a short straw to sniff cocaine from the reflective surface of a hand mirror. The time had been three o'clock in the morning. Complaints had come rolling in, a dozen calls, unusual for a weeknight. It had been a slow evening, so

Maréchal, who was strictly homicide, had gone along as senior officer. The tennis player had been sentenced to a year in prison, and the sentence had been suspended.

Maréchal was a conservative man who wore a three-piece suit even in summer. He drank Vichy water for lunch. At dinner, he allowed himself two glasses of red wine, but only off duty. He viewed the world as a dark place, with occasional flashes of bright and blinding light. He believed innocence was a temporary condition, and that, sooner or later, everyone wanted to kill someone else.

The Inspector thought Armando Reyes had been murdered. Eventually, the State Coroner would arrive at the same conclusion. Meanwhile, Maréchal had been taken off an important case—a lonely and moderately attractive woman from the 14th Arrondissement was being tried for a triple ax murder—and had been asked to investigate the death of a Peruvian playboy.

There were pressures here from the Peruvian embassy, and from the man's brother. On the other side, the people from the lofty tennis establishment, from Monsieur le Président Clavier down to the lowliest circuit gypsy, seemed to want to ignore what had happened.

It was Maréchal's intention to bring reality to bear on the situation.

Who would profit from the death of Reyes? Tigrid, the mad Yugoslav? Comrade Polak, the dour man with dual residences in Dallas and Gdansk? Pantakoras Belynkas, who would have had to play Reyes in the final? Jack Di Rocca, the Italian-American with the prison record? David Cooper, who seemed to take orders from his mother? One of the managers—Bell? Ortega? Fenwick? Or perhaps the strange man with the albino hair and the temper, Terry Laville?

Now being driven through the early morning traffic to the Hôtel Sofitel, Maréchal lit a Gauloise and rolled the list along the tracks inside his head.

"I recognize that name. Terry Laville," he said to Sergeant Demetz.

"He is the one I bet on. Two thousand francs."

"His face, it is everywhere."

"My sister says Laville will be on the cover of *Paris Match* in a week. He is becoming the long-lost Frenchman."

Maréchal looked out the window. "Laville must be French Canadian, no?"

"Yes. I hear he's from Montreal. They say he is part Indian."

"They have incredible accents, those French Canadians. My cousin Bertholde married one, a bureaucrat from Quebec, and her opinion is that they should all be forced to attend grammar school in Paris. Or, at the least, take a semester of Berlitz."

Demetz laughed, turned a corner. They were at the Sofitel.

The concierge was very tan, a typical travel-industry type who probably spent his lunch hour with his shirt off on the banks of the Seine, staring at the topless girls. He wore a blue jacket with a soft collar, set off by a striped tie. He irritated the Inspector by spending time examining their credentials. At last he looked up, a sardonic smile crinkling the corners of his mouth.

"Well, how may I be of service?"

"We need a list," Demetz said, "of every tennis player staying here, along with room numbers."

"That will take some time."

"You have a half hour. Is anyone down for breakfast yet?"

"Yes. Mr. Di Rocca and his manager. They went in a quarter of an hour ago."

The Inspector knew the name Di Rocca, but he checked the list anyway, part of the routine of doing his job. "The sergeant here will stay with you, to expedite that list." Maréchal smiled at the concierge and walked into the breakfast room. He was looking forward to ruffling the feathers of Monsieur Di Rocca.

FIVE

Jack Di Rocca was not a tall man. His immense power stemmed from a fund of nervous energy that was always seeking release. On Monday, following the finals at Stade Roland-Garros, he wore his navy-blue track suit bearing the name of

Ryker, his main sponsor, and the La Rocca–brand shoes he wore as part of a contract with Distaff Inc., a shoe firm in California. It had often been rumored on the circuit that the contract was bogus, a simple cover allowing Di Rocca to be paid for unspecified acts he rendered for unnamed, but powerful, criminal interests.

When possible, Di Rocca left public-relations talk to his coach, the moon-faced Paco Ortega. Ortega's answers were as evasive as Di Rocca's silence. Once he had been interviewed for *Racquet World* by a pretty staff member who had played two years on the Avon circuit. The staffer had a degree in political science from a prominent women's college on the East Coast, and she prided herself on possessing the only conscience in America.

Question: "Is your man Di Rocca the Mafia's man on the circuit?"

Ortega's answer: "Yeah, that's right, and I'm their Ambassador, which gets me more power than the Secretary of State, the Secretary of Defense, and the President. Jackie and I are also working for the CIA, FBI, DIA, DOD, and three secret groups that I can't name here. If you think about it, it's a wonder we find time for the circuit."

Di Rocca and Ortega had the same stocky build. Di Rocca wore a black beard. Ortega's face was clean-shaven and gleamed with sweat. Di Rocca kept in shape, running three miles a day, working out in the gym. Ortega, on the other hand, was fifteen pounds overweight and preferred to limit his athletics to the bedroom.

Ortega had been named in rigged games in hockey and horse racing, and the gossip followed him into tennis, where he managed a half dozen South American players, as well as Di Rocca. Nothing had been proven, but neither Ortega nor Di Rocca attempted to dissipate the criminal reputation that surrounded them.

The speculation made them visible in a sport where personality flourished. It also got them interviews with the police. Often.

At eight-thirty that Monday morning—too close for comfort after Di Rocca's pitch to Armando and their meetings before the semis—they were interviewed by a fussy French cop in plainclothes, who came to their table in the breakfast room, pulled up a chair, and sat down. His identification said his name was Inspector Maréchal. He wore an amply cut charcoal wool suit and a subdued blue-and-gray silk tie. He asked to speak to Di Rocca alone, so Ortega moved to another table.

The Inspector was heavy-boned and deliberate. As he asked his questions, he made notes in a small black notebook. His English was careful, with a heavy French accent.

"Where were you on Friday, the day of the semifinals?"

"Before you ask another question," Di Rocca said, "I'd like a lawyer."

Maréchal looked up. "What for?"

"When policemen ask questions, a person is allowed to have a lawyer present."

Maréchal smiled. "At this stage, monsieur, that is unnecessary. You are in France, not the United States."

"Still, I'd like a lawyer."

Maréchal widened his smile and shook his head. "Would you prefer to answer questions here, or at the Préfecture?"

Di Rocca took a sip of coffee. "Okay. So it won't hurt to answer a few questions."

"Your whereabouts, monsieur? For Friday, the day Reyes died?"

"In the morning, I was with a lady."

"Her name, if you please."

"Danielle."

Maréchal wrote it down. "And her surname?"

"Nightingale," Di Rocca said.

"I beg your pardon?"

"Danielle Nightingale."

Maréchal allowed a small smile to creep across his lips. "Pretty name. What was her address?"

"We went to a hotel, off the Rue St. Denis. I paid cash for a room. I met her Thursday night. We were together Friday morning."

Maréchal knew the section of Paris frequented by young and beautiful prostitutes. "This is quite an alibi, monsieur."

"Did I break the law, Inspector?"

"No. I was merely thinking that with so many pretty women

about, it seems strange that a man like you should—" He let the idea sit there.

Di Rocca leaned forward. "Inspector, do you know the difference between phony and real?"

The Inspector sat back in his chair. He could see that Di Rocca was inverting the ordinary notion about prostitutes.

Di Rocca finished his coffee. The pot was empty, so he signaled for more. "There are a lot of phonies on the circuit. After a while, they get to you, and you need to get back to reality."

"Yes." The Inspector wrote down the word *réalité*. "This Danielle, would she remember you?"

Di Rocca gave the Inspector a look, man to man. "If necessary."

"Very well. How well did you know Señor Reyes?"

"Armando and I saw each other around the circuit. We played pretty much the same tournaments, and we're both over thirty, which segregates you from the younger players. But his real buddy was Milo Tigrid."

"And what was your opinion of Señor Reyes?"

"I thought he was a grade-A gigolo."

"In what way?"

"Reyes operated like a fancy whore. You never saw him without a lady on his arm. Have you seen his wardrobe?"

"Tell me about that."

Di Rocca grinned. "Reyes was the first guy on the circuit to have a silk warm-up suit. For a couple of years there, he wore tennis shorts that shimmered, like running shorts. He had them especially made, in Hong Kong."

Maréchal made a note. Fancy dress, the victim. "Did you see Señor Reyes the day he died?"

More coffee arrived, with a cup for Maréchal. After the waiter had gone, Di Rocca looked the Inspector in the eye. "Mind if I ask why you're asking all these questions?"

Maréchal shrugged. "A simple inquiry, m'sieu, brought about by the request of the Peruvian Embassy."

"Who have you talked to so far?"

"I would prefer to ask the questions, if you don't mind."

Di Rocca sipped his coffee, then added two cubes of sugar. "That means I'm the first, doesn't it?"

"Let me repeat my question. Did you see Señor Reyes the day he died?"

"Sure."

"Where was it?"

"I talked to him outside the locker room."

"What time was this?"

"Around noon. Maybe half-past."

"And what was the topic of conversation?"

"I wished him luck against Tigrid."

"Did you mean it?"

"Sure. Tigrid's no friend of mine."

"How did Señor Reyes appear? What was his mood?"

"He seemed high as a kite."

Clavier had not heard that expression. "Depressed? Sanguine?"

"He seemed confident as an elephant stepping on an ant bed. His eyes were all lit up. He told me he had a good chance of winning the French Open."

"You say that as if it surprised you, monsieur."

"Well, he hadn't won a big title in four years, maybe five. Hell, he partied too much."

"So, you had a brief meeting, and then you went your separate ways."

"That's right."

"And where were you when he died?"

"In the stands."

"Were you alone?"

"Davey Cooper was with me. And Terry Laville. And that movie starlet, Shirley what's-her-name. Reyes's brother. And a French lady named Muriel."

The Inspector wrote down the names.

"What do you know about Señor Reyes's companion, Madame Broussard-Gauthier?"

"I only met her once before, at a party given by that Arab."

"Saadi?"

"Yeah."

Maréchal checked back through his notebook. "Reyes seems to have been quite friendly with Saadi, and also with the Princess von Heidelberg."

"Yeah. Armando palled around with the quality."

"You sound envious."

"I wish I knew his secret for getting along on not much sleep."

"You are aware that drugs have been found in his bloodstream, are you not?"

"That's the rumor going around."

"What do you know about that?"

"About drugs?" Di Rocca put up his hands. "I know nothing."

"Did you ever use drugs, Monsieur Di Rocca?"

Di Rocca thought back to Houston five years ago, the tournament at River Oaks, when Terry Laville had popped a couple of sleeping pills into his beer the night before a major semifinal. He still owed Laville. "Not since I was a kid. They screw up your head."

"Did drugs have anything to do with your incarceration in New York?"

Di Rocca grinned, took another sip of his coffee. "Have you been digging into the Interpol files, Inspector?"

"Please answer the question."

"No. It was armed robbery, pure and simple. I was a dumb kid, scared to death. I paid my dues on that."

The Inspector paused in his note-taking, made an underline to emphasize a key word. He stood up. "I must ask you not to leave Paris, monsieur."

"What?" Di Rocca stood, too, gripping the table.

"An investigation is under way."

"What are you investigating?"

The Inspector answered with a small smile. "There are those of us who believe Señor Reyes was murdered."

"That's a crock!"

"I beg your pardon?"

"You're crazy!"

"Perhaps. In any event, do not leave Paris."

"But I've got a tournament coming up, in Palermo! I'm scheduled to play."

"I am certain that your manager, Monsieur Ortega, will be able to manipulate something."

Di Rocca was tight-lipped with fury. "This means over a hundred thousand dollars, Inspector."

But Maréchal walked away, as if he hadn't heard. Di Rocca knew he should get out of Paris right away, before the police stumbled onto his deal with Armando. He had Sally's money, and he'd given the bag with the pills to Milo. There was more to find out, especially now that he was making deals with Sally Vicenti.

As Ortega came up, Di Rocca was ticking off alternate scenarios. What if Sally had had Reyes killed? What if Muriel hadn't been sleeping with Reyes? What if there was another woman between the sheets with Reyes? What if Reyes had been killed for another reason, something to do with his brother and Peru?

"What did he want?" Ortega asked.

"Just practicing his interrogation techniques."

"Can we leave for Palermo?"

"Not just yet, apparently."

"How long?"

"Until they're finished."

"I'd better make a call. You're the second seed, behind Koras. They can't start without you."

"Yeah," Di Rocca said. "Remind them my mother was Sicilian."

"I'll tell Clavier. Maybe he knows somebody who can pull strings."

"Come in!"

Standing in the corridor, Maréchal knocked again, to make sure he had been heard, then opened the door. He found Koras Belynkas, who had beaten Milo Tigrid in the finals the day before, on the floor in the middle of the small sitting room of his suite. He wore a bathrobe of white terry cloth. In front of him on a tray was enough food to feed a battalion—ham, cheese, scrambled eggs, white bread, dark bread, croissants, butter, jam, and a large pot of coffee—a Scandinavian breakfast.

"Yes?" Koras said.

"Inspector Maréchal. We met briefly, yesterday afternoon."

"I remember, Inspector. Come in. Have some bacon, some eggs. How about a slice of ham?"

"Thank you." The sight of so much food so early in the morning made Maréchal nauseous. "What a magnificent meal."

"Yes. I love France. But I cannot abide your petit déjeuner."

"How do you get them to prepare such an . . . extravaganza?"

"A little persuasion," Koras said, in French. "A little silver across the palm."

"Your French is excellent, Monsieur Belynkas."

"Thank you. I have lived here, off and on, for years. It is a beautiful country, full of charm, good wine, and beautiful women."

"Thank you. On behalf of my country, I accept."

"Sit down, please."

The Inspector sat. "Again, congratulations on your victory."

"Thank you. Perhaps we should not have played, considering the circumstances. Milo was certainly distraught. But we are all entertainers. And the show must go on."

"In my opinion, the continuation of the tournament helped to stabilize the spectators. And the spectators, in turn, helped to stabilize Paris."

Koras smiled. "I didn't know tennis had such far-reaching import."

"The world of sport, Monsieur Belynkas, is a microcosm of civilization. Arenas lie at the very center of our collective subconscious."

Koras bit into a piece of dark bread. "That's a little over my head, Inspector."

Maréchal pulled out a notebook. "I was wondering if you might be willing to answer a few questions?"

"Of course. What about?"

"About Señor Reyes. And the events surrounding his death."

"I'll try. What do you want to know?"

"How well did you know Señor Reyes?"

"Not as well as Milo Tigrid. They were buddies. But we had a drink together. And up until a year ago, Frank Fenwick was Armando's manager."

"Oh? Why did that end?"

"Armando thought Frank was taking too much of a percentage. They parted company."

"As friends?"

"Sure. Business is business. Armando hadn't been winning much, and he was always a big spender."

"Who was his manager these days?"

"He didn't have one. He got business advice from his brother."

"Did he also obtain pills from his brother?"

"You mean the vitamins?"

Maréchal watched him. "Yes. The vitamins."

Koras poured a half cup of coffee, then sat with his back against the hotel sofa. "When I first came on the circuit, back in the mid-seventies, Armando had a chauffeur named Raul, whose main job was to seek out the herb shops, so that Armando would have a good source of vitamins."

"Do you have any idea what he took?"

Koras shook his head. "No. I know he was a vitamin freak."

"Were you aware, Monsieur Belynkas, that Armando Reyes was taking aphrodisiacs?"

Koras put down the coffee cup slowly, a look of surprise on his face. "Aphrodisiacs? Are you kidding?"

"No." Maréchal was leaking the information one piece at a time, sorting out his subject's reactions to each. "Traces of a cantharis derivative were found in his bloodstream, along with another drug."

"Jesus Christ. Then the rumors are right."

"What rumors?"

"That Armando died of an overdose."

"Yes." Maréchal nodded. "That is correct."

"There's something else, isn't there?" Koras asked. "You're asking these questions because—"

At that moment, the door leading to the bedroom opened and a naked young woman appeared. From where she was standing, she could not see Maréchal. Except for a strip of white across her bikini area, she was tanned everywhere. She was tall, with long legs and tight, firm breasts. She walked unembarrassed into the center of the room to the breakfast tray.

When she saw the Inspector, she stopped. "Oh! I am so sorry." She turned and hurried back into the bedroom. When she came out again, she wore a man's shirt, the buttons left undone. It made her look far more sensual than she had naked.

She sank down to pick at the breakfast tray.

"This is Inspector Maréchal," Koras said. "Inspector, may I present Mademoiselle Evelyne Dumont."

"Enchantée, mademoiselle."

"How do you do, Inspector."

"The Inspector is here investigating the death of Armando Reyes."

Maréchal lit a Gauloise and puffed on it. The girl had a lovely face, skin as smooth as the butter she was spreading on a croissant.

"Did you know Señor Reyes, mademoiselle?"

"No. I saw him play a few times."

"Mademoiselle Dumont is in marketing," Koras said. "And public relations."

"Sorry to interrupt," the girl said. She had fashioned a sandwich out of ham and cheese and a croissant. Holding the sandwich, she walked back into the bedroom, trim hips obvious behind the hem of the shirt. The door closed. Koras turned to Maréchal.

"You think someone murdered Armando, don't you?"

"That is correct."

Koras stood up, to pace the room. "Tennis players aren't worth killing. There's nothing to gain."

Maréchal waited before replying. Then he asked, "What did you think of the Sven Skaar interview? The one that was broadcast around the world via satellite?"

"I only caught part of it. I was working out when it came on."

"There was a point he made, about hating one's opponent, about using the hate to build momentum for the ultimate victory."

"Sven's always been full of theories. Most of them are crap."

"Yet, in this, he seemed altogether serious."

Koras stopped his pacing.

"My theory," Maréchal went on, "is that someone got angry

enough to kill him. Perhaps the competitive hatred boiled over."

"Well, you do build up some steam when you're out there. But it blows off when the match is done."

"A pure anger," Maréchal said. "An anger for athletes and Olympians?"

Koras grinned. "You make it sound silly. But yes, that's what it feels like. Pure."

Maréchal smiled. He loved playing cat and mouse, and this man Belynkas was intelligent. "Do you know the Parsifal legend, Monsieur Belynkas?"

"He was off saving the world from dragons, wasn't he? Hauling maidens out of trouble?"

"Yes. But his mental state reminds me of the way you and Sven Skaar think about tennis."

Koras smiled. "Well, don't tell it to the newspapers, Inspector. They'll never leave us any peace."

"Are you aware of any players on the circuit who use drugs, Monsieur Belynkas?"

Koras waited before replying. "There was a player named Eddie Trowbridge, from California. He had to drop off the circuit last year. He used uppers and downers to keep himself leveled out. Eventually, it caught up with him."

"No one else."

"No."

"Have you ever used drugs, M. Belynkas?"

"Penicillin, when I was in the service."

Maréchal stood. "Well, thank you for your time. I must be going." The two men shook hands, and the Inspector walked to the door. "Oh, I must ask you not to leave Paris."

"What?"

"Yes."

"For how long?"

"A day. Perhaps two. Until we have finished our investigation."

"But I've got a tournament! In Palermo!"

"My regrets." Maréchal opened the door and walked out, leaving the American to his breakfast and his pretty young woman.

* * *

On Tuesday, President Clavier and Peter Abraham were at a table in the restaurant of the Hôtel Sofitel, waiting for the arrival of Inspector Maréchal. Until the Reyes death, which the police were now calling a possible homicide, tennis had been a cloistered world, and the impresarios had been able to clamp down on problems before they became public knowledge. Now the situation called for some delicate liaison work.

Clavier, who seldom allowed anything to dissuade him from a good lunch, had eaten everything. The fish course had been excellent; the wine, superior. Abraham, a moody man, had barely touched his food.

"How long can they keep us here?" Abraham asked.

"Another day. Perhaps two. I spoke with my friend, the Minister. He is working to allow the players to move on."

Abraham poured more wine. Since the announcement about Reyes being murdered, he had been drinking too much. "They're talking about another strike, Alain."

"Mon Dieu! Please ask them not to. It would damage what little unity we have."

"Sven Skaar called, to tell me he's doing another interview. The public trusts him, and we've been getting some good mail and a lot of phone calls about it."

"Skaar is a good man."

"You don't sound convinced."

"What I am sensing, my dear Peter, is that people want to hurt us. We have such a positive image, and some people will stop at nothing to tarnish us."

Abraham sighed. "I keep feeling as though this happened behind the Iron Curtain. Cops everywhere, poking around. A gray Renault followed me when I went shopping yesterday."

"My main worry," Clavier said, "is that the problem will spread to the other tournaments and damage the entire season. Archer Bell has been speaking to me about this. So has Saadi."

"You know, when I was in my twenties, I wouldn't have minded hanging around Paris for another week. I had time to burn. But each year I think: Pete, this season is your last. And that's why I want to get out of here. I've got a tournament to play in Gstaad. Wimbledon's less than a month away, for God's sake!"

"Patience, my dear Peter." Clavier looked beyond Abraham's shoulder, to see Inspector Maréchal making his way toward them. He came up to their table and shook hands with both men. Clavier invited him to sit down, and a waiter hurried over to take his order. "Would you like to order something, Inspector?"

"Perhaps a small apéritif."

Clavier ordered a cassis. The men made small talk until it arrived.

Maréchal sipped his drink, then held it up between himself and Clavier. "Well, Monsieur le Président, I toast your political connections."

"What does that mean?"

"I had a call this morning from the assistant to the Minister. While I do not appreciate the intrusion, it appears that your tennis players will probably be able to depart, flee to all corners of the universe—if I get cooperation with my remaining interrogations."

"Ah, very good." Clavier glanced at Abraham.

"The Minister, you see, has become convinced that the death of Reyes was an accident."

Clavier had hoped as much.

"But I, on the other hand, differ."

"It's your job to think he was murdered."

The Inspector took a healthy sip of his drink and stood up. "So. I shall keep all players here until tomorrow morning. After that, they should be free to leave Paris."

"Terrific," Abraham said.

"However, if the inquest should take a different turn . . ."

Clavier listened carefully to the veiled threat.

". . . then I shall have to contact Scotland Yard and pursue the investigation to London."

"You don't mean you've got the jurisdiction to harass us in England?"

"Police cooperate with one another, Mr. Abraham. In today's terrorist climate, we must be on twenty-four-hour alert."

"In the middle of the tournament?"

"I'm afraid that our time schedules can't always coincide, and it would be extremely difficult for me to align mine with yours. I think you are forgetting that this is a criminal case, and that the murderer might very well be among you—"

"Impossible!"

"Or," Maréchal went on, "among those who follow the circuit."

The Inspector quickly stood, bowed, a stiff little motion, and walked away from the table, leaving both men with a vague sense that things had somehow become worse.

"I'm going to pack."

"Not yet, Peter." Clavier put a hand on his arm.

"Why not?"

"We still have an internal problem. We need to do something about it."

Abraham looked at his watch. "There's a plane for Switzerland at two. I'm going to be on it." He stood up.

"Give me half an hour," Clavier said, as he dropped a sheaf of French francs onto the table. "To call a war council."

Abraham walked out. Clavier went straight to the office of the concierge, where he used the telephone.

A huge traffic jam extended from the Avenue George V to the Champs Elysées. The taxi containing Archer Bell and Peter Abraham was stuck. They were about ready to get out and walk when the taxi squeaked through an opening. The driver sped to the Rue Quentin Bauchart, turned left at the next corner, and stopped in a swirl of curbside water. Abraham got out. Bell handed the driver a banknote.

"Keep the change."

Bell and Abraham walked up Avenue George V until they reached Fouquet's. A fussy maître d'hôtel led them to a private sitting room where the other guests were assembled. It was Clavier's party. Fenwick was there, along with Sven Skaar, Abdul Saadi, Paco Ortega, and Harrison Cabot, the President of the U.S. Tennis Association. A worried Sir Francis Malcolm, the chairman of the All-England Club and the man who would preside at the Wimbledon Championships, had arrived that morning from London.

These were the men who controlled professional tennis.

A waiter served the champagne. Saadi had Perrier, with a twist of lime. Clavier opened the discussion.

"Gentlemen, we have a problem."

"I hope we can get on with it, Alain," Fenwick said, looking at his watch. "This meeting just cost me a half million. I was due in Geneva three hours ago."

"And I've got to catch a plane myself," Abraham said.

"Gentlemen, we are all making sacrifices."

"What's the latest from the lab?" Abraham asked. "On the drugs?"

"There is nothing, I'm afraid. A new drug that acts as a stimulant, and a second drug, which is an aphrodisiac."

Bell cut in, leaning forward in his chair, frowning, using his bulk. "Drugs are what we've got to worry about. We need to squelch this drug connection, here and now."

"I agree," said Ortega. "We don't want the newspapers to run with this."

Tension was rising in the room.

"Gentlemen, please." Clavier held up his hand, palm out. "We are in accord, but we must keep cool. The French Open is over. We have a winner, and a *grande crise* has been averted. But the Season, it is ahead of us."

"Hear, hear," said Sir Francis, looking at Harrison Cabot.

Wimbledon was coming up next. Already, the publicity generated about drugs was dirtying the air, and ticket scalpers were doing a huge business. What happened at Wimbledon in mid-summer would affect what happened at the end of the summer, at Flushing Meadow in New York.

Clavier made an attempt to summarize. "Our problem, as I see it, is that we are being invaded. The police. The press. There has been a line outside my office for two days, photographers, television people, magazine writers. The phone never stops ringing."

"What we need," Archer Bell said, "is some protection."

"I don't buy this murder theory of Maréchal's," Abraham said. "Who would want to kill Armando?"

"I agree with Pete," Bell said. "We need to play this as an accident, and not a murder. Everyone knew that Armando was a vitamin freak, and it's not that big a step from vitamins to the hard stuff."

Abraham turned to Fenwick. "When you were managing Armando, F.F., how did he seem?"

Fenwick thought a moment before replying. "He started taking a drug last year, something for his anxiety. Hell, I've got friends back home in their sixties who take the same kind of thing, and they don't collapse."

"But Reyes was mixing drugs," Abraham said, "letting them combine in his bloodstream."

Fenwick shook his head. "I didn't know about that. He must have been on the edge, more than I knew."

"What we must do," Saadi said, "is protect the game as a whole. Reyes is dead. Others live on after him."

"Hear. Hear."

The talk swirled through the room. It was a closed meeting, with no waiters admitted, so Clavier poured more champagne all around. Archer Bell leaned back in his chair and studied the situation. Bell had a single priority—keeping his own players out of trouble. In the past, there had been talk that Terry Laville had dropped something into his opponent's food, but so far as Bell knew, it was just a rumor. If it had happened, it had been before Bell and Terry got together as manager and player. But Laville was crazy and highly strung, and when he got desperate, the man was capable of anything. It was too late this year for the Grand Slam—Koras had the momentum there—but Laville could win his first Wimbledon and go on to take New York. Laville needed a personal watchdog.

Bell, watching the momentum of the discussion shift and wobble, seized his moment. "I have a proposal, gentlemen."

"What?"

"We need information. We don't know anything, and that makes us a hostage to rumor, to speculation, to the investigators leaking exaggerations to the press to make themselves look heroic. If the police do come sneaking in undercover, we want to be informed. If someone's pushing drugs, we want to know which players before we read it in *Le Figaro*. Am I right?"

Information was a safe topic. For the first time, the men agreed. So Bell laid out his strategy.

"All of you know I own a basketball team. Three years back, we had a similar problem come up—drugs, doped players, threats of a news leak, which would have generated some rotten publicity, not to mention fines, suspensions, maybe jail terms for some of our people. We hired a private investigator. He nosed around, posing as a writer, found out who was using, who was clean. We had some private talks with our users— there weren't many—and the threatened criminal investigation never went anywhere."

Clavier nodded. Ortega looked at Bell, suspiciously. Abraham looked around the room. Saadi smiled, an enigmatic smile.

"Who is this man?" Clavier asked.

"Malone's his name. Matt Malone. He's ex-Army, ex-police. Had a year or so of law school. He's tough and reliable."

"Is he available?" Saadi asked.

"I can check." Bell looked at his watch. "If you gentlemen give me the go-ahead."

"What will this cost us?" Fenwick asked.

"Money's no object, F.F., if he does the job. When he worked for us, he got four hundred a day, plus expenses."

"This is International Tennis Federation money, I presume?"

"I suggest a private fund," Bell said. "With everyone at the table contributing. That way we keep the ITF out of it."

"A sound plan," Clavier said, glad to be insulated from this business.

"Who will Malone report to?" Abraham asked.

"Let him talk to Mr. Bell," Clavier said. "And Mr. Bell can report to us."

Abraham stood. "Three days ago, I would have voted no. But since that insinuating cop Maréchal has been breathing down my neck, I think it's a good idea. I vote yes, and if I hurry I can catch that plane."

"Good luck at Gstaad, Pete."

"Thanks."

Abraham walked out, and Archer Bell turned to face the impresarios. "I have one vote for Malone, gentlemen. What is your pleasure?"

The Advisory Group voted to buy themselves a little discretion.

SIX

It was midafternoon and the Avenue de Breteuil was calm at last. Even so, Sergeant Demetz could not find a parking space. Paris was getting too crowded, even for Parisians.

"Stop in a double lane," Maréchal ordered. "For heaven's sake, we're the police."

"Yes."

Demetz complied, but Maréchal knew it was against his principles. Demetz was a man who went by the book. He dressed precisely, and his reports were works of art. Maréchal smiled. He could bend the law here and there. But his aide, never.

Inspector Maréchal was ten minutes early for this meeting with Muriel Broussard-Gauthier. He had done his homework and had discovered that her husband was an attorney with close associations to high places in the city. Maréchal's task was to impress her with the fact that, without her husband's connections, she would have been taken to the Quai des Orfèvres and questioned there.

As the elevator rose, Maréchal flipped briefly through a file that contained photographs of Reyes with a dozen beautiful women. They were from magazines and from the files of professional and amateur photographers. One had caught Reyes at the moment of his death, collapsed on the red earth at Roland-Garros. Several photos showed Reyes and Milo Tigrid, who was one of the last players left in Paris. Maréchal had an appointment with Tigrid later that afternoon.

Another series of photos, from a glossy magazine covering a society party, showed Muriel between Reyes and her husband, the powerful attorney. The husband had a long, sad face, typically French. It was clear he did not like being photographed.

In the photo, Muriel was resplendent. She was much younger than her husband. Her hair fell like silk over naked shoulders, and the low-cut dress did little to hide the voluptuousness of her breasts. A discreet set of diamonds—a choker with a matching bracelet and a glittering ring—perfected the image of wealth and eternal beauty.

Maréchal knew that face, from an investigation five years ago, a scandal involving twenty important people from the fashion world, politics, the military. Drugs had been involved then, and a call-girl network had been uncovered. And in the center was the beautiful woman named Muriel X. She had not been married then. As he stepped off the elevator, the Inspector wondered how much her husband knew about her past.

If the husband knew nothing, Maréchal would have his leverage.

She lived in a sumptuous apartment on the fifth floor. Maréchal rang the buzzer, looked around the hall, which had floors and walls made of marble. A maid answered the door. She was dark, and her accent told Maréchal she was from the French Antilles. She led him to a sitting room furnished in authentic Louis XV, and left him there. In a moment, Madame Broussard-Gauthier, alias Muriel X, appeared. She wore a viridian-green dress that brought out the color of her eyes, and carried a hat in one hand. The hat, reminiscent of Paris in the thirties, told Maréchal that she was going out.

He stood. The lady greeted him and sat down, carefully, on the edge of a silk brocade settee. She crossed her legs, an experienced move by a woman conscious of her sexual allure.

"Thank you for taking the time to see me, madame."

"Not at all. I try to cooperate with the police. My husband is an officer of the court."

"Yes, madame. I know that. I am here to ask a few questions about Armando Reyes."

"It was terrible. I saw it, from the stands. One moment, he was playing beautifully, looking exceptionally strong, and the next he—"

"Are you aware that the case has been turned over to Homicide?"

"No." Her pretty features registered shock. "Why?"

"We think Reyes was murdered."

She put her hand up to clutch her throat. At the same time, her face grew pale, making her look older and more vulnerable. "It is not possible! Who would want to *kill* Armando?"

It was just the reaction he wanted. Maréchal pulled out his notebook. "Madame, it is well known that you were seen with Reyes in the days preceding his death. You drove him to the stadium the day he died."

"Is that a crime?" She recovered her composure by adjusting her position on the settee. She had excellent legs.

"There are rumors that you and the victim were lovers."

"The rumors are only rumors."

Marechal brought out the file of photographs. "How did he appear? That day?"

"He was nervous. It was just before the match."

"Was this a change in his behavior?"

"I cannot be certain. We had lunch a few times. We saw one another at parties."

Maréchal tried putting on more pressure. "I was wondering if your husband might be able to help us dispel these . . ."

Muriel stood up. "You are threatening me, Inspector." Her eyes flashed, and a tremor passed through her body. When angry, she was magnificent. A man might be tempted to treat her badly, just to see her this way. Maréchal wondered if that had been Reyes's mistake. "Now," she said, "I must ask you to go."

Maréchal stayed where he was and showed her the picture of herself, between Reyes and her husband. "I take it your husband was friendly with Reyes."

"My husband was interested in getting Armando's opinion on some investments in South America."

"Where is your husband, madame, in case we need to question him?"

"Singapore," she said. "Now, Inspector, if there is nothing else?"

She trembled, and the green dress rippled, settling neatly on her figure. Maréchal suddenly considered that if she was telling the truth about herself and Reyes—they saw one another over lunch and at parties—that meant there was another woman.

"I understand that you are doing a collection of your photos for a book. Une histoire de tennis?"

"Yes."

"I should like to see the photos."

Muriel walked into another room. When she came back, she

carried two albums of photos. As the Inspector leafed through the pages, he kept up his interrogation. "What can you tell us about Reyes's habits?"

She looked at her watch. "I can tell you I am late for an appointment."

"Who else did he see? What did he do when he wasn't playing tennis?"

"He was very debonair. He loved having a good time. His secret ambition was to be a race-car driver."

Maréchal noted that. "Were you aware that he took drugs, madame?"

"I knew that he took vitamins. He was what the Americans call a health nut. Frankly, I thought he drank too much."

Maréchal wrote that down in his notebook, then closed the photo album and stood up. "This photo book you are doing. Will it take you to other tournaments?"

Her answer was clipped. "Yes."

"In that case, I would appreciate it very much if you would keep your ears open." He handed her a card.

"I am not a police informer, monsieur."

Maréchal gave her his special inspectorial smile. "Oh, there is one small matter. A scandal five years ago, involving M. Bretton and some members from l'Ecole Militaire."

The woman blushed, then grew pale. "What about it?"

"I was just wondering how much your husband knew of that affair?"

"He knows enough."

Marechal nodded, pointed to his business card, and closed his notebook. "I bid you good day, madame. And good luck with your publishing venture."

The Inspector let himself out. Standing at the door of the elevator, waiting, he noticed that Madame Broussard-Gauthier had not yet come out. Perhaps she had forgotten her urgent appointment.

Going down in the elevator, he wondered how many pictures she had held back from him.

Milo Tigrid was sitting at the deserted bar, thinking about the death of his friend, when Inspector Maréchal appeared at the door. He waved the policeman over. The Inspector sat down and ordered a half beer on tap.

"We do not have beer on tap," the barman said.

"An Amstel then."

The barman opened the beer, poured half of it into a tall glass. Maréchal drank, then turned to Milo.

"Monsieur Tigrid, thank you for granting me this interview."

"I am here. You are here. What is it that you want?"

"You were good friends with the deceased, were you not?"

"The best. We drank together. I taught him everything he knew about tennis, life, women, having fun."

"What did he do for you?"

"Years ago, Armando loaned me money, so I could continue playing. I was on a losing streak. I had not won anything in more than a year. He kept me afloat."

"A good friend, then."

"The best."

"What did you think of his vitamins?"

"They were horse shit. But Armando could not function without them."

The Inspector switched subjects. "How well do you know Muriel Broussard-Gauthier?"

Milo gave the Inspector a look. "Not well enough."

"May I take it that means you and she were not intimate?"

"You put it delicately, Inspector, and my bruised ego thanks you. We were not intimate."

"And how did that make you feel?"

Milo shrugged. "You win some, you lose some."

"Could you be more specific?"

Milo signaled for another beer. "Women are like buses. If you miss one, another will be along in a quarter of an hour."

Maréchal smiled. "You are a philosopher, monsieur. Do you think Señor Reyes was intimate with her?"

"Who knows? If she could not have Tigrid, she might as well settle for the Peruvian."

"Does that mean you tried with her?"

"Is the world dark at night? Does a duck swim? Listen. Armando and I had a pact. If he so much as looked at a woman, I would try for her. And the same for him, when I looked."

"It was a game, then?"

"Yes. A small competition, off the courts, to keep us amused on the eternal round."

"This competition with Reyes, did you keep score?"

"Informally."

"Who was ahead?"

Tigrid grinned. "I was. I am older. But Armando was closing in on me."

The fresh beer came, and the Yugoslav held his glass up. "To Armando, you handsome bastard, wherever you are."

"Do you know for a fact that Reyes and Madame Broussard-Gauthier were intimate?"

"I would bet my life on it. Why do you ask?"

Maréchal knew someone was lying, so he tried a police ploy. "A woman was seen leaving Reyes's room the night before the murder."

"Why are you calling it a murder?"

Maréchal sipped his Amstel. "Do you have any idea who that woman might be?"

"Muriel, of course."

"What if it wasn't Muriel?"

Tigrid brightened, then grinned at Maréchal. "I see it this way."

"Yes?"

He held his glass up to the light and intoned to the room and the world at large. "For Armando, women were like buses . . ."

Maréchal stopped him. The man was drunk and a clown. How best to use him? "What would you do if you could locate the person who killed Reyes?"

Instantly, without thinking, Tigrid's eyes blazed and he smashed the empty beer bottle against the bar. "If I find the sonofabitch who killed him, I swear I'll throttle him with these two hands."

And they were big enough hands to do the job.

There was a dream girl on the jumbo jet to Paris who kept Matt Malone's attention, all the way from the takeoff at Chicago to the landing at Charles de Gaulle. She was a college junior from Beloit College, a liberal arts school in Wisconsin, just above the Illinois-Wisconsin border, north of Rockford. Malone, who worked out of Chicago, knew the area. A couple of years back, he had handled a case for a doctor from Rockford, Illinois. The doctor spent seventy hours a week in the Emergency Room, and he was certain his wife was cheating on him, with a good friend from college days. The lady in question, a stunning blonde who jogged in pink warm-up suits and who appeared in the society pages in a dazzling sable fur, had led Malone a chase across a landscape that resembled his nightmares about Siberia—Milwaukee, Madison, Chicago, Kenosha, Dubuque, Peoria—wheeling her pale-blue Seville down the narrow winter roads like a crazy woman.

The doctor had been right about his wife stepping out on him. But he'd been wrong about the college friend. The lady was seeing three different men, and having one hell of a time doing it. At the end of the case, the doctor refused to honor Malone's travel expenses, and had to be taken to small-claims court.

Oh, yes, Matt Malone remembered that winter. He'd drunk many boiler-makers, and the wind-chill factor had often been fifty below.

The honey-skinned girl on the plane, however, washed all the cold memories away. She was sunny and warm. Her name was Deborah Hansen and she was majoring in sociology. She had perfect white teeth, clean hair the color of an Iowa wheatfield, blue eyes that smiled at you, and a healthy chest that punched her sweater out in front, like two sharp mountain peaks. The sweater was pink and fuzzy, reminding him of how things were back in the fifties, Malone's own heyday.

Ah, sweet memories.

So he chatted with Deborah Hansen. They had a complimentary cocktail, then one more.

And when she excused herself, squeezing past him, brushing him with her knees, letting the touch linger for just that extra split-second that made him think she might be coming on to him, Malone told himself to calm down. He was old enough to be her father.

Malone had known a few girls like Deborah Hansen, but mostly from a distance. He'd had his first crush on a distant dream girl when he was a boxboy at the A&P in Skokie. She was an untouchable teenager on her way to being a pristine clean college girl. She had shining hair and the confident walk that came from money, like she owned half the world and was making plans to buy the other half on Saturday. He'd stare at her when she came in to shop, getting out of the car, flash of leg, walking into the store with a little knowing smile, standing in the aisles, hips tight and compact inside her plaid skirt, while she studied a label. She dressed casually, but Malone could tell the clothes were expensive. Her name was Sally Atkinson—he found that out after seeing her twice—and she represented money, wealth, power, the never-ending good life. Malone reckoned Sally was about his age, but that only made her more distant, more unreachable. When she went away to college, somewhere back east, he spent September and October waiting for her to come back to the A&P. When she didn't, Malone joined the Army.

Sitting there, on the jumbo jet, Malone could still remember Sally Atkinson getting out of her car, swinging those pretty legs, the skirt climbing up, like a class television commercial for women's stockings.

Now, at forty-seven, Malone still marveled how easy it was to close your eyes, reach back, and connect to teenage longing, teenage pain. Here he was, a veteran of the U.S. Army, the Chicago police force, Marshall Field's department store, the United Insurers Limited of Northern Illinois, Malone's Typing Service at the University of Illinois, and the Niles Center A&P in Skokie. And he was still lusting after college girls who smelled faintly of Ivory soap. The weighty emotion made him reflect on longing and hunger and appetite.

He'd enlisted in 1957, for Airborne training at Fort Bragg, North Carolina. The Army had shipped him to Germany, where a girl named Ilse Hausmeier had fallen in love with him. Ilse came on to him, icy blonde, with cold blue eyes and a frigid way of holding her mouth when she spoke. She had money from her father, who turned out to be your friendly neighborhood black-marketeer. Out in the world, Ilse walked stiffly and inspired chills. In private, between the sheets, she was all passionate action—serpentine legs, lips, sweat, moans, warm skin.

That dream girl had lasted four months.

After Germany, he spent some time in France, training French airborne troops to jump out of transport planes. From France, he went to Vietnam, where he was wounded. In 1963, he framed his discharge papers and entered the University of Illinois at Urbana, majoring in political science. After a semester of theory, Malone switched to criminology. He'd always been a jock when he had time, so he tried out for the baseball team and played catcher on the varsity. He was older than the average college boy, so he got elected captain. For a couple of years, the dream girls swarmed, nice, clean college girls, none as pretty as his vision of Sally Atkinson—where was she now?—but enough to let him know the world was there for the taking.

He was twenty-seven when he graduated and entered law school at the University of Chicago. He married Gretchen Hill Finch, from Evanston. Gretchen reminded him, from a distance, of sweet Sally Atkinson. After four months of bickering, Malone knew he shouldn't have tried to marry a dream. Gretchen divorced him and took a plane to New York. Her dream was making it big on Broadway.

Depressed, Malone dropped out of law school and became a skip tracer for Marshall Field's department store. He went on from Field's to insurance work, investigating arson cases, tracking insane firebugs who sent whole city blocks up in flames, and then were dumb enough to try to beat the insurance company. Malone enjoyed tracking the types who thought they could get away with it, and he kept meeting all kinds of people, the best and the worst his metropolis had to offer.

There was a certain circle of men in Chicago, most a few years older than Malone. They dressed in suits from Brooks Brothers. They had seats on the commodities exchange. They arrived at meetings in long black cars, piloted by polite chauffeurs in sharply tailored uniforms. These men lived in Evanston, Grosse Pointe, Kenilworth. Their wives were good clean college girls like Sally Atkinson, now grown into mature society women.

And these men came quietly to Malone, asking him to fix this, or to hide that, or to do a little coverup. They trusted Malone.

They needed him. And that gave him an idea for his own business.

He left United Insurers, Ltd., and went into business for himself. Matt Malone, Investigations. And that's how he met Archer Bell . . .

"Hi!" He looked up to see Deborah Hansen starting to slide back into her seat. "Did you miss me?"

Coming out of his memory, he smiled. "How about a refill?" Malone rang the buzzer for the flight attendant.

Deborah pointed back down the aisle. "I met the nicest man, a doctor, from Madison. He works for the Med Center in outpatient care. Would you believe he wanted me to interview for a job?" She showed Malone a card, James G. Belton, M.D. The guy wore five-hundred-dollar shoes and an expensive cashmere jacket. He was the type who would hire Malone to pick up after he tooled through the world, hurting people.

"You're picking up the work, flying to France."

"Isn't it wonderful?"

"Yeah. What's the job?"

"Research." Deborah Hansen's smile was bright enough for a Gleem ad. "I would interview people in the Emergency Room. Ask them questions. For a national survey he's putting together."

"Sounds great."

She hugged herself, which brought on a pretty shiver. "This is my day, I guess. Meeting two exciting men. Getting an actual job offer!"

"Yeah." Malone stretched, yawned. When you were young, you could still stabilize the dream.

Leaving the aircraft, he and Deborah Hansen got separated. He was in one transparent tube, heading down to Customs, and she was in another, behind him, off to the right, with the doctor from Madison. One more dream girl gone.

The Customs police at Charles de Gaulle had guns and duck-billed caps and little mustaches. They held out their hands for passports, and their eyes kept flicking over the passengers, and every so often they would pluck someone out of the line and take them through a door.

Customs made you realize you were a foreigner.

Archer Bell was there to meet him, with a driver in a snappy gray uniform who spoke French. Mr. Bell had gained a few pounds. He wore a three-piece suit. As they shook, Malone felt Bell's eyes, scanning him, measuring.

In minutes, they were heading south in Bell's deluxe Mercedes, away from the airport. Malone could see Paris, the famous skyline. It was after ten in the morning. He'd lost eight hours, flying against the sun. Jet lag fuzzed his mind. Bell handed him a manila envelope. Inside were photos of the principals of the case, mostly tennis players. They were handsome athletes with showboat smiles, strong faces, and deep-set eyes.

"This is Reyes," Bell said. "The man who died. This is Pantakoras Belynkas. This one is Milos Tigrid. Here's Polak with his wife, a Chicago girl. Fenwick manages them. Here's Fenwick."

"He always dress like that?"

"F.F.'s a Texan. You know how they are."

"Who's this?" Malone pointed to a photo of a man with a mustache.

"That's Jack Di Rocca. Our ex-con."

Malone flipped through the photos until he found the picture of Reyes. "They played his death up on national TV. Is the official Paris verdict still heart failure?"

"Yes. Brought on by a drug overdose."

"What were the drugs?"

"One was an aphrodisiac. The second was something to calm his nerves. He was an emotional player, a real party boy. A hot-dog cop named Maréchal thinks it's murder."

"Who would want to kill Reyes?"

"There are several ideas kicking around. I put my money on a French hit man, hired by the husband Reyes was cuckolding."

"Sounds promising."

Bell handed Malone a piece of notepaper containing a name and phone number. "His wife, Madame Muriel Broussard-Gauthier, is busily putting together a book of tennis photos. You might interview her."

Malone studied the note, then put it in his pocket. "Who else?"

Bell looked out the window at the scenery, then shifted his eyes to Malone. "Your official job for the Advisory Group is to find out who's using drugs before the police do. For the fee we agreed to over the phone. Four hundred a day, plus expenses."

There was something else, so Malone waited.

"Your unofficial job," Bell went on, "is to keep my top players out of trouble."

"Laville and Cooper."

Bell nodded. "The rival camp is headed by Fenwick. If any of his players should turn up with drugs, or if Di Rocca should make a small slip . . . well, you understand."

Bell handed Malone another envelope that contained a stack of business cards identifying him as a writer with Andrews, Livingston, a publisher with a New York address, plus five thousand dollars in French and Swiss francs. Malone understood—this money was from Bell, extra pay for moonlighting.

"So I'm off to Zurich?"

"Gstaad. There's a tournament there."

"Who do I watch in Gstaad?"

"My players. Also Tigrid and Polak."

"What about this other guy, Koras?"

"He's going to Palermo."

Malone tucked the money into his jacket pocket. "Do the Paris police know about me?"

"Yes. I'll drop you off at the quai des Orfèvres. To see Maréchal."

"What's he like?"

"A bloodhound."

Malone sat back against the cushions of the Mercedes. Great way to start your day in Paris, a visit to the gendarmes.

"Who did Reyes hang out with?"

"Tigrid was his friend. So was Koras. The woman is your best lead."

"I'm a writer. What if she wants us to write a book together?"

Bell looked directly at Malone. "Do what you have to."

"I saw Laville on the tube, giving it to the umpire. How's he holding up?"

"Terry is a vast talent. When he's on, a genius. As an artist, he needs protecting. This Reyes business has unnerved everyone. Terry told me, privately, he had a terrible nightmare about Reyes's death."

Screwballs, Malone thought, as the Mercedes turned a corner, heading for the Paris police station. Screwballs who paid his fee, and his way to Paris.

The police made Malone wait for nearly an hour. He sat on a wooden bench, which had held untold millions of tired, but guilty, derrières, distracting himself by reading an old Perry Mason novel. He was starting Chapter 7 when they came to fetch him.

"The Inspector will see you now."

"Thanks."

Maréchal stood on the threshold of his office, a short man with a neatly pressed suit and an expression of watchful disdain. The tidy little man made Malone think about his own clothes, rumpled from eight hours in an airplane seat. He needed a hot bath, some sleep, a drink, and a working girl who spoke ten words of English. Malone was ushered in.

"Do you speak French, Monsieur Malone?"

"A little. I taught some of your elite troops over here how to jump out of an airplane."

The Inspector smiled. "We have a background report on you, and on your detective business in Chicago." He sat down, waving Malone to a chair. "It seems you also were a policeman?"

"Yes. In Chicago. I worked vice for a while. Then homicide."

The Inspector nodded as he lit a Gauloise. "Might I get to the point?"

"Sure."

"This is a serious crime. I don't welcome foreign investigators who are not licensed here and who have no standing."

"I won't get in the way," Malone said.

"Perhaps. But if you do not overstep, perhaps we can cooperate."

That sounded like a break. "I'd like to help, Inspector. What can I do?"

"Where do you go when you leave Paris?"

"A place in Switzerland. Gstaad."

Maréchal smiled at Malone's difficulty with pronunciation. "Mr. Malone, how would you like to be our man in Gstaad, insofar as sharing your information with me?"

Malone knew a good deal when he heard one. "What do I get out of it?"

Maréchal spread his hands. "We have a small fund available, for operations of this sort. But I thought perhaps we might be of service to you in other ways. For example, if you required a background report on a certain player, we could get it for you. How does that sound?"

"It's a deal."

The Inspector smiled, then walked to the window and looked out. He had a fine view of the Quai, a privilege of his senior status, and when he leaned out he could see the Institute's cupola. He watched two *bateaux mouche* sliding downriver. "Is there anything you need from our information system today?"

"Yes. There's a player named Di Rocca. His first name is Jack."

"Ah, yes. We are aware of Mr. Di Rocca. There is a file already assembled. It may contain what you want."

"Terrific," Malone said.

The Inspector pressed a button, then spoke French into an intercom.

While they waited, Malone asked, "Have there been any public threats?"

"No. Surprising, isn't it?"

"Yeah. Death brings out the crazies. We had a butchers' strike back home early in the spring, and all kinds of people got into the act, throwing stink bombs in supermarkets, shooting at delivery trucks. This Reyes thing could attract a lot of what we call 'tangential activity.' "

"We shall be on the alert. And I have alerted Superintendent Weston, my counterpart at Scotland Yard. He is preparing security for Wimbledon."

The door opened and a man in uniform brought in a file, which he laid on the Inspector's desk. The name on the folder was DI ROCCA, J., USA. Pushing the file across the desk to Malone, the Inspector said, "You must read it here, in my office."

"No problem."

The Inspector left the office and Malone opened the file and began to make notes.

Archer Bell's French secretary made the appointment with Madame Muriel Broussard-Gauthier for seven that evening. Malone was tired, but working on a complex case helped him over the hump, and when the interview with Madame was over he planned to get a good night's sleep. He'd made a promising contact with the Paris policeman, Maréchal. Moreover, his wallet was full of money, and if he could stay ahead of the intricacies of the case, he could keep working until mid-September, when the tennis season was over. The break so far was the dossier on Jack Di Rocca. Malone had an appointment with Di Rocca tomorrow morning, at Stade Roland-Garros. Malone wanted to meet there, so he could get a feel for what went on in a world-class tennis arena. If he was going to masquerade as a sportswriter, he would have to learn the keys that unlocked the game.

There were always keys.

Malone rode up in the lift, got off on five, and found himself in a ritzy foyer with shining black marble walls. He located number 502 and rang the buzzer. An eyeball appeared in the security port.

"Monsieur Malone?"

"Oui, madame. Bonjour."

The door opened and Malone handed her the business card that said he was a writer. She was attractive, with high heels and a platinum jump-suit that showed off an excellent figure. She wore a silver bracelet on her right wrist, and her shining red hair was piled up on her head. The jump-suit had exaggerated shoulder pads, making her resemble a magazine model from a very expensive women's magazine. Her smile was dazzling.

She looked at the card, then stepped aside. "Won't you come in?" Her English was better than his French.

Malone followed her into a beautifully furnished room, where she invited him to sit down. She poured a glass of wine for each of them, and he tried his pitch about the photographs and the New York publisher. As he talked, she asked occasional questions, and he noted a faint gleam of amusement in her eye.

"Would this be, as you Americans say, a deal of fifty-fifty?"

"I was thinking more of thirty-seventy."

"Seventy for me?"

Malone smiled. The lady could deal. "Seventy for me, madame. That is, if my publisher likes your photos, and if you can get more for the rest of the season."

"I was planning to leave for Gstaad soon. Let me show you the pictures first."

"All right."

She left the room and came back with two photo albums and three white cardboard boxes full of photos. He took his time going through them until he came to the shots that showed Armando Reyes approaching death.

Muriel's photos captured Reyes as he was about to serve. There was the ball toss, the racket about to climb toward contact, and then a grainy close-up of his face, beginning to contort, a look of horrified surprise. The next shot showed Reyes dropping the racket, and then Reyes falling, crumpling, his legs giving up the effort to stand. Malone stopped to look at Madame Broussard-Gauthier. She had tears in her eyes. The next photo showed Reyes on his knees, dropping face-first into the dust. Then another series of shots of the men carrying the stretcher, and one of a stout man in tennis clothes standing a few feet away.

"This one is Tigrid, right?"

"Yes. A wonderful clown of a man."

"Tigrid was close to Reyes?"

"They were like brothers."

Malone was impressed. "This is superb work. I think we can make an arrangement with my publisher, with no trouble."

"Thank you. I must tell you, however, I am not satisfied with your seventy and my thirty."

"No? What would you suggest?"

"Fifty-fifty, monsieur."

Malone lifted his wine glass. "We can discuss that. After I talk to New York."

Muriel sipped her apéritif. "Are you an *investigative* journalist, Mr. Malone?"

Now that was a surprise. "Why do you ask?"

"You seem so intense. Like a policeman."

"Have you known many policemen, madame?"

"Once. But that was in another life."

They smiled at each other.

"It is the way you ask the questions. So confident. So questing. So like a . . . flic."

"I used to be a cop, back in Chicago. I didn't know it showed."

"I suspected as much. And how did you become a writer?"

"I got tired of getting shot at."

Nervously, she stood, making the platinum material of the jump-suit shimmer. "Are you by chance free for dinner?"

"Sure. But I thought . . ."

She put a hand on his arm. "I know a quiet place, a neighborhood restaurant where the tourists do not venture. If you would allow me to be your guide . . ."

"Hey. Great. I'd like that."

They walked through the soft May evening to the restaurant. Two policemen passed, on bicycles, wearing short capes that made Malone think he was in a Humphrey Bogart movie.

"*Les hirondelles,*" Muriel said. "With the tails of swallows."

Over a carafe of red wine in the restaurant, she asked him questions about his life in America. He fudged on the answers. Then Muriel told him some things. "Armando and I were not lovers. I met him in Rome, three weeks ago. I found him attractive, a charming man. At another time, we might have become intimate. But we did not."

"How come?"

She shrugged. "I am particular with my friends. My husband is some years older than I. We have a sensible marriage. He has his other interests, I have mine. But with Armando, I could sense the presence of another woman. It was as if we met . . . for purely social reasons."

If Reyes was using someone this beautiful as a decoy, it was a sad waste of resources. "Any idea who the woman was?"

"None."

"Too bad."

With the flickering candlelight between them, Malone felt

closer to this strange woman. He watched while Muriel refilled their wine glasses.

"Do you like a good mystery, Monsieur Malone?"

He knew then she didn't buy his cover, the writer from the States. All the talk about flics, the way he asked questions, *les hirondelles.* "Sure."

Muriel hesitated for a fraction of a second, then slipped a photo out of her handbag. This one was not of the same quality as the others. It showed Armando Reyes leaning against a wall while he talked to Jack Di Rocca. It was clear to Malone that Di Rocca was putting the arm on Reyes.

"When did you take this?"

"An hour or so before the semifinal."

"What was going on?"

"All I know is that Armando was under terrible strain. And that he didn't want me to hear what he and Jack Di Rocca were saying."

"Why did you show it to me?"

Muriel shrugged, then looked him directly in the eye. "I feel something from you, trust—something."

"Thanks."

"One day, perhaps, you will trust me enough to tell me who you are, Monsieur l'Ecrivain."

Thinking she should have been a cop herself, Malone touched his wine glass to hers. The book idea had been a way to get him inside, for a look at her photos, but now he was thinking he might as well pitch the photo book to New York. He'd done some writing in college and it would be dumb to turn down a coauthor as good-looking as Muriel. With her in tow, his cover might hold.

The food came. Malone was no gourmet, but it was excellent. Across from him, Muriel was eating European style, using her knife to pack a piece of duck on the back of her fork. He enjoyed watching her eat. She had sharp instincts. Maybe fifty-fifty was worth considering.

Abdul Saadi had dinner with four friends from Damascus, then returned to his penthouse suite on the top floor of the

Hôtel Paladin, on the Right Bank of the Seine. The tournament was over, and he was still engrossed in an elaborate corporate takeover of the tennis equipment firm of Sport City. Things were at a standstill because the stockholders wanted too much per share. There had to be a way to bring the price down.

Entering the penthouse, he went first to Athena's room, but the Princess was not there. If he decided to marry the Princess, he would make certain that she stayed at home, as befits a wife.

Saadi walked through the penthouse, which was vast, to his private study. There were two phone calls from Leonardo Reyes, the brother of the dead man, but when Saadi called Reyes's hotel room, he got no answer. Good.

He sat down at his desk, made two phone calls to Damascus, and then tried clearing his mind of business pressures by writing a few sentences on his monograph. The subject of Saadi's research was an enlightened Arab view of the Crusades, and his mission was to show that race hatred and a lust for plunder had motivated the "Holy Wars" of the Middle Ages to a much larger degree than had been conceded by Western historians.

The words refused to come.

Saadi pushed away from the desk and thought about Clothilde, then about Laure Puget. Thinking about Laure made him angry, so he shifted his thoughts back to what he was about to achieve for Sahara Sports, the conglomerate empire of the Saadi family.

From a small operation of less than a million annually, Sahara Sports had mushroomed into a huge corporate umbrella for a sporting goods empire that specialized in tennis equipment. Sahara made rackets, balls, nets, shoes, clothes, string, stringing machines, wind screens, sweatbands, energy packs—anything and everything for the game of tennis. Market share had grown from 1.3 to 35.7. As a child, Saadi had hoarded coins. Now he hoarded corporations. It was a matter of scale. Saadi liked growth.

The next step was to buy up the competition. Sport City, then Laval Sportif, then Ryker.

Saadi's dream was to turn Sahara into a complete sports equipment system—all the way from marketing and production to distribution and retailing. In the next year, he planned to build the first Sahara Stadium in Dallas, and then spread other arenas like a string of diamonds across the major cities of the world. His tournaments would rival Paris, Wimbledon, New York.

The world wanted entertainment. Saadi was there to provide.

Sitting at his computer console, Saadi leaned back to stare at his books—scientific treatises, business books, economics, political science, accounting, a complete collection of the works of William Blake. Here, in Paris, there was a special collection of 517 volumes of pornography, in French, Swedish, and English.

His histories of the Crusades had been duplicated for each penthouse study. Several shelves were devoted to this subject, and Saadi had a team of scholars from Harvard who were busy putting all the data from the books into his computer system. The task would take three more years.

Now Saadi unlocked the top drawer of his desk. A dozen bottles of red pills were there, arranged in a neat row, along with a recent copy of *Racquet World,* the premier tennis magazine. He suspected Athena had given some of these pills to Reyes, as he had hoped she might. Saadi smiled at the thought. Nothing ventured, really, yet everything gained. It had been an easy way to rid himself of a nuisance. Only a nouveau-riche Peruvian would mix aphrodisiacs with his other medication. The man had a heart condition. He had been a fool. Good riddance.

He set the magazine on his desk, then brought out scissors, a piece of typing paper, a bottle of glue, and a pair of plastic gloves. He put on the gloves and began searching through the magazine for the right words.

Abdul Saadi was going to let the media help him hype tennis to a frenzy. He was an economist and a businessman, and he had been the first to notice how the death of Reyes increased ticket sales—and more sales meant more exposure.

This was a way to boost tennis into an even bigger sport. The biggest.

Finding the words he wanted, Saadi went to work.

* * *

When Di Rocca entered the stadium, accompanied by Sergeant Demetz, he saw Malone waiting halfway up in the bleachers. Di Rocca climbed up to where Malone sat. Down below, the nets were gone and the net posts had been removed; the grounds crew worked on the orange clay. Today Roland-Garros seemed ghostly and deserted, like Yankee Stadium after the fans had gone, leaving their hot-dog wrappers and beer cans.

Di Rocca wore an expensive business suit, light gray, with a conservative blue tie. Because of the heat, he had removed the jacket. His white shirt was spotless and freshly pressed. By contrast, Malone looked disheveled, and his blue shirt was unbuttoned at the collar. His brown wool tie hung loose.

Fifteen rows below, Detective Sergeant Demetz sat alone, smoking a cigarette.

"All right," Di Rocca said. "Your name is Malone. You had the cops bring me here by special escort, for a fireside chat. I have a plane to catch for Palermo."

"I need something from you, Di Rocca."

Di Rocca sighed. "What?"

"Like I said, I've been hired to track down the source of the drugs that killed Reyes, before they kill another one of you people."

"Why tell me?"

Malone showed Di Rocca the photo of himself talking to Armando. "So?" He handed it back.

"With this, the Paris cops could put you away."

Di Rocca sighed, looked at his watch. "If I'm your idea of a big connection, you're dumber than I thought. What do you want?"

"There's a player I want you to watch for me."

"Who?"

"The one who wound up winning the French Open after Reyes got killed." Malone checked his notebook. "Belynkas. Pantakoras Belynkas."

Di Rocca grinned. "Why didn't you say so? What kind of stuff do you want?"

"The little things. If he owes money, who to. If he's seeing a woman, who is it. If he's dealing in drugs, who does he get them from. Just the little things."

Di Rocca stood, looked around. To the west, a group of clouds gathered. "What do I get out of it?"

"The police stay off your back, so you can get out of Paris."

Di Rocca took two steps down, then stopped and eyed Malone. "You really think you can pass as a writer?"

"I did it before."

Di Rocca shook his head. "You move like a cop, talk like a cop. You couldn't fool me."

"That's why I didn't try." He handed Di Rocca a business card with a telephone number written on the back. "Call me in Switzerland."

"Sure."

As Di Rocca reached ground level, Malone called, "How well did you know Armando Reyes?"

"He was lucky with women."

"Did that tick you off?"

"Not enough to kill him, if that's what you mean."

Malone watched Di Rocca walk out with Sergeant Demetz, then stood up for a good stretch. A player had lost his life down there on the court, less than a week ago. Today a mechanized court-roller chugged by, smoothing the sand where the man had died, blotting out every trace. Thinking about Koras, whom he had not met, Malone started down. Koras was getting old, maybe feeling desperate. Reyes had been on a tear. If Koras had felt threatened enough, maybe he had slipped the Peruvian some pills. Here, compadre, these will give you a jolt. Malone sighed. It was great to be working. Maybe Di Rocca would find out something useful in Palermo.

PART II

WIMBLEDON

Death in an English Garden

SEVEN

On the grounds at the All-England Lawn Tennis and Croquet Club on Church Road in the village of Wimbledon, the head groundsman ordered the careful watering of courts 1 and 2. Already, the grass was yellowing, and the tournament had not yet begun. This catastrophe had not been seen for nearly half a century.

The head gardener was also worried. His hortensias were in full bloom, and he feared they might die from lack of water. That week, the centenarian ivy climbing over the red brick walls shading the Royal Box had been completely reclipped. There was a plan to sprinkle the ivy at the last minute on opening day in order to revive the lovely green. They were hoping for some cool weather, typical of England in the summer. Why was it so hot?

The head gardener stood in the shade thrown by the stadium in center court, discussing his problems with the head groundsman.

"Do you see any chance of a break in the heat?"

"No. It hasn't been this bad since right after the War."

"Twelve days of sun. That is a record, what?"

"I should say. I heard there were drops of rain over Greenwich yesterday."

"We need more than drops."

Wimbledon was the cathedral of professional tennis, and since the day the tournament ended last summer, the grounds crews had been busy getting ready for this year's Wimbledon fortnight. They tilled and raked and replanted, while the head groundsman, an expert at horticulture, went down on his hands and knees, not to pray, but to inspect every blade of grass.

Soon everything would be ready. The opening ceremony had been rehearsed several times. The Guards Band would be present because the Prince of Wales was appearing in person. That day would probably be the most important in Wimbledon history, ranking with 1977, when the Queen herself appeared for the tournament's centenary.

Wimbledon had a regal history. Built in 1877, the club was a meeting place for royalty and the upper class. After World War I, the future King George V had accepted the presidency of the All-England Club, and since then sovereigns had been seen more frequently at the matches. In 1926, the Duke of York had actually competed in the doubles. Eliminated easily in the first round, he still remained a stout and stalwart supporter of the tournament. These days, the Duke of Kent presided over the honorable association. Tradition required that Her Majesty's Drawing Room beneath the box be decorated with fresh flowers every day, just in case. Unfortunately, the Queen had r.ever used the room, but the flowers were nonetheless changed each day.

This year, however, there were to be significant changes at the All-England Club. Security, in the capable hands of Superintendent Leo Weston, was to be tightened, firmed up. And at that very moment, Weston sat in the stands, across the yellowing grass from the Royal Box, while he made a rough sketch of the seating area, the aisles, the exits. Scotland Yard had received reports from Paris, where that Peruvian had died, that there might be attempts at violence, to disrupt the games. It might have happened in Paris, but this was England. Nothing like that would happen here.

A few miles away, at the Queen's Club, Matt Malone was walking the grounds with his new friend, Muriel Broussard-Gauthier. They both wore identity cards with the words JOURNALIST AFFILIATED TO WIMBLEDON. This badge of entrée was coveted by journalists the world over, and it had taken the Chairman's personal intervention to obtain two extra passes. Muriel was grateful to Malone for it.

For the last three weeks, Malone had researched the sacrosanct world of professional tennis, reading books by all the great players—Tilden, Riggs, Kramer, Budge, Laver, Ashe—and reading back issues of *Racquet World, World Tennis,* and *Tennis* magazine. He understood now that the most important variable in the game was surface—clay-courters had a hard time on grass, hard-court players had an impossible mission on clay—and he had become adept at picking seedings, which is the way players are distributed, like seeds at planting time, throughout the draw. A proper seeding meant that the best players would meet in the later rounds of play. Malone could reel off statistics—the longest match in history, the scores of the final in 1977, Tilden's score over Lacoste in the 1925 Davis Cup—and he knew every circuit player by name.

In the stands by the first court, they spotted David Kollmore, the tennis writer for the sports page of the *Financial Times.* Kollmore, who was sitting with Nora Laville, waved him over. Terry Laville was down on the court, working out with Davey Cooper. Malone introduced Muriel to Kollmore and Nora, who was sipping something cool and alcoholic from a tall glass. Down on the court, Laville drilled a ball past Cooper, who grunted as he made a dive for it. Muriel excused herself while she made her way to the far end of the court, to take some action shots of the players.

"Laville's looking good," Malone said.

Kollmore said, "I was just telling Mrs. Laville here how good his chances are for winning the tournament."

Nora glanced up at Malone. "Terry's been very edgy, because of the Reyes business."

"Yes," Malone said. "I've been interviewing players for the book and I've noticed the same thing."

"I heard an odd story," Kollmore said. "This morning, at the Gloucester, this man Mikhail Polak made a scene by refusing to eat some oatmeal. The manager had to be called."

"I was there," Malone said. "And it was quite a scene."

Nora shivered slightly and hugged herself. Today she looked pretty in a pink tank top and white trousers. Her shoulders were tanned, and they helped to distract attention from the circles under her eyes. Malone knew from circuit gossip that Nora Laville had been in the States and Vancouver for a couple of weeks. Nora had a reputation for sudden departures and unexpected arrivals. She also had a reputation for appearing drunk in public, and everyone said she used to be much prettier before the drinking started. She had family in Kansas.

Kollmore pulled out a pack of Craven A's, which he offered around. Nora took one.

"Have you been a writer long, Mr. Malone?" Nora asked.

"Five years."

"I had someone check in the library, when I was in Vancouver. They couldn't find anything you had written. Not a single word."

Malone smiled at Nora. "I wrote a lot of financial stuff before. They don't give you a byline for that, most of the time."

"I thought," Kollmore said, "that you had done a book on another sport. Basketball? Baseball? Something along those lines?"

"Basketball," Malone said. "It was a series of articles. I wrote those under a pseudonym."

"Really?" Nora asked. "Why is that?"

"There were mob connections. I didn't want to turn on my car ignition and be blown into fish food."

"Really?" Nora's hand stopped, holding the smoldering cigarette.

"It was an exposé of the corruption behind the glittering exterior of professional sports."

Kollmore turned to him. "Is *that* what your book on tennis will be about? Corruption?"

"I just write about what's there," Malone answered.

"Isn't it ironic," Nora said, "that you happen on the scene just after a man dies on the court in Paris."

"That did have something to do with the idea," Malone said. "Publishers like it when it's hot."

Nora turned back to concentrate on her husband's workout.

Terry and Davey stood near the net, hitting quick volleys with the staccato reflex of boxers working with a small bag. From the stands, Terry looked far superior to Davey. Both men were large, weighing over two hundred pounds each. David Kollmore took a notebook from his jacket pocket and wrote down impressions.

When the workout was over, Terry and Davey gathered their extra rackets and came over. Terry's lean features were flushed with excitement and the white hair was wet beneath his Indian headband. He and Davey shook hands with Malone and Kollmore. Laville remained standing while Davey took a seat next to Kollmore. Malone reminded Laville of their interview date.

"How did I look out there, Mr. Malone?" Laville's eyes were blazing.

"You looked great, Terry."

From the side, Davey Cooper let out a feigned groan. "He's trying to get me to kill myself before the games start."

"Davey," Nora scolded. "That's not funny."

Muriel shot several photos of the group as they stood talking. Davey rubbed his leg and grinned into the camera. "They'll record this workout in history, and put it right up in the Wimbledon Museum. Davey Cooper, speared by Terry Laville in a pre-tournament exercise session."

Everyone laughed.

"I've got a topic for you, Malone. A chapter for that book."

"What is it?"

"Food poisoning," Davey said. "At the Wimbledon Games."

Malone whipped out a ballpoint and an envelope. "Tell me about it, Davey."

"Well, my eggs this morning were green, and the bacon tasted like shit."

"That was the beer you drank last night," Laville said. "How can an entire country like warm beer?"

"Seriously," Davey said. "A lot of the players are jumpy about the food. If something tastes the least bit off, they're sending it back. If there's one case of turista during the next two weeks, the hypochondriacs will come right out of the woodwork."

Malone and Muriel said goodbye and headed over toward the clubhouse.

"Wait until you see these photos of Laville," Muriel whispered, when they were out of earshot. "He looks absolutely to be in a trance. As if he saw nothing except his opponent. When I started taking pictures, he played as if I weren't there."

"He's a strange one, all right. Part genius, part timber wolf."

"The look in his eyes was mad," she said.

Muriel gripped his arm as they walked along. Up ahead, a girl stepped out of a phone booth and walked away from them. She had long blonde hair, and she wore high heels and a light-blue frock that dramatized her elegant long legs. Malone recognized her as Shirley Nash-Winters, the Hollywood starlet.

"I would like a bite of lunch," Muriel said.

"Okay. Let's head back to the hotel. I have a little research to do."

At the Gloucester Hotel, Malone used his lock picks to let himself into Davey Cooper's room. The hotel maids were working down the hall, vacuums whining, and that gave Malone about ten minutes for his search. He had timed the maids for two days, learned their names, made a schedule chart of their routines. It took them twelve minutes to do a room, unless the room belonged to Davey Cooper. There was dirty laundry everywhere—socks, Ryker shirts, soiled shorts, sweaty jocks, towels slopped over chair backs. When his mother wasn't around, this Cooper was one messy kid. The bed looked like it had been hit by a tornado. In a frame on the bedside table was a photograph of the legendary Mother Cooper—Lorraine, her name was—standing in front of a big house somewhere on the East Coast of America.

The framed picture was the only neat item in the place.

Malone found some Colombian weed in the top drawer, underneath three mismatched socks. What would Mother Lorraine say to that? Surprisingly, he hadn't found any pills. From the way Cooper acted, he'd picked the kid as a user-loser.

This was Malone's fourteenth unauthorized room search. So far, he hadn't found pills anywhere, but he had some ideas. His main suspect was the Yugoslav, Milovan Tigrid, mostly because of what Malone knew about the Albanian Connection. New drugs were coming out of the Middle East, and the Albanians were starting to compete with the Sicilians for a share of the market. As a Yugoslav, Tigrid might have easy entry into that particular pipeline.

Malone brought out an envelope with some names printed on it in his square, predictable hand.

Belynkas.

Laville.
Cooper.
Tigrid.
Polak.
Abraham.
Colombier.
Di Rocca.
Leroy.
Which player would have wanted Armando Reyes dead?

The book Malone was doing with Muriel had developed from a quick idea into a partial reality. Malone had called the publisher, Andrews, Livingston, and had roused some interest at that end. He had mailed off two hundred photos, with some hastily written captions, and the publisher was talking about a contract. Now Malone had to decide whether to try to write the chapters himself—he'd done plenty of rewriting of term papers back at the University of Illinois—or to hunt up a writer he knew in Chicago to do the job for him.

One thing was certain, he liked working with Muriel. After Paris, they'd been together for a couple of days at Gstaad, and then again in Munich, and when she'd joined him in London she'd given him a quick kiss on the mouth and one of those lingering looks with the faint measuring smile that told him she had hanky-panky on her mind. Malone was careful not to rush Muriel. She was a lady, and ladies always took their time. With Muriel, the wait was going to be worth it.

Later that afternoon, after a long lunch and some talk about chapters and divisions in the book, Malone spent some time going over his notes on Terry Laville. As he studied the folder, Malone turned the facts around inside his head, thinking about Laville and the woodcutting myth, and how it enhanced his place in the tennis spotlight, and how Malone could help keep that spotlight bright.

Here was the bottom line: Malone had been on the job just over three weeks and so far he'd grossed almost nine thousand dollars for his daily services—he worked every day and got paid for seven days a week—and more than three thousand dollars for expenses. The twelve thousand dollars came from a secret pool filled by the big hitters from professional tennis. No names had been mentioned, but Malone understood that even Harrison Cabot, the President of the United States Tennis Association, USTA for short, had kicked in his share. On top of the twelve grand, Archer Bell had sweetened the pot with three thousand in foreign currency, Swiss, French, British.

The money was good, and Malone wanted to keep the cash flow positive. The way to do that was to study Laville, who was Archer Bell's hope for the future.

The best part of his writer's cover was that every player, even Laville, wanted his name in a book. The players got used to seeing their names in the newspapers and even in the three top tennis magazines. But books were permanent. All Malone had to do was mention he'd like an interview, wave the tape recorder, and the players would come hunting for him.

Everyone so far had been easy. Except Pantakoras Belynkas, still the number-one player. Belynkas kept to himself and was elusive. He worked through his manager, Fenwick, and stayed out of the range of television cameras.

Walking down the hall to Laville's suite in the Gloucester, Malone thought about tennis. Since the game began, power and control of tennis had been vested in a few men, wealthy gentlemen who had altruistic notions about the beauty of competition and the purity of the game. Today, with tennis more than a hundred years old, the impresarios still paid lip service to the notions of honor and purity.

The noble image of tennis was what made Wimbledon tick along, like a grandfather clock in the hallway of time.

Toney magazines with slick covers were devoted to its promotion. Every major tournament had blanket TV coverage, the time bought by car companies and stockbrokers. Tennis public relations was a Technicolor slow-motion film of The Good Life, with happy, smiling tennis stars taking a leisurely swim in the Bahamas with their pretty smiling wives, a small blonde child or two in the frame for proper balance. To the public, tennis was America—the clean life-style, special diets, health, keeping in shape.

But tennis was changing as big money entered the arena. Big corporations wanted to sell rackets to the weekend hackers, starting at two hundred dollars, shorts at fifty dollars a pair, shoes at seventy-five. They'd lowered the price of tennis balls over the years, to keep the weekend players out there burning up rackets and breaking strings. And in the seventies, the equipment makers had penetrated the market with new products, changing the material with which they made rackets—wood, metal, graphite, boron, krypton, oversize, mid-size, illegal spaghetti-string jobs—and they'd tied in the magic myth of the equipment, hooked it right in to winning, an ego trip.

This ceramic racket, the ads implied, can save your game out there, for only $250. Playing your boss this weekend? Get a demonstration of a Koras Boron. Got a tough match coming up at the Club? Pulverize the enemy with the new Sport City Polak Autograph.

Malone had hefted several rackets, and they seemed pretty much the same to him, which was why the equipment makers needed the names of tennis players.

Koras. Laville. Polak. Cooper . . .

At the interview, Laville wore a leather jacket, blue jeans that looked new, and hand-tooled cowboy boots. His white hair was slicked back, and the crazy look had receded from his eyes. Malone had learned how to interview while working with the Chicago police. As he asked his questions, he studied the person giving answers. Several times, Laville's eyes drifted out of focus, as if he were staring at a place hidden somewhere in the dips of his memory.

Q: So, Mr. Laville. How does it feel to be coasting into your seventh Wimbledon at the ripe old age of twenty-six?
A: Great.
Q: Planning to win?
A: Absolutely.
Q: You're a Canadian, right?
A: Right.
Q: I'm from Chicago. That's right across the lake from me. Where are you from, originally?
A: I was born in Ontario, at a place called Six Nations Reserve, but grew up in Calgary. My mother was part Iroquois.

Q: Canada. Is that why they call you the Woodcutter?

A: I worked as a logger for three years. They would fly a gang of us up north to the logging camps, a place called La Manique. Using an ax helped me with my service motion, but it also makes these neck muscles tight, right here. When my service starts to go, I drag back the memory of swinging that double-edged ax.

Q: So how did you get started in tennis?

A: I played sports in high school—football, ice hockey, soccer —but there was no money in it. I used to devour the sports pages, and I suppose I hoped sports would help me escape from logging. The summer of my junior year, the logging company went broke, leaving me out of a job. My high-school coach helped me find a job in New Hampshire, at a camp for boys. One of my jobs was sweeping the tennis courts. I watched these kids hitting, watched the coach, saw what he was telling them. It looked smooth and kind of beautiful. One day I picked up a racket, hit some serves. The coach saw me, told me I was a natural. I took lessons from him. In two weeks, I was beating him. I liked hitting hard. It gave me—a real thrill. I won my serve 98 percent of the time. The coach said I had a natural swing, a motion like Pancho Gonzales. I was a Canadian, man, and all I knew about Gonzales was that he had a temper on the court. Back home, I quit the winter sports and concentrated on tennis. When winter came, I hitchhiked twenty miles to an indoor court. Five bucks an hour, way outside my budget. I read tennis books. After my senior year, I cruised to Florida. For a year, I lived on my tennis, hitting with anyone, working at odd jobs around Miami, scrounging lessons. I played in college for a year, won an open in Florida, decided to turn pro. The first biggie I qualified for was River Oaks, in Houston.

Q: How did you feel?

A: Man, I was scared shitless. All the hoity-toity crowd. Koras was there, sopping up the spotlight, along with Mad Milo and Armando the Sword.

Q: Sounds like you had a chip on your shoulder.

A: Those guys owned the world, man. I was hungry for just a tiny piece.

Q: How far did you get? At River Oaks, I mean?

A: Second round. I met Koras, almost had him by the short hairs, but he got lucky. Hell, they wouldn't have let me win, first time out.

Q: Who do you mean by "they"?

A: The fat cats who ran River Oaks.

Q: You're implying that the tournament was fixed?

A: Not *fixed*-fixed. But when they're after you, they manage to schedule your singles back to back with your doubles. You have to play at the crappy hours, on a court way the hell away from everything.

Q: What did you do about that?

A: Only one thing to do, and that was get famous.

Q: Are there other fat cats, at other tournaments? Care to name names?

A: No. I'd better not. This is a secret, okay. I just let it slip.

Q: Okay. You wouldn't regard Archer Bell as a fat cat?

A: Arch is my manager. He takes a piece of my action. I sweat on the court. Arch does his sweating in the meetings, where he makes deals that keep us going.

Q: Did you have a coach?

A: There was Joe Slater, that summer in the camp. The college coach was zero help.

Q: There's a story going around that says you were coached by Pantakoras Belynkas. When you first appeared on the circuit.

A: Did he say that?

Q: No. It's just, like I said, one of the myths of the circuit.

A: Koras was the King. He might have given me some tips. But not enough to say I was coached. Man, I learned most of this by myself, the hard way, the only way.

Q: You and Koras are real rivals now, wouldn't you say?

A: He's finished. The guy's thirty-four, he's over the hill.

Q: So you don't think he'll get his Grand Slam?

A: Someone will stop him.

Q: You?

A: Why not? Yeah. I'll stop him.

Q: Mind talking a little bit about the off-court rivalry?

A: Where do these rumors start?

Q: Any truth to some little altercation at Régine's in Paris?

A: No comment.

Q: What drives you, Terry?

A: I want to be known as the best. I got a late start. Not like these country club fellows.

Q: The fat cats?

A: Okay. Sure, the fat cats.

Q: Are you out for revenge, Terry?

A: Revenge. That's crazy.

Q: Would you say you were getting back at them?

A: Getting back at? I wouldn't even say that.

Q: What about the idea broached by Sven Skaar, in the TV interview, about having to kill your opponent?

A: Skaar had to retire from the circuit. He's a big quitter, in my book.

Q: It's too late for a Grand Slam this year. But say you win it next year. What happens after that?

A: First, I've got to win it. Some very good players stand in the way.

Q: Like who, for instance?

A: On grass, Davey Cooper. He hits harder than I do. When he's on, and the court is burnt out, you can't see his serve. In New York, on the hard surface, it would be Cooper again. He loves New York, and they love him back. Micky Polak is tough in New York, too, especially since he married a girl from the States. The other players who could win? Maybe Colombier, if he gets it together. Maybe Abraham, who's from Buffalo. Maybe this new kid, Heinz. He's a big hitter. Maybe Ivan Leroy.

Q: I notice you didn't mention Koras.

A: Okay. Koras.

Q: If you do win the Slam, how much do you think it will increase your gross?

A: I'm just the player, Malone. You'll have to ask Arch Bell about numbers.

Q: They're saying a Slam could triple your endorsements.

A: I've heard that.

Q: Mind telling me which companies are after you to sign?

A: That's Arch Bell's area. I just go out there and try to win.

Q: Terry, I was wondering what you thought of all this drug talk.

A: I don't pay much attention to gossip. I took some hits on the weed when I was younger, traveling around, wondering whether or not I'd make it. But now that I'm up there on the ladder I wouldn't touch anything like that.

Q: How do you feel about mandatory blood tests, for all players, to clear them to play?

A: I think it's a matter for lawyers. I wouldn't object to a test, personally. But I have a feeling it's a violation of our civil rights.

Q: What did you think of Armando Reyes?

A: I liked Armando. He had a great sense of humor. He was a legend when I came onto the circuit. I thought he was a little off the wall with the vitamins. I guess it's only another step to other pills. I didn't know Armando was a user until it came out in the papers. He was a great guy, but he drank too much, spent a lot of time chasing women. Everyone knew it. That was Armando.

Q: Think anyone would want to kill him?

A: A husband, you mean?

Q: Something like that.

A: I don't think so. Those things happen only in the movies.

Q: You're married, aren't you?

A: Yes.

Q: Any children?

A: No. Not yet.

Q: Does your wife travel with you on the circuit?

A: Most of the time. She likes it back home. We have this great place in Vancouver.

Q: Nice place, Vancouver.

A: Yes. It is.

Q: Well, I've got about enough, Terry. Good luck with Wimbledon.

A: Thanks. What are you going to do with all these interviews?

Q: Put them in a book, with pictures.
A: I'd like a full-page spread.
Q: You've got it, Terry.

The day before the opening of the Wimbledon fortnight, Abdul Saadi held a dinner party at his fashionable Victoria Intercontinental Hotel in London's West End. The Victoria Intercontinental had been built by a German architect named Stoller, then leased to a British hotel firm, which had sold it in the late seventies to the Sahara Corporation, which was owned by the Saadi family. When Saadi was in London, he and his entourage, including his current mistress and half a dozen servants, stayed in the lavish penthouse, with a view of the city and its tableau.

The meal that evening was French, prepared by a chef from the Cordon Bleu school. The guests sat around an oval table, bathed in soft light. Athena, as hostess, was at one end, Saadi at the other. The table was lit by candles, supported by complex contemporary ceiling lights on separate rheostats. There was a waiter for each diner. The waiters were monitored by Joshua, a huge Kenyan majordomo in a white tuxedo.

Athena wore conservative black, a dress with a high neck and long sleeves, and a diamond bracelet belonging to her mother, Helga von Heidelberg. The bracelet was rumored to be worth $1.5 million. Circuit gossip held that Athena had worn it in Los Angeles to attract Saadi, who had a sharp eye for jewels. The dress was new, and attracted comment for the simple reason that it failed to reveal Athena's attractive assets. Archer Bell even remarked to Frank Fenwick that Athena looked as if she'd just come back from a funeral in Monte Carlo.

"She did go to Austria for a couple of days," Fenwick said.

"How do you know?"

"My secret, Arch."

The conversation that evening was about tennis, how the sport was changing, more crowds, more pressure on the facilities, crowd control, ticket prices, and the constant search for new stars, fresh talent.

Filtering through the chitchat was the theme of Armando Reyes's death, and what it boded for the game. Some athletes had begun to avoid the food at the Gloucester, and even here at Saadi's table, Mikhail Polak, who was the strictest player on the circuit about diet, examined every mouthful of food with suspicion. His pretty wife, the Chicago girl Gail Hofstedter, kept blushing with embarrassment, explaining to Archer Bell and Malone about Polak's diet.

"Micky read this book on high-carbohydrate efficiency and he just can't seem to eat enough to keep him filled up. Last night, he got me out of bed at two in the morning, and we drove around until he found an all-night Italian place where he could get some spaghetti."

Polak looked up from his plate long enough to agree. "Is called the loading of the carbohydrates," he said. "Is recommended for all athletes."

Malone cut a piece of beef, put it into his mouth, and chewed thoughtfully. "Sounds like a good theory. What's the name of the book?"

"*The Clean Burn,*" Polak said, between mouthfuls.

"Oh, Micky," his wife said. "You are the dearest man."

Down at the other end of the table, Sir Francis Malcolm addressed himself to Frank Fenwick's question about security during the Wimbledon fortnight.

"We've been alerted, of course. Scotland Yard is on the job, as usual."

"I was out at the stadium today," Fenwick said. "I didn't see any signs of it."

Sir Francis smiled. "That, of course, is the best kind of security."

Fenwick disagreed. "The police back in the States work on a different theory. It's called high visibility."

"I am certain that Scotland Yard will handle things to your liking, Mr. Fenwick."

"I lost a good friend in Armando Reyes. I'd hate to see it happen again." He looked down the table at Milo Tigrid and Mikhail Polak. Koras had not been invited, because of Saadi's insane jealousy about Athena's past.

It was well known on the tennis circuit that Saadi's favorite dessert was cherries jubilee, which he had discovered in a Paris restaurant during his student days at the Sorbonne. People who were invited to dinner with Saadi either developed a taste for burnt brandy, cold ice cream, and cherries, or they skipped dessert. After a huge dish, Saadi had seconds.

After the meal, Saadi excused himself and withdrew for a long business talk with Mikhail Polak and Frank Fenwick, Polak's manager. Mrs. Polak was not invited. Terry Laville, who was there with his wife, watched the men leave the dining room and head toward Saadi's study, at the opposite end of the penthouse. Archer Bell, on Laville's left, blew smoke from his cigar into the air.

The three men sat in Saadi's study, a mirror duplicate of his study at the Hôtel Paladin in Paris, the walls lined with books on French literature, the Crusades, economics, nineteenth-century Impressionists, sixteenth-century Dutch landscapes, and erotica. Behind the books, on a mechanical platform that worked with the press of a button, was the closed-circuit TV system that monitored every room in the penthouse, in Technicolor. The TV monitor was hidden until Saadi wanted it visible.

"Well, gentlemen. To business." Saadi did not smoke, and was obviously grateful to be away from Archer Bell's acrid panatelas.

"A magnificent dinner, Mr. Saadi." Polak had eaten too much, and he felt like burping.

"Yes," Fenwick said. "Great food, Abdul."

"I have something for you, Mikhail." Saadi walked to a cabinet, opened it, came back carrying a handsome wooden box, hand tooled. He handed it to Mikhail. The box contained a Colt revolver, .45 caliber, dated 1868. It was a vintage model. Polak's contract with Sport City was about to run out; Saadi was trying to woo him. The gun was magnificent. Polak had seen one like it the year before, at an auction in Dallas. The price had been twenty-five thousand dollars.

"For me?"

"Yes. As a token of good will."

"I am overwhelmed."

Saadi sat back down. "Gentlemen, I make no secret of why you are here. His obligation to Sport City terminates next Friday. I am interested in signing Mr. Polak for Sahara. I will offer half a million dollars, with a proviso that if he should win Wimbledon, the offer will rise to six hundred thousand."

Fenwick looked at Polak, who was having trouble with his digestion, then at Saadi. "It's a good offer, Mr. Saadi."

"Well, when may I have your answer?"

Polak took a sip of brandy.

Fenwick pulled a notebook and a pocket calculator out of his jacket. He ran a few numbers, then looked up. "What did Sahara do last year?"

"Just under eight million."

Fenwick grinned. "I heard it was just *over* ten million."

Saadi spread his hands, a gesture of peace. "A matter of a few thousand."

"Tell you what I'm thinking, Mr. Saadi. Micky here is about to become a higher-ranked player. He's got a good chance of making the semifinals here, and that would boost his ranking to number three, maybe number two. Last year, Tigrid was the best-known player from the Eastern Bloc. This year, it's Micky."

"I am well aware of these numbers," Saadi said testily.

"Just for starters," Fenwick said, "we're going to ask you to raise your ante a little."

"How much?"

"A million up front, and a percentage of the gross."

Saadi leaned forward to study Fenwick. "A percentage of the gross is unheard of."

"It's done in Hollywood all the time."

"In Hollywood, stars take less up front."

"We think Micky's worth it. He could be the next Koras."

"Don't mention Koras Belynkas to me."

"All right." Fenwick looked at Polak, who nodded.

Saadi sat back, a stricken look on his face. "You've been talking to someone else."

Closing his notebook, Fenwick stood. "Micky and I need to talk over the numbers, Mr. Saadi. My daddy always warned me, never make a money decision on a full stomach."

Saadi's eyes narrowed. He did not appreciate philosophy lessons from someone like Fenwick. When he spoke, his voice was a whisper. "How big a percentage of the gross?"

"Half of one percent."

"Madness." Saadi swiveled around in his chair, to face the window overlooking London. "Utter madness."

Fenwick and Polak got up from their chairs and walked out, leaving Saadi alone.

When they were outside, with the door closed, Polak asked Fenwick what he thought. "Does the Arab go for the deal?"

Fenwick grinned. "I think we've got him, Micky. He needs you, and the board back home in Damascus would rather have your name on Sahara's products than anyone else's."

Polak smiled. It was one of the first times in his life when his Polish heritage had been profitable.

The sun was hot the day the Wimbledon ballboys were given their mauve-and-green uniforms, the colors of the All-England Club. Ballboys were chosen by strict ritual from the most deserving students of the London tennis clubs. They were all players who understood the rhythms of the game. They had dreams of one day playing on the sacred grass. This year, a black boy had been selected, and seven girls.

The All-England Club was moving with the times.

EIGHT

President Alain Clavier had set up temporary headquarters in the Chairman's office, where he and Sir Francis Malcolm were going over the timetable of matches. In Britain, Wimbledon was referred to simply as "The Championships." Like the tournaments in Paris and New York, it took two weeks to get an army of players through seven rounds of play, and Clavier and Sir Francis were drawing lots for the three early rounds that led to the all-important Round of Sixteen. As they worked, they tried to foresee the worst possible delays. Their ultimate goal was the second Sunday after the opening—the men's final had to be played on that day, at two o'clock precisely.

As always, the two men argued, precise French logic against steadfast British tradition. Clavier saw no reason that matches should not start at ten in the morning or at noon. Sir Francis, known to the press as "Lord Wimbledon," was horrified at the mere mention of altering the starting time.

The sacred rule at Wimbledon was that no match would be played before two o'clock. This rule was the backbone of the tradition which set the tempo of studied and classic leisure that made Wimbledon the premier event of international tennis. Yet in their discussion today, Clavier's logic had swung Sir Francis around, and they were already planning a scenario for early-round matches starting at midmorning. Sir Francis shuddered at what the membership would say.

"But not on Opening Day, understand, Alain. Opening Day must begin at two o'clock, on Centre Court."

"Yes, yes. I understand."

Clavier remembered that the stodgy club members had put up a fuss when colored shirts and dresses with red piping had been introduced onto the hallowed courts. There had almost been a revolution when the white balls provided for years by Jeffries and Company, of Woolwich, had been replaced by greenish-yellow balls of questionable provenance.

But colored costumes had arrived with the advent of professional play, which allowed the competitors to use their names to promote certain brand names in sportswear. Colored tennis clothes had enlivened the scene, and Milos Tigrid had been able to expand his range of stunts. Everyone at the Club, for example, remembered a doubles match when Milo had been paired with Walter Tray, a black player, and it had been required that both partners wear the same colors.

Tray had come onto the court first, wearing shorts and a matching shirt of sky blue. The spectators waited. When Milo bounded onto the court, he did indeed wear the same costume, but his face was done up with black greasepaint. Once it became clear that Tray was in on the stunt, the referee laughed so hard that he nearly fell out of his chair, and decided to inflict only the minimum fine.

"At least the weather report is optimistic," said Sir Francis.

"Yes. If it keeps up, Wimbledon will be the focus of the Grand Slam, as usual."

"How good are Koras's chances?"

"I thought he was off his game at Roland-Garros."

"Before the Reyes death? Or after?"

"In the finals, he seemed to be playing with less zeal, less energy."

"Hmm. What about our man Laville? Could he win here?"

"He is a brittle player, despite his brute strength. One always feels Laville needs an extra weapon before he can win."

During his time as President of the Federation, Clavier had mastered the art of diplomacy. The thing that tired him most was the barrage of contradictory interests, and the fact that he had to tend to them all personally. Each of the Grand Slam tournaments—Australia, Paris, Wimbledon, New York— wanted to see itself as the supreme test for players. The Grand Prix, which took place during the winter, wanted equal time. And now Saadi was broaching plans for his Sahara Circuit, an echo of the World Championship of Tennis, a professional circuit developed several years ago by a wealthy Texan. Clavier, who wanted Roland-Garros to be the ultimate in tennis, had to keep peace by humoring them all.

"Buckingham Palace has confirmed that the Prince of Wales will be opening the tournament."

"Excellent." Clavier looked out the window at the solid-blue sky, so rare for England in summer.

"Yes, but we have not seen Her Majesty since the Centenary. She is not as enthusiastic about tennis as Queen Mary was."

Clavier had little patience with British royalty, so he made some notes on a yellow pad, then walked to a map of the stadium that had been unfolded on a table. The matches were shaping up. The draw was complete. "Have we confirmed the meeting with security?"

Sir Francis consulted his pocket watch, an heirloom. "Four o'clock, precisely. Security will confer with Special Branch."

"Is Scotland Yard necessary?"

Sir Francis made a fatalistic face. "We tighten up a bit when members of the Royal Family come as our guests."

"I suppose they are keeping track of any random members of the IRA?"

"They always watch the Irish. And the terrorists."

"What is the police theory?"

"We shall know in a moment."

"Good." Clavier was thinking of not-so-distant times, only a few years past, when tennis tournaments had attracted thousands of well-bred and well-dressed aficionados who would not have dared to breathe, much less whistle or utter catcalls, while a player was preparing to serve. Then tennis had been a religion. Here at Wimbledon some of the religious zeal had been preserved, and there remained fond memories of that transitory period between the wars when women played in skirts, Suzanne Lenglen was the rage, and all the dandies resembled the Great Gatsby himself.

An intercom buzzed, and the secretary announced that the police had arrived. Clavier prepared himself to see them.

The door opened and the secretary came in, followed by Superintendent Weston. The Superintendent had sandy hair, shrewd blue eyes, and the seasoned look of a gunnery officer at the battle of El Alamein. He was tall and lean, the perfect caricature of an English country gentleman, with clothes tailored on Bond Street. His shoes had a high polish. Before taking a seat, he shook hands with Clavier and Sir Francis.

"Well, gentlemen. I've had a look around, and we've developed a plan."

"Good show," said Sir Francis.

The Superintendent leaned forward as he spread a chart of the All-England Club on the desk. "We are vulnerable here, in the Royal Box, from these points." He pointed out a dozen places in the stands. "These will be covered, as will the roof."

"What if they are after the players, and not the Royal Family?" Clavier asked.

"Well, sir, for us the Royal Family must come first, and the players second."

"But Armando Reyes wasn't a member of the British royalty."

"We're increasing our security forces around the courts. As

you know, we use off-duty servicemen as ushers. This year, we're arming them."

"Good show," Sir Francis said again.

A buzzer rang on his desk. He pressed a button and answered. "What is it, Gardiner?"

"A letter, sir. It's just arrived. I'm afraid it's marked urgent."

"Very well. Bring it in."

The Superintendent went on with his explanation of the security measures, which were elaborate, while Sir Francis walked to the door to get the letter from his secretary. "Thank you, Gardiner."

The letter was in a plain envelope, with the address of the All-England Club typewritten across the front, and the name Sir Francis Malcolm in the lower left-hand corner. He tore the letter open and a single sheet of paper fell out. It was a photocopy of an original, composed of words clipped from a newspaper or magazine. The message read:

REYES WAS ONLY THE FIRST.
CANCEL THE WIMBLEDON MATCHES OR
A SECOND SEMIFINALIST WILL DIE.

Sir Francis passed the letter to Clavier, who read it and handed it on to Superintendent Weston. Sir Francis had already begun to tremble.

"A madman!" Clavier exclaimed.

"I shall get right on this," the Superintendent said. "I recommend that we keep it between us."

"We are certainly in no position to cancel The Championships," Sir Francis said.

"Agreed," said Clavier. "You will report back to us, won't you?"

"Of course." Weston said a hasty goodbye and hurried out, carrying the letter by one corner, using his handkerchief.

Wimbledon, Opening Day.

The resplendent conductor lifted his arms and fixed his eyes on the person who was to indicate the exact moment of entry of the Prince of Wales into the Royal Box. The musicians of the

Royal Guards, also in full uniform—red jacket, golden epaulets, white leather baldric, black trousers bearing double stripes— stood sweating in the sun.

At precisely ten minutes to two, the Prince of Wales arrived, in the company of the Duke and Duchess of Kent, an unidentified admiral, three pretty women in colored frocks, seven attendants, and a full plainclothes security force. Princess Diana had not accompanied her husband, as an added precaution against terrorists. The week before, an IRA terrorist had been convicted and sentenced at the Old Bailey, and there was fear of an act of violence as a counterattack.

The spectators arrived early to eat picnic lunches on the lawns beneath the lovely summer sun. Fans without tickets had spent the night on Church Road, queuing up for the privilege of buying one of the three hundred tickets put on sale each day for Centre Court. There was an ironic justice at work here. Some stood in line, or slept outdoors in foul weather and fair. Some paid hundreds of British pounds for tickets. Others were given free seats in the official stands.

One had only to know the right people. Matt Malone sat in Saadi's private box, with Muriel and the Princess Athena. The women looked glorious.

At exactly two o'clock, Koras came onto the court, followed by his opponent, Ramesh Nanda, of Bangalore, India, a short man, dark and spare. This was the high moment of his life, to be playing on Centre Court, before the Prince of Wales, against the best player in the world. The spectators, to be fair, gave the Indian the same attentive applause that they gave Koras.

Koras began the match by winning his serve, but then his concentration vanished and he lost the first set, 2–6. To the spectators, sitting high above, the defending champion seemed to lack the magic touch that had won for him last year. Koras rallied in the second set to win, 6–4. The third set seesawed, 2–all, 3–all, ending in a tiebreaker won by Koras, 12–10. The fans were excited now, because first-round matches are not noted for their excitement and drama.

In the fourth set, Koras was behind all the way, when his right knee gave way beneath him and he fell to the turf while running down a wide forehand. He was forced to take the three-minute time-out, while his opponent paced nervously about near the umpire's chair. Down 5–3, the champion regained his precision at last, climbing back up the scoreboard with a masterful execution of drop shots and well-placed lobs that forced Nanda away from the net. A tentative overhead smash drifted wide on the Indian at 5–all, and Koras moved ahead with three sizzling backhands that left the spectators breathless.

The fourth set ended in a tiebreaker, 11–9, in favor of Koras. As the opponents shook hands, the champion was observed to be pale and shaken.

Koras had almost lost to the Indian.

The spectators were now waiting for Tania Pikeste, already a legend because of her performance at Roland-Garros. Tania was to open the women's tournament, and it was another break in tradition to have the women start on the same day as the men. Tania, in a white dress with blue trim, came onto the court, followed by her opponent, Beth Brookfield, from Hudson on Thames, the hope of the British.

The Rumanian would give her no chance.

Back in the dressing room, a weary Koras found his friend Milo Tigrid, dressed in white flannels from another era, a checkered bow tie, and a white cap with a soft ball. The burly Yugoslav was grinning, his face flushed. He had just won his first match on the so-called "Upset Court."

"Ho, Koras. Did you win?"

"Barely. The Indian let me live. And you?"

"Chalk up one dead Australian." Milo snapped the end of a towel at Koras, who dodged.

"What was your score?"

"Oh, 6–4, 6–3, 3–6, 7–6. I thank the tennis gods it did not go to five sets."

"How did they like the Big Bill Tilden costume?"

"It is not Tilden."

"Okay. Who is it?"

Milo gave Koras a condescending look. "Have you visited the hallowed Wimbledon Museum? Try something further back."

"All right." Koras unlaced one shoe. "Major Wingfield?"

Major Walter Clopton Wingfield had invented lawn tennis.

He took the net from badminton; the ball from a handball game, Eton Fives; the court from court tennis, an indoor game; the scoring from hard rackets. He named his game *Sphairistike*, a Greek word meaning lawn tennis. Wingfield got a preliminary patent in Britain in February 1874. Britons were mad for sport. By the end of the century, they were deeply in love with lawn tennis.

"Too far back. Try the Renshaw era."

"Willie or Ernest?"

Milo swished the towel at Koras. "Which Renshaw was more savage, more vengeful, more competitive?"

"Willie. Ernest always lost in the clutch."

Milo shook hands with Koras, then struck a pose. "Announcing—Sir Willie Renshaw."

Koras laughed. "The cap is the coup de grace, Milo."

Milo swept the cap off, bowing to Koras. "From the races, Your Highness. How was Palermo?"

"Hot. The women were handsome and proud, with gypsy eyes and breath like wine and garlic. How was Gstaad?"

"Weary. Those bloody Swiss, and their bloody banks." Milos pulled out a piece of monogrammed stationery and showed it to Koras. It had the name Jessica on it, and a phone number.

"What's that?"

"A love note. I tell you, Pantakoras, it's this costume. They see me out there, they see Tradition walking. Let me describe her, as she walks in beauty. She is blonde, sturdy but with well-rounded limbs, of good English stock, a lady archer riding with Sir Robin Hood. I know she will smell like loam, the good English earth." He paused. "I had an instructor once in school who claimed Robin Hood was the first communist."

Koras grinned and untied his other shoe. His right knee hurt. "How was the condition of your court?"

"Perfection itself. They say Centre Court is already showing wear. Laville has complained, thinking words can grow fresh grass. So has Polak."

Koras thought of losing. He had almost lost today. Opening round, and two close tiebreakers. "Maybe we won't have to worry about that this year."

"Huh! Speak for yourself, my sagging Lithuanian."

Koras opened his locker. "How is Muriel?"

"She has deserted me for a man passing himself off as a writer."

Malone. "You're kidding," Koras said.

Milo nodded, pushed his cheek out with his tongue. "They are writing a book together. He has contacted his publisher."

"What does the husband say?"

For an answer, Milo stuck his cheek out with his tongue. "The husband is French. He has his mistresses. Malone has consoled the lady about Armando."

"I have a tough time seeing them together."

"So do I."

"No. I meant Muriel and Armando." Koras turned to look at his friend. "They just didn't seem to be right for each other."

"That Peruvian was God's gift to women. Oh, how I miss the bastard."

"Yes. Me, too."

"Speaking of Armando, I have something for you."

"What?"

Milo sat down next to Koras, reached into his tennis bag, and brought out an envelope. He passed the envelope to his friend. "Tell no one. In Montenegrin, they call this magic." His voice was a whisper.

Koras looked into the envelope, saw a dozen red pills. "Where did you get these?"

"From Armando's tennis bag. The day he died."

"How did you get the bag?"

"Di Rocca gave it to me. The pills spilled out."

"They're what killed him!"

"Because he took too many. I, Tigrid, am a careful man."

Koras felt a quick flash of anger. One friend dead was enough. "How do you know there's no residual effect, no buildup?"

"Trust me, Pantakoras. I can feel the Montenegrin magic, feel the power coursing through me." He made a fist of triumph, then shook it in the general direction of the universe. "Down with Laville, all these pimpled latecomers! You should have seen me, Pantakoras. I tell you, I was superior out there. I was Milovan the Magnificent, not Milo the Mad."

Koras handed the pills back, shaking his head. "Be careful, old friend."

"Take them. I have more."

"No, thanks."

"I have been waiting for this magic for years. I may even take this tournament of the English."

"They're working now, Milo, making you hallucinate about English blondes with an earthy smell."

Milo leaned close, his eyes very intense. "I can tell you, they help one's performance between the sheets of love."

"Since when did you need help there?"

The door opened and they heard voices coming their way. Milo tucked the envelope back into his tennis bag as Davey Cooper walked in, dressed in street clothes. He was followed by Matt Malone, who carried his writer's notebook.

"Well?" Malone asked Milo.

"Another victory for the geriatrics."

"Drinks for the victor. I'm buying." Malone shook Milo's hand, a genuine gesture, then turned to greet Koras. "Hello, Koras. Good to see you."

"Hello." Koras shook hands with Malone, who seemed to be Milo's new pal.

"When can we get in an interview?"

"End of the week."

"How about tomorrow? I have some time."

Koras hesitated. "Phone me at the hotel."

"Pantakoras is incognito," Milo said. "He has his own news blackout."

"Milo does enough TV interviews for both of us."

"One of the legacies of being old," Milo said, "is that they don't think you are interesting anymore."

"Hell, Milo," Malone said. "You'll always be interesting."

"Any word on the Magnelli contract?" Koras asked.

"They may renew. They may not. One never knows. While they decide, it leaves one free to dress as one pleases."

"You look like a real fruit, Milo," Davey Cooper said.

"Brat."

The men laughed.

"Well, I'm buying the drinks," Malone said. "There's a bar over by the Gloucester with a waitress who has her eye on Milo."

Milo spread his hands, a mock gesture of helplessness. "What can I say? They love Tigrid."

"The waitress has spiked hair," Malone said. "Purple to the roots."

"Only on the right," Milo countered. "The left side is green."

"World's full of fruits," Davey said and walked around the corner, shaking his head. Koras and Milo laughed with Malone, then headed for the tubs.

Malone stayed where he was and listened. He could hear what sounded like Will Channer singing one of his Aussie drinking songs, slamming a locker one aisle over. Malone dropped his notebook onto the bench and started to go through Tigrid's tennis bag. Channer would be coming up this aisle on his way out to see Koras. Malone figured he had about fifteen seconds to find out what was in the envelope he'd seen in Milo's hand.

While Will Channer waited for Koras to come out of the tubs, he checked through his notebook for strategy pointers he had gleaned from the match against Ramesh Nanda. Koras had been distracted and his game had not been sharp. Channer was thinking of ways to tell him.

In a few moments, Koras came out, wearing a blue towel wrapped around his waist, and the two men talked strokes and strategies. Channer thought these postmortem sessions were valuable as a training device, because they helped Koras with an overview of his own game that was not possible when he was out on the court, stroking and sweating and surviving. Both men agreed that Koras had spent too much time in the back-court, and that his topspin forehand needed more shoulder turn. Finally, Channer closed the notebook and handed Koras a shoe box from Laval Sportif.

"They came."

"Almost too late." Koras opened the box and brought out a pair of Laval shoes, leather uppers, with hundreds of tiny rubber spikes on the soles. They had been especially designed for him by the people at Laval, strictly for grass play. Koras had been waiting for them for weeks. "The footing was tricky out there today. It will be worse when it rains."

Channer nodded. "If these help you win, Laval will go into mass production."

"They're only good on grass."

"I saw Micky Polak earlier. He's trying out a pair from Izanagi."

Koras knew Micky's contract with Sport City was up at the end of the week. "Are they after Polak?"

Channer shrugged, then brushed a shock of hair away from his face. "Musical chairs in the endorsement arena. Micky didn't say."

Koras held up the shoe. "What this shoe needs is a grass court circuit."

"The Sahara Grass Court Championships?"

Koras grinned as he leaned down to tie his shoelaces. "Saadi could mass-produce that stuff they used in the Astrodome, for Houston football." He tossed the shoe box into the trash bin and stowed the shoes in his tennis bag.

They heard Milo's voice from around the corner, shouting hello to Frank Fenwick. In a moment, the Texan appeared. He carried a manila folder stuffed with papers for Koras to sign. Koras signed, quickly noting the amounts but not grasping the strategy. A million three to one account in Boston. Six hundred thousand in a money-market fund. A signature card for a new market-rate account at a bank in Houston. It was a shell game, and only Fenwick knew where the money was. Koras handed the papers back. He'd been poor half his life, then rich. These days, however, he felt constant pressure to perform, to hang in there, to keep making money.

"What's up, F.F.?"

"You want detail? Or the bottom line?"

"How about the current strategy?"

Fenwick sighed, pointed to the papers with a long finger. "We owe the contractors a million two. In a week, we'll pay them seven hundred and sixty-five grand, a number I nego-tiated. Until then, the money draws top-dollar interest. If I can get these finalized, you might stay out of jail until September."

"Good timing."

Koras knew he'd spent too much money on the Westhampton house. A million to expand the house. Almost a half million for the two tennis courts, so he could work out year-round.

"One reason we're tight," Fenwick said, "the check still hasn't come through from Palermo."

Koras dipped into his tennis bag, brought out a handful of Italian liras. "Did you talk to Di Rocca? He's got pull down there."

Fenwick and Channer laughed. Koras stuffed the liras back in his bag and zipped it up.

"I heard Laville outside," Channer said, "beefing about the grass."

"How does Laville seem to you?"

"Edgy. He hasn't killed any linespeople yet."

Koras hefted his bag and looked at the two men who held his future in their hands. There was a faraway look in his eye. "Did you see Milo and his lawn tennis rig?"

Channer laughed. "I like that crazy guy. We played a match at Kooyong back in the sixties, in hundred-degree heat. Milo wore cabbage leaves in his hat to keep his head cool and he kept telling me he was Jaroslav Drobny reincarnated."

"Milo's a treat."

"Did they renew his contract with Magnelli?" Koras asked Fenwick.

"Not yet. But it's in the works."

The three men walked out together.

"Let's have a beer," Channer said.

"Sorry," Koras said. "Got to hit a bookstore."

"See you at Queen's Club, eight sharp."

"I'll call to confirm," Koras said, and left Channer and Fenwick strategizing about the Wimbledon fortnight.

On his way out, Koras ran into Princess Athena. She wore a conservatively draped dress of white muslin, which did not have the usual number of revealing vents and startling gaps. She forced a smile and tried to look vivacious, but she seemed subdued, pensive, sad. Koras hadn't seen her smile since Armando had died in Paris.

"Oh, Pantakoras. I watched your match against Ramesh. You seemed so sad."

He looked at the dark circles under her eyes. "I was just about to say the same about you. Have you had some bad news?"

"A little." She gripped his arms in both hands.

"Do you want to talk about it?"

"Perhaps." The Princess bit her lip. "Walk with me. I'm meeting Saadi and Nora in the box."

"Has Saadi decided to lock you in a dungeon and throw away the key?"

"Always perceptive, Pantakoras." She clung to his arm, a memory of old times.

Koras walked beside her for a moment. "I need directions to Alesia."

"Alesia?" Now she smiled. "What about the matches?"

"I don't play tomorrow. I'll be back for my daily workout."

"You rascal, Pantakoras. It is some fifty kilometers to the north." She told him to fly to Dijon, then rent a car. "Are you madly in love then?"

Her intensity made him wonder if she had sensed his urgent need to see Laure. It was crazy leaving the matches, risky. It was a measure of the pull Laure exerted on him.

Instead of answering directly, Koras said, "Give my regards to Nora."

Athena squeezed his arm. "You be good to Laure. She is young. She does not have the benefit of your experience in love."

"She's a woman. That starts her out at 5–love, 40–15 in the last set."

Athena started to protest, but Koras kissed her on the cheek and made his exit.

NINE

The hired Bentley stopped in front of a dilapidated building labeled "Special Air Travels." It was located behind the Gatwick air terminal, near the maintenance warehouse. The chauffeur carefully set the hand brake before stepping out of the car to open the door for his passenger.

"Here we are, sir."

Koras put on his sunglasses and left the car. There were clouds to the east, but the London weathermen had reversed themselves and now no rain was predicted for tomorrow. He wanted one sunny day in France. Picking up his briefcase, he entered the building. The young woman behind the counter recognized him.

"Oh, Mr. Belynkas, your pilot is waiting in the lounge. And your aeroplane is getting its final check."

"Thank you. What is the weather in France?"

"There is light rain, sir, all the way from the Alps to the French Coast. I certainly hope it does not spoil your visit."

"Thank you. Were you able to arrange for a car at the other end?"

"Yes." She handed him his papers, asked for his passport and credit card. He handed over an American Express card. After he had signed seven separate forms, the young woman smiled.

"Did you win today?"

Koras thought of his tough match. "Yes. Thank you. Do you follow tennis?"

"My boyfriend does. He's a player himself."

"Good. We need all the tennis players we can get."

Outside again, Koras beckoned to the driver to follow him with the suitcase, heavy with books. The plane was a Falcon 10, twin engine, with the insignia of the rental company. A hostess in a sky-blue uniform stood at the bottom of the steps. She had a pretty smile. He reminded himself to tip her.

Koras told the driver to come back the following morning. As he was giving his instructions, a taxi pulled up outside the

Special Air building. Koras noticed that its light was off, but no one got out. For a moment he waited, feeling the hairs stand up on the back of his neck, wondering if all the talk of murder was making him jumpy. Then he shrugged it off and handed his driver five pounds. The driver touched his cap in salute.

"Right you are, sir."

Seven minutes later, Koras had boarded his plane and was settled in his seat. He was the only passenger. He asked for a cold beer, which brought another smile from the hostess, and opened a book he had picked up in a used bookstore—*Critical Essay on the de Bello Gallico,* by Sir George Wallensborough. His bag contained a paperback edition of Caesar's *Conquest of Gaul,* a map of central France, around the Côte d'Or, and *Europe's Wonderful Little Hotels and Inns.* When he had the time, Koras was a planner.

When the plane was taxiing out to the end of the airstrip, Malone emerged from a cab and walked inside Special Air to inquire about Koras's destination. He left Muriel waiting in the cab. He was back in less than a minute with the news that Koras had chartered a plane to Dijon.

"Where is Dijon?"

"Southeast of Paris."

"He's going to see the cousin of the Princess, then?"

"If Jack Di Rocca is right."

"What's the quickest way to get to Dijon?"

"Why not charter a plane ourselves?" Muriel's tone was ironic, playful.

"Bell would kill me."

Muriel laughed, crossed her legs. "We can fly to Paris. From there, you can drive to Alesia."

That meant she would stay in Paris. "How the hell am I supposed to find him there?"

Muriel smiled at Malone. "France is a small country. Have you not found men in places much more vast?"

He had sworn her to secrecy and told her he was a private investigator. Every chance she had, she dropped a reference about his tracking abilities.

As Koras's plane roared over their heads, Malone asked the driver to take them to British Airways.

It was late afternoon when the rented Falcon 10 landed at the airport of Neuilly-les-Dijon. Rain was still falling, and the air was fresh and clean. Koras came out of the book, closed it, put it back into his case. He stretched, yawned. Wimbledon was behind him. He looked forward to seeing Laure.

Koras made sure the plane would be ready to leave the next morning, sometime before noon, and then said goodbye to the captain and the hostess. He tipped the hostess ten pounds, which brought forth a pretty smile.

He cleared Customs in five minutes. A white Renault was waiting in the parking lot. A driver was available, but Koras wanted to drive himself. He produced his international driver's license, which still had three months before expiration. He verified the location of Alesia, which was on a rising elevation of ground near Mont Auxois. The correspondent at the car rental desk advised Koras to book a hotel in Dijon for the night. But Koras hoped to spend the night closer to Laure.

Twenty minutes after landing, in his rented car with its slightly wobbly steering, he was on his way to Alesia.

He drove through the village of Alesia, and took the first turn on his left, toward the small mountain he took to be Mont Auxois. At its base lay the vast excavation site. Many foreign cars, German makes mostly, along with a Volvo and some Saabs, were parked in a level areas with a sign that read STATIONNE-MENT. He found a parking spot and slid the Renault in. Behind the parking, a gravel path, slick with rain, rose to a series of levels, where people in yellow rain slickers moved about. He counted eighteen tents, their tan canvas sagging and darkened by the weather. The activity reminded him of a movie set.

More people in slickers walked quickly from the tents up to a higher area, great piles of dirt turning to mud, where wooden scaffolds stood. Alesia was on a rise above the village of Alise Sainte Reine. A grove of trees there, a dark-green copse, off to the left. Below him lay the road, yellow and white in the rain, winding up from the village.

A man wearing a yellow rain jacket passed, and Koras asked in fluent French about Laure Puget.

"Up there." The man pointed up the hill, toward the scaffolding. Wearing his own rain jacket, Koras rummaged in the trunk of the car until he found his collapsible umbrella, black with a carved wooden handle, bought in Vienna, five years ago. It was getting old now and he should replace it.

Up here, the rain slanted, driven by the wind. The air, though, smelled fresh and clean. Koras took in a deep breath and realized he was nervous about seeing Laure. It was, after all, her arena, and Koras was more comfortable in the surroundings of the tennis circuit.

He found her working with two men under the shelter of a canvas lean-to. Damp brown hair was plastered around her long face. She wore a blue rain jacket, open to reveal a white safari blouse with two large pockets, and khaki shorts. Her lace-up leather boots, and bare calves, tanned from long hours in the sun, were stained with splotches of mud. They were excellent legs.

"Well. Mr. Belynkas." Laure looked surprised.

The formality did not deter him. "I came to buy you that drink."

She recovered her composure and introduced him to the two men. One was a young, sharp-faced fellow with wire-rim glasses, a white lab coat, and a protective intensity about Laure. Laure introduced him as Dr. Jean-Luc Benoît. The other, Professor Evarts from the Free University of Berlin, had gray hair and a matching beard. Both men frowned at the interruption, and Koras sensed a certain amount of tension, not so different from what could be felt in the dressing room while a major tournament was being played and there was a lot at stake.

"We are just finishing up, if you don't mind waiting. In a few moments, I can show you around."

He waited under an overhang in the scaffolding, listening to the voices, Laure's sharp and female, in contrast to the two men, who were asking lots of questions. They spoke in German, English, and French, and the topic was money, which they were running short of. She came out after a few moments, her frown changing to a soft smile as she approached. Her blue hood was up, to keep the water off her hair.

Laure led him to a promontory, where she pointed out some of the landmarks of the fortress and the battle where Caesar defeated Vercingetorix. They stood together under Koras's umbrella.

"There were ramparts along there," Laure said, pointing, "and a wall two meters high. The Gauls were up here. The Romans had eight camps, laid out at strategic points. These camps were connected by two dozen redoubts. The Roman lines extended nine and one-half English miles."

He had the sense she was avoiding the reason he'd flown over. "Incredible."

She turned to face him. "I'm surprised you came."

"I wanted to see you."

"What about Wimbledon?"

"I won earlier today, a very tough match. I owed myself a visit. I won't play again until Wednesday."

"How did you get here?"

"I hired a plane. From Dijon I took a car, a white Renault with French steering."

"Are you staying the night?"

"Yes. Can you have dinner?"

She shook her head. "I wish you hadn't come. We are having terrible problems."

"Money?"

She nodded. "There are arguments all the time. Everyone is on edge."

"How much do you need?"

She laughed at that, smirking before she turned away to stare down the valley. "Three million francs might fund us for the short run."

Koras wondered if he could raise even a quarter of that before Fenwick slipped it beneath another tax shelter. "It's like making a movie, then?"

"Yes," Laure said, "only much earthier."

Koras laughed. She wanted him to know she was turned on by the past. As she kept on talking, he began to get the feel for what the Gauls had gone through in their defeat by Caesar. It was getting dark by the time she finished, so he repeated his invitation for dinner.

Laure hesitated while she thought the matter over. "All right. I could use a night off from the bickering. Give me a moment."

Before he could answer, she trotted through the rain to the tent where the two men waited. Koras had the feeling she was breaking some kind of date with the intense Jean-Luc.

At the house where the excavation crew stayed, Koras called the Hôtel Metz in Montbard, while Laure took a quick shower and changed. He got a room, $27 US for the night, making him realize he was in the provinces, and not in Paris. She came out wearing leather knee boots, a dark skirt, a red blouse that highlighted her hair. As she hugged Koras, a fresh, clean smell came off her. Laure Puget was the eternal springtime girl.

In moments, she had worked her magic and had transformed herself from a toiling academic archaeologist to a very desirable woman. Over her shoulder was the leather bag, too large for a purse, too small for a suitcase, that Koras remembered from Paris. She stowed the bag in the back seat of the Renault. They drove to the Hôtel Caesar in Alesia for the evening meal.

The main course was a Bourguignon, red and succulent. For that, the waiter recommended a Bourgogne red. By the end of the meal, they were into the third bottle. Laure's cheeks were flushed and the conversation had swerved away from Caesar and Alesia to Koras and his life on the tennis circuit.

"I was sorry to miss seeing you in the finals in Paris."

He heard the words, but her mind seemed to be elsewhere. "I was sorry, too."

"You won a lot of money, didn't you?"

Koras was thinking of Armando, dead from an overdose. And also of Fenwick, with his talk of bank loans. "My manager takes it away." He reached into his briefcase, produced his copy of Wallensborough. "I've been reading detective stories."

Laure was delighted. "You are always surprising me."

"I saw you reading. I knew that the way to your heart was through books, moldy old ones."

Laure blushed and took another sip of wine.

She stood close to him as he brought out his wallet to pay the bill. When Koras handed the proprietor a credit card, the man shook his head.

"Sorry, monsieur. We cannot accept."

Koras turned to Laure. "Damn. I forgot to bring French money."

Laure rummaged in her leather purse and came out with three hundred francs. She paid the bill. In the car, he handed her some British pounds. She shook her head.

"You owe me a *dinner* now. At a very good restaurant." Was money one of her interests? She seemed to like having this hold over him.

"I have American money. Liras. Even some German marks, traveler's checks."

"Sorry, the debt can only be paid in food."

At the house where Laure stayed, she gave him a quick kiss, soft lips on his cheek. He wanted to ask her to drive to Montbard, to the Hôtel Metz, to spend the night. Her good-night was firm and he felt suddenly empty.

"Tomorrow?" he asked. "Breakfast?"

"I must work," she said and hurried into the house.

The moon came out as he started north toward Montbard. Far behind him, Koras picked up the occasional flash from another pair of headlights, but except for them he had the road to himself.

At the hotel in Montbard, they gave him number 9, le numéro neuf. As he walked up the stairs, he saw the image of Laure, the shorts, the boots, the tanned legs, her hair wet with rain, and loneliness flooded his heart.

He felt chilly from the rain and the wet night, so he showered, a long hot one, in the *douche* down the hall. Dressed in his favorite robe, a blue terry cloth given to him years ago by Athena, he unpacked. There were Levis and a shirt for tomorrow, socks, fresh underwear. He liked not being at Wimbledon, immersed in the matches, competing, grinding along, clawing up through the draw. Koras had never left a tournament before.

He read for a while, his paperback copy of Caesar's *Conquest of Gaul.* He read the speech of Critognatus twice, wondering what it would be like to eat roast baby. What could make you hungry enough to eat human flesh?

He was about to turn out the light when there was a soft knock on the door. He opened the door to find Laure Puget, leather bag over her shoulder.

"I came to inspect the room," she said. "Le numéro neuf."

She was so beautiful he could not speak. His legs trembled as he held the door open for her.

Laure brushed him coming in, swinging the leather bag with confidence, yet edged with a certain nervousness. She set the bag down on the bed, opened it to bring out a bottle of brandy. "A local cognac, très formidable, or so they say." She handed him the bottle. One-quarter gone, he noticed. Who were her other drinking partners?

Koras brought glasses from the ancient armoire and poured them both a cognac. As they clinked glasses, he could see her watching him over the rim of her glass, studying him.

They had a drink. Then Laure excused herself to go to the W.C. When she came back, her eyes were thoughtful. She poured more cognac and handed Koras his glass. "Have you recalled the moment when I first saw you?" she asked.

"Of course. In Paris. You were reading while I played my heart out."

"You don't remember our tennis lesson?"

"What tennis lesson?"

"I was fourteen. You were in love with Cousin Athena. The lesson was in Salzburg, at Aunt Helga's."

Koras remembered. The skinny kid with the legs and the shy smile. Her forehand had been a natural, but he hadn't taught her to serve. "I feel stupid."

She touched his lip with one finger. "Ah, the great Koras Belynkas, off balance for what must be the only time in his life."

He sipped his cognac, which burned going down. "Only fourteen. Are you sure?"

"A very romantic fourteen. I thought you were the handsomest man in the world. And Athena, the luckiest woman." She took a step close to him. He touched her and she did not move away.

"Laure, I—"

He kissed her then, covering his confusion with instinct, tasting her mouth, pressing the truth of his desire against her. She pushed closer, then broke off the kiss to lick the edge of his mouth, one subtle flick with her tongue. After a long sighing moment, she broke away to put one foot on the edge of a chair.

She unzipped one boot. Laure was a pretty sight with her leg up, her skirt hiked high, long lines of absolute beauty. "An assist, if you please."

Koras helped her with the boots. Touching her took him deeper into fantasy.

"Ahh," she said, as she flopped back on the bed. "Wonderful night. Wonderful bed."

As she lay back, he noticed that three buttons on her red blouse were undone, a clear invitation. He saw the mounds of her breasts, gentle slopes, lightly tanned. His breath quickened, and she smiled. He admired her way of controlling the rhythms of love.

When he took her by the wrist and pulled her close, she came willingly. Her movements were supple. Her mouth searched his, probing, her tongue running along his teeth. She put a hand on his leg, caressed him gently. Her neck beneath his lips was total smoothness. She cried out when he bit her ear. "My skirt," she whispered. "Let me take it off."

They separated. Koras, short of breath, threw off his robe. The lights were still on. Laure noticed his arousal, and smiled, unzipping her skirt, allowing it to fall to the floor. Koras flipped the light switch, throwing the room into semidarkness. Light pushed into the room, the pale-green moon of France. Laure moved to the open window, used the moonlight to finish undressing. Watching, Koras held his breath. It was a beautiful moment, hushed and still. As she bent to remove her stockings, her hair swung down around her face, hiding it. The red blouse, unbuttoned, draped open, bathing her in moonlight. He caught his breath when she slipped out of her panties, the long legs bare, sensual. She tossed the blouse away and came to the bed, naked.

His eyes filled with tears. She kissed his face, pausing to nuzzle the blond mustache.

"You are crying."

"Because you are so beautiful."

He licked her toes first, making her writhe as he continued up one leg, then the other. They made love playfully, then seriously, then playfully once more. Twice, he made her cry out. When he was inside her, he felt safe, home at last, all the loneliness from his gypsy life falling away . . .

When they were finished, Laure left the bed to refill their glasses. Her face was soft, but again he sensed distance. Her mind was somewhere else. The brandy warmed him.

"Tell me."

"Hmm?"

"What are you thinking about?"

For a moment, she didn't answer. "You won't be hurt? Or angry?"

"I promise."

"I was thinking about Greece, actually."

"Why Greece?"

"There is a man in Athens. Professor Colicos, at the University. He sees Alesia as the French Troy. He may help us raise money to expand the work here."

"Money again?"

She touched his glass with hers. "Money, always."

Koras put a hand on her bare shoulder. Her skin was smooth, flawless. She stared at him a moment in the moonlight, then looked away. Koras got up from the bed.

"Where are you going?" Her voice was sharp.

He flipped the light on. "Let's make a list." He returned to the bed with his notebook and a ballpoint pen. "My coach pumps me full of strategy. I'm supposed to keep notes in here. Writing it down helps." He flipped past his notes on other players. "Ready."

"This is silly."

"Ready," he said again.

"I feel foolish, burdening you."

"Because you hardly know me?"

"No. There is something—"

He poked her lightly with the end of the ballpoint. "You said three million francs." He wrote that at the top of the page.

"Let's break it down. Salaries? Dig permits? A fresh white frock for young Dr. Benoît?"

Laure kicked him with her bare heel. At the same time, a small smile played at the corners of her mouth. "All right. Permits for the expansion, for a year, 360,000 francs. Two million francs for salaries. Then we have 46,000 for insurance, 86,000 for our meals, 29,000 to upgrade our X-ray equipment. The diesel generator died Friday and a new one costs at least 70,000. The lab takes 260,000 a quarter, if we don't bring in experts from Paris and the States."

Koras made a neat list. The total came to 2,803,000 francs. At the current exchange rate, that was roughly $400,000. He put the pen and notebook aside. There was one sip of brandy left.

"Now, do you feel better?" Laure asked.

"Immensely. You?"

"I'm not sure."

"When will you go to Greece?"

"Why? Is there a tournament there?"

"In the autumn, perhaps."

"I must go sooner than that."

He touched her then and she smiled and turned to him.

"Come to America," he said. "I'll introduce you to rich people."

"The Peabody is in Massachusetts. Are you near there?"

"An hour. Maybe two."

She set her glass down and rolled on top of him in a movement that seemed innocent, natural, and playful. "Do you always make lists, monsieur?" Her voice mocked him, gently.

"When it's something important."

"My excavation at Alesia is important?"

"A noble cause."

She moved, subtly. In the pale moonlight, he saw the smile on her face. "Did you really read Wallensborough?"

"I skimmed it."

She moved again, making him catch his breath. "Sometime, I would like to read your lists."

"All right."

She touched his face. "I did not expect this."

"What?"

"The list. Your interest in my work."

"Neither did I."

She laughed and that made him laugh and then he was lost in touch and perfume and exploring their mutual desire.

Morning in Montbard, at the Hôtel Metz.

Koras woke to find her side of the bed empty. The sight made his heart race. He sat up in bed and saw the note on the dresser. He rolled out of bed and put on his robe. The note said she had to leave early for the excavation. Sun streamed through the window. Koras was disappointed, depressed. One night of love, and then emptiness. He wanted her more than ever.

After doing his knee exercises, he called Will Channer in London, to tell him he would be late for their workout. Will said he was insane for leaving London during the Fortnight. Then he called the airport in Dijon, to tell them to get ready to leave around noon. He cashed a check with the hotel and paid his bill. He spent an hour at breakfast, drinking coffee and ordering more croissants while he read the papers. When breakfast was over, he waited another fifteen minutes for the national bank to open. Then he called his bank in New York, with instructions to wire money to a bank in Dijon. He wanted half a million. All they could advance him, drawing from the construction account, was four hundred thousand dollars.

Malone waited until Koras had settled in with his second pot of coffee and his newspapers. Then he sneaked past the desk of the concierge to room number 9. There was no one on the floor. The locks looked seventy-five years old, not much of a match for a special set of skeleton keys, made up for Malone by J. D. Griswold, an ex-con who lived three houses down, in Skokie. Griswold had done time for burglary, breaking and entering. He made the best lock picks and skeleton keys in the business. In the last couple of years, Griswold had built up a reputation for developing a system that could defeat the new electronic hotel locks, the ones that changed combinations with every new customer. A computer punched out a key card, changed the locks, automatically.

Griswold's system was secret. It was also for sale for ten thousand. Two days ago, Malone had ordered a Griswold system.

Inside the room, he went quickly through Koras's gear. The man traveled light, only one bag for clothes, a custom-made leather job with a strap for the shoulder and wheels for long hauls through airports. A laundry bag. Two pairs of sneaks. The bag was empty. The clothes were stowed in the dresser, an antique from the look of it, and in the armoire against the wall, by the window. Koras had a good view from his room, right onto the picturesque street. Not a bad life, being a tennis star. Malone worked fast, finishing his search in less than seven minutes. Not a trace of a recreational drug anyplace. So far, Koras was clean.

Malone was out of the hotel and into his rented car before Koras returned to pack up. As he drove south toward Dijon, Malone had a choice. He could take a flight from here back to Paris. Or he could wait for Koras to finish up with the girl and try to hitch a ride with him.

Thinking about that, Malone grinned.

In Dijon, Koras picked up the bank draft for 2,803,000 francs, made out to Laure Puget. At the current rate of exchange, that was what his four hundred thousand dollars would buy on the currency markets. With the draft tucked into his jacket pocket, he made the drive to Alesia. The sun was bright. It was a magnificent day.

With the sun out, activity at the excavation seemed diligent and serious. At least a hundred people were working and today the careful surgery on the earth seemed part of a grand plan. It took him fifteen minutes to find Laure, at the bottom of a deep trench, on her hands and knees in the mud. With her was Dr. Jean-Luc Benoît, wearing a mud-spattered lab coat and rubber knee boots. As Koras appeared at the top of the trough, Dr. Benoît looked up, sunlight winking off his glasses. Laure was in shadow, examining a shard of pottery. They were excited, but they stopped talking when Koras arrived.

"Oh!" Laure said.

"Good morning." The check was in his pocket. He felt like a Gallic hero coming to save France.

Laure spoke briefly to Jean-Luc and then climbed a ladder

out of her ditch. She was blushing as she came up to Koras. A strand of hair fell across one eye and she brushed it away. Was she glad to see him? Or embarrassed? He couldn't tell. She took his arm and walked him away from the trough.

"Did you get my note?"

"Yes."

"I—" she began, then stopped.

"It was a lovely time," Koras said.

"Yes. But you have your life, I have mine. Don't we?"

She was in love with the past, all this digging, all these tiny bits of pottery and charcoal. "I want to see you again."

"It is not pos—" She stopped, looked around. "It will not work."

"I think it will."

She held out a hand to shake. "You do owe me a dinner."

Koras reached into his pocket and handed her the bank draft. She unfolded it, stared at the numbers, looked at him. A blush crept up her throat. From deep in the trough, her name was called, but she did not answer. Her eyelids fluttered as she looked at Koras.

"This is a joke."

"No joke. It's for-real francs. On a real French bank."

"But it is so much money! You can't possibly—"

He was feeling better now. "It's only half what you need to finish the summer. I'll wire the rest."

"But why?"

He had control now, so he smiled at her. "A noble cause. The French Troy, you said."

She tried to hand the check back, but Koras put up his hand, palm out.

"It's yours."

"Can you afford it?"

He couldn't. "Yes."

Laure's face changed then, from a frown to a smile of ecstatic happiness. She threw her arms around Koras's neck and he felt her lips on his. The kiss lasted for a brief moment. Just then, Dr. Benoît appeared on the ladder, his head sticking up over the edge of the excavation. With hopeful promise and yielding finality, Laure pressed herself against Koras before letting him go.

"I have a plane to catch," he said.

"Goodbye. And thank you."

"Come to London."

"I shall try."

He turned and walked away, toward his rented Renault.

As Koras departed, Laure felt a fluttering in her heart. He confused her, knocked her off-balance. She was attracted to him and at the same time wary. She had spent her life studying, reading, cloistered by schools and universities. He, on the other hand, was a man of the world, cynical, experienced.

"What is it?" Jean-Luc asked as he came up.

Laure tucked the bank draft into a shirt pocket. "He came to say goodbye."

Jean-Luc glanced at Koras, who was almost out of sight. "Good. Now you can get back to work."

She almost told him then, almost flashed the check in his face. Instead, she ran after Koras, her eyes stinging with tears.

When she reached the parking lot below the excavation, she was out of breath. The white Renault was out of the lot and pulling away. Laure called out, but the Renault kept going. She felt her heart would burst. Waving, she ran behind the car, which was picking up speed. Then, abruptly, it stopped as he saw her in the rearview mirror. She slowed to a walk and Koras put the car into reverse, backed up, and parked on the edge of the road.

"What is it?" He was out of the car, moving toward her. "Laure, what is it?"

The sun was hot now, burning down. Her face felt flushed and she wondered how she looked. "There is something," she began. "I had to tell you."

"All right."

"Let's get in the car. Out of the sun."

He opened the door for her and she slid into the passenger seat. Her lip trembled. He walked around and got in behind the wheel.

"You know Saadi," she said.

"Yes."

"Much of our money was coming from him."

"From Saadi?"

Laure nodded. She hated talking about this. "Athena helped us persuade him. Saadi fancies himself a historian. He came to visit in the winter, after he and Athena—" She left that sentence unfinished. "He met Professor Evarts and Jean-Luc. He knew quite a bit about stratigraphy and carbon-dating. He wanted a small plaque for his Sahara company. And he started giving us money."

"But it stopped, right?"

"Yes." Laure didn't know how to tell Koras the rest. "In Paris, he invited me to visit his yacht, which was in Juan-les-Pins. I refused. When I arrived here and mentioned it to Jean-Luc, he insisted we go down there to see Saadi. I did not want to go, but at last we did, for a weekend. The yacht is lovely and the area is charming, but Saadi—" Laure paused to wipe her eyes. She was crying now, unable to stop, and the tears felt necessary. "And Saadi made advances."

"This is making my skin crawl."

"When I refused him, he stopped the money."

"Does Athena know?"

"She was in Austria. Perhaps she suspects. I don't know."

"A man like Saadi would count on your being too ashamed to say anything to her."

Laure wanted to be held then; she came into Koras's arms. Why was life so complicated? Why couldn't one live with emotions that came one at a time, with motives that were better than the ones she saw around her?

"Is that why you didn't want to take money from me?" Koras asked.

Laure nodded and another sob escaped. "We had a lovely night. I hated to spoil it."

Koras patted her on the shoulder. "It *was* lovely. And you didn't spoil anything."

She stayed in his arms a few more minutes. He kissed away her tears. They made tentative plans to see one another after Wimbledon, and she wrote down the number for her grandparents in Choisel, in the Chevreuse Valley. Then she gave him a deep, searching kiss, got out of the car, and watched him drive away.

* * *

When he turned in his rented Renault at the Dijon airport,
he made a comment about the loose steering. The man behind
the desk said he would have it looked into. Then Koras made
his way out of the car rental office. His plane would leave in
twenty minutes, something about maintenance, so Koras went
into the airport cafe for a beer. He was sitting there, getting
ready for Frank Fenwick, when he heard an American voice
and looked up to see Matt Malone standing there in a rumpled
tweed coat. Malone always looked as if he had slept in his
clothes for a week.

"Malone?"

"Mind if I join you?"

"What are you doing here?"

Malone pulled up a chair. "I need that interview."

"You followed me to France for an interview?"

Malone nodded. "Got lost last night, so I hung out here, a
rowdy hotel in Dijon. I thought maybe I could hitch a ride back
in your private jet, interview you on the way."

Koras laughed. He knew he should have been angry, but
Malone sat there grinning. It was a mad world. He held out a
hand and the two men shook. "It's paid for. Welcome aboard."

Malone pulled out his notebook, ready to get down to business. "I know how busy you sports jocks are." His grin was
infectious. "Have I got time for a beer?"

Koras turned to the waiter to order one.

"How come you speak the language so well?"

The interview had begun.

Koras smiled. "My only gift, I guess. We spoke Lithuanian at
my granddad's house, back in New York. I was a college drop-
out, but the Army sent me to Monterey, to the language school.
I studied Russian, and while I was there I dated a Vietnamese
teacher who taught me French. Picked up a lot."

The beer came. Malone lifted his glass before taking a sip.
"Good way to learn a language."

"The best."

"To women, then."

They clicked glasses. Koras's beer was half gone. Malone
finished his in three easy swallows. Then they walked out onto

the tarmac and boarded the Falcon. Once they were airborne and heading back for England, Malone continued the interview.

"I've been curious about how it feels, being you. You're the star, the number one. What do you do to keep beating a guy like Laville? He's going strong, steamrolling, driving the crowds wild, while he does everything to distract you except dynamite the umpire's chair. You're not as young as you used to be. This could be your last chance for the Grand Slam. How do you handle the situation?"

"Just lucky, I guess. Judson Garwood says I've got the whammy on Laville."

Malone chuckled. "What about Polak?"

"Against Micky, I go to the net all the time. Against Cooper, I lob, to take the pace off the ball. Cooper loves pace."

"What about the trick knee?"

Koras thought about that. "It hurts a lot. Went out from under me yesterday, against Nanda. I tried a brace once. Now I try to exercise it every day."

"How old are you?"

"Thirty-four."

"What keeps you going?"

"My manager."

"I hear you owe some money on a house you built."

"Correction. Rebuilt. And I'd like to keep that confidential."

"Okay. How long have you known Tigrid?"

"Thirteen years. I won my first major title with Milo, back in the early seventies."

"What keeps *him* going?"

Koras waited before answering. "Milo's turned himself into the circuit clown."

"You think he's on something?"

"Besides women?"

"I was thinking of drugs."

Koras shook his head. Malone's eyes watched his every move, made him feel trapped. "Not Milo."

"When did you start playing tennis?"

"I was about twelve, a late starter for a player. But I'd honed my hitting eye on stickball in the streets, and a tennis racket seemed easy after that. I used to hang around Central Park, with nothing but a racket and corduroy cutoffs and two paper-thin tennis balls, waiting for someone to ask me to hit. Tennis kept me off the street."

"That's why you stuck with it?"

"Yes. But it felt right, being out there, hitting. It felt, well—beautiful—when you did it just right, the feet and the shoulder swing and the power traveling through your wrist. That sweet spot felt just right. A man named Al Moscowitz coached me after a while. He taught me spin, balance, footwork. He helped me enter some tournaments, where I got whipped pretty badly. My father's business wasn't doing well, so I had to work delivering groceries. When I got better, Al Moscowitz paid for some lessons with a real pro, at the West Side Club."

Koras paused. "I learned how to dream at the West Side Club. All those gorgeous girls."

"What happened to Moscowitz?"

"He died, three years ago."

Koras was feeling sad now, remembering Al Moscowitz. Malone switched topics, turning the conversation to drugs.

"Did you know Reyes was on something?"

"Just vitamins."

"He was mixing two drugs, an aphrodisiac and some anti-anxiety stuff. What about you?"

Koras grinned. "I'm not a race horse, Malone."

"What about Laville?"

"With Terry, anything is possible." Koras did a quick shoulder roll, feeling the weight of the universe bearing down on his neck and shoulders.

"How did you get along with Reyes?"

"Armando was a friend. He was closer to Milo than he was to me."

"I heard that you and he and the Princess were pretty thick, back in the old days."

"Yeah. But the circuit back then was even smaller. You knew everyone."

"I heard she went from you to Reyes and then back to you."

"In between, there were others. She's a volatile woman!"

"What I'm getting at is Saadi. They say he's got it in for you."

"When Saadi has a party, I'm not on the guest list."

"Has he ever interfered with you professionally?"

Koras grinned. "No. But if he gets control of every company, he can squeeze me on endorsement contracts."

"How much did you make last year?"

"You'll have to ask Frank Fenwick. He's my numbers guy."

Malone wrote notes for a moment before going on with the questions. He was very thorough, like a cop, coming back to clarify points. They were over the Channel, starting their descent.

Koras shook his head, but didn't answer. Malone kept probing.

"The aphrodisiac is a cantharis derivative, right out of the Middle East, through the so-called Albanian Connection. It's supposed to turn a simple sexual encounter into a space mission."

"You've done your research, Malone."

"When I ask around, it's like those three monkeys. No one knows a thing."

"Tennis players are superstitious. We protect our turf."

Malone waited a moment before he started again. "What if this is a way to sell tickets?"

Koras stared at him, then turned to look out the window. "Like a ritual sacrifice?"

Malone nodded. "The arena is right for it. Upper-class audience. Bored. Jaded. Make a good movie."

"Is this just theory?"

"So far. What do you think?"

Koras was thinking of Laure and her tales of Celtic sacrifice. Maybe civilization hadn't moved so far away from those times, after all. "Sounds too grim for tennis."

The plane was descending rapidly now. Koras looked at his watch. The time was one-fifteen. At Wimbledon, with the new schedule put into effect by Clavier, the matches had been under way for three hours.

Polak was on Centre Court, sweating through the moist afternoon in a match against Paul Harper, a lanky Californian with a surfer's tan and a smile that he doubtless wore while sleeping.

Micky's forehand was on, but his backhand was off. He'd hit his cross-court and it would sail out by a foot. He tried taking the racket back early, but then he seemed slow getting to the ball. Across the net, Harper saw Micky's problem and kept chipping his approach shot and coming to the net for an easy volley.

The score was 5–3 in the second set and Polak was losing. He'd lost the first set, 6–1, and as he struggled to revive himself on the skittery grass courts of the All-England Club, Mikhail Polak, the Archangel of Gdansk, came to the conclusion that his wife was to blame for his sagging tennis game. After courting for a year, Mikhail and Gail Hofstedter had been married in Rome, just before the Italian Open began at the Foro Italico. Mikhail, the runner-up at the Italian Open the previous year, had been seeded number 2 at the Foro. He was a clay-court specialist who had taught himself the game by pounding tennis balls against a gray wall at the soccer stadium in his native Gdansk.

Micky had been discovered by Ferdi Wrezowski, the Polish champion of yesteryear and then the Davis Cup coach of a fledgling team. Micky had developed under Wrezowski, had played his first French Open at seventeen, where he had been catapulted into international fame by defeating the reigning champion, a Frenchman by the name of Alphonse Arbintoir, in the Round of Sixteen. Two years later, Polak had won the French title, and great things had been expected of him. This year at Rome, the tennis world—and especially his manager and wellwishers back in his native land—had been surprised and disappointed when he lost in the Round of Sixteen to the American, Jack Di Rocca.

Mikhail's wife, Gail, was an American. Her maiden name, Hofstedter, told the financial world she was the daughter of T. Jason Hofstedter, a senior partner in the powerful law firm of Hofstedter, Stein, and Barkman, of Chicago. Jason Hofstedter's specialty was corporate takeovers. Gail had grown up in the upscale suburb of Kenilworth, on the North Shore, a few miles above Chicago. She was pretty, a blonde debutante whose bland ideas hid completely her outré sexual capacities. She had surprised Micky with her ability to flirt and distract him. To bury the distraction, and to prove himself a man of the world, he had courted her, fallen more deeply under her spell, and then married her. It had been a major error.

As they wheeled around the circuit, it became clear to Micky that his wife was not happy coping with hotels and dirty laundry and his fluctuating moods. On airplanes, Gail babbled constantly of the house they would live in, near her parents on the North Shore. Micky didn't like it. Chicago was cold, like Poland. It snowed there in November. The ice was miserable. He preferred Dallas, where he owned a house already. There was country near Dallas, and Micky liked to hunt. His idea—they argued constantly about this—was to make their headquarters in Dallas. With Frank Fenwick's help, Micky had purchased some shares in a new shopping mall on Interstate 30, just south of the Dallas–Fort Worth airport. Already, the shares had made money.

Now, inside his mind, Micky was distracted from his best tennis by these endless arguments with his wife. Suddenly, his opponent, the grinning insolent surfer, sent the ball deep to Micky's forehand. Harper was tall, with a huge forehand and a backhand that he hit with two hands. Micky did not like Harper, his beach-boy good looks, his manner of speaking with a constant smile. To Micky, Californians were a race of mutants, the result of electromagnetic breeding techniques, who had mastered two arts—staying tanned all year around and making conversation without unclenching the teeth.

Micky hit the return into the net.

Down three games to two in the final set, Micky decided to send his wife back home. It was too late for Wimbledon, but he might save his focus for New York. He knew there would be a scene. She was a spoiled female, the product of a capitalistic economic system plagued by waste and decadence. Still, he would do it.

Now he was losing in the first round to Paul Harper, and the only thing saving him was a new pair of shoes by Izanagi, a Japanese equipment manufacturer. Through the soles of these shoes, he could actually feel his toes gripping the slippery grass-court surface.

Then Harper's service came, the ball flattening out like a

thick saucer. Micky got it back, topspin, always topspin. Harper volleyed. Micky retrieved, a high lob, into the gray sky, pushing Harper deep. Micky charged, volleyed away the return.

He won three more points the same way, hammering away the return as he thought of sending his wife off. Just the idea made him feel free. He won the second set, drawing even with the American. There were other women in the world. Before his marriage, he had received love letters from strange women who had enclosed photos. Most of the photos had been portraits, but a few women had sent along photos of themselves in bikinis. One had even dared to send a nude. Micky wondered where she was now.

Without his whining wife, Micky would be free once more to roam. He was a hunter, and that thought appealed to him.

He won the next two sets, 6–1, 6–2, to take the match from a surprised Paul Harper. After the match, in the dressing room, Harper came up to him as he was feeling the sole of his right shoe. It was covered with hundreds of square rubber nubs. Micky liked these Izanagi shoes.

"I thought I had you out there, Polak. What happened?"

"I came to some decision," Micky said.

"You turned into a stroking machine."

Polak nodded, but said nothing. In the shower, he began singing in Polish.

TEN

At breakfast in the Gloucester Hotel, Matt Malone was back on the late, late schedule of the circuit. As he drank his coffee, he realized he had adopted the way of life and the impossible schedule of people in the tennis world. In the afternoons, they played tennis, or waited to play, or watched. After the matches, they stayed up late, to unwind. After unwinding, they slept late, so they would be fresh for the afternoon's matches. Every day he promised himself he would be up early. Yet every day he arose later, had a good breakfast while he read the *Chicago Tribune,* and looked forward to the day at Wimbledon, or at the Queen's Club out in West Kensington, where the players practiced.

Today was Tuesday, the second day of the Round of Sixteen. Koras had advanced to the quarterfinals, but everyone was remarking how the defending champion wasn't playing his best. Each time Koras played, his matches had gone to five sets, and yesterday he had won in an extended fifth set, 10–8, over Ivan Leroy, from France. As a result, the bookmakers had changed the odds on Koras from 2–1 to 13–3.

The two players who were soaking up the media time were Milo Tigrid and Mikhail Polak. Tigrid was playing out of his mind, beating players half his age with shots that were both powerful and accurate. And Polak hadn't lost a set since he'd sent his wife back home.

Malone looked up from his breakfast to see Laville come in, with Shirley Nash-Winters, the pretty starlet, and Mikhail Polak. Laughing and talking like old friends, the three took a table across the room from Malone. Laville waved, but Polak kept his attention fixed on Shirley's valentine face. Today Shirley wore a soft yellow dress, made from velour, tight around the hips and thighs, with a deep neckline that threatened to spill her bouncy young breasts.

So Polak wasn't the only player who had sent his wife back home.

Malone sipped his coffee while he smelled the aroma from the ham and eggs. It was amazing. You cross the Channel in an airplane and you get different food for breakfast. The French liked bread and buttery croissants. In Paris, you had to fight the chef for a boiled egg. The English, on the other hand, liked bacon, toast, and eggs. Malone liked it all. Traveling made him curious about what the Germans ate for breakfast, and the Swiss, and the Dutch, and then the Swedes and the Norwegians and the Finns. Koras was Lithuanian. What did they eat in Kaunas, Lithuania? It was after ten, and the dining room was almost deserted. Milo Tigrid appeared in the doorway; Malone waved him over.

"Ho, you jackal of the press. What news from the world?" Milo sat down.

"This coffee isn't bad."

A waiter came over to take Milo's order for coffee. When he had gone, Milo turned to Malone.

"Have you seen Pantakoras?"

"No," Malone said. "Isn't he at the Queen's Club, practicing?"

"Oh, probably. I think Pantakoras practices too much. His Australian coach is a slave driver."

"Have you eaten?"

Milo nodded, then leaned close. "Did you notice the barbarian Laville with Miss Nash-Winters and Comrade Polak?"

"Yeah."

Across the room, Shirley leaned back and laughed, a tinkling sound, filled with the beauty and promise of youth. The waiter brought Milo's coffee.

"I knew a woman like that once," Milo said, "the same gray eyes, the same sleepy intelligence. She was from Montana, land of mountains. Do you know it?"

"I hear it's cold and beautiful."

"You poet!" Milo slapped Malone on the back.

"What happened to the girl?"

"I taught her the Kama Sutra. She has doubtless gone on to produce consumers for your decadent marketplace."

"Been teaching any Kama Sutra around here?"

Milo grinned as he added sugar to his coffee. "A woman keeps staring at me from the Members' Stand. On Saturday she used binoculars."

"Have you met her?"

"No. She keeps eluding me."

"Well, they say you're playing well. The bookmakers have increased the odds."

Milo grinned, then pounded his chest. "Tigrid, the Eternal." He stared at Malone as if he had something important to say, then changed the subject. "How would you like to accompany me on a shopping spree?"

"Shop? What for?"

Milo sighed. "I have two sisters who are in love with English wool. In Yugoslavia they pass themselves off as party dignitaries simply by exhibiting the colorful cashmeres I send them."

"Hey, I could use a little shopping myself."

"You! Look at you! You are the perfect capitalistic journalist. Those crumpled trousers, that jacket with the elbow patches flawed to perfection."

"I could use some socks, maybe some underwear, and a new shirt."

"Spoken like a man." Milo slapped Malone on the back. "Let us depart."

"Where to?"

"Burlington Arcade."

Milo turned out to be an efficient shopper. When they reached Burlington Arcade, he led Malone into the first sweater shop they saw, where he gave the nervous shopgirl precise English sizes. Milo could create a flurry on any stage, and soon they were joined by another shopgirl, older and prettier than the first.

"One of my sisters is about your size, but not as radiant. Are you a Yugoslav, my dear?"

"No, Mr. Tigrid. I'm from Hampstead."

"A beautiful area, Hampstead. I often practice at a club there."

"Oh? Which one?"

"The Cumberland. Have you been there?"

"Oh, no, sir."

"Well, then, I must invite you to be among my guests, the next time I am there."

"Oh, sir. That would be lovely."

While Milo energized the shop, Malone leaned against a counter to watch the Yugoslav examining sweaters. Forty different varieties were laid out on the counters. Milo went through them, feeling for softness and quality. When he had made his selection, eight sweaters costing over 650 pounds, Milo asked that they be shipped to Yugoslavia, and that meant forms to fill out. The manager had to be called, to help with the intricate paperwork.

They were no sooner out of the sweater shop than Milo spotted a pet store. He dragged Malone in, looking around with his supercharged energy, and picked up a young bobtail dog. It was white, with gray hind paws and a long coat of hair that surrounded it in an indistinguishable mass. Malone thought the dog was the ugliest one he had ever seen.

"Well, journalist, what do you think?"

"If he has teeth, he'll make a good guard dog."

"He has teeth, my dear Matthew."

"Can't see them, under all that hair."

Milo handed the dog to Malone, then stepped away. "Consider this dog as a gift. What do you think of it as a gift?"

"Great. Especially if you ship it to Yugoslavia. The paperwork shouldn't take more than a couple weeks."

Milo's face lit up. "I'll take it," he said to the attendant. "What is its name?"

"Swash," said the attendant.

"A lovely name, as in Swashbuckler."

"He wants it gift wrapped," Malone said.

The dog cost another 250 pounds, which Milo paid without a blink. There were more papers to fill out. The dog had a pedigree, with a number tattooed on the inside of its left ear. The attendant said the pedigree made the bobtail worth 450 pounds, and urged Milo to register the animal at the Dog Club.

"Hell," Malone said, "you've already made a profit, and you haven't even had to feed him yet."

"I could not sell Swash. What do you take me for?"

Malone laughed.

"Now," Milo announced, "I am famished. Let's go to Harrod's."

"Hey, I just had breakfast."

"A man must keep up his strength. And there are beautiful women there."

Malone thought of Muriel, who would be arriving tomorrow. "All right. But then we need to get out to Wimbledon."

As they entered a taxicab, Malone thought he saw Mikhail Polak, driving the other way.

"Did you see him?"

"See who?"

"Polak."

"With a woman?"

"No. He was alone."

"I saw him yesterday, with the actress Shirley. Laville was not around. She was captivating, turning on her charm. You'd think she had just been introduced to Roman Polanski."

"Maybe she wants Polak for a leading man."

Milo sighed. "She is gorgeous, is she not?"

"Too young for you!"

Milo stared at Malone with sardonic laughter in his eye. "There are few too young for Tigrid, my capitalistic Puritan. And that is because Tigrid has the remedy to remove sadness in the heart of a woman."

"Okay, what's the remedy for sadness?"

"Tigrid," he cried, and thumped his chest.

With his wife gone home to America, Mikhail Polak had time to himself once again. The morning after his second-round win, he took some time off to pursue his hobby—fine guns.

Mikhail's favorite firearm emporium in the world was Purdey & Sons, London, a temple of gunsmiths. The place exuded tradition, history, the solid weight of monarchy. The organization dated back to 1763, when the first Purdey had been named official court armorer. Back at his home in Dallas, Mikhail had a superior gun collection. He paid the Polish government a handsome retainer so that he could return to Poland to do some hunting. There was something about hunting—especially the stalking phase—that made him feel alive.

He was well known by the salesmen at Purdey's, which he always visited when in London. Last summer, Mikhail had purchased an antique Franchi Falconet shotgun, twelve-gauge, made by hand at the factory in Brescia, Italy, in 1901. The piece was one of a matched set, and Mikhail had asked the store to search for its mate. He had been disappointed when they hadn't turned up the twin shotgun.

Two salesmen, dressed in well-cut suits, greeted Mikhail by name. The store manager, Mr. Jessup, came forward with a smile and a handshake. Mikhail talked with Jessup a few moments. Mr. Blade, who usually helped Mikhail, was away from the store because of a cold. This morning, Mr. Whitlington would take care of Mikhail.

Mr. Whitlington was thin, with gray eyes and a receding hairline. He knew his weapons, however. In the first five minutes, Mikhail bought a Soviet Margolin sport .22 pistol, which he asked to have shipped to Dallas. While he was looking at shotguns—he had his eye on a Harrington and Richardson over-and-under twelve-gauge, dated 1894—Mr. Whitlington vanished for a moment and came back with a Franchi, dated the same year.

"Our Mr. Jessup just informed me, Mr. Polak. A customer finds he, ah, cannot acquire this weapon at this time. It is, if you will permit me, a beautiful piece."

Mikhail felt excitement shooting through him even before he hefted the weapon, touched the butt to his shoulder, sighted along the top barrel. Thirty seconds, and Mikhail was in love. He asked the price, but barely heard the answer. This Franchi was beyond money.

Mikhail told them to add it to his account. He would take the shotgun with him, do some shooting after he'd won Wimbledon. Shooting relaxed him.

With his purchase, Purdey's included a handsome leather case and two boxes of custom shells. As he rode back to the Gloucester in his taxi, he was already planning a morning at the skeet range in Hertfordshire. There was a better range in Scotland. Perhaps he might go there. He knew a man who knew a man who raised game birds, a private preserve, where one could get in some shooting off season.

When he won Wimbledon, he would deserve a rest. Mikhail smiled, settled back against the seat cushions, watched London glide by. With his wife seven thousand miles away, he felt almost weightless.

When Princess Athena got depressed, she began dressing in darker clothes, high-necked sweaters, blouses that were not see-through, and loose-fitting slacks that her mother would have declared totally lacking in style.

She had never really analyzed her behavior—the Princess

simply acted and left interpretation to the tabloids—but since Armando's death she had felt closed in, caged by gloom. She dressed to fit her mood, buttons buttoned, zippers zipped. She knew people were talking, asking questions, making snide remarks. But Athena, while a darling of the mob, was not of the mob. She lived life as she pleased. And right now, the object of her life was to get away from Saadi. Life in his entourage was oppressive, and in his penthouses—identical quarters in his family-owned hotels, no matter what the city—Athena felt both incarcerated and spied upon.

She had taken up with Saadi because she felt she could control him. At first, he had smothered her with presents and allowed her to live her own life. But as they came to be regarded as "a couple" on the circuit, Saadi had become more possessive, demanding to know where she was going, where she had been, who she had been with. At first, she had found it tiresome, then nerve-wracking.

Her decision to leave had been made in Austria, after the end of the tournament in Paris. Shaken by Armando's death, Athena had slipped away to Salzburg. Saadi had showed up, landing his private jet nearby, with orders for Athena to join him in Zurich. When she had refused, Saadi had revealed that he had purchased some outstanding loans owed by Athena's mother. If Athena did not comply, Saadi would bring pressure to bear.

Making the decision to escape was easy. The hard part was finding a way to neutralize Saadi's power.

On the surface, Abdul Saadi was smooth, a manipulator with a slick smile who shook hands and wore Western clothes and made people feel at ease. Down deep, however, he was jealous and vengeful, a man who flew into rages at the least provocation. When the time came to tell him goodbye, she wanted to make certain he understood why, and she was planning to use a particular issue of *Racquet World* she'd found in his trash basket as leverage.

She needed a willing accomplice, someone shrewd and tough. She thought first of Pantakoras, her old friend, and then she ran into Jack Di Rocca on the second day of the Round of Sixteen. Di Rocca, who had won his match the day before, putting him into the quarters, was dressed in an attractive leather jacket, gray slacks, and a wool tie. Smiling warmly, but without her usual flamboyant charge of sexual electricity, Athena invited Di Rocca to sit with her in Saadi's private box, which was practically next door to the Royal Box. Saadi was the honorary president of his country's tennis league. His private box was one of the many perks of Sahara Sports.

"Nice view," Di Rocca said.

"Yes. Saadi lives well."

"Where is Saadi? I haven't seen him around today."

"When I left the hotel, he was on the phone, making some deal or other. Saadi is frequently on the phone."

She felt him watching her as she talked, his eyes measuring her. It was not a new feeling. Men had been measuring her since she was a girl. Today she wore khaki linen slacks, a dark-blue blouse, a navy shantung jacket, and a tan scarf around her throat. In her handbag, she carried a blue sweater and an umbrella. The weather was gray, with clouds hanging low over the arena, making the green of the courts even more intense. She could smell the rain about to start, and here and there she could see umbrellas blooming in the stands, then folding up again like flowers in the dark.

A waiter appeared as they were getting settled. She ordered a brandy.

"Make that two, waiter."

The waiter bowed and went away.

"Congratulations on winning yesterday."

"I keep getting lucky. The quarters promise to be tough."

Athena gestured toward the court, where Davey Cooper was fighting it out with Jean-François Colombier. "Who do you pick to win here?"

"Cooper."

Athena looked at the scoreboard. Davey was behind a set, and losing to Colombier in the second. "I pick Jean-François. At least he is not American."

"A pound on Cooper," Di Rocca said.

"Agreed."

They shook hands and she noticed how strong he was, how firm his grip. The waiter came back with the drinks, and they settled back to watch the match.

"That was a fine party you and Saadi threw the other night."

"Oh?" She responded to the tone of his voice, which sounded slightly mocking. "Are you so fond of cherries jubilee?"

Di Rocca laughed. "Being around Saadi reminds me how the other half lives. He owns fifty percent of tennis and plans to own the rest by September."

She edged her own reply with answering irony. "If not September, then by Christmas."

"Where did you meet Saadi, anyway?"

"In Los Angeles, at the home of mutual friends. Saadi was decorating his house in Bel Air, having the statues painted, Persian rugs in the bath, all that dismal Arab taste. With a few simple suggestions, I dismissed his decorator, who was charging far too much, and dazzled him with my sense of style. His family, of course, does not approve. To them, I am a Teutonic infidel."

Di Rocca toasted her with the brandy. "To the price of oil."

She turned to give Di Rocca an appraising look. "How old are you, Mr. Di Rocca?"

"Thirty-two. And you?"

Instead of answering, Athena shifted in her seat, leaning toward Di Rocca. "I remember the first time I saw you play, in Gstaad. It was one of your first clay-court tournaments, and yet you seemed to have mastered it."

"I remember seeing you in the stands, and thinking you were the most beautiful woman in the world."

Athena acknowledged the compliment with a smile. Perhaps this was the kindred spirit she needed to help her with Saadi. "Why, thank you," she murmured.

At Harrod's, Milo's dog was the object of several wicked glances. Well-dressed Londoners kept turning up their noses. Milo gave them the benefit of his clown face as he handed the leash to Malone and led the way to a table. A waitress appeared and they ordered tea and cakes.

"I don't think they like the dog, Milo."

"Perhaps it is my beard, or your clothes."

"No one ever talked straight to me about my 'look.' Maybe you could help me put together a new wardrobe."

"I would consider it a duty to society to help you dress like a gentleman."

Their tea came. Milo sipped, made a face. "Tea, blah! This is good reason for the British Empire to sink forever into Sargasso Sea."

At the next table, two gray-haired ladies turned to glare at Milo.

"It was your idea to come here," Malone said.

Milo leaned across the table to look Malone in the eye. "I don't think you are a writer, Malone."

Malone decided not to work at making denials. "You're right."

"So. You admit?"

"Sure." Malone sipped his tea. "The Federation hired me, after Reyes died."

Milo looked offended. "You are a private eyeball, like Mike the Hammer?"

"That's right."

"What is your charge, if I might ask?"

"Two things. One was to find out if Reyes killed himself, or if something else did him in. The other was to find out who."

"And?"

Malone shook his head. "I'm working for the Federation, Milo. Not you. And I'd appreciate it if you didn't say anything. I don't want my cover blown."

"Why should I help you? You are a snake in the house of chickens, as Frank Fenwick likes to say."

Malone reached into his jacket pocket and brought out an envelope with the logo of the Gloucester Hotel. He upended the envelope and a red capsule fell out onto the table. Milo's face got pale. "This is why."

"What is it?"

"It's a red pill, an aphrodisiac, like the one that killed Reyes."

"Where did you find it?"

"Your tennis bag."

Milo looked sick, then his face became angry. "You search my stuff?" His voice was loud.

"Easy, Milo. Easy." Malone put a hand on Milo's arm.

"No. You are a—" He finished with something in a language

Malone did not understand and hurried out, yanking the dog along roughly.

Malone dropped some money on the table and went after him. Outside, on the sidewalk, Milo was stalking away. Malone had to run to catch up.

"Goddammit, Milo. I just got you off the hook with the Paris police."

Milo turned. "That scum. How?"

"I told them you were innocent. I sure as hell didn't mention the red pills."

"You must be on good terms with that fascist Maréchal."

"We made a deal. I'm nosing around. If I find something useful, I'll let him know."

"What do you mean, useful?"

Malone shrugged. "Depends."

Milo was scowling at Malone. "Why do I listen to you, after you search my private stuff?"

"Better I found it than someone else. Where'd you get these, anyway?"

Milo sighed. "From Armando's bag, the day he died. I saw how he played. I knew there was something. They were super-pills." Milo looked away from Malone and down at the dog. "Listen, detective. They help Tigrid shove back some years. Okay?" He grabbed Malone by the lapels. "Do you know where I am? I am in the quarterfinals of Wimbledon for the first time in six years!"

Malone nodded. There were tears in the Yugoslavian's eyes. "Do you see what I am telling you, Matthew? Do you?"

And before Malone could answer, Milo shoved the dog's leash into his hand and hurried off, running across the street, through the heavy London traffic.

ELEVEN

"Match point," intoned the chair umpire.

Down on the court, Davey Cooper was close to being eliminated in the Round of Sixteen by Jean-François Colombier. The young Frenchman, with a ranking of only 72 on the ATP computer, had won the first two sets and was leading 6–5 in the third, 40–15. He was one point away from victory.

And then there was a hint of rain, drops misting down. In the stands, a few colored umbrellas were already open.

Colombier took the balls from the ballboy. In one minute, he would become a tennis legend. He shut his eyes to the crowd, to his coach's words, to the contracts that would come his way if he eliminated a seeded player. His girlfriend would shower him with love.

He laid the toss-up carefully, muscles tense, and came down on the ball with immense force. He wanted an ace to end this match on television. The ball slapped the tape. Fault. He served the second ball with a high kicking spin, but the wet grass kept it low and Davey took the point with a screaming backhand, to climb to 40–30.

It was still match point. The sky was a metallic gray, and more rain fell. Colombier was sweating now with the tension. He had to end it now. His serve skimmed the tape for a let call.

"Let," said the umpire. "First service."

The rain came harder now, slanting silver against the dark green of Centre Court. Colombier served. Cooper moved in for a damaging return, sent the ball whistling down the line to Colombier's backhand. The passing shot was high. Cooper clipped it off for a sharp cross-court volley.

"Point to Mr. Cooper. The score is deuce."

Now the raindrops became showers, falling in sheets. In the stands, the umbrellas flourished suddenly, exploding into red, blue, yellow. They played two more points, with Colombier losing his footing and crashing into the net, before the umpire adjourned the match. Before he left the chair, he made certain that the ground crew unrolled the heavy green tarpaulin that covered Centre Court.

When the rain began to fall in earnest, Athena and Jack Di Rocca left Saadi's box and hurried to the Players' Tea Room, a place of wicker chairs and wicker tables, where the atmosphere seethed with deals and deal-makers. The bar here was first-class.

Outside the entrance, a regal blonde hurried up to pluck at Athena's sleeve. She was a friend, Lady Jessica Coatkey, and she whispered to Athena that she was dying for an introduction to the fierce Montenegrin Milo Tigrid. Always ready to play Cupid, Athena brought Lady Jessica in as her guest.

Once inside, she spotted Milo and Koras standing at the bar. Di Rocca went off to speak to someone, which gave Athena her chance. She marched over, leading the blushing Lady Jessica.

"Milo," Athena said, "an admirer of yours was outside in the rain." And as Milo turned to beam at both women, Athena made her introductions.

Milo grasped Lady Jessica's hand. "A wondrous beauty. How nice to meet you, dear lady. Are you by chance a Yugoslavian?"

"Oh, Mr. Tigrid. I so admire your prowess on the court."

"Did you hear that, Koras? Did you hear that?"

"It's a real compliment, Lady Coatkey. Milo only passes out a dozen or two Yugoslavian passports per year."

Watching Jessica and Milo, Athena smiled benevolently. Meeting Di Rocca had given her new hope, and now there was this tête-à-tête between two people who were attracted to one another. She gave Koras a quick hug while Milo worked his magic on Lady Jessica. Athena felt alive again, and began to plan a few changes in her wardrobe.

"So," Athena asked Koras, "are you in love at last? Will you admit it to me?"

Koras laughed, but his eyes were serious. "I've got a long way to fall."

"Laure is très charmante. So young. So full of possibility."

"She's a beauty, all right."

"I remember," Milo was saying to Lady Jessica. "You are the vision from Opening Day."

"Oh, Mr. Tigrid."

Jessica blushed as Milo took her hand in both of his.

"Please. Call me Milo. My friends all call me Milo."

"Oh, I say."

Everyone laughed. Milo did a quick handstand, and coins fell out of his pants pockets. When he stood up, his face was red. He led the blonde off, so he could whisper sweet somethings in her ear.

A loudspeaker announced that the match was starting again. Athena said goodbye to Koras and walked with Jack Di Rocca back to Saadi's box. She felt better than she had in weeks.

By the time they reached Saadi's box, Davey Cooper had broken Colombier's serve and was taking over the momentum in the quarterfinal. The sun was out and in the stands people were removing their rain gear. Athena folded her umbrella, took off the shantung blazer, and, when Di Rocca wasn't looking, unbuttoned the top two buttons on her blouse.

At the changeover between games, she drew closer to Di Rocca. "Is it true that you were in prison?"

"Yes. I broke into a gas station and took twenty-four bucks."

"And how long were you in prison?"

"Thirteen months."

She was shocked. "That is severe punishment."

"Ortega got me out. He offered to coach me for a percentage. I would have chewed nails to get out of there."

"Do you like the game?"

"I like the life!"

"Are you married, Mr. Di Rocca?"

He grinned. "No, ma'am. It ruins the circuit. Talk to Micky Polak. Talk to Laville."

"Pantakoras says tennis is his wife, his mistress."

Di Rocca nodded, but said nothing.

"Did you by chance see the film *Belle de Jour?* With Catherine Deneuve?"

"Nope. Can't say I have."

"A curious film. The plot is interesting. A woman, a married woman, is persuaded to spend one afternoon a week in a house of prostitution in Paris. Her curiosity grows toward her work. After a time, she enjoys herself, for the power, I think. Her favorite client turns out to be a thief and a murderer."

Di Rocca stared into her eyes. "Crazy."

She smiled at him and drained her glass. "Can you find the waiter? I seem to need another drink."

Di Rocca signaled the waiter, three boxes away.

Down on the court, Davey Cooper took the third set, 7–6. Athena clapped for both players. She felt warm from the exchange with Di Rocca and the sudden sunshine. Her body hummed its pleasure at being alive. The waiter came with the drinks. When he had gone, Athena continued her conversation about films.

"Would you like to view the film?"

"Any time." His dark beard highlighted his ready smile.

"I have it on cassette."

"Is there popcorn?"

"With butter?" Athena asked. "Or without?"

"I like it with a beer, maybe two. You eat the popcorn. You drink the beer."

"German beer? Danish beer?"

"Dos Equis. It's Mexican."

Cooper finished off the fourth set. The Princess took a look at the scoreboard. "I love Mexico, all that fierce heat. It's so primitive."

Di Rocca touched his glass to hers. "Here's to Mexico and old movies."

"To popcorn," she said, and felt herself smiling.

On the court, Jean-François Colombier wiped his legs with a towel. He had lost his momentum because of the rain delay, and now he had to start again. At this moment, he should have been under the shower singing in ecstasy. Instead, here he was, on the court, with another set to play. The universe was against him. There was a fading headline in his brain: YOUNG FRENCH HOPEFUL DEFEATS DAVID COOPER AT WIMBLEDON. Could he still do it?

He tossed the towel aside and readied himself to receive

serve. Cooper served; Colombier shot back a return. Cooper volleyed like a madman, driving, rolling on the grass to make an impossible shot.

Cooper took game after game, the score mounting against Colombier on the scoreboard until the match was over. Final set, Cooper, 6–0. Colombier was finished. He left Centre Court in tears.

Within two minutes, Koras came out to play Peter Abraham. The winner would play Mikhail Polak tomorrow.

In Polak's room at the Gloucester, Malone found a tennis bag full of dirty clothes, an electric teapot and a good collection of herbal teas, an antique Colt cavalryman's revolver in a wooden presentation case, and a shotgun. The shotgun was fancy, an Italian job with the name Franchi of Brescia in Gothic letters on the plate above the trigger guard. There was a date in Roman numerals that Malone could not decipher—eighteen-something. He snapped the gun to his shoulder a couple of times, noting the terrific feel. This fellow Polak knew his firearms.

A quick search told Malone there were no pills here either. And that surprised him, because up until a couple of days ago, Polak had been having a lousy tournament, playing five-setters against unknowns, the bookies in their little booths cranking up the odds. Smart money had it that Polak would lose to Tigrid, but in fact he'd killed Tigrid in four sets. Now, the bookmakers thought, Polak had an excellent chance of beating Koras in the semis, and they were giving 7–3 he could take either Laville or Cooper in the final.

In Polak's tennis bag, Malone found a photo of his wife, a debutante with a knowing smile and a mean gleam in her eye. Gail Hofstedter Polak was an American girl from Kenilworth, Illinois, outside Chicago, a girl born into money. She looked like Daddy's favorite, the right schools, the right clothes, first puff of a cigarette at twelve, marijuana in junior high, swinging her bottom around in her private-school skirt, testing her power, dating college boys, Europe in the summer, a diamond for Christmas, nothing too good for Daddy's girl.

Malone tossed the photograph back. She reminded him of

Sally Atkinson, his first dream girl, and that brought up a certain amount of pain he thought he'd escaped. Seeing the girl, all that money, the special cared-for look, reminded Malone that a few lucky people lived, while the rest of the world worked for a living.

He checked his watch, ten-fourteen. As he was leaving the room, the phone rang. Probably Polak's impatient bride, calling from the States. Malone walked out, letting it ring.

He was an Eastern Bloc player, innocent, puritanical, fastidious about sex, and it was Mikhail Polak's first experience with a real *ménage à trois*. And, he vowed to himself, his last. He felt drunk, guilty, deranged. His head pounded and his desire seemed endless, jagged, decadent. Laville was there, in the bed, and the woman was coiled like a golden snake between the two men.

Earlier in the evening, they'd begun at the Hard Rock Cafe, celebrating their wins in the quarterfinals. From the Hard Rock, they had gone on to a discotheque Laville knew, where Micky had danced with Shirley Nash-Winters. The starlet was sad because she was leaving London to return to Hollywood. Her beautiful face, her larger-than-life gray eyes floated in front of him on the dance floor. Tears glistened on her soft cheeks. "I'll be back," she kept saying. "You'll see."

Her mood opened Polak up, so he told her about his contract decision. "I am signing the contract with Izanagi Ltd.," he whispered as they were dancing. The drinks had made his mind absolutely clear, allowing him to see around corners. He felt infallible. Tonight, he could do no wrong.

"What's that, hon?" She was soft in his arms, pliable. He was aware of being watched from the darkness.

"I am not signing with Saadi's Sahara Sports. It is a secret. Izanagi has offered me more than a million dollars."

Shirley smiled at that and gave him a complimentary little push with her thighs. "Your secret is safe with me, hon. My lips are sealed." For a while, they danced very close.

They left the discotheque for a round of pubs, and when he was thoroughly drunk and feeling heated by constant contact with the starlet, they had wandered back to the hotel, singing,

"Row, Row, Row Your Boat," and he remembered Laville send-ing him with a strange smile into the bedroom where Shirley lay, all warm and lovely and half-undressed, like the seduction scenes in her films, and then his hungers had overcome him, coupling him with the girl, and in the midst of his grand passion with beautiful Shirley the man Laville had joined them and for a while Mikhail had felt as if he and Laville were actually broth-ers and three people in one huge bed seemed the most natural thing in the world.

In his alcoholic daze, he remembered bright lights flashing, a synchronized clicking sound, a keening animal cry, high-pitched and savage. The voice was familiar. He had heard it often, in his dreams. It was his voice.

Now Micky Polak arched awake, sitting up in bed with a raging thirst. He stumbled into the bathroom. In the mirror, his face resembled a waxen imitation of a publicity photo in a museum somewhere behind the Iron Curtain. He thought of icy Siberia, the hateful Gulag. Would they send him there someday, when he was old? When he could no longer play? Would he grow cynical, like Koras? He drank, greedily, feeling sick to his stomach when the water hit the bottom. Tomorrow, he had a semifinal to play. His watch said 23:43, minutes until midnight. He felt terrible. There was still time to get some sleep.

Laville was waiting for him as he came out of the bathroom, a camera poised and ready, hiding his grinning face. Laville pressed the button to release the shutter, that clicking sound again, as of a small door being shut inside his mind, and at the same time the blinding light of the built-in flash. Then he knew —Laville had photographed him in his shame, naked, with this woman.

He rushed Laville, with an idea of getting the camera back, but the big man merely laughed and shoved him aside. Micky crashed into the bureau, but caught himself on the wall and pushed off as he was about to slam his eye into the corner of the chest.

Fear made him sweat. "What do you want?"

"Just having some fun, Micky. Or should I call you Micky Izanagi?"

Micky understood. "You want Izanagi for yourself."

Laville answered with a short laugh. "Forget it." He aimed the camera and shot another picture. The flash hurt Micky's eyes.

Feeling unsteady, Micky took a hopeless swing at Laville, who danced out of the way. On the bed, Shirley Nash-Winters slept through the drunken fight with her mouth open, long golden legs tucked up in the fetal position. Dread closed in around Micky as he stumbled to the living room, dragging his clothes, and began to dress. Laville, wearing a short silk prize-fighter's robe, sauntered out to watch. The camera dangled in one huge hand. His tousled white hair threw his left eye into shadow.

"Why you do this?"

"I was just screwing around. But now I'm wondering what would happen if Saadi knew. About your hot deal. The man has a temper, Micky."

The woman had told Laville. Micky felt sick. His manager, Frank Fenwick, always warned him. No leaks, he said. "What do you do with pictures?"

Laville sat down on the sofa with his legs spread. "Well. They'd go great in the London tabloids . . ."

"You are crazy, like they say." There was no way Micky could handle this now. There was a gun in his room. He jerked open the door and stalked out, feeling dizzy.

Malone was watching TV with Muriel when Milo rang up, wanting to go pub-crawling.

"Ho, you American Eyeball. It is I, Tigrid, calling you and your beautiful lady. The Lady Jessica thinks you are a writer. She wishes to meet you."

Muriel was about to return to her own room for the night. When Malone told her about the invitation, she was interested.

"Oh, I would like to do that."

Malone turned back to the telephone. "Okay, Milo. Shall we bring the dog?"

"We are coming to get you, for creeping the London pubs. Not needing more dogs."

They rode in Lady Jessica's chauffeured limo to the Dove, where Milo led the crowd in a Montenegrin dance. They went on to the Dickens Inn, where they were joined by a skinny blonde with spiked hair and her boyfriend, a black with a Jamaican accent. The six of them went on to the Cutty Sark, where Milo got into a fight about the beauty of Yugoslavian women, and then from there to the Dirty Dick. By then it was closing time, and they had lost the Jamaican, so the five of them drove out to Lady Jessica's house, which turned out to be a castle thirty miles west of London. They were doing Greek dances when the blonde passed out. Lady Jessica went off with Muriel, somewhere upstairs, and Milo turned from the wet bar, where he had been pouring a drink, to stare at Malone.

"You, detective. You know what you are?"

"The owner of a bobtail dog worth over four hundred pounds if we can figure a way to get him to Sarajevo."

"Ha! You think you are so smart, police lackey. No, that is not what you are."

Malone could take abuse from Milo, because he knew that, down deep, Milo was the original softie. "Okay. You tell me. What am I?"

Milo brought his drink over and sat down on the sofa next to Malone. "You, my American capitalist dupe, are Tigrid's alibi."

"Alibi? For what?"

The Yugoslav waved his drink at the stairs in a wide sweep. "For whatever comes to pass."

"Do you know something I don't, Milo?"

He leaned close to Malone's face. There was the smell of alcohol, rank, repelling. "Someone wants me dead, detective. I pay you to figure it out who." He handed Malone a five-pound note.

Malone grinned. "You've had enough to drink, pal."

The women came back downstairs. Muriel was smiling. Lady Jessica took Milo by the arm and led him away, back up the stairs. At the top of the stairs, he turned and yelled down at Malone. "Sleep well, my little alibis."

Milo and Lady Jessica vanished, and they could hear his voice singing in his own language, and then a door closed. In the lower cabinet of the wet bar, Malone discovered a half bottle of brandy with the date 1895 on it. He uncapped it, and the smell was wonderful. Muriel agreed. They sat on the huge gray sofa, talking, and then Muriel led Malone up to bed.

He had found his dream girl at last.

TWELVE

Micky Polak slept badly, tossing through the night, and when he woke it was almost ten. His head ached. His stomach swarmed with poisons. If he lost today to Koras, it would be his own fault. Hands shaking, he brewed a pot of strong tea. While the tea was steeping, he strategized about how to deal with the Canadian. He was worried about his sanity, nervous about playing today, and furious at Terry Laville. A cup of tea gave him strength. He dressed in his yellow warm-up, then marched to the closet and pulled out the antique Colt. When he tried tucking it into his waistband, the weight of the pistol was too much for the elastic of the warm-up, so he cinched himself up with a hand-tooled leather belt he'd bought last year in Dallas.

Armed and ready, he took the stairs to Laville's floor. Outside the door of Laville's suite, he waited, letting his resolve gather. He had to knock several times before the door was opened by Shirley Nash-Winters. Her face was pale. She wore a floor-length green robe with long sleeves that covered her, made her look ill. Her eyes stared at him as if he were a stranger. The radiant beauty had left her face.

"Terry's not here."

Micky brandished the Colt at Shirley and walked into the room. Shirley backed away as Micky stomped into the bedroom. The bed was mussed and the room smelled of decadence. Shirley came to the door and leaned against the door frame. He wondered how she felt about last night.

"What is it, Micky? What's going on?"

"He takes the pictures. Where is camera?"

"Oh, God, I don't know. I feel awful."

He pawed through the closets, the drawers in the bedside table.

"You better go. He'll be back any minute."

"He is mad. Photos will not destroy Polak."

Shirley laughed at his use of English, which did not improve matters. Micky glared at her and walked to the dresser. He found the camera in the top drawer, with two rolls of exposed film. He had no way of knowing how many rolls Laville had taken. He put the film into his pocket, then tried opening the camera. His hands shook.

"I'm warning you, Micky. You'd better not."

Micky smashed the camera three times on a corner of the dresser. The lens shattered and the back popped open. Micky jerked out the spool of film. That made three.

When he reached the doorway, Shirley was sitting on the sofa, staring at him. The robe had fallen open to reveal her bare legs. Last night, he had gone to hell for those legs. But now the sight made him sick that he had allowed himself to fall so low. He brandished the Colt at her again.

"You slut! You told him!"

Shirley shook her head and began to cry.

Early in the morning before the semifinals, Koras and Will Channer worked out for an hour at the Queen's Club. In the dressing room afterward, Channer brought out his notebook and went through a series of strategies Koras would use to defeat Polak. The information was not new, but Channer was a conscientious coach, as well as a brilliant one. Like Koras, he left nothing to chance.

"On the approach, keep the ball down the middle to cut off Polak's angle on the forehand. Off both wings, volley deep and down the line. If you want to drop volley, hit it cross-court, to make him cover the long distance to reach it. Let the topspin lobs go, unless they fall short. He may win a couple of points, but with the wind today the percentages are against him."

Koras nodded, sipped some water. His knee hurt, and he wanted a beer more than anything. Those were not championship thoughts, and he knew better than to drink beer before a tough match.

"Polak got tougher the minute his wife left town."

"Yes. The same thing happened to me, back in 1963, when I sent my wife back to Melbourne."

"That's the Aussie way, right? Leave the wife at home?"

"What's the Koras way? Not to get married?"

"Right." Koras nodded, thinking of Laure and the money he wanted to send her.

He was aware of Channer studying him carefully, with a frown. "How's the knee?"

"Hurts. I think it will hold out."

"Pace yourself. You want to stay sharp for Laville."

"All right. Let's have some breakfast."

"Bloody good idea."

Micky had just reached his room and was thinking about ordering breakfast when someone knocked on his door. The antique Colt was still in his belt. He zipped up the yellow jacket and opened the door to see Jack Di Rocca standing there. Di Rocca wore a dark-blue suit, a white shirt, and a striped tie. Even with his dark beard newly trimmed, he reminded Micky of a Spanish buccaneer.

"What is it?"

"I just need a minute, Micky. Mind if I come in?"

Micky stepped aside so Di Rocca could come in. Di Rocca had lost his quarterfinal. Probably he had come to wish Micky luck in the semi. He left Di Rocca for a moment while he went back to the closet to put the revolver away. When he came back, Di Rocca was standing at the window, looking out. Micky took a moment to call room service and order breakfast. His headache was fading. He needed to concentrate on beating Koras this afternoon. Di Rocca took a chair. Micky, however, remained standing.

"I must get ready, Jack. What is this that you want?"

"Micky, I have a friend in New York who'll pay you a hundred thousand to lose to Koras."

Polak was astounded. "What friend?"

Di Rocca repeated his offer. "A hundred thousand dollars, in cash. Half now. Half after the match. We want you to make it look good by going out in the fifth."

Micky was stunned. He forced a smile that hurt his face. "You make the joke."

Di Rocca nodded. "It's no joke."

"What kind of friend?"

Di Rocca shook his head. "It won't help you to know any more."

The tennis term for losing intentionally was "to tank" and he hated the sound of it. Micky was enraged that anyone could even think he would throw a tennis match. Eastern Bloc players did not tank.

"You lose your match, so you come to me," Micky growled.

Di Rocca shook his head. "That's got nothing to do with it."

Micky marched to the door and flung it open. "Get out!"

Di Rocca hesitated, then shrugged and started out. "I'll be around until noon or so. My room number's 402. If you change your mind—"

"Get *out*, I said."

Di Rocca stepped into the corridor and Micky slammed the door behind him. Micky stood there, staring at it. His world had suddenly gone mad. He was playing the best tennis of his life. And now Laville was threatening him with lurid photos, and some faceless man in New York had offered him money to lose in the semifinal at Wimbledon.

He could deal with the photos now. Micky marched to the tennis bag and dumped the contents onto the bed. Hands trembling, he pried open the first can of film, unrolling it, exposing the frames to the light. He tossed it onto the bed, dug for the second roll, and went through the same process. Cursing in Polish, he probed for the third roll, but with no luck. Quickly, he searched the bag. There was no third roll. Perhaps he had been mistaken? He jammed the two exposed rolls back into his bag and stared outside at the summer sunlight. In two hours he would meet Koras for the match of his life. How could they expect him to play under these pressures?

"Was the gun loaded?"

"Oh, God, Terry. I don't know."

"How many rolls?"

From the sofa, Shirley shook her head and continued with her bawling. Edgy now, Laville grabbed her shoulders, squeezing hard, and shook her, rattling her teeth, making her blonde hair fly and her breasts shake. It didn't stop her blubbering. Shirley was a wreck. Her face was blotchy with tears and she kept moaning, complaining she was sick. Finally, he threw her roughly onto the sofa and stalked into the bedroom. The camera was on the floor, empty, its lens smashed. At least two rolls of exposed film were missing from the drawer. Laville walked to the bedroom door. Shirley was still on the couch.

"What were you doing while he busted my camera? A strip-tease?"

Shirley stared at him. For a moment, the tears stopped. She dabbed at her eyes with a tissue.

"Stupid bitch." Terry walked back into the bedroom, where he picked up a handful of Shirley's clothes. "Get out!" he ordered.

"What?"

"I want you gone by the time I get back."

"Gone? Where would I go?"

"Back to that Hollywood fruitbag, what's his name. Pack up and get out."

Terry walked out, slamming the door on her tears. One thing he really hated was a wailing female. First Nora. Now Shirley. He moved quickly down the stairs, through the lobby, and into the street. His mind clicked through an endorsement scenario. He had some hot information. How could he use it to tilt Saadi's cage? Saadi had been counting on Polak. If Polak was out of the slot, maybe there was a chance for a Sahara contract for Laville. Would Arch Bell be surprised!

Terry walked several blocks, refining his script. Who the hell did Polak think he was, busting into Laville's room with a gun? Passing a telephone callbox, Terry fished in his pocket for coins. He had to wait a couple of minutes, while an old bearded fellow finished up his conversation. Then Terry stepped into the red booth and dialed Saadi's number at the Victoria Intercontinental. A butler with a French accent answered, and Laville was kept waiting several minutes before he got through.

"Mr. Laville, Abdul Saadi here. How are you, sir?"

"Hey, okay. You in the mood for some news?"

"What sort of news?"

"Contracts. Endorsements. What makes the world go round."

"Get to the point, Mr. Laville."

"You know my contract's running out with Ryker."

"Is it?" Saadi was playing hard to get. He kept books on the players and knew all the numbers on the contracts of his competitors.

"Yeah. And I was thinking maybe Sahara might want to make me an offer."

"You are tardy with your idea, sir. Everyone knows we are signing Mikhail Polak."

Laville grinned as a pretty girl walked by. "Hey, Abdul. That's what I'm calling about."

"What's that?" Saadi's voice had lost some of its confidence.

Laville let him sweat for a few seconds. Then he said, "Yeah. I heard Micky was signing with Izanagi. Loves their shoes, all those rubber spikes."

There was silence on the other end of the line. Then Saadi said in a cold voice, "How timely is your information?"

"It just surfaced. The last twenty-four hours."

"Are you certain?"

"If it's just a rumor, you can check me out."

"Why are you telling me this?"

"Like I said. I do you a favor, then you return it. I think we'd make a winning team, Mr. Saadi. Sahara and Laville. Laville and Sahara."

"I shall give it some thought, Mr. Laville. Goodbye."

Saadi hung up and the line went dead.

When Laville got back to the hotel, there was no sign of Shirley. Good riddance. A maid who did not speak English was cleaning the rooms with a vacuum cleaner so loud he could barely think.

The phone rang. It was Nora, his wife, calling from Heathrow. For a moment, Laville thought he was hallucinating. Nora wasn't due until tomorrow. Her unexpected arrival made Laville sweat.

"Why didn't you call, tell me you were coming?"

"I can barely hear you, darling. Is the maid right on top of the telephone?"

"I could have met your plane, if I'd known."

"It was a last-minute opening, Terry. I was on three waiting lists, and I wanted to see you play. John Greenwald booked it for me, through the agency. I told John to call and tell you."

Laville didn't like even hearing Greenwald's name. Also, he didn't want his wife here right now, pressuring him to be nice. He checked his watch. "Look, Nora. I've been working out, and I need to rest. Why don't we meet at the Members' Enclosure? Say, around one."

"Oh, I'd hoped we might have brunch." Nora sounded disappointed, but Laville didn't really care.

Suddenly, the vacuum cleaner stopped, and the maid came to the door holding the broken camera, a question on her face. Laville waved her off. "We can have a Perrier at one. I was awake most of the night, worrying about the damned grass."

"Oh, poor Terry."

Nora always drank on the plane, coming over. By one o'clock she would be drunk. He needed to get rid of Nora. When you were famous, and about to be more famous, the world was full of willing women. Nora's days with him were numbered.

Events had made Micky weary, so he lay down on the bed. No sooner was he down than restlessness came over him. He stripped to running shorts, shoes, and a T-shirt and went outdoors, for a slow, agonizing jog through St. James's Park. After a ragged mile or so, listening to the birds, puffing like an old man, he began to loosen up and his mood lifted. He kept up the exercise, feeling the toxins from the night before sweat out of his system. When he got back to the hotel, he felt better and his mind was made up. He would win today. No faceless thugs in New York could force him to lose. Today was his day.

The first spectators for the men's semifinal at Wimbledon began arriving at Church Road around midday. People in the standing-room queue debated whether or not Polak would beat the aging Koras. The British tennis fans, among the world's most knowledgeable, were well aware that this year was probably Koras's last chance for the Grand Slam. Heated arguments, tempered with logic, kept the time moving. Money changed hands, at three pounds on Koras to two on Polak. The sun was out, there was a breeze, and the grounds at the All-England Club were covered with picnickers.

It was a beautiful day for tennis.

Koras went to the dressing room. In a corner, protected from reporters by Will Channer, he examined his rackets, checking the strings, tapping them against the heel of his hand. He could guess the tension in a string job within three ounces. Each of these was strung at forty-seven pounds, a fact which always brought comments from the tennis writers. Koras was a touch player. A power hitter like Laville would have his rackets strung at seventy pounds.

Koras checked his watch. Almost two hours remained before the match on Centre Court. He closed his eyes and willed the usual careful emptiness to take hold of his mind.

Nora Laville was sitting on the terrace, getting some sun, when the Princess arrived. Nora was finishing a plate of strawberries with cream, feeling pleasantly loose. A half-finished highball sat next to her. The Princess carried her usual drink, a glass of ice-cold champagne. She wore a stunning dress of eggshell white, with slits and openings placed strategically. The dress gave Nora an idea.

"Athena, how would you like to pose for a series?"

The Princess sat down. "Pose? For what?"

"For *Elan*. I'm just back from New York. I know they'd go for it."

"So. You are going back to work."

Nora nodded. "Yes. On the fashion side. And you at the center of the series would be super."

Athena smiled her willingness. "It would be a pleasure."

The two women chatted some more as they waited for the matches to get under way. Then Athena saw Archer Bell and went off, leaving Nora alone with her thoughts.

She was worried about her marriage. Sometimes she even thought of hiring someone to watch Terry, to find out what he really did while she was away. Sitting there in the sun, she thought back to their first meeting, when Terry was playing the Canadian Open. . . .

Nora had been in Montreal, working on a layout for *Elan*. The photographer, John Greenwald, was her lover, and they had booked rooms at the Regent, the same hotel used by most of the circuit tennis players. In the lobby, she had been struck by Laville's facial structure, the harsh lines, the wide-set eyes that made him seem like a movie star, and she had approached him in the bar where he was sitting alone, nursing a beer. She had never watched more than a few minutes of television tennis, so what she said was a white lie: "I really like the way you play."

Over drinks, Laville had questioned her about her work. He had seemed genuinely interested in her modeling career—the intricate lighting procedures, the endless takes, the way she had to get herself "up" for a session. During a break in his tournament, he had joined her for an early-morning shoot at Ville de Laval.

"I've never been up this early in my life," he protested.

"Never?"

"Only in the logging camps. And I left that behind forever."

Because he was interested in her work, Nora fell in love. He was a big man, with heavy arms, heavy legs, a torso developed by endless exertion, but his smile was sad, disarming. It brought out the mother in Nora. She had expected a womanizer, all those tales about sports stars and their groupies. But Terry had been hesitant with her, distant. When he had stumbled over inviting her to dinner, she knew she had fallen in love.

Her photographer-lover warned her.

"Is this some kind of joke?"

"No. I met a man. I plan to spend time with him."

"How much time?"

"A stretch of time."

"What about us? What about your career?"

"They're not one and the same, John."

"Who is this guy?"

"A tennis player. A wonderful tennis player. His name is Terry Laville."

"I've heard of Laville. He uses women like light bulbs. First he screws them. When they burn out, he unscrews them and tosses them away."

"You don't have to get nasty with your mouth."

"There's a part coming up in Hollywood. Burt's casting for the role of Mary Anne in *Dreamer*. You're just right for it."

"Sorry. I have to go with Terry."

She had hurt John Greenwald and she was sorry. But she was madly in love with Terry. The "stretch of time" had lasted over three years. In that time, Nora had discovered fear, and now she was drinking too much and looking older.

Would she ever escape this vicious circle?

Frank Fenwick broke her reverie by sitting down beside her. He said he was just back from Rome, where he had renegotiated a contract with the Magnelli people for Milo Tigrid. Strips of paper protruded from his pockets.

"How nice for Milo," Nora said.

"Yeah. At his age, it's tough. But the Magnelli people like him, at least for one more year."

"Don't you get tired of all the running around, Frank?"

"I would if I didn't make money." Fenwick looked around. "Is Terry here yet?"

Nora looked at her watch. "He should be here soon. He's meeting me."

"How's his mood?"

"Fine." She knew she was lying. "Why do you ask?"

"He and Koras haven't said a civil word since Paris. I was thinking of getting them together with a peace pipe."

"That would be wonderful."

He looked at her. "Would you help?"

Nora nodded hopefully. "Oh. Of course."

Just then Athena came back from her talk with Archer Bell. She said hello to Fenwick and sat down. He studied her with his eyes. It was clear that he was attracted to her.

But what man wouldn't be?

Walking down the corridor toward the designated room, he noticed that the doors to several rooms stood open for the day's cleaning. Up ahead, he heard the high whine of an industrial vacuum cleaner. When it suddenly stopped, filling the hallway with silence, he stepped quickly into a room and waited until two uniformed maids passed, chattering in a language he did not understand.

It was just past midday, and the rooms were deserted. This was a tennis hotel, and everyone had gone out to watch the matches. He started walking again, moving efficiently, his mind alert. He came to the room, 512. The door was ajar. Inside, he heard the shower running. He opened the door. A breakfast cart from room service stood against the wall, next to the windows. A plate with the remains of eggs and bacon. A half-filled coffee cup. The bathroom door was closed and he could hear the Pole humming. The room key lay on the bedside table. He put it into his pocket.

The Pole was singing in the shower, humming, then launching out into words. The tune was familiar. The visitor had been told that Polak was a gun collector. He found a gun—an Italian-made over-and-under shotgun with a hand-etched brass nameplate—in the closet. Two boxes of shells were on the closet shelf.

The visitor loaded both chambers.

Before going into the bathroom, he picked up a big tennis equipment bag that sat on a chair near the bathroom door. He slid the muzzle of the shotgun inside the equipment bag, up against some dirty clothes, and then he zipped the bag up over the barrel. He waited until he heard the vacuum cleaner start up again, down the hall, then pushed through the bathroom door. Steam was thick in the bathroom.

At that moment, the man in the shower must have felt the breeze, or the change in temperature from the open door. He poked his head out, rubbed the water from his eyes.

"What do you want?" He saw the gun. "Give it to me!" As he reached out, grabbing for the gun, he stumbled and at the same time his visitor pulled both triggers.

The tennis bag muffled the blast. The force threw Polak crashing back against the wall. As he fell, he ripped down the shower curtain. Blood spurted onto the white curtain. The second blast, aimed at Polak's face, made him almost unrecognizable.

The murderer was sweating as he backed out of the bathroom. He set the tennis bag on the bed while he replaced the shotgun in the closet. He had worn gloves, so there would be no fingerprints. Now that it was over, he began to tremble.

One end of the tennis bag was burst open. He emptied the soiled clothes—scorched by the blast—onto the bed. Three rolls of exposed film fell out. He put them into his pocket and folded the bag, so that the hole would not show. When he opened the door, there was a vast silence in the hallway. The vacuum cleaner had stopped, and that meant the maids might have heard the muffled blast. Down the hall and around a corner, he heard their high-pitched voices, coming closer.

The door to the room across the hall was open. He crossed the hall, into room 513, eased the door shut, locked it, and stood with his back against it, breathing harshly, trying to control the trembling. They were hurrying from room to room, calling to one another. Someone tried the door to room 513. He heard them fumbling with a bunch of keys, and he hoped he would not have to kill anybody else. There was a scream then, as one of the maids found the body, and footsteps rushing clumsily away as they ran for help.

He counted to ten before opening the door. The corridor was empty. Holding the folded sports bag to hide the gaping hole, he walked to the stairs, feeling the excitement start, now that it was over. He felt pumped, ready for anything. What a feeling!

Koras was waiting in the men's dressing room for Mikhail Polak to appear, when Frank Fenwick showed up. It was the custom at Wimbledon for the players to walk out together as a symbol of gentlemanly competition, and when one player was late, the other one felt the pressure. The time was 1:45 P.M. and Polak still had not showed.

Fenwick marched up to Koras and Channer with the familiar half smile that did not hide his anger. "Give me a minute with Koras, would you, Will?"

Channer moved away and Fenwick sat down on the bench next to Koras. "I was in Italy when I got word from New York. You withdrew four hundred grand?"

Koras nodded. There was nothing to say.

"That four hundred was earmarked for your Westhampton place, for the construction people."

Koras started to sweat. "I'll just have to make some more money."

"Huh," Fenwick grunted, as he brought out his notes. "That ain't the half of it. You *have* to win here. You *have* to win in Ohio, at the ATP. New York is not negotiable." Fenwick pointed at numbers on the back of an envelope. $100,000, $145,000, $200,000. And then the words GRAND SLAM and LAVAL SPORTIF underlined three times. Koras felt the pressure mounting. He would have to keep playing forever, on knees that buckled when he ran wide.

"I can do it, F.F."

"You damn well better." Fenwick stuffed the envelope into his pocket and brought out some legal papers. Koras signed them without reading them, but he knew they would prevent his giving more money for Laure's dig at Alesia.

He had just signed the last document when a court official approached. "Mr. Belynkas, perhaps you'd like to walk out on the court?"

"Is Polak here?"

"No, sir. But we're told to go ahead."

Koras gave the man his rackets and Laval tennis bag. Fenwick and Channer wished him luck. And then he followed the man out through the passage between the Royal Box and the West Open Stand. The head groundskeeper was there, on a folding chair, ready to rush out and plug up divots during the course of the match.

The stands of Centre Court were packed. As defending champion, Koras received a standing ovation. Where was Polak?

Koras sat down, dropping into his yogic emptiness, and tried some deep breathing. Just before he closed his eyes, he saw Frank Fenwick join Athena and Nora Laville in Saadi's box. Fenwick had blocked his promise to Laure of more money. Yet he knew his manager was right.

The crowd grew impatient. This was the men's semifinal, traditionally the best match of the tournament, and many of the fans had placed bets with their bookmakers. Since Polak had been playing so well, the odds had risen in his favor. In the chair, the umpire, Geoffrey Smith, kept talking on his telephone to the head umpire. So far, there was no sign of Polak.

At two-fifteen, Sir Francis Malcolm himself emerged from the locker-room door to speak to the umpire. Koras came out of his meditation. Something was wrong. Sir Francis whispered to the umpire.

"What's wrong?" Koras stood up.

"Your opponent has been scratched!"

"Scratched? What for? Is he sick?"

Sir Francis hesitated. His face was ashen. "No. He's not coming. We've had word."

"What kind of word?"

"In a moment, Mr. Belynkas. Please be patient."

Above his head, Koras heard the announcement that Polak had been defaulted. The umpire was invoking the fifteen-minute rule, one more of Wimbledon's hallowed traditions, and awarding the semifinal match to Mr. Belynkas.

Koras didn't like it. He was ready to play. The crowd was expectant, eager for the duel that would decide the Sunday finalists. Now thousands of fans would be disappointed.

To scattered applause from the stunned spectators, Koras walked off the court with Sir Francis.

The atmosphere in the men's dressing room was reminiscent of the bleak day Reyes had collapsed on the center court at Roland-Garros, only worse. Small groups had formed. There were mutterings about terrorism and death threats. The air crackled with tension, and Koras smelled the stink of fear.

He walked up to Channer and Fenwick.

"We just heard," Fenwick said. "Polak is dead."

"What?"

Fenwick nodded. "A chambermaid found him dead, in the goddamn bathroom at the Gloucester."

"What was it?" Koras's first thought was a drug overdose. "A heart attack?" He knew that sounded crazy. Polak was only twenty-six.

"We don't know. What we do now is get you the hell out of

here. Sir Francis has called a War Council in the big room. You and Will scoot before the reporters start swarming around."

The Advisory Group had met before at Fouquet's in Paris. The occasion then had been the death of Reyes on court. The men who made the decisions in tennis had convened again: Archer Bell, who managed top players like Laville and Cooper; Frank Fenwick, the Texan who managed Koras, Tigrid, and Polak; Paco Ortega, who managed Jack Di Rocca; Peter Abraham, a player himself and President of the Association of Tennis Professionals; Alain Clavier, President of the International Tennis Federation; Sven Skaar, the great Scandinavian player, now retired, who acted as ombudsman, and sometimes the collective conscience, of the players; and Abdul Saadi, his country's representative on the ITF, who was there mostly because he was rich and powerful.

Sir Francis Malcolm, Secretary of the All-England Club, seemed in deep shock. Alain Clavier stared out the window at the milling spectators. They did not know what had happened and were waiting restlessly for the next match. Would there *be* a next match?

While they awaited the arrival of Inspector Weston from Scotland Yard, they discussed strategies to keep the tournament going.

"I think we should stop play," Abraham said, "while the police conduct an investigation. Send everyone home with a rain check. Play the damned finals on Tuesday of next week, if it comes to that."

"It would be awkward," Sir Francis said. "The men's final is always on Sunday."

Paco Ortega, wearing a red tennis shirt from Sport City, swung his massive shoulders to speak to Archer Bell. "I thought we hired a detective to nose around, keep us informed."

"I'll request a report, on the double."

Clavier joined the discussion. "He has been working, but I have seen only one report."

"You want a report," Bell said, "we can have a report."

"*I'd* like to see a report," Frank Fenwick said. "Especially since he seems to be reporting mostly to Arch Bell."

"Goddamn you, F.F. That was uncalled for."

"I call 'em like I see 'em."

Bell sighed. "If you remember, we hired Malone to check on the death of Armando Reyes because we were concerned about drugs. He's working closely with the Paris police. So far, he hasn't found any drugs. I don't see how we can hold him personally responsible for Polak, or for any player."

"If there are facts, Arch, we should be getting them," Fenwick growled.

"Gentlemen, gentlemen," Sir Francis broke in. "Let us not bicker amongst ourselves when there are larger issues."

Bell and Fenwick glared at each other, but stopped talking. Sir Francis went on.

"Here is the problem, as I see it. We have a sellout crowd, waiting to see a semifinal match. Outside, there are an estimated 9,540 people standing in line for tickets. You saw them when you drove in."

"Took half an hour longer today," Fenwick said. "Just getting here from the goddamn hotel."

"Yes, well. I have been informed that Mr. Laville, who was to play the second semifinal, has not yet arrived. We must tell our spectators something. . . ." Sir Francis looked around the room bleakly. "I was thinking perhaps we might assemble a men's doubles?"

"Laville will be here," Archer Bell said.

"He was supposed to be here already."

"Terry hangs loose. He knew Koras and Polak would take two hours, perhaps three. He got tied up in traffic and stopped off to phone me."

"All players should use our limousines."

"Terry likes driving on the wrong side of the road."

No one laughed. Sir Francis stiffened.

"Anyway, he'll be here."

"All right," Sir Francis said. "We'll announce the Laville-Cooper match."

"What will you say about Polak?"

"We'll say he defaulted. We shall hold a formal press conference following the match."

"I vote for that," Fenwick said.

Bell leaned toward Fenwick to whisper, "And your guy gets a day off."

"Knock it off, Arch."

Sir Francis buzzed for his secretary, a young man wearing a rumpled blazer. "Can you find Davey Cooper for us, Gerald? Ask him if he would mind terribly playing a bit earlier. There's a good chap."

The secretary went out.

"This means Koras is in the final?" Ortega asked.

"Yes," Sir Francis said. "Unless there is an objection."

"Polak had been playing well," Archer Bell said. "What are the chances Koras could have beaten him?"

"It was fifty-fifty," Abraham said.

"I disagree," Fenwick said. "Koras is on his way to a Grand Slam."

The men around the table were quiet. At last, the secretary came in, followed by Superintendent Weston. The Superintendent wore a tan suit that fit perfectly. His lean-jawed face showed signs of strain. His shoes had their usual high polish. Weston elected to stand. Before starting out, he looked fixedly at each man.

Weston removed a notebook from his jacket pocket and put on a pair of half-moon reading glasses.

"Let me bring you up to date on events, gentlemen. This afternoon, at twelve-nineteen, a chambermaid named, ah, Mika Franulovich heard an explosion while running a hoover on the fifth floor of the Gloucester Hotel. When she checked round, she discovered a dead body in the bathroom of number 512. The room belonged to a Mr. Mikhail Polak, a tennis player and also a citizen of the Eastern Bloc. The body, nude, was his.

"There was another maid, Cosima Branko, who was helping Miss Franulovich do the rooms. Upon seeing the body, both maids ran down the hall, screaming, leaving the door open. Between the time the maids ran down the hall and the hotel security man arrived, at least half a dozen persons, including, I'm sorry to say, at least one freelance photographer, entered the room. Any one of them could have removed the man's wallet, which was missing. The murder weapon, by the way, was an Italian shotgun. This has been corroborated by Dr. Sims, our medical examiner. The time of death was shortly after noon, which means the murderer may still have been close by when the body was discovered.

"As for access, the windows are five stories up. One was open, the others had been latched from the inside. The fire escape is around the corner and three rooms away, and we are therefore presuming the murderer simply entered through the door from the corridor. Since there was no sign of forced entry, we must presume he had a key. Or he was let in by the victim. We know that the victim purchased the shotgun, a Franchi, from Purdey's three days ago. The victim was a collector of small arms, some for target shooting, some for sport. He has had an account with Purdey's for the past six years. We have begun a background check on Mr. Polak, but information is scant so far, which is usually the case when we deal with law enforcement in Eastern Europe. He is married to an American woman in Chicago. I am informed he pays his bills on time, through a bank in Dallas, Texas. He paid fourteen hundred pounds for this Franchi, made in Brescia, Italy. Records from Purdey's show the shotgun was manufactured in 1894."

Weston closed the notebook and looked around the table. "That is all we have at the moment, gentlemen. We are giving this case top priority."

There was rustling around the table, as the men shifted in their chairs.

Superintendent Weston was an orderly man who hated violence. He was not a tennis player himself, but his brother Clifford had played at university and still managed to get in a game of doubles twice a week. Weston knew that The Championships was the premier event in professional tennis, and that these men would bring pressure to bear to clear this case quickly.

"What I wish to know from you, gentlemen, is who would want this man dead? It's sticky for us, his being a foreigner."

There was silence in the room as the Superintendent looked from one man to another.

"Well, at least it wasn't drugs," Paco Ortega said.

There was a general murmur of assent, but the horror of the moment was still maddening.

* * *

Following the general meeting, Superintendent Weston stayed on for a moment to confer with Clavier and Sir Francis. Clavier asked about the threat note that had been received a day before Wimbledon started—a development that Clavier, Sir Francis, and Weston had kept under wraps.

"We worked on it, of course," Weston said. "The words themselves could have come from any one of a dozen magazines devoted to tennis. The paper is the type used by copying machines all over the world. Our lab technicians think the copy machine was made in Japan, but that does not narrow it down terribly."

"But we should have taken it more seriously!" Clavier said.

"Yes." Sir Francis looked solemn. "The only thing now is to increase security for the players."

"That's being done," Weston said. "They'll be watched by rotating two-man teams until this is over."

"What about alerting the New York police," Clavier said, "in case this madman decides to continue his violence at the U.S. Open?"

"We've already seen to that," Weston said.

"This is terrible!" Sir Francis said.

"It is like a bad dream," said Clavier.

"A recurring one, too, I'm afraid," Weston said.

Coming out of the dressing room, Koras met Terry Laville, dressed in shorts and his bright-red warm-up jacket. Laville had a crazy look in his eyes. He stared at Koras for a long moment.

"This story about Polak. It can't be true."

Koras nodded. "It's true. A chambermaid found Polak dead, in his bathtub."

"How did it happen?"

"No one knows yet."

Laville's eyes darted behind Koras's shoulder. He clutched his rackets to his chest as if about to explode. His face looked haggard. He needed sleep. Was the circuit getting to him already?

"I heard a news flash while I was driving down. I couldn't believe the radio!"

"Stay cool, Terry. There's a reasonable explanation."

"How the fuck do you know everything?" Terry lashed out. "As a matter of fact, isn't that some kind of record, Koras?"

"What?"

"You make the finals at the Big W without hitting a single ball in the semis?"

"This isn't the first default in tennis, Terry."

"It's the first default by a corpse."

Koras turned away. Laville was behaving worse than usual, probably from the strain of hearing about poor Polak. A crowd of reporters and television people had surrounded them. Koras started walking away, but Laville turned with a forced smile to take advantage of the moment.

"You want a statement? I'll give you a statement. I'm going to beat Davey," he announced. "And then, even though the odds aren't in my favor, I'm going to kill King Koras."

A question came from one of the reporters. "Just what sort of odds are we talking about here, Terry?"

Laville swung to face the questioner. "It's simple. Koras didn't have to hit one ball today, so he'll be fresh. I've got to go out there and face the number-four player in the world."

"What do you plan to do about it?"

"Take it up with the boys upstairs," Laville said. "As soon as this match is over."

"But what if you don't win?" asked another reporter.

"Oh, I'll win," Terry said. "I've got that part planned."

A ripple of uneasiness spread through the knot of reporters as Laville brushed by them and vanished into the dressing room.

In the fourth set of his semifinal against Davey Cooper, leading two sets to one and tied up at 4–all, Terry Laville saw the ball out. He was running wide on the baseline for a forehand and he saw the ball drop down at least five inches outside the chalk. He played the shot with an open stance, hitting short with topspin, catching Cooper coming in. In the back of his mind, he was listening for the line call that would verify his own judgment, but it never came. Cooper hit a drop volley, soft with backspin, just over the net. Listening for the call had made

Laville hesitate, so he was late starting forward for the intercept.

The sun was out, fleecy white clouds slipping across the sky, and Laville could really see the ball, pale against the green grass. It was definitely out, but Cooper still won the point. Feeling the anger pound in his head, Laville marched to the umpire's stand to complain.

"That ball was out. Five inches, at least."

"The lines person disagrees, Mr. Laville."

Terry felt the anger build. The legend on the circuit held that when he got hot, he played better.

"He's blind," Terry said. "I was right there. I saw it."

"You are a player, Mr. Laville. Players do not call lines."

"Listen, you moron. That line judge is incompetent. He's been making mistakes all day. I want the bum replaced." Terry wanted the crowd to hear. Someone hissed at him from the stands on his right. He turned but couldn't see who it was in the vast sea of faces.

The umpire's face was becoming flushed with anger. "Play is continuous, Mr. Laville. Please play on."

"Are you telling me that ball was in? Because if you are, you're blind, too."

"Please, Mr. Laville. Your time is up. I shall have to issue a warning."

Furious now, Laville kept on grinning. Up in the stands, the fans buzzed. He was the big name out here, the player they recognized, the one hackers stood in line to watch. In Paris, they had his face on a billboard, and it was only a matter of time before his face was on billboards everywhere.

"Ahh, have it your way." He turned his back, stalked stiffly to the baseline. Down at the other end of the court, Cooper was pacing, gesturing with his elbows, muttering to himself. Laville knew those signs—Davey's concentration was shaky, and he was begging for the old coup de grace. Laville's tactics had worked: Cooper had won the point but was about to lose the set.

Cooper weighed 220, a few pounds more than Laville. He was the same height as Terry and he played the big game, hitting big ground strokes and charging the net to put away the volley.

But Terry had learned to analyze opponents by listening to old Koras, when he first came on the tour. And now, back in the match, temperature up, he stroked the ball low, heavy with topspin, and Davey would come in and pick up the ball off his shoe tops and Terry would glide in to whistle the shot by him. Three times in the fifth set he hit Davey with the ball. Each time, Cooper grinned, like he still thought this was a friendly game.

Terry took the fourth game to surge ahead, 3–1. All that stood between him and the Wimbledon title was this awkward player with the boyish smile and the huge feet. And then a nemesis named Belynkas. That thought gave Terry confidence. He made his toss and hit a slice serve, pulling Davey wide. He charged to the net to knife away the volley for a clean winner. Laville was almost home free.

Sitting with Archer Bell in Bell's private box, Malone half-watched the men's semifinal while Arch summarized what had gone on in the War Council in Sir Francis Malcolm's office. Malone took notes on the way Polak had died.

"They want another report, Malone. What have you got?"

"Nothing on Polak."

Bell turned to look at Malone. "What about his room?"

"Nothing there but a teapot, a picture of the wife, and a fancy shotgun."

"Where was the shotgun?"

"In the closet."

"Did you touch it?"

Malone nodded. "I wore gloves."

"Keep that out of the report, about searching the rooms. We don't want to upset Clavier."

"Don't worry. I'm not adding myself to Weston's list of suspects. It's between us, Mr. Bell."

"I suppose you had to search rooms?" Bell's pudgy face wore a look of pain.

"It's tough to find recreational drugs without pawing through some dirty underwear."

"But you haven't *found* any drugs."

Malone thought of Milo Tigrid and his pills. "Some marijuana is all."

"Where?"

"Harper. The two crazy Argentinians. Cooper."

Bell's eyes narrowed. "Cooper? Are you certain?"

Malone nodded. "Bet his mama doesn't suspect, either."

"Well, keep quiet on that, too."

"Right."

"What else are you doing?"

"I'm working on my theory."

"Oh?" Bell arched his eyebrows. "What theory is that?"

Malone leaned close. "I think Reyes was sacrificed for the glory of the game. Polak, too."

"That's ridiculous, Malone. Who would profit?"

"Whoever sells tickets. Whoever sells equipment."

Bell's face turned pale. "Jesus! Are you crazy?"

"Maybe. But the theory fits. Just look at the attendance numbers since Reyes dropped dead. Look what the scalpers are getting out there today."

"You realize what you're saying?"

Malone stood up restlessly, stuffed his hands in his pockets. Down on the court, Terry Laville was loudly disputing a line call and the umpire was trying to bring the match under control.

"Yeah."

"Sit down, Malone. You're making me nervous."

Malone sat down. Terry Laville walked back to the baseline to receive serve. The crowd got silent again. Malone knew that his job depended on being able to predict what would happen next.

Davey Cooper lobbed over Laville's head. At the last possible moment, when the ball seemed to have drifted out of reach, Laville leaped into the air with the extraordinary trampoline action known as the Jungle Jump. His face, as he stiffened his arm to bring the ball down out of the sky, was a mask of harried intensity, an echo of darkness. This was what the fans came for. It didn't matter who Laville was playing; his desire to win was so intense, so obvious to the spectators, that his victory vibrations reached from the most exclusive private box to the highest seat in the great cathedral, to the fans packed in the standing-room-only section. It was, Malone knew, this single quality that had convinced Archer Bell to draw up a contract with Laville in the first place. The other players were wearing out, or getting blown away, and Terry Laville's time of greatness was coming.

"Laville's playing well today, don't you think?"

"He's putting on a real show."

"This excitement is unreal."

Death did that to people, but Malone kept this observation to himself. His conspiracy theory had no appeal for Mr. Bell. And Mr. Bell was paying his way this summer.

Down on the court, Laville crunched away another forehand volley, and Davey Cooper went down on his knees in the yellow grass and buried his face in his hands. Malone wondered what were the chances that Laville was on something heavier than Irish coffee. The man was playing like a maniac.

THIRTEEN

From the first, Superintendent Weston was not happy about the arrival of his counterpart from Paris. The French were natural meddlers who draped their investigations in a mixture of logic and innuendo. When Weston took his vacations, he went to Spain or Italy or Scandinavia, but seldom to France.

The body of Mikhail Polak was barely cold when he got word that Inspector Pierre-Aimé Maréchal was flying over, for a "professional" consultation. There was an assumption, unspoken by the French and not yet buttressed by solid evidence from Paris, that the murder of Polak was related in some way to the death of Armando Reyes at Stade Roland-Garros a month ago.

While he waited at Gatwick for Maréchal's plane, Weston remembered a case he had handled back in 1979. A top member of the Conservative Party had been caught in a hotel room with the body of a twenty-six-year-old homosexual barman from Manchester. Weston had kept the official lid on, with extreme difficulty, and a scandal had been averted. His circumspection had gained him a promotion. This death of an international celebrity bore the same earmarks as that case. If a man worked, there was always the possibility of advancement.

The flight arrived from Paris and Weston felt a little better when he got a look at Maréchal. The Frenchman was short, stocky, with a barrel chest and beady policeman's eyes. Even though it was midsummer, Maréchal wore a three-piece suit. His handshake was firm, and he regarded Weston with a no-nonsense gaze.

"Have you had lunch, Inspector?"

"Beer nuts, on the flight across. It was nothing."

"I have a place in mind."

Maréchal smiled warily. "Excellent. I accept."

Weston leaned forward, to speak to his driver. "Let's drive around to my club, Jenkins."

"Yes, Superintendent."

Weston's club was located in a somber buiding a few minutes' walk from Westminster Abbey. The lobby of the club was dark, its walls decorated with portraits of dour-looking Englishmen from the glorious days of British colonial power. A gray-haired maître d' led them into the dining room, where a few old gentlemen nodded as they saw Weston come in with a guest.

Once they were seated, Maréchal stared at the menu, which had been handwritten earlier that morning. He ordered sole, but was informed they were out. He ordered Welsh rarebit, but was informed they were out. He ordered kidney pie. They were out.

"This is embarrassing," Weston said, turning to the waiter. "What *do* you have?"

"The curry is quite good, I'm told."

Maréchal made a face, but there was no choice. Both men ordered curry. To smooth things over, Weston ordered a bottle of white Bordeaux, the best the cellar had. He wasn't accustomed to drinking at lunch, but several trips to Paris had taught him that it might be worth his while to bend a little.

The wine came. After a glass, the two policemen began discussing what they referred to as the Tennis Murders. "What sort of gun was it?"

"A Franchi, hand-crafted, 1894. Barrels above and below. Perfectly balanced. Quite a weapon."

"A cousin of my wife's collects guns. He owns a Franchi Falconet."

Weston checked his notebook. "The firm of Franchi ventured into the submachine-gun business. In the sixties."

Maréchal nodded. "The LF-57. I saw a demonstration when I visited a friend in Rome. The Italian Navy used it for three years."

"Their shotgun made a mess of the victim."

Maréchal had finished his wine, so he refilled his own glass. "Polak had the look of a victim, all that anguish on his face."

"We were fortunate to obtain the weapon," Weston said. "Immediately after the killing, several people entered the victim's room. We think there was money stolen. We don't know what else."

"How long before the scene was sealed?"

"Seven minutes. Perhaps eight."

Maréchal drank half a glass of wine. "Polak was cut down at an ironic moment. According to the papers, he was playing well."

"Yes. Brilliantly. The bookmakers were giving him good odds against Koras in the semifinals, and also against Laville in the finals."

"It seems quite extreme, doesn't it, for someone to murder his next opponent?"

"Perhaps a player has gone mad."

"Where were these two when it happened?"

"Koras was at Wimbledon, with his coach, in the dressing room. Laville was enroute, in a rented car."

"What about the others? Tigrid? Di Rocca? Cooper?"

"Cooper was at the All-England Club, practicing. Di Rocca was on the telephone in New York, from a telephone exchange. This man Tigrid swears he was with a lady, but refuses to give her name."

"Never trust a Yugoslav, is my motto. Could I have another glass of this, please? It's not a bad wine."

Weston frowned as he poured some wine. If the Frenchman kept this up, they would finish this bottle before the food came and be forced to order another, to accompany the meal. They kept on discussing the case. At last, the food came. Weston found it pleasant, but he could tell from Maréchal's face that the Frenchman did not agree. The French found it patriotic to dislike English food. Weston gave in and ordered another bottle. When it came, the Frenchman kept on with his questions.

"What time was the murder again?"

"Noon. Perhaps a quarter past."

"And the maid found the body?"

"Two maids, actually. One of them heard the gunshot. But the other one found the body. We've had to use a translator. All they speak is Serbian."

"Perhaps you could enlist the services of Tigrid."

Weston smiled as he chewed his curry. "Should I get you something else?"

"I am not so hungry as I thought. This wine gets better, however."

"I was wondering if I might ask you a few questions, Inspector?"

Maréchal waved his wine glass. "By all means."

"Did you have a chance to interrogate either Di Rocca or this man Malone?"

Maréchal looked beyond Weston's shoulder. "I suppose you know about Di Rocca?"

"The criminal record, yes. Is there something else?"

Maréchal shrugged. "When one speaks with him, there appear to be large portions of the fabric that have holes."

Weston agreed. "Di Rocca seems capable of having someone killed. Anyone."

"Yes. But with what motive?"

"Envy? Perhaps Di Rocca was humiliated on a court somewhere by Comrade Polak."

"Perhaps. Have you interrogated Malone yet?"

"Later today. Why?"

Maréchal poured more wine for himself and his host. "We have been working together, in a small way. Malone has a theory. Has he told you?"

"What's that?"

"He thinks someone in power is having players killed to enhance the visibility—and thus the profit center—of the game."

"Extraordinary!" Weston covered his shock by drinking more wine. The second bottle was almost gone, so he signaled the waiter for more. Maréchal smiled his approval. Both men liked their work and they were warming to the discussion.

"The implications are interesting, wouldn't you say?"

"If there's anything to it, think of who it would implicate."

"All those at the top."

Clavier. Sir Francis. Archer Bell. Fenwick. Abdul Saadi. Perhaps even the American, Harrison Cabot. It was quite a list. "My word," Weston murmured.

They stopped talking while the waiter opened the wine. Weston tasted it, nodded at the waiter, who filled both glasses. As the waiter walked away, the two policemen toasted one another.

"This wine has insights," Weston said, aware that he had slurred his words.

"It accelerates the thinking process." Maréchal pushed the curry around with his fork. "There is another angle, which could be related."

Weston was ahead of his guest. "Gambling, you mean?"

"Precisely."

"We have a team investigating that, but it is difficult, as you know, to find reliable data where so much cash is involved. What are your thoughts, Inspector?"

"It was discovered, after the tournament was over at Roland-Garros, that major speculation had been taking place."

"In Paris?"

"Yes. They were using a room out at Longchamps."

Weston smiled. "How much money are we talking about?"

"Three hundred million francs. Three times as much as last year."

"Any idea where it came from?"

"Yes. From Zurich. From South America. And from New York."

Weston knew that could mean the American Mafia. "Who was the favorite in Paris?"

"Koras. Who is favored here?"

Weston hesitated. "Since Polak died, it is Koras, with Laville closing."

Maréchal finished his last swallow of wine and looked around for the waiter. "Do you think we could order a coffee, Superintendent?"

"Of course. Of course." Weston caught the waiter's eye. When he had given the order, he said, "Koras would have had to hire it done. That's not his way."

"Why not?"

"Koras is an American. Don't they prefer doing things for themselves?"

Athena von Heidelberg was a sexual creature whose identity and sense of self were directly tied to the men she could attract. She was beautiful, and beauty was a commodity in her world, and as she aged, searching for telltale worry lines in her mirror, she remembered how she had looked at eighteen and twenty and even twenty-five. The memory made her feel vulnerable, and now she realized why her mother had chosen cosmetic surgery at forty-two. Athena was a dozen years away from that age, but already she was worried. She needed men, their smiles, their admiration, their money, their dynamism. In her lifetime, she had been admired by millions, loved from afar by thousands, courted by hundreds.

Athena had a recurring dream about her first encounter with a man. In the dream, she was a little girl again, wearing a peasant's blue-and-white dirndl as she danced around the room with a dozen little girls her age at a birthday party in a castle at the peak of summer. The voices echo and there is the sound of music, harpsichord, the deep throb of a cello, and as the chain of little girls circles around the table where the presents sit, Athena glances up into the eyes of Uncle Fritz, a friend of her mother's. Uncle Fritz is smiling. Athena remembers him because he gives her presents—pretty jewelry, a red saddle for her pony, dolls that talk and wet their pants—and at night he steals into her room and sits on her bed and touches her, very lightly, underneath the covers.

From Uncle Fritz, Athena learned what men want from women, always. At thirty, she had no illusions. She had been married twice and in love many times. Men were necessary to her existence. She could handle them. They were her life. And life could be difficult.

She was remembering her dream as she rode the train to Oxford, for a rendezvous in a modest hotel with Jack Di Rocca. Earlier this morning, Saadi had flown to Zurich for a meeting. Later today, the women's final would be played at Wimbledon. Athena regretted missing the final, but this meeting with Di Rocca was important. She needed his help, and she was prepared to entice him with promises, pleas, fantasy, sex.

The room was on the third floor, overlooking a brick courtyard. When she arrived, Di Rocca was already there, watching a replay of the Cooper-Laville match from yesterday. As she entered, the announcer made a reference to the death of Mikhail Polak. There were two bottles of champagne on ice and a videocassette player. Di Rocca opened the first bottle, but was careful not to rush her into anything sexual. She drank the champagne and tried to relax. They watched the cassette of the film *Belle de Jour*, but she could not concentrate. As he poured more champagne for her, Di Rocca asked why they were here.

Athena was offended. "Would you rather be somewhere else? *With* someone else?" She brushed a strand of hair from her face.

"No. But I know when I'm getting the deep freeze."

She hadn't expected this. Nervously, she walked over to him, put her hands on his shoulders, and gave him a questioning kiss. When he did not respond, she reached behind herself, to grasp the zipper on her expensive beige dress. She pulled the zipper only halfway down, then turned around so that her back was to Di Rocca. He did not offer to help.

She glanced at him over her shoulder and her lip quivered. Had she lost her power over men? Di Rocca was not a handsome man, and his coarseness reminded her of the physical beauty of Armando. Suddenly, she sat down on the edge of the chair and cried. Di Rocca moved to stand beside her. She felt his hand on her hair and she knew that her face would be red and splotchy from the tears. After a moment, she broke away from Di Rocca and retreated into the bathroom.

She took some time repairing her face. Then she opened her purse and brought out the vial of red pills. As she nervously popped the cap, four pills rolled from the vial into her palm. She was putting them back in when the door opened and Di Rocca stood there. She tried to hide the pills, but it was too late. He entered the bathroom and grabbed her by the wrist. The pills scattered onto the floor.

"Where'd you get them?"

"None of your business."

He squatted down easily to pick up a pill. Then he turned to her, a hard smile in his eyes. "You gave them to Armando."

Feeling faint and sick to her stomach, she brushed past Di Rocca. He followed her into the bedroom.

"Answer me, goddammit."

"Yes. I gave them to Armando. But not before I took them myself."

"Yeah. But you didn't mix them with anti-anxiety pills." Di Rocca shook his head, then walked to the window and looked out. "Where'd you get them?"

"From Saadi. From his desk."

"You stole them?"

"I have a key."

"Where did you get the key?"

"I had one copied. For my own protection. You don't know what he's like."

Di Rocca turned to stare at her. "What if Saadi wanted you to find the pills? What if he knew about you and Armando?"

"Impossible," she said. But then the idea chilled her and she began to cough.

Di Rocca refilled their champagne glasses. On the screen, the videotape of the movie seemed pale, surrealistic. She took the glass from Di Rocca.

"So. You want to tell me why we're here?"

She waited before replying. "You are a man. You came. I thought you understood."

"I was curious. And you're a good-looking woman."

That made her feel better. She crossed her legs and tried to regain her composure. "You knew my reputation. You wanted to see if the gossip was true."

"Okay. You turn me on. But I can tell when a woman likes me, or when she needs me for piano-moving up some twisted stairs. This is a baby grand. And the stairs are steep."

Athena shook her head as she felt the tears starting again. She got up to leave the room. She would find some other way. "This won't work." Di Rocca caught her by the arm before she reached the door.

"Tell me about it."

His face was rugged beneath the beard. He was an ex-convict with rumored connections in the American underworld. The fierce light in his eyes told her he was attracted to her. She needed his help, so she brought out the copy of *Racquet World* she had taken from Saadi's study in Paris. As Di Rocca thumbed through it, she explained about the words that had been cut out. And then she showed Di Rocca the list: SEMIFINALIST, WIMBLE-DON, CANCEL, REYES, SECOND, ONLY, WILL, FIRST.

Di Rocca frowned as he read through the list. "A semifinalist will die?"

"And Mikhail Polak was a semifinalist."

"But there's been nothing in the news."

She walked back to the chair and sat down. "Perhaps he waits to send it. Perhaps it has been suppressed by the police."

"You think Saadi killed Polak for going with Izanagi?"

"I don't know. He was enraged when he heard."

They finished the first bottle of champagne and Di Rocca opened the second. Athena was feeling better now that she had shared her secret knowledge with someone. They still had no plan.

"Okay. Let's play what-if. What if Saadi knew you were see-ing Armando? So he slips you the pills. You slip them to Armando. Armando plays out of his head, takes too many, and dies. Lucky break for Saadi. But does he have that kind of knowledge about the pills?"

"It is possible. He has doctors on staff at his research facility in California."

"I read about that. They do research on health drinks?"

"Yes."

"Okay," Di Rocca said. "So that's a possible. Now, what if Saadi was counting on the Polak deal and Polak lets it out that he's signing with Izanagi, and someone tells Saadi and Saadi hires a pro to blow Polak up?"

Athena shivered. "That is not Saadi's way."

Di Rocca sipped his champagne. "Okay, let's talk about the way you lured me here to see a movie about a lady and a thief."

Athena smiled at his light tone of voice. "You were right. I do need help."

"With Saadi?"

"Yes. I want to leave him."

"Why don't you just walk out?"

"He has a hold on me, through my mother." She told him about the pressure Saadi had put on her through his Swiss bankers.

"What you need is some leverage." Di Rocca picked up the issue of *Racquet World*.

"Exactly."

"And what we need is for Saadi to make a dumb move."

"Something he seldom does," Athena said.

"Well, maybe we'll get lucky." He held out his glass to touch Athena's. "Here's to luck."

They sipped their champagne. Athena went to the bathroom to repair her face. When she came out, Di Rocca was on the bed with his shoes off, a good sign. "I'm still working on the what-ifs," he said.

She sat down on the edge of the bed and did her best to look alluring. "And what are you coming up with?"

"Let's say we get lucky. I help you escape the penthouse world of Abdul Saadi. What's in it for me?"

Athena smiled. She liked negotiating. "Saadi has lots of money. Perhaps you could take it away from him."

"An annuity," Di Rocca mused. "Payable every quarter."

"A hundred thousand a quarter?"

"Make it a quarter million a quarter. A million a year. In

tax-free bonds." The figure made him smile. He was enjoying this. "So. What does Saadi want the most?"

"He wants to control everything in tennis—equipment, clothes, tournaments."

"Saadi wants to be Mr. Tennis."

Athena nodded.

"So," Di Rocca said, "maybe all we have to do is threaten to derail him. Hurt his projections just a little."

"Excellent." Athena leaned down to give Di Rocca a brief kiss. This time, she felt him respond. When she left the bed to pour the last of the champagne, she kicked off her shoes. She could feel his eyes on her as she returned to the bed.

"What we need to do," Di Rocca said, "is to pick the perfect time. Saadi's chugging along toward his goal. We take over the switching station."

Athena smiled then and climbed up onto the bed next to Di Rocca. She felt the flutterings of relief. She smiled and her eyes became watery, a sure sign that she was getting ready to make love. For the first time since Armando had died, she knew the stirrings of desire.

"All right, Jack."

On Saturday afternoon, during the women's singles final, President Clavier called a special meeting to order. Koras was there with Fenwick and Channer. Laville and Cooper came with Archer Bell. Sir Francis Malcolm sat behind his desk, frowning. A policeman, stationed outside the door, was killing time with the security guards who had followed the top players since Polak's murder.

"Let's run Koras around the track, five miles," Laville said. "That will assure us an evenly matched final."

Archer Bell laughed, but no one else did.

"I'm tired enough, Terry. Have a heart."

"I'm serious," Laville said, leaning forward. "I just played over three hours out there, and because of Polak's murder the number-one seed has a whole day of rest on me. How do you call that fair?"

"Please, Mr. Laville. Please."

"I'm lodging a protest, and I want the world to know. Just

because a player dies is no reason to screw another player in the match of his lifetime."

"Is that how you see the final?"

"You're goddamned right that's how I see it." Terry's eyes blazed up. He was restrained by Archer Bell, who put a hand on his arm. Laville was not acting like a winner. Everyone in the room could sense it.

Back at the Gloucester Hotel, after the abortive meeting, Koras found a message to call Laure Puget at the home of her grandparents, in a village called Choisel, in the Chevreuse Valley, outside Paris. While he waited for his call to go through, Koras wondered whether he should tell her there would be no more money. Should he tell her now? Or should he wait until after Wimbledon?

Since he had seen her at Alesia, he had thought about her often, the firm, sun-bronzed legs, her face in the rain, her loveliness in the moonlight. She resisted him, resisted his world. That part was hard to grasp. He had worked hard for a foothold in tennis, had fought for stardom and everything that went with it. For a dozen years, women had been attracted to him because he was famous. But Laure seemed, if anything, suspicious of it. Perhaps, if he saw her again, he could sort things out.

"Koras?" Her voice was breathless. "Are you all right?"

"Yes. I'm fine."

"On the news they said a tennis player had died at Wimbledon. I was so afraid it was you."

"No. It was Micky Polak."

"Was he a friend of yours?"

"I liked Micky. We had the same manager."

"What will happen now?"

"They've beefed up security. A policeman is with me even in bed."

She did not laugh. "They won't cancel the matches, you mean?"

"No. People are shaken up. But they've sold too many tickets. We have to go on."

"That sounds just like you."

He thought of Frank Fenwick, and the money. "How are things going at the dig?"

"Very well." From her tone of voice, things sounded worse. "Everyone was impressed with your generosity."

"Even young Dr. Benoît?"

"Of course. He even suggested a commemorative plaque."

"I feel like a ruin."

She laughed, but still sounded far away. "Does the tournament finish on Sunday?"

"Yes. Why?"

She hesitated before saying, "I am in Paris until Wednesday. Then I go to Greece."

Koras's money had run out. "For Professor what's-his-name?"

"Colicos. Yes."

"Then what you got from me has run out?"

"Please. We must look to the future. Professor Colicos knows people at the Peabody who may be able to help."

Koras stared at the wall. His first year on the circuit, he'd made seventeen thousand dollars, barely enough for expenses. "Wednesday, you said?"

"Yes."

"How is Monday for you? We could meet somewhere. I could pay you back that dinner."

"I know a lovely restaurant. On the Rue St. Denis. The proprietor is an old friend. And you can meet my grandparents."

Koras was hoping for more, but she sounded so far away that he knew talking about it would not help.

She had to go, so she gave him directions to her grandparents' house in Choisel, and then they hung up. Frustrated, Koras listened to the buzz on the telephone line for a moment, then put the receiver back and lay on his bed. He closed his eyes and tried to think of Mademoiselle Dumont, the lady with the Peugeot in Paris, but images of Laure Puget kept blocking her out.

Was Laure simply playing hard to get? Or was she as uncertain as he was about how she felt? Perhaps, in Paris, he would find out.

FOURTEEN

The Superintendent sat behind his mahogany desk, a seventeenth-century piece signed William Kent. Had the desk been an authentic Kent, it would have been worth at least twenty thousand pounds at Sotheby's, but it was part of a haul the police had made in the cellar of an Elizabethan manor house where a group of forgers had installed an operation to bilk the public with the aid of bogus furniture. By the time the criminals were unmasked, they had flooded the London antiques market and had gone into the business of exporting with more success than the Beatles, British Leyland, or Princess Diana.

The Superintendent sat in an executive swivel chair, also an item of booty retrieved from thieves. Maréchal was at the window, staring out, hands clasped behind his back. A few feet from the desk, Milo Tigrid sat in a hard chair. Instead of his usual outlandish costume, Milo was dressed conservatively in gray flannel trousers, white shirt and tie, and a blazer bearing the shield of the All-England Club.

He looked positively elegant.

"If you keep me here more than six hours," Milo joked, "my chauffeur has instructions to contact my attorneys. What is it you call them here? Solicitors?"

"I am sure that won't be necessary, Mr. Tigrid. Just a few questions, and then you can be on your way."

"You think I killed Polak? You are crazy."

Maréchal turned from the window. "An odd word, coming from you."

Milo swung to confront Maréchal. "What's that? What do you say?"

" 'Crazy' is a strange word, coming from the self-appointed clown of the sport."

Milo folded his arms and glared at both policemen. "Tigrid is innocent."

"Yes, well. Would you mind telling us where you were from

ten in the morning until thirteen hundred hours, yesterday?"

"I was with a lady."

Maréchal looked at Weston. "A lady in Paris. A lady in London."

"Is it against the law?"

"We should like to have her name."

"She is a lady. You won't get her name from me."

Weston sighed, then tapped his pipe against the brass ashtray, which was in fact the base of a shell casing belonging to his predecessor, Superintendent Nigel Curzon, who had served in the Royal Navy during World War II. The shell had been fired by H.M.S. *Prince of Wales* during the sea battle which led to the sinking of the *Bismarck* in 1941. Weston was proud of this symbol of British might and vigor. "Were you aware that Polak's murderer used clothes stuffed into a Laval tennis bag to muffle the sound of the gun going off?"

"No. I know nothing about murder."

"The bag is missing. We were wondering whether or not you knew its whereabouts?"

"Tigrid knows nothing."

"The bag was a Laval. Isn't that your brand?"

"Laval is everybody's bag. They make the good bags, like nobody."

Weston smiled cordially. "Inspector Maréchal assures me you were very close to Armando Reyes, the man who died in Paris."

"We were friends. I did not kill Armando either."

"Tell me about this competition with Reyes."

Milo glared at Maréchal. "It was no secret. If Armando liked a woman, I would do my best to steal her away. It was a game."

"Who did you compete for in Paris?"

Milo sighed. "She is with Malone. Her name is Muriel Broussard-Gauthier."

"Do you compete with this man Malone?"

Milo emitted a snort. "Do not make me laugh, okay?"

"If I do not have this lady's name, Mr. Tigrid, you will very soon become acquainted with our accommodations for recalcitrant foreigners."

Milo reached for the phone. "I call my embassy now."

"Later," Weston said, holding out a hand, palm forward.

Frowning, Milo leaned back and squeezed the arms of the chair. "Malone knows where I am yesterday. He can tell all."

"Really? Where was that?"

Milo gave them a trickster's smile. "We were in bed. Together."

The two policemen looked at each other. Then the Superintendent pressed the button on his intercom. "Get that detective in here."

"Very good, sir."

Malone arrived at Scotland Yard after six, and was kept waiting for forty minutes. When he was admitted to Weston's office, he found himself shaking hands with a smiling man dressed like an ad for *Country Gentleman*. The Superintendent had a ruddy face, as if he spent a lot of time outdoors. He poured Malone a B&B.

"This is a tradition in my family, a B&B before dinner. I try to wait until later, but tonight, as long as you managed to pop round, well . . ." He handed Malone the glass of gold liquid. The drink was too sweet for Malone, but he drank it, in small sips.

"Nice."

"We're investigating this murder at the Gloucester. Thought you could help us out."

"Okay."

"Mr. Tigrid gave us a statement. In it, he implied that you and he were . . . ah . . . shall we say, in the same bed together."

Malone laughed. "That goddamn Yugoslav. We were together, all right. But in separate beds. And with separate women."

Weston's face showed vast relief. "Oh, I say." He drank off his B&B and stood up to pour another. "Could you be a good chap and describe the time, with a chronology?"

Malone ran the Superintendent through a travelogue of the pubs from Thursday night. As he talked, Weston made notes, nodding as he recognized a name.

"Then when the pubs closed, we went on to Lady Jessica's manor house."

"Where was it?"

"Outside London, maybe thirty miles west."

"Does it have a name?"

"Coatkey."

"*The* Coatkey Manor?" Weston suddenly set his glass down on the desk.

"I suppose. We had a late supper. Lady Jessica took Milo up to bed around two-thirty, maybe three."

"And when did you see him next?"

"Midmorning, Friday. We had lunch. Around one, we piled into the Coatkey limo and drove out to Church Road, for the matches."

"Will you testify to that in court?"

"Sure." Malone paused. "Any idea who killed Polak?"

Weston sipped his drink. "Maréchal told me of your theory, if that's what you refer to."

"What do you think?"

"It has possibilities. But one would want to be extremely certain before one in your position attacked a position so high up."

"Big guys are easier to bring down than you think, Superintendent."

"From your expression, it would seem that you relish the thought."

Malone raised his glass. "Aim high, Superintendent."

After leaving the office of Superintendent Weston, Malone took a taxi to St. James's Park, where he got out and walked through the evening to the White Horse Bar. He had a meeting with Jack Di Rocca, and later on he planned to take Muriel to dinner at a fancy Indian restaurant. Malone reached the bar before Di Rocca. He ordered a pint and made a call to Lorimer's, one of the large London bookmakers. The phone rang three times before it was picked up.

"Malone here."

"You're late. You were supposed to ring earlier."

"What have you got for me?"

"The day in question, Mr. Milo Tigrid was quoted at thirty to one."

"How heavy were the bets?"

"Someone placed fifty thousand pounds."

"Here? In London?"

"No. From Paris."

"What was the total placed on the matches?"

"Just over two million pounds."

Malone whistled, did some quick calculations. At the current rate of exchange, two million pounds was close to three and half million dollars. The basketball games he'd worked on for Archer Bell had sometimes pulled down two million. Tennis was in the big-time gambling arena.

"How much was bet on Polak?"

"There was a large pool bet on Mr. Polak, in the semifinals. The largest individual amount our office have ever seen."

"How large is that?"

"Eight hundred thousand pounds."

"What were the odds on Polak?"

"Seven to one."

Malone considered. At 7–1, that meant a payoff of over five million pounds. "How do the finals look?"

"Actually, more money is arriving for the finals. We were forced to put a ceiling on it."

"Any idea where the money's coming from?"

"The largest amount is from banks in Zurich. The next largest is from New York, in the States."

It was the mob. Malone could smell them a mile away. It would take some proving.

"Thanks. I'll call tomorrow."

"Yes. You do that."

Malone went back to his table, where he watched the English girls. He was halfway through his schooner when Di Rocca showed up, wearing Levi's with a sharp crease and a tan flight jacket. Jackie looked relaxed, eyes lazy, a smirky smile. "Almost didn't recognize you, Jackie. Where's the coat and tie?"

"I'm incognito." Di Rocca sat down, looked around. "You like this place?"

"Reminds me of Ireland."

"You ever been to Ireland?"

Malone grinned. "Nope. But I'm visiting right after we're finished here."

A waiter appeared and Di Rocca asked for a gin. "So. What's up, Malone?"

"I just saved your butt from being tossed in the Tower of London."

"Gee, thanks. That means I owe you another one, right?"

"I spent a couple of hours with the top cop in charge of the Polak case. His name is Weston, and he's working with your Paris shadow, Inspector Maréchal. Maréchal wanted to haul you in for the sweatbox treatment."

The waiter arrived with Di Rocca's gin, no ice, slice of lemon peel. He sipped it before arching his eyebrows. "Malone, the fixer."

Malone spread his hands. "Hey. What are friends for?"

"You want something special, Malone." Di Rocca readjusted his chair. "Well, I don't know who wasted Polak."

"Jackie, there's big money coming into tennis. Something tells me you're leading the charge."

"Big money, meaning what?"

"Gambling. Endorsements. Ticket sales. Knocking over a player or two whets the public appetite."

Di Rocca twisted his glass in a pattern on the table. "You come on so squeaky clean, Malone. But you don't fool me."

"Don't change the subject."

"You're cozying up to Arch Bell like Siamese twins."

"Well, you've got Ortega."

"Compared to Bell, Ortega is small potatoes." Di Rocca finished his gin in one swallow, then shoved his chair back and stood up. "Bell's dirt, Malone. He's scum in a suit from Brooks Brothers. As long as you're with him, expect zero from me."

Di Rocca walked out, rolling his thick shoulders. Malone looked at his watch. He had thirty minutes before meeting Muriel. Time for another pint, while he gave some thought to the slant on his report to Clavier and Sir Francis, tomorrow.

FIFTEEN

"Are you ready, gentlemen?"" said the dressing-room attendant. "May I have your rackets, please?"

The question was part of the timeless ritual of Wimbledon, and it came from the attendant with all the solemnity of the opening of Parliament.

He took three rackets from each player and led the way outside. Two uniformed policemen accompanied the players, and security men in plainclothes were stationed at strategic positions around Centre Court.

It was a sunny day, not much breeze, sedate, and quite beautiful. Koras had always loved walking out onto Centre Court at Wimbledon. The tennis writers called it a cathedral, and that's what it felt like to the players. On finals day, it was hushed, expectant, waiting. The Royal Box was full of royalty. The stands were so packed that there was barely room to stand. The grass was in fairly good shape, considering the pounding it had taken over the last two weeks. The blue sky reminded Koras of a final he had played here six years ago, against Gustav Romanec, the brilliant Rumanian. The match had lasted three and a half hours. Koras had won, final set, 14–12, after being driven mad by topspin lobs.

The crowd stood as they caught sight of the players, and the umpire asked for a moment of silence, in memory of Mikhail Polak, the dead Polish player.

The players kept standing as the band played "Oh, Canada," then "The Star-Spangled Banner," followed by "God Save the Queen."

Milo Tigrid and Frank Fenwick sat in the Players' Box. During the playing of the anthems, Koras could feel the seconds ticking by, and he thought back to earlier that morning, in his suite at the Gloucester, when the chambermaid had found him ironing the black warm-up suit he would wear to the matches. The maid had tried to do the work for him.

"I always do it," Koras explained, "on the day of a final."

Like most tennis players, Koras was superstitious. This particular warm-up suit was one he had worn for the first leg of the Grand Slam, at White City, in Sydney. He clung to this old ritual, pressing his vestment by using a table, a folded blanket, and his compact travel iron.

So far, the ritual of the ironing had worked.

"Gentlemen, if you please."

The applause rained down. Koras started for his end of the court, and just at that moment Laville fell back into his chair, leaving Koras to walk out alone. Koras looked back at Laville, annoyed. Laville answered with an insane smile, and Koras knew he would have trouble winning today.

Koras kept walking, making certain he did not step on any of the lines until the ball was in motion. That was another ritual.

A plainclothesman was directly in his line of sight as he turned the corner and moved a few feet behind the baseline. He took three balls from the ballboy, and stroked a forehand to begin the warm-up. In the stands, a uniformed policeman moved horizontally, along the aisle, and he found himself thinking about death as he warmed up. Armando had died. Polak had died. Who was next?

He felt stiff today, with occasional sharp twinges from his right knee, and he thought back to those early days on the circuit when he could stay up all night, drinking and dancing and singing, and then come out at ten the next morning and play brilliantly with only three minutes to get loose. These days, he needed at least fifteen minutes. The muscles in his right leg pulled tight, warning him to slow down. He slowed himself down and began counting from five down to zero, calming himself with yogic breathing.

Across the net, Laville had never looked better.

As the players warmed up on Centre Court, Matt Malone was summarizing his findings to Sir Francis and Alain Clavier. The three men sat in Sir Francis's office, above Centre Court. Malone could tell from the frowns and the stony looks that he was not getting through with his theory. He had two pages of numbers to accompany his report. When he finished, both Sir Francis and Alain Clavier stared at the wall. Sir Francis was the first to speak, and Malone figured he had just talked himself out of a job. The ax would fall in the next five minutes.

"Are you seriously asking us to believe that there is some sort of . . . conspiracy . . . on the part of the tennis establishment, as you call it, to heighten visibility in this game?" Sir Francis's voice was overcontrolled and tight. His eyes were ice cold.

"The numbers are there, Sir Francis. All I did was try to figure out who would profit from the deaths of two tennis stars."

"But, my God, man, this is incredible."

"Look." Malone focused on Sir Francis. "Players don't have that much to gain by knocking each other off. I mean, the balance at the top seesaws. Koras was a tiger in Australia, but he starts to fade in Paris, and Polak starts to come alive. Now what if Koras kills Polak?"

"He advances to the finals of Wimbledon," Clavier said.

"Yeah. But he's taking some kind of risk, just to win one tournament. He's got to plan carefully, and there's not much to gain, because another tournament's coming. He can't kill everybody off, or there won't be anyone to play."

Sir Francis nodded. "There was the year of the players' strike," he said. "The field was fairly thin."

Malone went on, building his argument. "I've spent the last five weeks interviewing, nosing around, talking to the players. They're stand-up guys, juvenile, moody, anxious, irritable. They might kill a linesperson over a bad call, but they're not going to kill each other."

"Even if you were right, how does that leave us with the larger establishment?"

"Look at page two," Malone said. "I've condensed the recent trading activity of the major equipment manufacturers. All of them—Sahara, Sport City, Laval, Magnelli, Ryker—are trading like hotcakes on the New York Exchange. Their stock prices are up across the board. In sales, I compared some figures from five years ago, when they were small. Now, with the new interest in tennis as a sport with violence attached, these companies are expected to be grossing more, and that means they can act big-time."

Malone had them looking at the figures on the second page of his report. It was now or never.

"We have three areas that gain from the violence, gentlemen. First, the equipment people. Second, gamblers, if they can control things. And third, the arenas themselves."

Sir Francis lowered the report to the table. "How dare you?"

Malone waved a hand outside. "Have you ever felt tension like you've got today?"

"We are not here to assess feelings, Mr. Malone. We are here to verify facts."

"Feelings are what it's all about, Sir Francis. Death, or the promise of it, breeds its own fear and excitement."

"I am intrigued by your assumptions about gambling," Clavier said hurriedly. "Do you have any facts to support that thesis?"

"The bookmakers here say it's the biggest year ever. And the bets increased dramatically after Polak's death on Friday."

Clavier looked at Sir Francis, who had walked to the window and was now staring out, with his back to the room. "Why should we keep you on our payroll, Mr. Malone, when you bring us reports such as this?"

"Because we'd better get to the bottom of this before the tennis writers do. Anyone can gather these numbers, and good investigative people like Judson Garwood and David Kollmore are nosing around."

Sir Francis spoke without turning. "I would love to muzzle that man Garwood."

Clavier nodded, then swung to face Malone. He was not a large man, but he raised himself up to seem larger as he spoke. "Mr. Malone, I feel that I speak for the Federation when I say your services are terminated, as of this moment. I will confer with Mr. Bell about the money still owed to you."

"Yes," Sir Francis said. "And leave your journalist's pass with my secretary."

"Okay." Malone was resigned. He'd gambled, and he'd lost. He didn't like losing his golden egg. But he had been fired before, usually when he cut too close to the bone with his view of the truth. He went out of the office without shaking hands.

* * *

Malone had just dropped off his journalist's pass with the unsmiling secretary when Superintendent Weston showed up. Today, the Superintendent wore a three-piece suit, gray, with bankerly cap-toed shoes and a flower in his buttonhole. He carried a manila envelope and his face looked tired.

"Mr. Malone. Just the man I wanted to see. Come with me."

Weston took Malone's arm and guided him back into the office, where Sir Francis still stood at the window, staring out onto the grounds of the All-England Club. Alain Clavier was at the bar, pouring himself a glass of sherry.

"I asked Mr. Malone to come in with me. I trust you gentlemen don't mind."

Neither Sir Francis nor Clavier would look at Malone. "What is it, Superintendent?"

Weston opened the envelope and produced a single sheet of paper. It was a note, addressed to the "Tennis Owners." It had been photocopied from an original made by assembling words cut out of a magazine. The note resembled the one that had arrived in Sir Francis's office just two weeks ago.

AFTER REYES, POLAK HAS PAID FOR IGNORING OUR WARNINGS, AND IF THE PLAYERS STILL REFUSE TO PLAY BY OUR RULES, A THIRD SEMIFINALIST WILL DIE IN THE NEXT GRAND SLAM EVENT. BEWARE, NEW YORK.

"Great Scott!" cried Sir Francis.

"Incredible," said Clavier.

Malone indicated the note. "Where did this come from?"

"Four London papers received the same message this morning, deposited in the box of a private distribution company which sends urgent mail, seven days a week. All four envelopes were contained within a larger one, along with three ten-pound notes for the postage."

"Are they being published?"

"Yes," Weston said. "In a matter of hours, the world will know."

"Do you have the original?"

"No. All were photocopies. No fingerprints."

"Pretty clever," Malone said.

"Let's not give them any more credit than is necessary," Sir Francis said.

The Superintendent spoke to Clavier and Sir Francis. "Has Mr. Malone explained his theory to you, gentlemen?"

"Briefly," Sir Francis said.

"I spent much of the night considering it," Weston said. "It seems to have some validity. At least, I am directing our murder investigation along those lines."

Malone smiled and decided to wait to see what the big hitters said. Sir Francis cleared his throat, preparing to speak. Clavier was faster. "It is a shock, of course, to think that someone would manipulate an entire sport in this way. But we have retained Mr. Malone for the rest of the Grand Slam season, that is, if he is willing."

"Well, Malone?" Weston arched his eyebrows. "It's your theory. May we continue to rely on your absolute discretion?"

Matt Malone grinned. He liked being in the catbird seat. "Do I get my press pass back?" he asked.

Koras lost the first set, 6–4, playing sluggishly, favoring his right knee. Laville exploited every weakness, and it was obvious from the opening point, which Laville won with a booming passing shot down the line, that the Canadian was playing his best tennis of the season, and perhaps of his career.

Laville took the second set, 6–2, and the people in the stands tried to rally Koras with solid rounds of applause. For the first time in several years, Koras was the underdog at Wimbledon.

A disputed line call distracted Laville at 3–all in the third set, and he began a protracted argument, forcing the umpire to call the tournament referee, a certain Lord Dunham, said to be related to the Royal Family, who had arrived guarded by a policeman.

Koras, who knew all of Laville's tricks, wrapped a towel around his neck and stepped to the sidelines to begin chatting about the weather with a cameraman for the BBC. Behind the cameraman sat a pretty young woman who reminded Koras of Athena, as she had looked twelve years ago.

"Hello," Koras said.

"Hello."

"Are you enjoying the matches?"

"Oh, yes. Quite. Very much."

By now, the people around Koras were craning their necks to hear the conversation. The cameraman had alerted his director in the control booth, who was focusing on Koras and the spectators. The sky was slightly overcast, but blue patches showed through the gray.

"Are you from around here?" Koras asked the girl.

"Cambridge, actually."

"Nice town, Cambridge."

The girl hesitated, then took the plunge. "Might I ask you a question, Mr. Belynkas?"

"Of course."

The camera focused on the face of Pantakoras Belynkas, veteran of almost two decades of tennis. The girl was about to ask her question. "Well," she said, her voice low, "I want to know who you think will be next?"

She wanted to know which tennis star was going to be killed. His smile widened, got tighter, as his face paled behind the blond mustache. "No one, I hope."

"How can you keep on playing, knowing it might happen?"

"It's my job. This is what I do."

"I think you are very brave, Mr. Belynkas."

"Thanks." His voice cracked.

"Good luck out there." Her words carried a terrible double meaning.

In the control booth, an assistant director flipped a switch that sent Koras's conversation with the girl flashing across the world —a legendary tennis star, a pretty young girl, talking about death in the arena.

"Are you getting this?" the director whispered.

"Every word."

Sweating with the effort, the umpire brought the match back under control by announcing he had awarded the point to Mr. Belynkas. The crowd applauded. Terry Laville made an obscene gesture and walked back to serve. For the first time in the final, Laville was momentarily off his game.

Koras won the third set on a tense tiebreaker that went to 12–10. His knee was bothering him, so he asked the referee for a time-out. In tennis, that meant three minutes.

"What's going on?" Laville wanted to know. He stood like a white-maned colossus, legs spread, chin upthrust, to accent his question.

"Mr. Belynkas is entitled to three minutes."

"Jesus Christ!" Terry cried.

The official tournament trainer came out to examine Koras's knee. There was talk of a knee brace, and Laville could taste victory. Koras looked tired out, worn down. Taking advantage of the break, Laville jogged over to chat with some people in a private box at courtside. When Koras resumed, it was with an elastic knee brace. The veteran was coming apart.

The fourth set was the best set of the tournament. Koras won the first game, Laville won the second. They fought their way to 6–all, and Koras won another extended tiebreak, 11–9.

In the fifth set, Laville made a special effort to end the see-sawing struggle, and he took the first four games to lead his opponent 4–0. It was clear the knee was bothering Koras. Twice he fell, accompanied by groans from the stands. When he got back to his feet, he limped slightly.

Laville kept playing the ball to Koras's forehand. With the bad right knee, Koras could not put much power behind his shot. He lobbed to Laville's backhand. As they passed each other at the changeover, Laville taunted Koras. "Play like a man, why don't you?"

Koras pulled even with Laville with three brilliant service returns and a wicked topspin lob. At 4–all, Laville started his last argument of the Wimbledon fortnight. The chair umpire listened patiently, but it was clear that Laville was merely stalling. At last, the umpire ruled that the point be replayed, which did not pacify Laville. He won that point, but his concentration had been shattered. Twelve minutes later, Pantakoras Belynkas won the men's final at Wimbledon. It was the third tournament for Koras, out of the four needed for a Grand Slam.

Terry Laville's handshake across the net was a sham. His mouth was tight and he glared at Koras with hate in his eye.

As the reigning champion held the trophy high to make a slow symbolic turn around the packed stadium, the fans rose to their feet to shout themselves hoarse with praise. Many of them were crying.

Laville stayed on the court long enough to shake hands with the Duke of Kent. The Duke wore a club blazer and gray flannel slacks.

"Good show out there, Mr. Laville. You played well."

"I'll play better, next year," Laville growled. "And I'm going to win in New York."

The Duke smiled his official smile. "I'm sure you will."

Shaking hands with the Duke, Koras felt only the ragged edge of fatigue.

"Congratulations, Mr. Belynkas. You always do us proud here at Centre Court."

"Thank you, Your Grace."

Koras had met the Duke before, when he and Athena had been invited to a small supper party at Kensington Palace. There was more chitchat, about the circuit schedule, before the Duke wished Koras luck in his quest for the Grand Slam and then left the court, surrounded by his security people.

Laville stalked toward the dressing rooms three steps ahead of Koras. Suddenly, when he was a few feet from the door, he stumbled, sank to one knee. An official asked what was wrong.

"I've got a bad pain," he said. "Right here." He pointed to a spot on his left leg, high on the thigh, near the crotch.

"Can you walk?"

"I'll try."

Koras came out of the baths to find a doctor with a short beard closing his black medical bag. Terry Laville was spread out in a leather chair against the wall, his left leg propped up on a folded towel on one of the benches.

"I can't find a thing, Mr. Laville."

"Then why does it hurt?" Terry growled.

"It could be psychosomatic, part of the pressures of playing under stress. If you'd like to come to my offices tomorrow, I'm certain we can do a proper job." The doctor did not sound sympathetic.

Terry waved him away. "I'll be there."

The doctor handed Laville his card and walked out. Laville sat up, with a look of faked pain on his face. Koras opened his locker and began to dress. He knew Laville was up to his old tricks. If the Canadian could talk to some reporters about his alleged injury, it would dampen the victory Koras had just won.

"You played well, Terry."

"Up yours, Koras. I was beat from playing Davey."

"You didn't seem tired to me."

"How would you know?" Laville pointed at his leg. "I pulled a muscle out there, at 3–4, in the fifth. They'll have it on tape."

"Hope it gets better."

"You don't believe me, do you? You're not the only guy with injuries." Laville stood up, moved over to stand close to Koras. His face, huge and hate-filled, was inches away. "You think this is your year for the Slam, don't you?"

Koras didn't answer. There was no percentage in talking to a crazy man. He finished dressing. Laville went back to his chair, sat down heavily, his left leg out in front of him.

Koras turned to him as he prepared to leave. "See you in New York."

Without moving from his chair, Terry gave Koras the Italian fuck-you sign, a clenched right fist, the left hand tight against his bicep.

"I'll see you in hell, Koras."

PART III

FLUSHING MEADOW

In the Arena

SIXTEEN

The barrel of the pistol, a shiny, chrome-plated .357 Magnum, was less than six inches away from the head resting on the pale-yellow cushion of the chaise longue. Koras lay on his stomach, arms by his sides. He was daydreaming, thinking about Laure in Paris, when he had told her about the money. The vision of Laure went away, the sky darkening and Koras sensing danger. He forced himself not to move. There was the clear, metallic click of the hammer being pulled back. Koras turned over. He wanted to see who was going to kill him. Blinded by the glare of the sun, he saw only the huge black hole of the barrel, distorted by his perspective, then the hand holding the weapon, and beyond that a thick, hairy forearm with black hair. Koras squinted. Beyond the arm, he made out the features of Milo Tigrid, the Mad Montenegrin, grinning profusely at the sight of Koras, petrified.

"Are you insane?" Koras cried.

"Only a scenario, my friend." Milo waved the gun.

"A scenario?" Koras felt sick to his stomach.

"Yes. I only wanted to prove to the world how easy it would be to kill the great Koras, here, beside the pool at glorious Court's Court."

Koras was sweating now and feeling white shocks of relief. "The gun is real, isn't it?"

"Yes. But there are no bullets." The Yugoslav removed six bullets from his pocket and showed them to Koras. He counted them off. "One, two, three . . . six bullets, six famous tennis players, all gone, eliminated from the ATP computer."

"Milo, you're crazy!"

"Touché, my friend." He slid the weapon under his belt.

Koras did some deep breathing and tried to stay calm. The two men sat beside the swimming pool at Koras's house in Westhampton, on the South Shore of Long Island. Koras had bought the house three years before, because Frank Fenwick had explained they needed a tax shelter. It was a three-story home, built in the New England style, with Cape Cod ornamention, a central cupola, and eight dormers across the front. Koras had modified the house, putting in a swimming pool outdoors, and another swimming pool indoors, on the ground floor. There were ten bedrooms, a modern kitchen, and a dining room that could easily seat forty guests. The indoor pool was linked to the outdoor pool by a canal. From above, the pool system resembled a giant tennis racket, with the racket head constituting the main basin of the pool.

There were seven acres of land around the house. The oversize lot sloped off as it neared the seacoast, and halfway to the beach Koras had built a helicopter landing pad. A hundred yards to the east, forming a triangle with the house and the heli-pad, Koras had built two courts, one above the other. The upper court was where he worked out during the summer. The lower court, with a fifty-five-foot ceiling, was enclosed and heated for the winter months.

"Do you carry it all the time?"

"Since Wimbledon." Milo plucked the gun out of his belt, aimed it at an imaginary intruder. "If a murderer enters Tigrid's room, let him beware. Boom. Boom."

"What do you do on the court?"

"It is in my tennis bag."

"What about airports?"

"In my checked luggage, and packed in foil, like a camera."

"Why don't you find one of those gunsmiths who work for the Mafia and pay him five thousand dollars to build you a two-shot derringer hidden away in the butt of your racket."

Milo beamed. "An excellent idea. Then, when one's opponent got the upper hand, one could aim the butt of the racket at the opponent and strum the strings, and suddenly—no more problem."

"It's time you retired, Milo. The pace of the circuit is getting to you."

"I shall save the last bullet for myself."

"What do you think of this threat? About the semifinals?"

Milo sighed. "What does an old dog like me care? I haven't reached the semis here in this godforsaken capitalist place since 1976. Remember? I played Armando in the quarters. I bested him."

"That was at Forest Hills, right?"

"What a lovely place. Why did they do away with it?"

"We needed a showplace. The House That Slew Built. Remember?"

"Speak for yourself, my friend. You are a transplanted comrade. I, Tigrid, am not an American. All is not well here, in this land controlled by Mafia dons and Republicans."

"You always get grumpy in New York, old friend."

"I need a woman."

Jack Di Rocca lingered in London for ten days after Wimbledon was over. Saadi was out of town—Zurich, Rome, Damascus—making headlines in the financial papers with big-money deals like his recent takeover of Sport City by the Sahara Corporation, and the Princess Athena had decided to stay in London to irk Saadi and to catch up on some shopping. Di Rocca had her escape plans taking shape. She had been thinking small. Now, with Di Rocca's support, she was planning to escape Saadi's clutches with an annuity of one million dollars a year, perhaps more.

The secret was in the timing. Athena was impulsive. When she felt something, she acted at once. Di Rocca had persuaded her to wait until New York and the U.S. Open. They had three instruments—the pills, the magazine, and the roll of film Di Rocca had picked up in Polak's room.

The Princess didn't know about the roll of film.

She was beautiful, inventive, seductive, and Di Rocca was surprised that he and Athena had become intimate. Everywhere she went, men ogled her, and it was clear that her sexual attraction gave her power and control. But she seemed to enjoy her afternoons with Di Rocca—three of them so far, plus one languorous night—and as they explored their mounting passion he discovered he was jealous of Armando Reyes.

She talked about Saadi but so far she hadn't said much about Armando. Di Rocca took her reticence as a keep-out sign. He didn't push her for information. But sometimes, his body locked onto hers, Di Rocca had the feeling Armando had joined them in bed.

When he saw her spend money, Di Rocca was glad Saadi was paying the bills. Five hundred pounds for shoes, ten thousand for a designer frock, rising to thirty for a Russian sable. Di Rocca had grown up poor in South Brooklyn. Even though he had money now, he hadn't forgotten what it felt like, being poor. It made you want to steal, to hurt somebody, sometimes even kill.

But the Princess was his first experience with the flamboyant decadence of European royalty. And she was a lot of woman, passionate, hot, healthy, with the smoothest skin he had ever touched and the ability to drink through the night, make furious love, and appear, bright as a summer morning, in her private box at the stadium the next day. She had a good mind. She could remember authors, lines of poetry, character actors from stage and screen, scores from tennis matches ten years ago. She introduced him to writers and movie people who knew his name from tennis. With Athena, Di Rocca discovered a new world.

Her favorite movie was *Belle de Jour*. His was *Last Year at Marienbad*, a black-and-white film from the sixties. Lying in bed, sipping champagne, sated, Di Rocca would let the screen roll across his mind.

There was this actor in the Marienbad film who had a face like Saadi, long, sad, with long fingers and a deliberate walk and cold eyes that nailed you to the wall. His name was M, and he was married to A, who was being courted by X, a youngish, almost handsome actor in an everyday European suit. X was an everyday guy. In the movie, M kept holding up a pistol and shooting at X, who was about to kiss A in another frame, lips close to her white neck. M knew X was after his wife. In the carpeted card room, the rivals played a game with matches. M always won, then slipped off to a shooting gallery, where he practiced with his dueling pistol, shooting at targets that were transformed on the screen into his wife and her lover.

The wife, A, was a pretty brunette who wore a dress made of white feathers. When the feathers flew, disturbed by M's gunfire, the Princess laughed, mostly from remembered shock, and her hands got cold. She had a kinky sense of humor.

Yves St. Laurent, the famous designer, had a dress of white feathers, slit up the back of the skirt, cut low, with a daring décolletage. On the day before Di Rocca left for New York for a meeting with Sally Vicenti, the Princess bought it in a fashionable shop for a thousand pounds, charging it to Saadi. "It might be my last," she laughed, swirling before the mirror. There were tears in her eyes.

The next day, Di Rocca flew to the States, while Athena took a plane to Austria to visit her mother. After Austria, she would spend a weekend on Saadi's yacht, in Juan-les-Pins, and she would be in New York the week before the U.S. Open. Saadi planned a party to launch Sahara's latest gambit. It would be Athena's last hostess act and she meant to depart on a note of gaiety and triumph.

Crossing over, Di Rocca's westward flight had very little headwind, which made it a six-and-a-half-hour trip. As soon as he got his baggage, he put in a call from Kennedy Airport to Sally Vicenti to set up a meeting. Di Rocca was an honorary member of the West Side Club, in Forest Hills. Sally, who owned stock in the fancy new Racquet Club of Oyster Bay, was hungry to be a member at the older club. Sally was a sucker for tradition, and Di Rocca knew he could soften him up with lunch in Forest Hills.

He and Di Rocca had made money betting on tennis. There was more in the near future. "I got this terrific plan, Jackie."

"It will be good to see you, Mr. Vicenti."

"Hey. Call me Sally, okay? See you tomorrow."

Di Rocca said thanks and hung up, his mind on the Princess. For the first time since he was sixteen and had a bad crush on Gloria Castelmonte, Di Rocca was hooked. Being hooked made you vulnerable. He needed leverage, an angle, something for his own protection. What kind of leverage would work on Salvatore Vicenti?

Sally Vicenti, the son of immigrants, was a good father, a standard husband, a jolly friend of the world who was nice to kids and dogs and widows, and a man who dearly loved to eat.

Eating made Sally feel joyously alive—rigatoni, lasagna, spaghetti with meatballs, veal Parmigiana. His mother, born Angelina Cavalcanti in the old country, was a terrific cook, and Sally always compared the commercial fare he found in the restaurants or in the houses of friends to the food he remembered, steaming, smelling like Italian Heaven, on his mother's table.

Unlike the ads on television, where actors ate Italian from a pink-and-white-checkerboard covering made of throw-away paper, his family ate off a white tablecloth, changed fresh after the meal.

Sally developed heart trouble early, at the age of thirty-four. He was walking down Broadway in the spring, a week before Easter, thinking of money and Doris Schuler, his current mistress, and here came the pains.

He tried to ignore them, but then he saw his brother's grave, which he took as a sign. Joey had died young, so at thirty-four Sally checked into the hospital for open-heart surgery. He was on the table twice, four hours a session. The scar was long and reddish-pink and ugly, and it took him six months to recuperate. Sally liked action. Wasting time depressed him. Lying in bed, hobbling around, he felt weak, not like a man. The doctors told him he'd have to cut back on his food, stop working so hard, get some exercise.

Stop eating, Mr. Vicenti, they said. You're killing yourself. He tried diets, raw vegetables, no wine, but he got more depressed.

The only answer was exercise.

When his strength returned, Sally looked around for a sport, something to keep his mind off food. His father, Nicola, had played a mean game of checkers. A cousin over in Jersey played an Italian version of that French game, Boule. But Sally liked killing, the comforting sound of gunfire, so he took up hunting, spent some scary times in the woods in Pennsylvania. Because of his weight, he had trouble climbing the hills. When an amateur crazy from the city let a gun go off in Sally's hunting area, barely missing him and splattering bark and yellow leaves all over, he gave up the woods.

He tried shooting at targets on the police range, two hands on the pistol grip, wearing earplugs for the noise, but target shooting bored him, so a friend in the business got him to take up golf. Sally spent two grand on equipment, four grand joining a club in Westchester, five grand on lessons from Ben Bolt, a smooth-stroking pro who'd spent his life playing on the golf circuit.

The only good thing about golf was getting away from home. A side benefit was the scenery—bottoms and brown thighs and young tits under tight sweaters.

When he was forty-two, Sally Vicenti discovered tennis. His daughter, Elena, a junior at Bryn Mawr, brought home her roommate, Julie Edwards. Julie was from California, blonde, outdoorsy, with clear blue eyes and terrific legs.

Julie Edwards had energy to burn. At school, Sally learned, she worked out every day, running laps in the snow, ice skating, doing push-ups, sit-ups. Her ambition was to play tennis on the women's circuit. Julie Edwards was a terrific model for Elena, who was already getting beefy, like her dad.

Because of all that tight muscle, so efficient, so nice to watch, Julie's body impressed Sally enough to watch a workout on the courts. Sally had a friend who had a cousin who had a membership at an indoor tennis club, the Tilden Club, right in midtown Manhattan. Outside, it was snowing, the first real weather of the season, making the streets slick. While Julie played with the local pro, Sally and Elena watched.

Sally found himself licking his lips as he fell in love with Julie's body. "How does she stay in that kind of shape?" he asked.

"She works out, Daddy. All the time. Isn't she beautiful?"

"Yeah. But so are you."

She hugged him. "Oh, Daddy."

Sally took his first tennis lesson at the Tilden Club from Julie Edwards, who was a superb teacher. She moved him around, huffing. She stopped when he thought he would die. Sweat streamed off Sally. During the break, Julie told him he had a natural swing on the forehand and a lovely hammer motion on the volley, and all the time he was scheming how to get into her pants without letting his daughter know.

He insisted on paying her for her time. When he handed her two twenties, her eyes lit up and she gave him a quick kiss on the cheek. There was no time to make a move. Julie went back to Bryn Mawr before Sally could execute a safe plan.

He dreamed about her at night, sweaty nightmares, with him

racing across the tennis court, huffing, dying for her, his wife asleep and suspicious in a bed that floated next to his in the dream. Julie would hold out her arms, come hither, Daddy, with Sally tripping, falling, the floor opening up, a sledgehammer crashing down on his heart, making him wake up, pajamas soaked with perspiration, his wife sitting up in her bed, dialing the doctor, her face on red alert.

Money was no object, so Sally found another tennis pro. He took lessons indoors all winter and dropped thirty-five pounds, then fifteen more. Exercise, imagine that, lifted his depression. He could eat more and still maintain the weight. What a deal.

At spring break, Sally played against Julie Edwards, his dreams coming true, a beautiful blonde across the net, the flight of the ball, young legs in short shorts, making his mouth dry. While Sally worked on the court, his daughter, Elena, sat up in the stands, unknowing, innocent, applauding for both players.

After the match, which Sally lost, 1–6, 2–6, he shook hands with Julie, who was amazed at his progress.

"Wow. Have you improved, Mr. Vicenti!" Her hand across the net was soft, warm, sexy.

"Meet me for a drink some time."

The cool blue eyes told him she understood, but she played it nonchalantly. "What?" As if she hadn't quite heard.

"You and me," he said. "Midweek. Anyplace. I'll come to you."

His daughter was walking over. Not much time.

A cunning look came into Julie's blue eyes. "All right, Mr. Vicenti. But just for a drink."

Sally smiled. He liked it, her calling him Mr. Vicenti. It showed respect.

So in May they met for a drink at a roadhouse in Upper Darby, Pennsylvania, well southeast of Bryn Mawr, far enough away that Elena wouldn't find out. Julie wore black, a diamond bracelet, a gold wedding band for the occasion, and knee boots for the Pennsylvania rain. He had the feeling this wasn't her first time, and that made him jealous. They had one drink in the bar, talking about tennis, the end of school, the summer circuit. They had a second drink in the room, water slicking the windows, sex brimming out around their words.

She talked about her expenses, how much it cost going to school, playing the West Coast Circuit. She wanted to hit the European circuit, summer on the clay courts, Cannes, Milano, Switzerland, but she couldn't begin to afford it.

Sally got the message, took out his billfold, and laid two hundred dollars on the table. "For your trip."

She left it there, her eyelids fluttering like butterflies. He laid another hundred on the table. She folded the bills into her wallet, put the wallet into her schoolgirl's shoulder bag, and slowly began to undress. She said okay when he asked her to wear the knee boots in bed. After a beautiful workout, Sally came through, heart banging, without cardiac arrest.

They met three other times before she took off for Europe. He paid her three hundred a visit, gave her a travel bonus for the trip. "Watch the European pretty boys," he said. "And come back soon."

Sally tried getting into the West Side Tennis Club, at Forest Hills. It had tradition, stretching all the way to the early twenties, and Sally wanted a club with class. But he had to settle for something less, and that summer, Sally bought his way into the Racquet Club of Oyster Bay, on Long Island's North Shore. He also had a membership in a club in Westchester, to please his wife, who saw herself as Lady Astor and liked to kill time mingling with the la-di-da society upper crust.

Becoming a member at the Racquet Club of Oyster Bay cost Sally $35,000, what with fees and considerations. He bought $50,000 of their stock, so he would have some respect. The head tennis pro, Johnny Florian, was an Italian-American from Chicago, whose biggest win had been the Italian doubles at the Foro Italico. From the pro, Sally learned first-hand how the sport had changed with Open Tennis. Johnny would tell Sally about the bets in the old days, circuit hot dogs playing for ten dollars a set, money under the table.

Johnny set Sally up in a doubles eightsome, four matched teams who met three times a week. Sally met stockbrokers, an entertainment attorney, a computer marketeer, a Broadway producer, a gambler who frequented Aqueduct. Sally had developed a wicked American twist serve that bounced high to the backhand. And he loved to kill the ball, put it away.

In midsummer of his second year at Oyster Bay, the stockbroker came to Sally for money. That fall, the Broadway producer made his move. By Christmas, Sally had loaned money to five of his seven tennis pals, and he and his wife were meeting a new class of people.

These were bluenoses with money troubles. Sally's business was mostly cash. He suggested a football pool, and they made 22 percent on their money. He suggested a basketball pool, and they made 20 percent. That spring, Sally began thinking of a tennis pool.

There was big money coming into tennis, and the scenario reminded him of baseball back in the twenties, when a friend of his grandfather's had fixed the World Series. Sally, who liked conquering virgin territory, wondered what it would be like to make a little pin money betting on some of these big tournaments.

To Sally, the marketplace was like a duck pond. The ducks were the suckers. The businessmen were the hunters. If you got to the pond early, or if you found yourself a new pond at the beginning of a new season, you could do some fancy shooting and leave with a full game bag, before the competition wandered out of the woods.

Tennis was a fresh new pond, swimming with suckers.

One day, watching TV, he saw a name he decided to follow up on. Jack Di Rocca was an Italian-American player from the New York area who'd done some time with one of Sally's soldiers. They were televising an indoor match from Dallas. The announcer was saying how Di Rocca had emerged from nowhere. Sally made some calls. Di Rocca was a survivor, had a clean record since getting out of jail, and seemed to do pretty well for himself playing the horses. Di Rocca had been in the Top Ten for three years.

For their lunch in Forest Hills, Sally wore a Palm Beach suit, cream-colored, with heavy-soled wingtips. His face and hands were dark, from three hours a day on the courts. He was happy about the money he'd made betting on tennis at Roland-Garros and Wimbledon. The U.S. Open was a week off and more money was filling the pot.

The trick now was to lock in a winner with long odds.

They had just shaken hands and were being seated when Drury and Margaret Matthews, the twins, walked by, their pleated tennis dresses curling around their tanned thighs.

"Nice scenery."

Di Rocca opened the menu. "Nice place."

Sally grinned, leaned close. "I tried getting in here. They got a waiting list."

"I could speak to the chairman, Mal Whitwood."

Sally nodded. "I'd consider it a favor. I like it out at the Oyster Bay facility, but it's nothing like this. I'm someone who appreciates tradition."

"Consider it done."

Di Rocca ordered a roast beef sandwich, rare. Sally ordered salmon, broiled. They decided together on a Valpolicella, 1979. When the waiter had gone, Di Rocca turned to Sally.

"Are we going ahead on schedule at the Open?" Di Rocca asked.

"Those threats in the paper. Whoever sent them didn't have such a bad idea. Guys on the street who never heard of tennis are following Koras and Laville like they played ball for the Knicks."

"I heard Koras was still two to one."

"Panties Koras," Sally said, and sipped his wine. "We need to talk to him."

"I'll set something up."

"Don't let him know I'll be there. A lunch, say, between the two of you."

"Where?"

Sally looked around. "I like it here. This is a good place."

Di Rocca grinned. The waiter arrived with their food. Both men were hungry, so for a few moments they were silent as they ate.

"The pool's up past four million," Sally said, "and growing. We need to bet it before opening day."

"What about this kid Heinz? He's hot enough."

"Nineteen to one. I like those odds. But I was thinking of another winner."

"Who?"

Sally chewed thoughtfully, making Di Rocca wait. "Jackie, how'd you like to be the next U.S. Open champ?"

Di Rocca started to laugh, but the look on Sally's face stopped him. "You serious?"

Sally nodded. "Seven to one. We could pick up a bundle."

"I play Koras in the semis. If I get that far."

"That's where he loses."

"He's going to love hearing that."

"He's in hock to the construction people. I bought some of his paper. About a quarter of a million. He gets indecisive, I'll buy some more."

Di Rocca refilled the wine glasses, then held up his hand to signal the waiter for another bottle.

"Where'd you stash the cash you were going to give Reyes?"

"In the Zurich bank. Fifty grand from Paris. Polak's hundred grand from London."

Sally dug into his coat pocket, came out with an envelope, which he shoved across the table to Di Rocca. "Hundred more in there. The money in Zurich, keep it."

Di Rocca had earned it, with sweat. "Thanks, Sally."

"Nothing too good for the next champ of the U.S. Open." Sally toasted Di Rocca. If he could afford to pay Di Rocca $250,000, Sally's take had to be ten times that. Maybe more. Di Rocca could sense control shifting to his paisano here. The price of his win would be steep and he didn't want to be locked in with Sally Vicenti the rest of his life. Di Rocca started to think about ways to protect himself.

"What about Laville?"

"Something will turn up."

Di Rocca reached into his pocket, pulled three photos out of an envelope. He handed them to Sally. "Maybe it already has." He owed Laville, for that time in Houston. Time to collect.

Sally looked at the photos, which showed Micky Polak without any clothes on in a bedroom scene with a very pretty girl. "Who's the doll?"

"Shirley Nash-Winters. She was with Laville in Paris, again in London. The guy is Polak. My guess is Laville took the pictures."

Sally's smile widened. "Where'd you get them?"

"Out of Laville's tennis bag, the day Polak was murdered."

"Laville would blackmail Polak?"

"With Laville, anything is possible."

"Can we tie them to Laville?"

"I got some blowups. There's a wristwatch and a headband on the bedside table."

Sally banged the table. "The important thing, Laville will know we know."

"Yes."

Sally handed back the photos. "Nice work, Jackie. You got talent."

"I'll try to set something up with Koras for the end of the week."

"Surprise him if you can. How do you think the player vote will go?"

"You heard about that?"

Sally gestured with one pudgy hand. "The mayor. The cops. The tennis bigwigs. I got people inside City Hall."

Sally's smile, coupled with the hard-eyed look, cinched Di Rocca's need for protection. "I think they'll vote to play."

"God, I love a democracy."

"You don't miss much, do you, Sally?"

Sally tapped his chest, above his heart. "When this almost went, I made a decision. Sally, I said to myself, don't rush around so much. Sit back. Check things out. Since I made that decision, I got rich. It's the key, Jackie."

SEVENTEEN

It was midafternoon. Out of the windows of the Mayor's office, Deputy Mayor John McKenzie could distinguish the high towers of the Brooklyn Bridge emerging through a haze of heat and smog. McKenzie, sweating with the task delegated to him by the Mayor, had just turned away from the window. "Gentlemen, let's get to the point. Will there be a Flushing Meadow or not?"

Ten worried men sat around the black conference table. The War Council from Fouquet's was growing.

Ross O'Brien, the Chief of Detectives of the New York Police Department, sat on McKenzie's right. He was an enormous man, solid, as though carved from a timeless block of granite out of the Irish past.

Next to O'Brien was Harrison Cabot, President of the U.S. Tennis Association. Frank Fenwick, his pockets bulging with paper, sat on Cabot's right. Fenwick shuffled two manila folders in front of him, then turned to his right to observe Archer Bell, who smiled as if he were cooking up a plan to save the world and make a profit doing it.

Peter Abraham sat at the end of the table, opposite the deputy mayor. Abraham, the President of the Association of Tennis Professionals, was the only player at the table. Paco Ortega, Di Rocca's manager, sat on Abraham's right, in the corner seat across from Archer Bell. Ortega had recently picked up three players from South America, eager young men who grinned into the camera, hit big topspin loopers, and partied a lot.

On Ortega's right, going back up the table, sat Alain Clavier, President of the International Tennis Federation. Beside Clavier was Abdul Saadi, President and CEO of Sahara Sports, which had just made a successful corporate takeover of a former competitor, Sport City. Saadi was at the meeting because he represented the Middle Eastern players. Next to Saadi was Sir Francis Malcolm.

The only man without a coat and tie was Peter Abraham.

For more than an hour, the deputy mayor and the others had listened to President Clavier's summary of the problems they were having in professional tennis.

Clavier looked down at his notes. The meeting was the second one in twenty-four hours, and no solution was in sight. In less than a week the tournament was scheduled to begin. Ticket sales had already outstripped last year's, and there was little doubt that it was because of the death threat published in the London papers. The entire circuit was steeped in a climate of tension, which grew worse each day.

After Wimbledon, the players had dispersed to less important tournaments, hoping a win would bolster their confidence for the upcoming struggle in New York's major arena. The immediacy and horror of Polak's death had come to the surface again here in New York, with the newspapers reprinting the grisly pictures of his body slammed up against the tub, and below the photos a facsimile of the note that had turned up on Finals Day in London. The *New York Post* headline blared out: WHO'S NEXT?

Now there was talk of letting the players vote on whether or not to hold the U.S. Open. As a player, Peter Abraham wanted the chance to vote. The other men in the room felt the situation was getting out of hand. Archer Bell had already mentioned analogies with big business and labor. "It's like letting the United Steelworkers call the shots at U.S. Steel," Bell said.

"Bad comparison, Arch," Frank Fenwick said. "This is entertainment and that's the Rust Belt."

"It's a power struggle, F.F. You'll see it when your balance sheet comes in for the season."

Fenwick pointed to his head. "I carry my balance sheet here, Arch. Right here. So it's handy."

"Gentlemen, please," said President Clavier. "We have two issues before us. There is the matter of the player vote, which seems to be the only solution. Second is the matter of player security, and here we need the help of the city."

Sir Francis broke in. "The last player vote was to boycott Wimbledon in the seventies. I hesitate to raise ghosts, but there it is."

"We don't want a goddamn boycott," Archer Bell said. "What is this, the United Farm Workers?"

"Let's say we vote to play," Abraham said. "What about security?"

"That," Clavier said, "is in the hands of the City of New York."

The deputy mayor smiled. "We'll do our best. But you've got 128 men and 64 women to watch over. If we start at the—what's it called right before the quarters?"

"The Round of Sixteen."

"Yes. If we start there, and try to cover the sixteen on both the men's and the women's, we might have some success."

Peter Abraham broke in. "We need a player referendum. It's easy enough to sit up here in air-conditioned safety and talk, but the players have to go out there on the court and face the possibility of getting killed."

Archer Bell turned to Abraham. "Polak was killed in his hotel room, remember?"

Abraham flared up. "If we walk out, Arch, there won't be a tournament. Remember Wimbledon, the year the pros struck? You people barely *had* a tournament."

"Mr. Abraham is talking about canceling the tournament?" the deputy mayor asked.

"Absolutely."

"You're crazy, Pete," Archer Bell said.

"A lot of people would lose a lot of money, Pete," Frank Fenwick said.

"Better to lose some money than to have one more player killed."

The deputy mayor walked back to the window. When the time came for him to make a crucial decision, he had to be standing. It was an old habit, one that hung on from his days as a trial lawyer. New York had protected the Pope, the Shah, even Yasir Arafat. If he allowed the U.S. Open to be aborted because of a lack of confidence in his police force, he could kiss the tournament goodbye, permanently, along with his job. McKenzie looked out at the teeming city without speaking, then returned to his chair. He turned to Harrison Cabot, the President of the USTA. "Will your people cooperate with our security measures?"

"We'll do our best, certainly."

The deputy mayor turned to his Chief of Detectives. "Can you do it, Ross?"

"It won't be perfect," O'Brien said. "Let me bring in my chief security officer. He can brief us." O'Brien walked to the door and opened it.

"We're ready, Lieutenant."

Lieutenant John Lucchesi was five foot ten, slightly built, with expensive taste in clothes and the trim look of a long-distance runner. His chief saw him as a man for the long haul. Although Lucchesi had not been home during the last forty-eight hours, his face, shadowy from long hours fighting crime, was freshly shaved. In fact, Lucchesi spent a lot of twenty-hour-days on the job, not sleeping, catching catnaps on a cot at one of his precinct houses. His eyes could have made him a musician, or a college professor. But when he spoke, showing the little glint of a smile that marked the professional policeman, Lucchesi was all business.

"Gentlemen, I can make this brief. We've talked to our counterparts in London and Paris. We've checked with Interpol, Treasury, the FBI. No one has a line on the killer—or killers. There are theories around, mostly terrorist talk. The IRA could be in it, but they don't operate in this sphere unless they get locked out of England. We've got a full task force working around the clock, even though no crime has been committed here. Anyone who has any information should get it to us. I'm leaving business cards on the table, and I'm planning to sleep at the National Tennis Center until after the finals. My people are setting up a command post now, in an RV near the entrance gate. If you know something, or even think you know something, give me a call."

"The Lieutenant will take questions," the Chief said.

Archer Bell spoke up. "There's talk of a player vote, Lieutenant. If that goes through, and our players vote to have this tournament, how quickly could your people set up security?"

"Are we talking individual security here?"

"Yes." It was clear Bell was thinking of his players, Davey Cooper and Terry Laville.

"So far, what we have worked out is to cover the top twenty-five men and the top twenty-five women. As we get closer to the semifinals, we'll blanket the players still left in the tournament."

"Oh, terrific," Peter Abraham said. "If a player doesn't get killed, *then* he gets protection."

"We're looking for ideas, doing everything we can. The people at the Tennis Center are being asked to beef up their security."

"Metal detectors?"

"If we have to. There are so many ways to fool them, they're not considered effective."

While Lucchesi answered questions, Fenwick leaned back in his chair and thought about the way things were going. Saadi had just bought up Sport City, adding it to his Sahara Corporation, and there was talk he was considering Laval Sportif for his next takeover. Laval held Koras's endorsement, and Fenwick knew Saadi would make things rough on Koras. Now there was a rumor going around that Saadi was about to sign Terry Laville, to replace the dead Micky Polak. On that, Arch Bell wasn't talking. The news would be leaked tomorrow tonight, at a party Saadi was giving at his new casino in Atlantic City. Koras wasn't invited, but everyone else in tennis who counted would be there.

The Lieutenant finished up and left the room. Fenwick walked out with Harrison Cabot, who was on his way to an interview with the garrulous journalist Judson Garwood.

"Garwood smells something," Fenwick said.

"Don't worry. I can handle him."

"What do you think of the overall situation, Harry?"

"Ticket sales are astronomical. Profits will double from last year. One is tempted to go on the black market."

"You don't have the temperament for a scalper, Harry."

"Yes. Quite right."

Cabot's black limousine slid to a stop at the curb. The door opened and Cabot got in. The day was typical of New York in the late summer, hot and humid and getting more so. Fenwick stood on the curb, watching the limo pull away, into New York traffic. Fenwick hoped Cabot could handle Garwood.

"The history of the largest and richest tennis tournament in the world is a recent one," wrote Judson Garwood in the *New York Daily News*. "Flushing Meadow began in 1977, after a disagreement between the USTA and the directors of the West Side Tennis Club, at Forest Hills. Since 1924, the U.S. national championships had been played at the West Side Club. But the tournament grew beyond the bounds of the club, and a new site had to be looked for.

"They called it 'the House That Slew Built.'

"Slew Hester, a businessman from Jackson, Mississippi, was the first USTA president to come from the Deep South. During the Second World War, Hester worked with the U.S. Army to develop a transportation system for France. Since then, he has served in several large firms at the corporate level, gaining the experience in leadership which would aid him in developing the new stadium at Flushing Meadow Park. Hester, an inveterate entrepreneur, left the corporate world to become an independent oil producer.

"The legend of the Tennis Center goes this way: Hester was flying in from Dallas to La Guardia when he spotted the site from the air. It was the Singer Bowl, site of the 1964–65 World's Fair, which had been renamed the Louis Armstrong Stadium in 1973. The new site had sixteen acres, and the plan was to save the original structure and to build on or around it, with a huge Stadium Court as the center, a Grandstand Court off to the side, emulating Wimbledon, and the two connected by a walkway, to accommodate spectators wishing to see what was going on next door. The National Tennis Center, as it was to be called, would have twenty-seven outdoor courts and nine indoor courts, all air-conditioned.

"It was a glorious dream—a symbolic site for the greatness of American tennis—but the obstacles were immense. To begin with, the plans had to be approved by nine municipal agencies. Then the winter before the opening was long, causing many work slowdowns. And as the warmer months came, and everyone looked forward to completion, the contracts the builders had with various unions ran out—this was in June—and seven different unions went out on strike. Things were brought under control by Hester and his Number One, Hy Zausner, who had founded the Port Washington Tennis Academy.

"It took just under a year to build, and Flushing Meadow became the most extravangant tennis tournament ever seen. The new national tennis arena is situated on the axis of the main landing strip at La Guardia. Planes taking off pass over the stadium every two minutes, making the players feel they are in the crater of a volcano always on the verge of erupting. The compact crowds sit in moist and heavy heat while the huge structure actually shakes. 'It is,' remarked three-time champion

Pantakoras Belynkas, 'the only tournament where one cannot hear the balls rebound, where the roar of the crowd is outdone by the roar of angry jets.'

"Players and spectators alike adapted themselves to Flushing Meadow, and it became the hardest, the most testing, the most ferocious tournament on the Grand Slam circuit. Here, defeat is most bitter, success the most triumphant. Part of it is shock. After the refined rustlings of Wimbledon, the players are plunged despite themselves into a game of killers, taking place in a climate of noise and furor, of heat and pungent odors, of thunderous tantrums and sudden despair. Here, Jack Di Rocca, a product of the Bronx streets, rediscovers the rough rules of his adolescence. In the U.S. Open's merciless struggle, Di Rocca's rage to win finds its proper expression. Here, at Flushing Meadow in Queens, New York, tennis becomes the sport of the toughest, and Di Rocca the idol of the rough-and-ready New York fans who flock to the stadium to consecrate their hero.

"A player like Davey Cooper, on the other hand, has never been able to conquer, or arouse, or placate the spectators. Cooper, more often than not, plays under the jeers which punctuate and exacerbate his faults, driving him further and further into a solitude close to martyrdom.

"Here, in New York, the ambiance of the Roman Circus has been revived, and the spectators, swigging beer from paper cups, devouring hot dogs and steak sandwiches, reject the losing gladiator, thumbs down. New Yorkers are winners. They will root for the underdog, but they reserve their cheers only for the hot victory of the winner.

"But the tenor of the game has been altered by the spectacle of murder. Peruvian Armando Reyes died of a drug overdose on the orange clay in Paris. The police are still pressing a homicide investigation. And Mikhail Polak was shotgunned to death in his hotel room in London. The deaths were tennis-related: Reyes collapsed during a semifinal; Polak was two hours away from a semifinal. And the threat sent to the London papers specifically mentioned semifinalists as targets.

"So what does this mean for tennis at Flushing Meadow? The police are on the job. Spectators at the massive Tennis Center will face metal detectors and the occasional security frisk. Players will be guarded, especially as they approach the semifinals. But while the machinery locks into position for play and for protection, one wonders what is going on in the minds of the person—or persons—responsible.

"The police theory is secret. Terrorism is a possibility. But if you are a tennis fan, you love the game for its pure arc, its flowing line, and the last thing you want to think about during a tennis match is a madman stalking the semis.

"And you have the feeling that's just what this madman wants, wherever he is."

Ross O'Brien, Chief of Detectives, put down his copy of the *Daily News* and lit a black cigarillo. The situation seemed increasingly tense, and he was worried that the threats against the tennis players would become epidemic, would spread until the sports world beyond tennis would be endangered. That was the way strings of assassinations got going.

The deputy mayor was standing at the window, looking out at his city.

"Okay, Ross. Let's bump lists. Who do you see for the murder in France? Then the murder in London? Then the crazy notes? Let's hit them one by one, see what we've got."

O'Brien shifted in his chair as he brought out his notebook. "We've got four possibilities. My number one is the Cavalcanti family. Tennis is ripe for those monkeys. My number two is the players. In no particular order, I've got Tigrid, this Heinz kid, Di Rocca, Cooper, and Laville."

"I've got Koras on my list."

"Maybe." O'Brien looked at his notebook. "Koras seems cool and above it all."

"Maybe he lets it build until it explodes in his face."

"Maybe. My number three is a lone crazy, a fan or a groupie. My number four is the Big Hitters Club—Clavier, Malcolm, Cabot. For my money, those guys couldn't deliver an order for lunch at Sardi's, much less a contract to a hit man."

"I've got them at number three," the deputy mayor said, sitting down again. "What's new with Lucchesi?"

"Security is tight. And there's money piling up, all right. A bundle is being bet in Canada, where we can't touch it. Another bundle in Switzerland."

"Maybe we should haul in that private cop. What's his name?"

"Malone. He's checked in with Lucchesi. Seems like your everyday ex-cop."

The deputy mayor swung his feet up on his desk. It was summer, and he had counted on Flushing Meadow to provide distraction. Now it was one more problem to cope with. "We need a clear motive. What about this idea? Maybe Reyes and Polak messed with Laville's wife."

O'Brien laughed curtly, then furrowed his brow as he looked at McKenzie. "Anyone ever tell you you've got a dirty mind?"

"Anyone remind you the tournament's five days off?"

EIGHTEEN

It was late afternoon when he sat up in bed, covered with sweat and unable to catch his breath. His temples were pounding relentlessly. In the glaring bright light of the bedroom, the objects around him assumed awesome and unfamiliar shapes. It was August, late summer, humid, and he had forgotten to shut the curtains that would close him off from the rest of the world.

He turned to stare at the numbers on the electric clock, flashing by like the alarming beating of his heart, his thumping temples. Sleep had not refreshed him. He felt worse now than he had before. But when he closed his eyes, he kept seeing the ghostly face of Mikhail Polak. It stared at him from out of the newspaper, alive, from a tennis court in the past.

He felt remorse for Polak, a pretty wife, a great career ahead of him. He rolled over now and tried to think about the party tonight, at Saadi's new casino in Atlantic City, and the money Saadi would pay him if he overcame the hex and won here in New York.

He clenched his sweating hand on the pillow. He could win. He had to.

"Terry?" Nora's voice floated in from the front room. She was back from shopping. Hoping she would leave him alone, he didn't answer. He heard a door close, then footsteps approaching. The bedroom door opened and Nora looked in. "There you are. Did you have a good rest?"

"No."

"Oh, you're sweating. Are you all right?"

"Yes." He hated answering her questions. They made him feel like a child.

"Can I get you something?"

Nora sat down on the bed, reached out to feel his forehead. There were times when Laville didn't like being touched. He grabbed his wife's wrist.

"Oh, you're hurting me."

He let her go, then rolled off his side of the bed and stomped into the bathroom, to wash away Polak's face.

Just before six, one of Saadi's limousines picked Laville and Nora up to take them to the heliport at South Street Seaport. In the limo, Nora had a highball while Laville looked at the story in *Racquet World* about his recent victory over Koras in Ohio, in the ATP Championships.

His photo was there, a color shot showing him hitting a winning forehand. A caption under the photo asked: "Can Lumberjack Laville stop Belynkas's quest for the Grand Slam?

He began studying the story, hoping to find the answer to the question. Laville was sensitive to what the press said about him. He assembled the adjectives that the writer used to describe his playing style. "Masterful" was a word he liked. "Artistry": that was good. "Black Magic" and "magician," however, made him vaguely uncomfortable.

Laville tossed the magazine aside, yawning, stretching out his muscles. He was glad to be out of the claustrophobic apartment. Two years ago, Nora had nagged him until he bought it, and they stayed there when they were in New York. It was small and dingy and reminded Laville of his poor-boy childhood in Montreal. What he wanted in New York was a posh suite at the

Meridien for now, and then a classy estate on Long Island, like Koras had. Someday he would own this city. He was looking forward to the evening, to Saadi's party, and to the big announcement about Laville and Sahara Sports.

He heard the steady throb of the helicopter as they pulled into the heliport. The chauffeur parked the car and got out to open the door. The sound was deafening, a heavy blast of sound that threw Laville back against the seat cushions. Nora didn't seem to notice. She was out of the car, waiting for him. A hand reached in for him and a face appeared. The face was Micky Polak's and he was grinning.

"Ready, Mr. Laville?"

"Don't touch me!" Laville backed away on the seat until he was up against the other door. Micky Polak leaned inside, his hand still out. He was saying something now, but his words were drowned out by the blast of the shotgun inside Laville's head. Laville grabbed for the door handle, missed, grabbed again. The door opened and Laville scrambled out. Micky was coming around the rear of the limo now. Nora stood on the other side of the car. Laville sprinted for the helicopter. A flight attendant held out a hand. Laville brushed that aside. He didn't want any ghosts touching him.

Nora joined him in the cabin.

"Terry?" Nora asked. "Terry, what is it?"

Laville was sweating. He looked out the window for Micky, but saw only the chauffeur in his uniform and peaked cap.

"It's nothing." He turned to the flight attendant. "When does this thing get going?"

"There are a few more in the party, sir. It will be a few moments."

"Terry. What is it?" She touched him and he took his arm away.

"I thought I saw Micky Polak," he whispered.

"Where?"

"Back there, in the limo."

"It's those awful pictures," she said. "In the papers. Poor Terry."

He was still sweating, but his breathing was under control. He was aware that Nora was watching him strangely. He didn't care. What the hell did she know? He was the one who had to go out there and risk everything.

During the helicopter ride down to Saadi's Atlantic City casino, Laville felt the morbid sensation lift, and he bounced himself into a better mood. He told stories about the early days on the circuit. As long as he talked, he could forget the immense pressures of being a tennis superstar.

There were seven people riding down with them: Malone and Muriel, and behind them Di Rocca and his manager, Paco Ortega. Also in the helicopter was Judson Garwood, the nosiest man in tennis, and Mr. and Mrs. Harrison Cabot. Mrs. Cabot wore an expensive necklace containing enough diamonds to finance Laville for the rest of his days.

"Oh, look!" Nora cried. "What's that?"

"Asbury Park, coming up," Malone said. "Behind us is Long Branch."

"It's gorgeous!"

"Right south of there is Point Pleasant."

"Terry, don't you think it's simply gorgeous?"

"It's the greatest."

The helicopter landed on the casino roof, setting down in the center of a big white circle with a cross painted in it. Laville felt shaky when he entered the penthouse and saw Polak again, walking toward him. But then the light changed and he saw it was Saadi, wearing a white dinner jacket and a red bow tie. Behind Saadi there was a poster of Laville, the Woodcutter, twelve feet high and ten feet across. He stood at the net in Ohio, holding up the trophy for the ATP Championships. "Hey!" he said, walking up to it. "Great!" The colors were good, bringing out the white hair, and also the red and the black in his headband.

"It is a good likeness," Saadi said.

Across the room, Nora chatted with her pal Princess Athena and Jack Di Rocca. After a month or so of dressing conservatively, the Princess was back to her old style, a sequined black suit with a cutaway front that left both breasts bare beneath a black see-through blouse. Against her husband's wishes, Nora was going back to work. The Princess was donating her time to help Nora get started.

"May I offer you something?" Saadi said.

"Yeah. An escalator."

Saadi chuckled. "We have escalators downstairs."

"I was thinking of one worth about half a million."

Saadi's eyes hardened. "That's an expensive escalator."

"My idea," Laville continued, "is a new clause in my Sahara contract. If I win at Flushing Meadow, I get half a million. If I win the Australian, I get a million."

"That was not our original deal."

Laville looked at his right hand, then at Saadi. "And I haven't signed yet."

"Does Archer Bell know?"

"This is between you and me."

"It's absurd." Saadi started to walk away, but Laville stepped smoothly to block him.

"How would it be if the people in this room knew you were the first to know about Polak's deal with Izanagi?"

Saadi stared at Laville. "You are mad," he said and walked away to give instructions to the servants.

Laville picked up a drink from a tray and strolled to the window, a huge curved wall of glass that gave the penthouse at Casino Paladin a view of the brightest sections of Atlantic City. Nora came up to take Laville's arm. She was excited about the dress the Princess was wearing. Her cheeks were flushed and he knew she'd had a couple of drinks already.

"It's from Metamorphosis. The blouse is from Norma Kamali. She wouldn't tell me how much the whole thing cost, but I'd say four thousand five, easily. Everything was custom-tailored. The choker is from Brandwynne of Los Angeles. Saadi just bought it for her."

"Just can't wait to get back to work, can you?"

"Oh, Terry. It's only part-time. Athena's being wonderful. And the circuit drives me crazy."

"What it drives you to is the nearest bar." He glared at her before walking away.

The second wave of guests arrived, including Archer Bell and

Clavier, the President of the ITF, and right behind them Milo Tigrid, accompanied by an attractive brunette in a blue dress, and Hammer Heinz, the tennis writers' hope for the future. Laville sipped his Scotch. He thought the Hammer was too cocky, too full of himself, but he had to admit the young player could hit when he was on. Milos shook hands with people, introduced his companion as B.J. Where did Milo meet these women? Di Rocca, wearing a dark-blue suit that made him look like a corporate CEO, came up to stand next to Laville.

"I just talked to my bookie. They've got you at seven to one for the finals."

"So?"

"So I wondered if you were voting to play."

Laville laughed, a derisive bark. "Get set to lose, Jack. I'm playing."

Di Rocca waved his drink at the room, indicating the symbolic poster, then regarded Laville with a thin smile. "Remember that time in Houston when we were supposed to play in the quarters?"

"No. I don't remember we ever played in Houston."

"Come on. We went out drinking after we'd won the Round of Sixteen. When I went to the men's room, you slipped something in my beer."

Laville didn't like Di Rocca's smile. "Get lost, Jack. You're making things up."

"As you go for the top, kid, remember Houston."

Laville brushed past Di Rocca.

Dinner for sixty was at a long table under a million lights. The table was black and shiny, darker than ebony, and when you looked down you could see your hands moving, the glitter of silverware and jewelry, the reflection of your face. Giant candelabra were positioned about every six feet, along the center of the table.

The Princess sat at one end, Saadi at the other. Laville, sitting on the Princess's right, wondered how much money you'd need to live like this, above the dirt, never breaking a sweat, buying up buildings, companies, people, anything you wanted. Down the table, in the bubbles of conversation, he heard his name, Terry Laville, Laville, the Woodcutter, Terry this, Terry that, the Magician, Wizard Laville. Already, there was talk of a new racket, a Laville Autograph. Saadi wanted to call it "the Brave," to highlight Laville's Iroquois heritage. Archer Bell said that had a crude, exploitative ring to it, that it was too obvious. Laville, on the other hand, thought "the Brave" matched the standup image he wanted to project to the fans. Archer Bell wanted to call the racket "Black Magic." That name made Laville jumpy.

The Princess was talking across him to Nora, about the layout for *Elan,* and Laville remembered back to that time in Los Angeles when he'd spent a night with her. He'd just come on the tour, and was struggling to stay afloat. The Princess had been on the rebound from another affair. On a smoggy day in September, Laville had clawed his way to the semifinals, where he'd been beaten by Koras the Surgeon. After losing, he'd had a drink with the Princess in her hotel room on the Pacific Coast Highway in Malibu. She was younger then, honey-skinned, reckless. She'd made Laville dress up in an Indian costume, rented from a costume rental place in Hollywood. He felt stupid, but the Princess gave him a pill to loosen him up, and he dressed in the buckskin pants with no back and no front. The Princess had worn a heavy white nightgown, which she wanted torn off her, in strips. Laville had obliged . . .

"I'm so glad for you, Terry."

He came out of his reverie. "Hey. Thanks."

"If you're careful, you can go a long way with Saadi."

Laville looked around the room. This room with the rich people and the ebony table was a long way from the dirty snow of his Canadian childhood. Behind the candle's reflection in the black table, he saw the face of Mikhail Polak. It made him sweat.

"Careful. What's that supposed to mean?"

Instead of answering, the Princess looked away, at a string of servants, wheeling in carts covered with white cloths. "Oh, here's dessert, everyone."

Dessert was cherries over ice cream with burning brandy.

"Saadi's favorite." The Princess was smirking.

"Crazy."

"I detest it," she said.

"Where do the cherries come from?"

"He has them flown in, all year round, to wherever he happens to be. These are from Michigan. Last week, he fired someone when his precious cherries didn't arrive on time."

Laville dug into his burnt cherries.

At the other end of the table, Saadi rose for a toast to the new contract Sahara Sports was about to sign with Laville. Everyone stood except Terry, who smiled bravely into the glitter.

"I'm sure you tennis illustrious have guessed why we are here tonight," Saadi said. "Which is to congratulate the next number-one player in the world. What you might not know is that Terry Laville and his manager, Mr. Archer Bell, negotiated a contract with Sahara for a million and a half dollars, the highest single amount ever paid to a tennis player by a sports equipment firm."

There were appreciative gasps from the dinner guests. Saadi paused before going on. His face was pale and he seemed to be having difficulty with his words.

"To underscore our confidence in Mr. Laville, Sahara has included a contingency clause which will pay him another half million the moment he wins here at Flushing Meadow." Saadi paused to let his guests gasp. Was Saadi offering hazard pay to get his players to compete in the most dangerous tournament in the world? "And if he can win the Grand Slam in the next two years—and this seems a certainty—he will earn five million dollars, making Mr. Laville the highest-paid tennis star—a luminary if you will—in the history of our beautiful sport."

Saadi coughed and then stepped away from the table.

"I'm glad Koras isn't here," Malone whispered to Muriel.

Applause swept down on Terry. He stood, red-faced, grinning, trying to look larger than life so he could fulfill his star potential, to say thank you, and to tell the people how he was going to win the Grand Slam.

At that moment, gasps exploded from people at the other end of the room, and Laville looked around to see four men in blue coveralls rolling a car into the room. At the far end, a section of the wall had swung aside, automatically.

The car was hidden beneath a tarp. Murmurs came from the guests as a flashgun went off, then several more. Carrying a portable microphone, Saadi walked to the car. "Terry, a token of our esteem. And our faith."

At his signal, the four men began lifting the tarp. Oohs and ahhs came from the crowd. The car was a custom Porsche 911, sleek, low to the ground, bright red and gleaming.

Saadi beckoned Laville forward to hand him the keys.

"Hey. You outdid yourself. This is the greatest night of my life."

The keys were hot in his hand. Saadi stood near him as the applause swelled. Laville opened the door of the Porsche and sat behind the wheel, with Saadi in the passenger seat.

"Enjoy it while you can," Saadi said.

"What's that supposed to mean?"

"This odd idea you have about my having anything to do with Polak. I think the authorities would be interested in how *you* came by your information."

Laville gripped the wheel. "Should I mention that on ABC's 'Wide World of Sports'? Maybe while I'm wearing equipment by Sahara?"

Saadi opened the door and started to get out. "I shall have the contracts delivered to Mr. Bell."

"Great."

"There's just one thing."

"What's that?"

"If you're going to be a household word, do something about your wife's drinking. It blurs your public image."

"I'll handle my wife. And thanks for the car."

Saadi got out of the car. Archer Bell, holding a brandy snifter in his right hand, stuck his head in. "Hey, you negotiating your own deals without me?"

"He needs us, Arch. No sweat."

Bell shook his head. "Nice going, kid." Before walking off, he toasted Laville with his brandy.

Laville was alone with his new toy.

NINETEEN

It was a large house six miles from the Verrazano Narrows Bridge, which links Brooklyn to Staten Island.

Davey Cooper had established his New York headquarters in this huge villa for the season, leasing first, then buying. Some people in the area thought the purchase price had been too high.

Davey's family was installed there—Lorraine, his mother; Nancy, his wife; Jody and Jane, his two children; and two cousins who worked for him, developing investment deals for his corporation, David Cooper Enterprises, Inc.

Lorraine Cooper was a widow in her early fifties. She was blonde, attractive, with a very good figure that she kept in shape by jogging three miles every morning before breakfast. Buying the villa had been Lorraine Cooper's plan. It was like living in the country, calm, peaceful, but Lorraine had inside information that the area was ripe for development, and already her investment had paid off. The villa, which had cost $1.7 million, had already brought an offer of $2 million.

Lorraine was in the study with Sean Hilary, the lawyer who ran Davey's affairs. Hilary had the mottled complexion of the perpetual heavy drinker. It was just after eleven in the morning, and he was on his second glass of whisky. He drank it neat, without water or ice.

"Are we ready for David?" Lorraine asked.

"Yes. I think so. Will he go along with this?"

For an answer, Lorraine looked at the lawyer with disdain. She got up from her chair behind the desk and walked to the French doors. Outside, in the pool, David was splashing water at Jody and Jane, while Nancy Cooper, looking soft and pliable, sat in a chaise longue reading the *Ladies' Home Journal*. Lorraine and Nancy got along, mostly because Nancy seldom put up an argument.

"David! We're ready for you."

"Coming, Mother."

Davey heaved himself onto the edge of the pool and pulled himself out of the water. He grabbed a towel from the white metal chair, kissed his wife on the nose, and walked inside. He didn't like money discussions, and he hoped Hilary would be brief.

"So. What's the verdict?"

Hilary indicated a map of the area, spread out on the huge walnut desk. "Seventeen parcels, David. We can pick the whole thing up for just under three million."

Davey whistled. Last year, he had made almost two million. His mother kept track of it for him. "Have we got that kind of money lying around?"

"We'll need to sell some stock. That will make us more highly leveraged than we are now. The chemicals are down anyway, and we can unload some of that Silicon Valley stuff."

"What do you think, Mother?"

"I think we should buy the land, dear."

Davey nodded, and pretended to be thinking. He stared out the window, saw Peter Abraham, the President of the ATP, talking with Nancy. He knew Peter was here to find out how he was voting. With this new burden, Davey had to play the Open. "How much can we make on this?"

"Our money should double in three years."

The lawyer handed him a pen. As Davey bent over to sign, his mother smiled over her son's head at Hilary.

Back at poolside, Davey got together with Peter Abraham. The two men were close friends. They walked out of earshot of Nancy Cooper, who smiled warmly. Abraham's face was serious.

"Most of the votes are in, Davey. Everyone's voting to play."

Davey took a moment to look at his wife, sitting there in the chaise longue, and at his children, frolicking in the pool. Then he nodded. "I'll play."

"You're seeded three. There's a good chance you'll get to the semifinals."

"I said I'd play."

"Okay. It's your decision."

"You're playing, aren't you, Pete?"

"Yes. But I don't think I'll make the semis. And that's where the heat is."

Koras had a lunch date with Frank Fenwick, at the West Side Tennis Club. But before he left his house, he tried calling Laure at the number in Choisel. Laure was not there. Koras spoke to her grandmother briefly, then hung up and headed west in his Mercedes on the Sunrise Expressway, toward Queens.

The U.S. Open would begin in a couple of days and things were already tense. A team of police had already examined the Westhampton house, and declared it indefensible. Once the matches got under way, security guards would appear at his gate and he would be escorted to and from the Tennis Center. Meanwhile, a Lieutenant Lucchesi had advised Koras to move into town, to the Meridien, where most of the players were staying. But Koras had refused. Better to die at home, if you had to die at all.

The call to France had brought back memories of Laure in Paris, that Monday after he'd won Wimbledon. He kept thinking about her, the charming grandparents, the tiny village of Choisel, the quaint restaurant in Paris . . .

The garden at Choisel had been hidden in the recesses of an overgrown park, just outside the small village. He had stopped three times to ask for directions before finding the low stone wall, the dry fountain, the impudent water sprites left over from another age. The driveway had been narrow and thick with summer growth, and he had parked close to Laure's car.

"Don't run over my pumpkin!" she had yelled, running to meet him. Her smile had been warm and she had kissed him on the cheek. The grandparents, people who cared for Laure immensely, were classic. Emile Puget was a retired cavalry officer, hero of the Liberation, and he still wore his civilian clothes with military precision and elegance. His wife, Viviane, was animated and beautiful, with a musical voice that put Koras at ease immediately. Both had treated Koras as Laure's suitor, framing him in a role he was not quite ready for.

They had an apéritif, an orange wine with a curious bittersweet taste that the old man called "the elixir of life." Koras tried to imagine how many of Laure's men friends had sat here in this same garden, sipping orange wine.

"This is the recipe of Laure's mother," the old man said.

"It's very good." Actually, the wine was too sweet for Koras.

"She was very beautiful," the old man said.

"Yes. I can believe that." Koras toasted them all with his raised glass. Across from him, Laure smiled shyly.

"What sort of name is that, Belynkas?"

"Lithuanian, sir."

"Wasn't there another Lithuanian? Also a tennis player?"

"Yes. Gerulaitas."

"Another curious name." The old man paused. "What do you intend, with my lovely Laure?"

"Sir?"

"Grandfather, please!" Laure cried. "Mr. Belynkas is just here for a visit!"

The old man sat back, undissuaded but smiling now, and turned to Laure. "I may be an old man, but I know love when I see it."

Laure stood up, her orange wine unfinished. "We have to be going." She was blushing.

"To Paris, I suppose."

"Yes. Just for the evening."

"Well, be careful driving. The roads are insane."

"We're taking the train."

"Be careful, those fools strike every week these days. Not like it was when I was your age. Today chaos is everywhere."

They had left the charming grandparents and then had boarded the train into the city. Laure took Koras to a pleasant restaurant on the Rue St. Denis, where she knew the proprietor. It was a warm evening, and they sat on the sidewalk, across from each other. The table was small, with a white cloth and inexpensive wine glasses. Laure's eyes were shining, and Koras had never been so happy. After a leisurely dinner of trout and cabbage salad and flan for dessert, they took coffee and strolled around the city. Koras wanted her badly, but she seemed distant, rather than dreamy and full of desire.

Laure had been in a walking mood. They walked west, up the

Rue St. Honoré to the Faubourg, where Laure pointed out a scarf shop in which she had worked while a student in Paris. Holding hands, they came to the Avenue Friedland, where they turned left toward the Place de l'Etoile. For a long, silent moment, they stood gazing upward at the Arc de Triomphe.

"God," Koras said. "I love this city."

It was summer and Paris was alive with tourists. A group of students passed, laughing, and one of the young men whistled and made wolf eyes at Laure, who moved closer to Koras and squeezed his hand.

From the Arc de Triomphe, they walked south to the Trocadero. They passed a small hotel where Koras had spent time with Athena during their fiery courtship. Twenty-five francs for a room back then, and he had to borrow money from Athena for coffee and hard rolls. Laure seemed to sense what he was about to ask and withdrew again, into herself, making it clear she was not in the mood for love.

Koras was frustrated. On the train riding back to Choisel, Laure's mood changed again and she rested her head on his shoulder.

At the door to her grandparents' house, she turned, suddenly, to throw her arms around his neck for a passionate kiss. She arched her body into his with surprising urgency. He held her.

"Laure. What is it?"

She said nothing, only a fierce shake of her head. She led him into the shadows and they continued to hold each other.

"Laure, I have to break a promise."

"Oh?" She stiffened slightly.

"The money. What I promised you, back at Alesia. I can't come up with it."

She kissed him lightly and he tasted salty tears on her cheeks. "You have done too much."

"I wanted to do more."

"I could not accept more."

Perhaps that was the problem. "Why not?"

He could feel her hesitate before she whispered. "It costs so much. Things are so expensive. I knew, yet I did not know."

"What do you mean?"

Her voice was husky, filled with emotion. "The check, it was in my name. And when I signed it over I felt strange, all those thousands of dollars you worked for. And then, poof, it was gone."

"Did you get a new diesel generator?"

She nodded, her head against his chest. "Yes."

"That's what counts."

She was trembling now. "I am sorry about—tonight. Walking around Paris, all those tiny hotels. They did beckon, didn't they?"

He grinned in the darkness. "They were probably full anyway."

"Please wait for me, Pantakoras." She was gripping his arms. "All right."

"I know there are other women around. Wait for me anyway."

"While you go to Greece?"

"No. It is not Greece. It is something . . . "

But she never finished her sentence. Abruptly, she kissed him, her final goodbye, and in seconds she was out of his arms and into the safety of her house.

And he was out there, heart pounding, confused . . .

So now Laure was in Greece with Jean-Luc Benoît, talking to Professor Colicos, and Koras was on his way to talk to Fenwick about the never-ending subject of money.

He continued west on the Expressway until he reached the traffic buildup outside JFK International, then turned on Rockaway Boulevard, which took him northwest to 678, and then onto Queens Boulevard. From about there, you began to smell the old money around Forest Hills.

In a few moments, he was off the Boulevard, onto the streets. The houses here were large, sedate in the sunlight of a waning summer. Even though it was hot, he could sense autumn on the air. Forest Hills had made him weak with envy as a boy—not too far from Brooklyn, as the crow flies, but worlds away if you were a poor kid fighting for survival on the streets.

Over to his right, he saw Station Square, the Long Island Railroad, one-way streets. He remembered the crowds packing these same streets in the seventies, when Forest Hills was the site of the U.S. Nationals. Koras had won here, three times. His career had really started here, and that made him feel old.

He passed the vine-covered front of the old Forest Hills Inn, memories floating in his head. He remembered Billy Walters from Texas, his doubles partner, killed in a plane crash. He remembered Jocelyn White Hodges, a debutante with rich parents, a yacht, a sassy rich-girl walk, and a terrific forehand, saying no and laughing—a mocking sound he would never forget—when he asked her to marry him. They'd made hectic, goodbye love all night. The next day Koras went out to win a semifinal against Armando Reyes, wealthy, handsome, the Playboy from Peru. Jocelyn and her partner had lost in the doubles against an Australian team, and Koras had not seen her since.

Memories.

He turned the Mercedes over to the parking valet and walked toward the clubhouse. He liked the building, the English Tudor façade, the steep gabled roofs. In Koras's book, Forest Hills would always be the site of the real American championships. The National Tennis Center at Flushing Meadow was garish, a carnival for the crowds.

Frank Fenwick was already seated at a window table. The Texan had his calculator out and was punching numbers into it. He looked up and smiled as Koras arrived. The two men shook hands. Fenwick got right to business.

"Hell of a figure, what Saadi's paying Laville."

"Like selling your soul to the devil."

"At least the price is good. I ordered roast beef."

The waiter came up and Koras ordered a salad and a beer. "How's the vote going?"

"I just talked to Pete Abraham. Davey Cooper's in."

"Any numbers on how much people are betting?"

"There are different numbers," Fenwick said. "Anywhere from fifteen million to fifty."

"Did you read the paper? Jud Garwood's 'Scenario for the Round of Sixteen'?"

"Garwood's a crock." Fenwick pulled a thick brown envelope out of his pocket and took some papers out, which he spread in front of Koras. "Here."

"What are they?"

Fenwick handed Koras a pen. "Deal with a new bank, to extend your loan and give us some cash to operate with."

Koras was waiting for Fenwick to mention the $800,000. He handed back the pen to Fenwick. "How much will I make this year?"

"When you add the win here, tie in the Grand Slam bonus and the promotional stuff I've got sitting with the endorsers, the gross will be just over four million."

"Why do I feel poor?"

Fenwick continued. "We pay off the construction people. And you keep the lid on expenses. You stay out of jail and hope that Saadi doesn't do a leveraged buyout of Laval."

"Should I sell the house?" Koras was joking.

Fenwick folded the papers and stuck them into his pocket. "Not unless you lose here."

"Is it that serious?"

Their food arrived. Fenwick busied himself with rare roast beef. "I wouldn't use the word 'serious.'"

"What word would you lose?"

"'Tight.' I would use the word 'tight.'"

"Terrific."

Fenwick finished first, gulped a quick cup of coffee, and left Koras alone at the table. He was due in the city at three for more discussions. Koras ordered a second beer. He was sitting there thinking about money and pressure and dying in the semifinals, when Jack Di Rocca came up with Sally Vicenti.

Jack wore a nifty pincord seersucker with a striped tie. Sally was dark from the sun and he wore cream-colored tennis shorts, a matching shirt, matching socks, and new leather shoes, Sport City, that retailed for a hundred dollars.

"Can we join you?" Di Rocca asked.

Koras knew what they wanted. "Sure." A waiter in a white coat and black pants came to clear the table. Sally ordered a bottle of Valpolicella.

Koras crossed his legs. He was having trouble getting comfortable and wanted to be out of there, in the fresh air, driving the Mercedes.

"You're looking good, Panties. A little gray in the blond hair, there. Mustache needs a trim. But fit and tight. This life, it agrees."

"Thanks, Sally. You look tough yourself."

"I got eight years on you, maybe nine." With a blunt finger, Sally tapped his thick chest. "Heart trouble almost did me in, but surgery brought me back. And tennis. I love this game. Wish I'd discovered it years ago."

"Jack mentioned your heart trouble. When was it, again?"

"Ten years ago. Or is it eleven? Yeah, there I was, on that fucking table with the lights, listening to myself breathing, and I said to myself, 'Sally Vicenti, it's time for a new leaf. If I get out of this, I'm changing.' So I took up tennis."

"Back in Paris, Jack said you wanted something."

"I have this friend at the Oyster Bay Club, who did some work on your house. Says you owe him some money."

"And?"

"He sold the paper to me."

The beer was almost gone. Koras was thinking of the new bank papers he had signed for Frank Fenwick. Jesus, did Sally have his dirty hands in that? Or rather the clean hands of one of his money-laundering fronts? Koras looked at Di Rocca. "How much paper?"

"Quarter of a million."

"So now I owe you?"

"Yeah." Sally sipped his wine. "Did I tell you what I see in the finals of the U.S. Open?"

"No. But you will."

"I see crazy Terry Laville *versus* Jack Di Rocca. Laville loses. Di Rocca wins."

"His first big win on a fast surface," Koras said.

Sally ignored the sarcasm. "What this means is that you lose to Jackie in the semis. We tear up your note. You keep the fancy house."

Koras leaned forward—$250,000, to lose. His head was hurting. "What about Laville? He's crazy to win here."

"Laville's going to be very reasonable. Just like you are."

Koras leaned back, drained the beer. It had a decidedly bitter taste. Two hundred and fifty thousand was more than he would make winning the tournament. If he didn't take Sally's deal and then lost, he would make even less. This was easy money, based on his reputation of a decade of trying for the fans. The pounding in his head was worse. He stood up. "No."

"Hey, don't go away mad."

Koras walked away from the table. He was out the door, heading for the Mercedes, when Di Rocca caught up to him. "You pissed Sally off, Koras."

"You're good enough to take the Open, Jack. Play it straight."

Di Rocca shook his head. "I'm in too deep. Anyway, this is guaranteed."

"You tried the same shit with Armando, didn't you?"

Di Rocca didn't answer, but just stood there, looking stolid.

"And Micky Polak, right?"

Again, Di Rocca refused to answer.

"I thought I knew you better, Jack." Koras kept moving.

Di Rocca grabbed his arm. "Sally's got a lot at stake here, Koras. If your end is two fifty, you can imagine what his will be."

"Yeah," Koras said, and kept walking. He did not look back at Di Rocca in his pale summer suit.

"He'll protect himself," Di Rocca called. "He's a tough one. He expects you to change your mind."

The Mercedes took several hits on the starter before coming to life. The sun had made the interior steamy hot and Koras was sweating as he swung the car out of the parking lot. His hands shook and he felt sick to his stomach. Only he knew just how close he had come to thinking seriously about Sally Vicenti's offer.

Milo's taxi stopped in front of the long red-and-gold canopy. The building was a perfect example of late-nineteenth-century New York architecture, the era of the Astors and the Rockefellers.

Milo handed the driver his fare, along with a handsome tip, and stepped out. It was a little past seven o'clock. The porter, resplendent in his gold braid uniform, opened the wrought-iron gates that led into the lobby. Milo addressed himself to the concierge, who announced him on a handsome brass interphone and then led him to the elevator.

"You are expected, Mr. Tigrid. Twelfth floor."

"Which suite number?"

The concierge smiled. "Mrs. Jameson has the whole floor, sir."

Milo was impressed. The elevator opened on the twelve, and he saw black marble, a curving staircase, fruit trees, expensively dressed people chatting, and beyond them an actual indoor garden. A butler took Milo in. The attractive brunette, B.J., came forward to greet him.

"Your flowers were magnificent," she said. "Let me introduce you around."

Her hands were warm, and she looked terribly beautiful, like a painting from an artist's imagination. Twelve stories above the New York streets, he met financiers and their wives, a mogul from CBS, a publisher of a newspaper, two stockbrokers from Wall Street, and a conductor in town to direct the New York Philharmonic. The publisher asked him about the tennis tournament, and Milo said he was playing.

"Only one player has opted not to play," Milo said, "and he was a Frenchman."

Everyone laughed.

They dined outdoors, at a table beneath the stars. Milo sat on his hostess's right.

The last guests left at one o'clock. Milo and B.J. stayed on the terrace awhile, contemplating the dark expanse of Central Park, dotted here and there with street lamps.

"Those were nice people," Milo said.

B.J. drew his face close, for a kiss. He smelled her perfume and her lips were terribly soft. Suddenly, he broke free.

"Where are you going?"

"To the W.C."

In the bathroom, Milo removed a silver pillbox from his jacket pocket. Six pills remained, Armando's legacy. Without hesitating, Milo flushed them down the toilet.

In a tiny private hideaway he had rented near Greenwich Village, Terry Laville poured himself a stiff drink, a Chivas neat, then settled down with the phone to make some calls to Canada. It was after one in the morning, and Nora was asleep in the Central Park West apartment after drinking too much wine. He phoned his Montreal connection Wally Dolan, who had taught Laville how to shave points in high-school soccer. It took seven calls to locate Dolan. Laville got right to the point. He wanted a name in New York.

"Don't tell me you need a bodyguard, Laville."

"Yeah," Laville said. "Somebody's killing off tennis players. I don't want to be next."

Dolan gave him the name Torelli. "You get around, Laville. London. New York."

"How's the weather up there?"

"Drizzle. Haven't seen the sun for a week."

"I remember," Laville said and hung up. He waited a moment, sweating with the thought of what he was about to do. Then he called Torelli to set up a meeting.

The man who answered the phone had a flat voice, emotionless. Laville gave his own name as Dick and said he wanted to talk, but when he dropped Dolan's name, Torelli wasn't impressed. He wanted a thousand dollars, just to meet. Laville agreed and they set a time thirty minutes away. They would meet in Brooklyn, at the Cherry Hotel.

Laville put on gloves, a dark windbreaker, and a small-brimmed hat. From his money cache, the only way he felt safe traveling the jet stream, he took ten thousand dollars in crisp hundred-dollar bills.

He was calm as he let himself out of the building. He wanted this settled tonight. As soon as the tournament began, security people would blanket the players, himself included. He took the stairs down to the ground floor. The new Porsche was parked in the garage, underneath the building.

Laville loved driving it, feeling the road when he cornered, cruising easily at 120 m.p.h.; but now, heading toward Brooklyn, Laville kept to the speed limit. There was no use getting pulled over for speeding on a night like this. When he reached the Cherry Hotel, he parked down the street, locking the car and making certain the alarm system was set. In a neighborhood like this, anything could happen.

The Cherry Hotel was miserable, with a façade so dilapidated and windows so worn it looked abandoned. Inside, the neon lights from the street drifted into the room through torn curtains. A fat mountain of a man sat behind the reception desk, as though imprisoned there by his own bulk. Two prostitutes, each with a nervous client in tow, asked for keys, and the fat man took his time handing them over. He liked watching johns perspire.

One of the hookers was a mulatto, sexy, with honey-caramel skin and wide, innocent eyes. She smiled at Laville, and then led her trick upstairs, hips moving nicely under the thin blue dress.

Laville paid fifty dollars for a room. "When a guy comes in, tell him Dick is in number thirty-two."

The fat porter watched him climbing the dark staircase. Gays, probably, he thought, who like to do it in a whores' hotel. Real kinks, because they had money and didn't need to come to a hole like this.

In the room, Laville made certain the lights were down. A knock came on the door in less than five minutes. By then, Laville was sweating.

"Come in."

The door opened, and he was face to face with an automatic pistol. Torelli was tall, with a hard and emaciated face, and built like an athlete, lean and muscular. His blond hair was short, his eyes clear and unmoving as though permanently fixed on some distant horizon. He wore tight-fitting jeans, a pale-blue shirt, and a black leather flight jacket. On his hands were Ranger driving gloves, also black, with holes in the back for ventilation. He put the gun away.

Laville stayed seated while he told Torelli what he wanted. "If he wins, hit him. If I win, you got paid to do nothing."

Torelli listened without expression until Laville finished, then he grinned, showing a broken tooth. "You think like God." He moved to the window, stared out at the brick wall next door. "It's a tricky hit," he said. "I have to be there, make a decision. Fifty grand."

"Forty," Laville said, trying to bargain.

"Fifty. If you want a cut-rate job, get yourself another mechanic." Torelli started to leave.

"Wait." Laville brought out the money. "Here's ten. I'll pay you fifteen more tomorrow. You get the other half if you do the hit."

"I don't like it this complicated." Torelli took the money, counted it. He told Laville he wanted to meet Monday, at the Tennis Center.

"Why?"

"To get a feel for things. You can point this guy out."

They arranged to meet at the Steak House, a sandwich pavilion.

Laville was curious. "How will you do it?"

"It's better you don't know. That way, you just see the result."

Without another word, Torelli walked out of the room.

Laville waited, his heart pounding. He took off the windbreaker, which was making him sweat. When Torelli had been gone five minutes, Laville left the room.

He was moving quickly, jerking the door closed, eager to get the Porsche started. As he whirled, he bumped into someone, smelled cheap perfume. His cap fell off and he caught it in midair.

"Jesus. Watch it!"

He saw a pretty face, a creamy shoulder, a swatch of blue dress, and a swirling black wig. He remembered the same dress, heading up the stairs. Laville pulled away from her, tugged the cap back down to hide his hair, and hurried on down the stairs.

He took the stairs three at a time. The Cherry Hotel reminded him of his childhood, the same smells, the same dead faces, and he wanted out.

Malone sat in his rented Plymouth outside the Cherry Hotel. The second R was missing from the blue neon sign, and the O in "Hotel" kept popping on and off. Malone was tired. He'd followed Laville on a hunch, from the apartment on Central Park West to a place in the Village, and now here.

At 2:42, a black man in a white three-piece suit and white shoes sauntered down the steps, taking his time. He looked up and down the street, then turned right, heading uptown. Under his left armpit, Malone spotted the bulge of a shoulder holster. Malone shot three frames of infrared film with the automatic camera. At 2:44, a man with a week's growth of beard hurried out, carrying a battered black suitcase. As he left the hotel, the man turned and stared up at the façade. He shook his head, then turned left and hurried away. Malone shot his picture, too.

At 2:48, a guy in a leather flight jacket came out. He was tall, rangy, blond. He wore new jeans, boots, dark gloves. Malone aimed the camera and took a couple of pictures.

The guy in the flight jacket climbed into a Ford pickup and drove away. Malone used a long-range lens to shoot two photos of the license plate.

His watch said 2:53. Laville had been in there twenty minutes. Was he seeing a hooker, or what? The Porsche was parked five cars away. At 2:58, Laville came out, walking like a jock, easy, with a ton of confidence. As he got into the Porsche and headed back toward Manhattan, Malone snapped his picture, with the neon Cherry Hotel sign in the background.

Malone put the rented Plymouth in gear and followed Laville back to his apartment. He was getting closer to something, but had no idea what it was.

TWENTY

Three days before the start of the U.S. Open, Chief of Detectives Ross O'Brien sat in his office getting a report from Lieutenant Lucchesi. As usual, Lucchesi wore a $700 suit he'd been given at wholesale. He looked like a movie cop on the way to the top.

"I love this." O'Brien stared at the numbers on the report. "I've got forty-one detectives on overtime, trying to tag one of these players as a murderer. And I've got your security force *protecting* the same guys."

"We've had a couple of snags, Chief. On moving the players."

"Like who?"

"Koras, for one. We're working with the county people to set up security at his place."

"I see him as a prima donna," O'Brien said. "Who else?"

"Di Rocca. He doesn't trust the police, and would rather rely on his own security force."

"Bikers with leather heads, I'll bet."

"Yes." Lucchesi nodded. "Di Rocca's old gang, the Rebels. And a coalition of blacks calling themselves the Royal Bloods."

O'Brien sighed and swung away from Lucchesi to stare out the window. "Keep on working on Di Rocca. Have we got everyone else at the Meridien?"

"We're working on this kid Davey Cooper. He's with his mother and family, out on Staten Island. They live in this unbelievable house, and I heard on the grapevine they spend all their time buying up investment property."

O'Brien turned back to his desk, so he could make a list of the three names. "Who does that leave?"

"Laville. Tigrid. Abraham. Colombier. Leroy. This Swiss kid Heinz. We've convinced Laville to move. He and his wife have an apartment over on Central Park West. The other top players are already at the hotel. We'll work a three-team rotation around the clock, eight hours per team. We'll chauffeur the players from the Meridien to the Tennis Center, using police vehicles. If that's not possible, we'll make sure we have escorts to the Center."

The lieutenant flipped a page in his notebook before going on. "Security wasn't visible enough in Paris and London, so we're using uniforms at the Center, with conspicuous firearms. We'll have a command post set up in a van, located near the entrance, and we'll monitor the crowds with a dozen TV cameras. We'll do stop-and-search at random, but without a couple of hundred extra people we can't handle the crowds with metal detectors."

Lucchesi closed his notebook. O'Brien sat in his chair, thinking. "What does the gambling look like on this show?"

"I have three reports. One says three million. Another says seven. Another, fifteen."

"There have to be connections. Are you watching the families?"

"Around the clock."

*   *   *

Milo sat up and blinked several times, feeling disoriented by his surroundings. The walls were hung with white silk; the ceiling of the bed was canopied with deep-blue curtains, held back by golden girdles. The carpeting was white, deep, and the furniture was modern, with low, straight lines. He had a nagging headache.

He smelled coffee, and then B.J. walked into the room carrying a tray with a pot and two cups. She wore a pale-yellow robe, tied loosely around the waist. The robe displayed the breasts that had given Milo such pleasure the night before. He watched her legs as she came forward, and the bottom of the robe parted.

"Welcome back, champion."

"What time is it?" he growled.

She set the tray down and kissed him. "It's morning. Why?"

"I have to meet Laville for a workout. If I don't, he will be grumpy for weeks."

"What do you care?"

He reached over to turn the clock around to where he could see it. It was 11:01. "My God! Tigrid has slept the day away!"

B.J. laughed as she poured steaming coffee. It smelled delicious. "You have time for coffee, don't you?"

Milo sat on the bed while he dialed the Tilden Club in midtown Manhattan and asked to speak to Laville. B.J. sat next to him, her bare legs crossed. Milo had trouble keeping his eyes off her. The yellow robe had come open all the way to her thighs, and she was happy to distract him. He could hear them paging Laville, the voices echoing over the loudspeaker. After a while, the man came on, saying that Laville was not there. Milo felt relieved as he set down the phone.

"Not there." He dug his thumbs into his temples. "This head of mine, it splits."

"Why didn't you say so?"

"Yugoslavs show no weakness. It is not manly."

"Silly," she said. "I have some marvelous headache pills." B.J. moved quickly to pull open the top drawer of her bedside table. "Oh!" she said. Inside the drawer was Milo's chrome-plated .357 Magnum. B.J. stared at the gun, perplexed, then turned to Milo. "Why are you carrying that around?"

"For protection, what else?" Milo's voice was angry, defensive. He did not have to explain himself.

"Oh, Milo!" There was alarm in B.J.'s voice.

He put down his coffee cup and took her into his arms. She was stiff at first, but then she gave way and collapsed onto him. "Hold me," she murmured. "Hold me."

The man with the pockmarked face wore green coveralls with big letters in yellow plastic stuck on his back. He was carrying equipment for cleaning windows—a plastic pail, sponges, assorted rags, a squeegee with an extension, a bottle of spray cleaner—as he walked slowly down the corridor reading the numbers of office doors.

A policeman passed, the seventh one he had seen inside the Tennis Center. There were cops everywhere, but he had his ID badge and they were leaving the hordes of workmen alone.

On the lawns dividing the field courts, enormous yellow-and-white-striped tents had been erected. Refreshment stands were being put up and there was hope of outdoing the previous years' records: 115,000 hot dogs, 200,000 hamburgers, four tons of steak, 18,240 helpings of strawberries with cream, 43,200 ice creams, 6,000 cases of beer, 40,000 coffees, 115,000 sodas—all this not including whatever treats the spectators brought themselves, loaded in picnic hampers. Huge trucks were parked in rows outside the buildings, from which food was being unloaded and then carried to the freezers.

The man in the green coveralls had studied the routes through the labyrinthine stadium. He had stopped in the locker room to stow a narrow suitcase, and he now stood outside the door to the office of Harrison Cabot, President of the USTA.

He knocked three times, and then opened the door without hesitating. A young man wearing a bow tie was bending over a huge desk. He turned around, his steel-rimmed glasses giving him the aspect of a clergyman. He was Cabot's right-hand man, Darrell Whisner. In one corner of the big room was a locked wooden cabinet.

"Well, it's about time."

"I was backed up down the hall," the window washer said. "I'll be out of here in a quarter of an hour." He walked to the window, opened it, leaned out, and began daubing the panes with cleaning solution, which he then sluiced away with the squeegee. While he worked, he watched Whisner from the corner of his eye. The young man sat at a smaller desk, working his way studiously through a file, taking notes in a careful hand.

The outside of the window was finished. He closed it, then walked casually to the trophies that lined one wall of the office. At the desk, Whisner looked up from the file.

"They're beautiful, aren't they?"

"Yes, especially the big one." The window washer moved closer, to examine the plaque on the trophy. It was time for the telephone call. "But there's no name."

"No. Not yet."

"This is the winner's trophy, then? For the whole tournament?"

"Yes. Half the players in the world would kill to have their name on that plaque."

"Only half?"

The telephone rang, half a minute early. He watched Whisner pick it up, then went back to his work and waited. The man in the glasses got up, took the file that he had been working on, and started for the door. "I'll be right back."

The window washer nodded.

When the door was closed, the window washer put down the scraper and crossed the room to the locked wooden cabinet. The lock was cheap and it needed oil. He had it open in less than twenty seconds. Inside he found a ledger and a box of official USTA entry passes that would get him inside the stadium once the tournament had started. The ledger had several names repeated. Forsyte, Alcock, Castelmonte, O'Ryan, Smythe. He used one repeated name for each pass, numbers 702, 803, and 904. By the time Whisner came back, whistling, the cabinet was closed and the man was finishing up the last window.

"There," he said, gathering up his equipment to leave. "Now you'll be able to see what's going on around you."

Whisner nodded. He was already back at work on his reports.

The restaurant was called the Catania, located at the end of a blind alley just off Charlton Street. The sign on the door indicated that service would not begin until seven o'clock.

Lieutenant Lucchesi walked to the door and knocked on the

pane. The curtain rustled and he recognized the face of his cousin Marco. The door opened and the two cousins embraced.

"Johnny. Papa's waiting for you."

"God, it smells great in here."

They crossed the main body of the restaurant. The walls were tiled white and decorated with florid photographs representing views of Vesuvius, scenes from operas like *Aida* and *I Puritani*. On the tables were fishing buoys that had been transformed into lamps. They could have been in any restaurant in Little Italy. Varied salamis and sausages hung from the walls, filling the room with their splendid scents.

Uncle Beppo sat at a corner table in the back room. He was a patriarch, dark and stocky, with a muscular body that was very unwillingly turning to fat. In his youth, Beppo had been a boxer, but he had realized after losing badly that it was never the boxers themselves who reaped the benefits of their combat. Now he owned boxing stables in upstate New York, where he bred and trained champions. When he saw Lucchesi, he smiled.

"Buona sera, Uncle Beppo."

"Sit, Johnny. Sit." Beppo turned to his son and pointed to a bottle of chilled Mammertino in the ice bucket. "Marco, serve Johnny some wine."

Marco poured the wine and handed glasses all round.

"How's your father?" Beppo asked.

"Fine."

"And the hardware store?"

"It's going well."

"And your beautiful wife? And the children?"

"More beautiful with each day."

Uncle Beppo smiled. "One Sunday very soon, you bring them all to my house. The children can run in the garden. The tomatoes are ripening. It will be good for them."

"I'll talk to Papa. We'll set a day."

Beppo and his older brother had not spoken to each other for twenty years. It had started with an argument over who got their mother's silver crucifix when the old lady had gone to live with Beppo during the last days of her life.

The two men ate with good appetite. In the middle of the meal, Beppo brought up the subject.

"I have asked around, about this business with the tennis. So far, there is nothing."

"There's a lot of money coming in to the bookies. Someone's controlling it."

"The families stay out of that. It's too new."

Lucchesi looked at his uncle. He knew about the draconian methods used by the Mafia to keep conversations like this from going anywhere. Tonight he had the feeling that his uncle was not being completely sincere. He himself was a policeman; his uncle was a very well-organized criminal. He speared a piece of meatball and washed down the meat with a swallow of red wine. Maybe Uncle Beppo was out of touch.

"Could this be something you don't know about?"

The old man filled the squat glasses. "Which Sunday do you bring the children? Next week?"

The matches began tomorrow. "Sorry. I have to work."

"The Sunday after?"

Lucchesi shook his head. The old man was stalling. "Maybe in three weeks."

"Such a business. A man should save Sunday for his family. Even your father doesn't work on Sunday."

"Weren't the Cavalcantis into football pools?"

Uncle Beppo paused in his eating. "This is not our style, notes in newspapers, that sort of thing. That's the style of a crazy man. Maybe a terrorist."

Lucchesi continued eating. The food was excellent. It was all Lucchesi was going to get out of Uncle Beppo.

On Monday, the first day of the U.S. Open, traffic was heavy going east into the Tennis Center. The guards recognized Laville and waved the red Porsche through. The escort vehicle, which had followed Laville from the Meridien, turned around. Inside the Center, he would still be watched, but from a distance.

Laville was discovering that he relished the sense of danger.

He swung into a parking slot reserved for players. He had a half hour before his meeting with Torelli, and he wanted to walk around while he got a feel for the stadium. He strolled by a tent occupied by the Steak House, an outdoor pavilion in the

Food Village with a striped awning and waiters in cutaways. He found a seat next to a table where three pretty girls were sitting, and he ordered a Coke. They were giggling, and finally one of them became brave enough to ask for his autograph. He signed it, "With Love, Lumberjack Laville." He was finishing the Coke when Jack Di Rocca, in tennis clothes, sat down at his table.

"Terry, there's a man in the stands who wants to talk to you."

Laville made a show of checking his watch. "Sorry. Got a date."

Di Rocca pulled a three-by-five photo out of his warm-up pocket and shoved it across the table to Laville. It was a shot, taken at a crazy angle, of Polak making it with Shirley that night in London. The flash illuminated Polak's face, made it look ghostly. Laville turned pale. "What's this?"

"Souvenir. From Wimbledon."

Laville crumpled the photo.

"Your girl. Your stuff on the bedside table. It won't take much police work to put you behind the camera."

Laville was sweating now. He looked around the pavilion, where the lights had suddenly become too bright. "You want something. What is it?"

"Like I said, a man wants to talk to you."

Laville looked at his watch.

Di Rocca leaned close, with a strange gleam in his eyes. "Torelli won't be coming . . . Dick."

Laville was feeling sick now. Gripping the table edge, he felt his future start to crumble. "So what they say is true?"

Di Rocca stood up. "Coming, Terry?"

Laville was frantic now. "My match. It's in an hour. I need to hit, loosen up—"

"Just take a minute."

Laville's legs were unsteady as he walked with Di Rocca into the noisy stadium. Policemen were all over the place, here to protect him! At the entrance to the stadium, he and Di Rocca flashed player's passes, which were scrutinized carefully by guards with walkie-talkies. There were gun butts peeking out everywhere. Di Rocca led him to a box right down on the court. Out on the court in an early-round match, Koras was playing Paul Harper, from California. According to the scoreboard,

Koras wasn't having any trouble winning. The box, which was the same size as the one Saadi owned, sat twelve people. The man he would talk to was swarthy and Mediterranean-looking, his age somewhere in the forties. He wore a tennis shirt with a crocodile logo. Two more men, wearing business suits, sat in the rear of the box. Bodyguards. One of them listened through earphones to a portable radio.

As Laville came into the box, the swarthy man stood up, smiling and extending his hand. "Mr. Laville. I'm Sally Vicenti. Have some wine." He spoke with a low, raspy whisper. As he poured wine into a stubby glass, he kept chatting.

Laville refused the wine. "Let's get on with it."

"I understand. Take a seat, please." Sally pointed down onto Center Court. "I was just watching your friend Mr. Belynkas give a lesson to the youngster from California."

Laville sat down, his edginess combining with a terrible curiosity.

"Mr. Laville, I'll get right to it. Our Mr. Torelli told us of a plan you have. To eliminate a competitor."

"I don't know what you're talking about."

"Mr. Torelli works for us."

Laville felt a cold chill on the back of his neck. "So? Call the cops, Mr. Vicenti."

Vicenti spread his hands in a gesture of helplessness. "Call me Sally. Everyone does."

"Okay. Call the cops . . . Sally."

Vicenti grinned, white teeth, but the eyes stayed cold. "I like your style, Mr. Laville. You are a man who goes for what he wants. Think you can win here this year?"

Laville watched Koras knifing the ball down the line, coming to the net behind it, putting away the volley. It was only the early rounds, but the stands were packed. People wanted to see who got killed on the courts. "Yes. I can win."

"Would you be willing to bet on it?"

"I already have. I put down five thousand on me, to win the final."

"We know about that. I was thinking of betting on something more valuable. Like your life."

"I don't have to listen to this."

"Mr. Laville, we have a big pool of money, put up by friends of mine, from across the country. We bet on Mr. Di Rocca here, to win the tournament."

Laville grinned. "At seven to one, right?"

"You're astute, Mr. Laville." He turned to Di Rocca. "Didn't I tell you, Jackie, this Mr. Laville is astute."

- Di Rocca nodded, but said nothing.

"Di Rocca has to reach the final first," Laville said. "That means he has to get by Koras."

"We're handling that part. If he reaches the final, we want to know we can depend on you."

"You want me to tank?"

"Yes. In four sets."

Laville barked out a short laugh. "Jack showed me the photos. They're yours, not mine. There's nothing to connect me with them."

"Show him the blowup, Jackie."

Di Rocca handed Laville a manila envelope. Inside was a blowup showing Polak and Shirley. On the bedside table was Laville's travel alarm with the date and time, and a tennis headband. The room number was clearly visible on the telephone dial. There had been three rolls, after all. Laville did some heavy thinking. Maybe there was money in this somewhere . . .

"You want Koras out of the way," Sally said. "So we might work together."

"Not a chance."

"The way you might lose, is to develop a symptom of your famous hex. The one that gets to you here in New York."

Laville leaned forward. "What's it worth to you?"

Sally Vicenti smiled. "How many good years are left for you in this game?"

"Half a dozen. Maybe more. I want the Slam."

"Your wife is a drunk. The Arab, Saadi, is pressuring you to straighten up, clean up the image for public relations. You have a hex hanging over you. Until Ohio, you hadn't beaten Koras in what, a year? How would it be if your tennis public—and maybe the eager-beaver police out there—got their hands on the photos you took of Polak, so shortly before he died? How would it be if we produced an eyewitness to your deal with Torelli? According to the newspapers, you and Koras hate each other's guts. Too bad, a couple photos screw up a hot career."

Laville's jaw was tight. "What eyewitness?"

"Hey. I'm just asking what-if here."

Laville shifted uncomfortably in his chair. "So you keep me clean if I tank to Di Rocca in the finals?"

"Yes."

"What about Torelli?"

"Torelli's ours. We'll handle Torelli."

Laville felt sick, but at the same time he felt smarter than Di Rocca and his chubby partner. Maybe there was a way out. "So like I said, how about a deal?"

Sally sipped his wine. "Don't keep us in suspense."

Laville swung away from Sally and Di Rocca to stare at the action down on the court. His confidence was building. He'd handled Saadi. "If Di Rocca slides by Koras in the semis, I let him have the final. But next season, you deliver a Grand Slam for Terry Laville."

Sally narrowed his eyes. "We get a percentage."

"How much?"

"Thirty-five. Of everything."

Laville shook his head. "Ten. Max."

They argued for a couple of minutes and finally settled on eighteen percent. They shook hands on it. Laville stood up.

"What if Di Rocca loses his semi?"

Sally looked at Di Rocca. "He won't."

"I'm just asking what if."

Sally smiled up at him. "If he does, you still tank. You got it?"

Laville hated the idea of throwing a match to Koras. He made himself think about the year after, the Grand Slam.

"Yeah, we're all set."

Sally smiled. "It's nice doing business with you, Mr. Laville."

Leaving Sally's box, Laville was wondering how he'd break the news about the percentages to Arch Bell. Maybe it was time for a new manager, as well as a new wife.

Di Rocca watched Laville until he was out of sight. Then he turned to Sally. His stomach churned and the harsh sunlight hurt his eyes. He didn't like what Sally was up to. Too many angles. Too much to go wrong. Sally wasn't telling him everything.

"You want me to call Torelli? Tell him to back off?"

Sally had a strange light in his eyes as he studied the court, his eyes glued to Koras. He did not turn his head to follow the ball as it crossed the net. As far as Sally was concerned, there was only one player on the court—Pantakoras Belynkas. He answered without looking at Di Rocca.

"I'll talk to Torelli."

"Okay. Sure."

Feeling edgy, Di Rocca leaned forward, hands gripping his knees. Down on the court, Koras slipped a passing shot past Harper's outstretched racket.

"Have fun, Panties," Sally whispered. "Have fun while it lasts."

There was silence in the box until Koras won the game with a cleverly disguised topspin lob. The score was 5–2, Koras leading. As the players changed sides, Sally frowned, rubbed his forehead, and beckoned to Enrico. Enrico left his chair, squatted down beside Sally. Di Rocca could not hear what Sally told Enrico, who nodded and left the box.

Sally turned to Di Rocca. "Tell me, Jackie. How you going to beat Panties Koras in the semis?"

"There's only one way. Take the net, before he does."

Sally indicated Koras's opponent. "Harper's having problems trying that."

"Harper's a kid. Keeps hitting wide to Koras. That sets up the angle for the pass. I'm coming in by hitting down the middle."

Sally stared into Di Rocca's eyes. "Think you can take him, Jackie?"

"Isn't that the plan?"

"I know the plan. What I want to know is, can you take him?"

Di Rocca nodded. "Sure. Sure I can take him."

"Sure. Sure. Everyone can take him. How come no one does?"

Sally's eyes grew cold. He patted Di Rocca on the hand and turned back to the match. A bank of clouds drifted eastward, blocking out the hot sun, turning the day a soft gray. Summer was almost over. Di Rocca told himself to relax, but it didn't keep him from worrying.

One thing was certain. Sally's reputation was at stake with the other families. Family capos from Vegas and Miami kept asking hard questions. They weren't sure about this big-money move into professional tennis. Football was safe. So was basketball. The take from the U.S. Open was important. Paris and London had been peanuts compared to the gross revenue Sally expected from these climactic two weeks in New York. A hundred million, Di Rocca had heard. A hundred fifty million. This was Sally's big test. If he blew New York, he'd blow two years of preparation. Sally had to protect himself or lose face with the other families. The TV cameras would be rolling, creating a perfect moment for a sacrifice, a symbol of Sally's control. Fear made people do funny things, and if that meant a symbolic sacrifice, some big-name player thrown to the wolves to make a point, Di Rocca didn't want to be down there on that tennis court.

The killer, Torelli, had a reputation for never missing a hit. Set in motion, Torelli was a murder machine.

Down on the court, Harper lunged for a backhand volley. The ball ticked the edge of his racket, spun off the white tape, and slid down the net. Koras was moving for it, angling in from the baseline, but the ball was too close to the net. Koras acknowledged his opponent's shot with a wide grin. A real tennis gentleman.

"Point for Harper," intoned the umpire. "He wins the game. The score is 5–3, with Mr. Belynkas leading in the set."

There was light applause for Harper's acrobatic dive. But after the applause had died down in the stands, Sally Vicenti was still clapping loudly. He wasn't clapping for the young Californian, Di Rocca knew. He was applauding anything that went against Koras.

Sally hated Koras. Was he losing control?

TWENTY-ONE

The stadium was filled to capacity when Milo Tigrid
walked onto the court for his quarterfinal match with Di Rocca.
Twenty thousand people were shouting and waving their arms
in the air like so many banners when the champion walked on.
The cries of the crowd competed with the deafening transit of
a Boeing 737 on its way out of La Guardia.

At the bottom of the crater, the humid heat seemed as concentrated as the focus of a solar oven. The clamor of the crowd
cascaded down the stands like a waterfall of noise. The great
American tennis fair had been in progress over a week now. So
far, there had been no incidents. In the excitement of the spectacle, the tennis fans talked less of the threats that had been
made and instead gossiped about the tennis. After a few days
of pure tennis, the media set aside the violence theme and
concentrated more on games, sets, matches, personalities—and
contracts.

To enhance the public-relations aspects of the matches,
Davey Cooper had practiced with a giant racket bearing the
logo of Ryker Equipment, his main sponsor. Pantakoras Belynkas had held a clinic on the grandstand court for a group of fifty
young black players selected by a Harlem Methodist church.
Milo Tigrid had played in the opening five minutes in a soccer
game with the New York Cosmos. There was a photograph of
Milo shaking hands with the famous Pelé, who was wearing
shoes made by Magnelli, Milo's main sponsor. In the Round of
Sixteen, Terry Laville had come onto the court carrying a large
cardboard tree trunk and the facsimile of a woodcutter's double-edged ax. Printed on the tree, the name "Laville's Forest
Country" identified the builders of Canadian chalets who had
given his name to their newest development outside Vancouver.

Even the diminutive Tania Pikeste had succumbed to the
mirages of advertising by dancing with the pompom girls of a
baseball team with its headquarters in the field adjacent to

the Tennis Center. For this U.S. Open, the spectators had been offered all the circus tricks that Madison Avenue could dream of.

Nothing had been modified in the natural development of the tournament. A close look might reveal many more plain-clothes policemen patrolling the stands, talking on hand-held radios, watching for suspicious behavior. In several instances, cartons destined for the refreshment stands were opened and their contents checked. None of this was overt enough to disconcert the crowds. In the skies above the stadium, two police helicopters hovered, compounding the din of passing airplanes.

Di Rocca had not appeared yet. Milo walked to the referee's stand, pointing up at a 747 in takeoff, a roiling trail of gray-black jet exhaust pouring from its engines.

"I see you still haven't managed to keep the birds quiet."

"We haven't given up hope. Mr. Cabot is talking about buying up La Guardia."

As the airplane passed, the stands shook, as if from an earthquake. Most of the crowd was standing, waiting for the entrance of Di Rocca. In the top rows, hundreds of youths in black leather were killing time drinking beer, silent for the moment. They had arrived in hoards, leaving their motorcycles in a parking area especially cleared for them. The security people had been worried about the invasion, but the Chief of Detectives said he had no basis to exclude them.

"They'll make a moving wall around Di Rocca," said O'Brien, putting the best face on it he could. Indeed, with their black casket helmets pulled down over Ray-Ban glasses, their lips dark from the sun, they were an impressive counterthreat.

Now, in the upper stands, people grew restless and began to throw beer cans. There were some outcries and a few minor injuries until policemen broke up the skirmishes and took the culprits away.

Milo checked the clock on the scoreboard, noting that Di Rocca was already five minutes late. A wave of panic seized the Yugoslav, as he remembered the death of Armando Reyes. He wondered if Koras had felt this way at Wimbledon, when Polak had failed to show up. Milo sat in his chair, his face buried in a white towel. Before the match, he had prepared a farce for the crowd, something to keep things moving, but now he knew he would not use his jokes today. Today he wanted to win.

As he sat there, he thought of B.J., his new lady. Sitting on her terrace, she had asked him to handle the sports service of a television station she ran in Chicago.

"I know nothing of television," he had protested.

"But you know sports, Milo. And you are lovely with people. You would be behind the scenes, organizing, smoothing rifts, giving counsel."

Inside his mind, he saw his face on a television set. It wasn't a bad idea, and certainly easier than sweating your heart out on a hot tennis court. "Let me consider it . . ."

Milo was jolted by a thunderous round of applause as Di Rocca came onto the court. Milo grinned. He had never before been so happy to see an opponent. The two men walked to opposite ends of the court and began to warm up.

When Nora Laville came into the players' cafeteria at the Tennis Center, Athena von Heidelberg was dreamily stirring a wilted straw in the remains of her strawberry ice cream soda. It was almost eight in the evening and the Princess wore a man-tailored silk shirt with three buttons undone and a pair of designer jeans. Nora was dressed in black, with a pearl necklace. Athena waved at Nora, who came over, trying to smile.

"How is the apartment?"

"It's . . . pleasant." A waiter came up to take her drink order. Nora's eyes were sunken, and she wore too much makeup.

"Terry wants a divorce," Nora said, as the waiter walked away.

"That brute. When did he tell you?"

"He came by this morning, looking terrible. I had a feeling he was with his little Hollywood tart, Shirley what's-her-name. I got angry, and he—" She paused. "He hit me."

"The bastard."

Nora nodded.

"Leave him," Athena said. "A judge would give you a nice settlement. And there are thousands of men around who would take good care of you."

"Yes. I should have married my photographer when I had the chance."

The waiter arrived with Nora's drink. She signed for it and took a long swallow.

At 5–all in the fourth set of the quarterfinal between Koras and Peter Abraham, play was halted because of a commotion in the stands, near the broadcast booth. Half a dozen plainclothes security men ran onto the court to surround Koras and his opponent. The crowd buzzed, and one could hear the sharp crackle of walkie-talkies.

The closest security man wore an ID badge that read RIVERA.

"What's up?" Koras asked.

Rivera surveyed the crowd with field glasses. "Guy with a rifle. Up there."

"Have they got him?"

"Yeah."

"Thanks."

Koras felt a sense of relief, like a too taut rubber band going back to normal. Rivera was dark, well-dressed, with even teeth and the poise of an anchorman on the evening news. He shook Koras's hand. "Tell you a secret, Mr. Belynkas?"

"Sure."

"I got a hundred on you, to win."

"Today?"

"No. Sunday. The final."

"You're a gambler. I'm not there yet."

"You'll get there. I seen you play before."

"Hope you don't lose your life savings."

Rivera grinned. "You can hurt Laville, or whoever. I'm betting on it."

"Thanks."

"Know what I think? That Laville's a bum."

The stands were buzzing as uniformed police brought down a man wearing a gray jacket and Levi's. His hands were handcuffed behind his back. He was normal-looking, someone you would never glance twice at on the street.

It took ten minutes for the crowd to settle down. People

returned to their seats. Rivera and his security force retired to the seats near the court. The umpire, voice shaking, called for play to resume.

As they started up again, Koras felt luck on his side. Abraham hit two shots out, one into the stands, showing that the delay had hurt his confidence. Sensing weakness, Koras strung the younger man out with drop shots and slices, pulling him wide to the forehand, dinking the ball across the net, forcing Abraham to sprint for the next shot. Abraham was fast. He got to everything. But the sting had left his spectacular returns.

Koras won the fourth set, 7–6, in the tiebreaker, which put him into the semifinals. The crowd chanted "King King Koras!" echoing the old days. As he walked off the court with Abraham, he thought about people like Rivera, the security man, guys who probably made only three hundred a week and who had bet a third of that on him. To win.

Malone had to call Archer Bell, who had a contact in the NYPD, to find out the gun wasn't loaded—the man hadn't bought the right-size ammunition. The gun was a Colt Commando, Army issue, telescope sight, so the police could hold the guy on that. Army weapons were illegal. His name was Alva G. Wreston, from the Chicago area. A computer check showed that he had a record for car theft, B&E (mostly upscale homes in Kenilworth and Evanston), and two convictions for pushing dope in high school.

"According to the police report, the man's a klutz, when it comes to weapons," Bell told him.

"The crazies are out as we approach the semis."

"Yes. Four players, three New Yorkers. The fans will be badgering us for a larger stadium if things go on." Bell was still at the Tennis Center, on Harrison Cabot's private line. Malone was at the hotel. Laville had won his semifinal against Colombier, but the match had not held the tension of the Koras-Abraham duel. "You've done a good job, Matt."

"Thanks, Mr. Bell."

"After this is over, let's sit down for a heart-to-heart. When Terry wins here, he'll start training for the Grand Slam. I have plans for making this a historic move. I'll need your help."

"I'd like that, Mr. Bell."

But after he'd hung up, Malone wondered. Did he really want to work for Archer Bell? The guy was prissy, rich, fussy as an old maid eating warm Jell-O.

And Malone still had a hunch about Laville.

Alain Clavier met Frank Fenwick at the entrance to the locker rooms, while Laville was playing Colombier in the semifinal. Fenwick was studying a memo card containing numbers in well-ordered rows.

"F.F., there is a rumor you are planning to sign Di Rocca, to bring him into your stable."

The Texan grinned. "The surprise of New York. A clay-courter doing this well on deco turf. That's made him worth more money."

"Sometimes, my dear Frank, you are disgusting."

"Heck, Alain, I just know where the money is."

Fenwick put away his card and rubbed his face, to churn away the fatigue. The players had been great so far, but Fenwick, an old hand at tennis, knew there hadn't been a really great match out there. He had personally been in on two cabinetlike meetings in the offices of two sponsors where all the talk had been of death at the semifinals. More tickets had been sold, and the profits of the sponsors were soaring. Now, if Koras could just win this Grand Slam, a cut of that money would be his.

As Fenwick and Clavier continued to talk, Milo Tigrid came in from his match with Di Rocca.

"Well, Milo. What happened?"

Milo grinned. "I have lost the match, but I have saved my miserable life." He began to undress.

"What was the score?"

"It was 12–10 in the tiebreak, fifth set. I was planning to win. In fact, I could taste the sweetmeat of victory. And then one of your damnable aeroplanes flew over, and I was momentarily disconcerted. That is the word, I hope. And my service lost its sting, and Di Rocca closed me out." Milo sighed. "I assure you, I tried my best, despite this threat of death we are under."

"I speak," said Clavier, "for the entire tennis community when I offer my thanks."

Milo waved a hand. "Now I shake these security guards. They follow one into a lady's very boudoir."

The men laughed. Milo kept on undressing. His voice was light, easy, full of mirth; but his face was serious. Perhaps the reason was that he felt this was his last professional tournament.

And now he was out of it, for good.

Malone's room was on the same floor as Laville's at the Meridien, so he could hang around without attracting a lot of attention. During the afternoon, when he saw the floor was deserted, Malone had used the electronic lock-picking system from Griswold to open the door of Laville's suite. It was late in the day of the men's quarterfinals. The maids had been there; the beds were made.

The suite was good-sized. A living room with a big sofa, three easy chairs, a wet bar, a wall-size TV. There was a bedroom off to the left, king-size bed, private bath. Sitting room, with a table, chairs for four. Small kitchen. A smaller bedroom off to the right, second king-size bed, a smaller bath. Laville's clothes were in the larger bedroom, still in suitcases. Apparently, Laville hadn't had time to unpack when they had moved him here for security reasons.

Malone walked through the living room to search the bedroom. He systematically worked the clothes, the pockets, the toes of the shoes. He went through three suitcases without finding anything. There was a separate tennis bag containing nothing but shoes. In the tip of a pair of Magnelli running shoes, he found a slip of paper with a phone number on it, and the name Dick. He jotted the number down on the back of an envelope, along with the name.

As he put the suite back the way he'd found it, Malone thought about his work during the summer.

This had been the best summer of his life as a private detective. He'd worked 87 days straight, making $200 a day from the ITF, which came to just over seventeen grand. He'd been paid fourteen already, with the rest to come after the U.S. Open. He'd used the money to buy the Griswold system. And if he kept Laville out of trouble, Malone would hook in another ten grand from Archer Bell.

* * *

When Malone got back to his room, Muriel was sitting in front of the dressing table, combing her rich red hair. On the small desk was a stack of photographs Muriel had taken at Flushing Meadow.

"There is something interesting, you might want to see it."

She walked over to the table and picked up three photographs she had taken of someone in the stands. Malone recognized Laville because he was so huge. The big Canadian was in a private box down near courtside, talking to a heavyset man in a tennis shirt. The man had a glass of wine in his hand. Behind the man and Laville sat Jackie Di Rocca. Behind Jackie, a man listened to a radio through headphones.

Malone looked more carefully. "Can we get a blowup of this? All the faces?"

"I think so. Does it mean something?"

"Maybe. How soon can we have it?"

"As soon as I can find a lab, if any are open."

"Great." Taking the envelope out of his pocket, Malone walked to the phone and dialed the number. After three rings, a mechanical voice came on the line to tell him the number was no longer in service and there was no forwarding number listed.

Chief of Detectives Ross O'Brien had eaten dinner with a U.S. Senator at the Four Seasons. There was a lot of talk about Flushing Meadow, which had taken over the headlines of major newspapers all across the country. O'Brien assured the Senator that things were under control.

He got back to his office around ten, where he sat down to do some paperwork. He took an hour to read through the daily report from Lieutenant Lucchesi on the security at Flushing Meadow. Everything had gone well, and the four semifinalists were known at last. David Cooper would play Terry Laville. Pantakoras Belynkas would play Jack Di Rocca. It was magnificent for the fans—three New York players among the four best tennis players in the world. That flattered O'Brien's civic pride.

But now these four men had to be protected as though the very future of America depended on their well-being.

Lucchesi arrived at a quarter past midnight. "Chief, I think we've got something."

"What?"

"There's word out on the street about a hit being set up. It's not much. But there's a bomber who goes by the code name TNT."

O'Brien leaned forward. "What about it?"

"No one knows who's going to be hit, or how. But this guy TNT is supposed to have learned his explosives with the military."

"What's his real name?"

"My people are checking Army records, but so far we haven't turned anything up."

"Well, keep going. How many men have you put on this thing?"

"Counting the plainclothes people, three hundred and change."

"An army." O'Brien puffed on his cigarillo. "Anything from your sources?"

Lucchesi shook his head. "Nothing yet. I've got my lines out."

"Do some rousting. I need results now. Tomorrow is too late."

"Right, Chief."

As Lucchesi walked out, O'Brien wondered if his right-hand man was telling him everything he knew.

TWENTY-TWO

Will Channer found his player in the downstairs kitchen at Court's Court. Koras was supposed to be concentrating on the semifinal match he would be playing in a few hours' time. Channer suspected he was waiting for a call from Laure Puget.

From the fanlight in the basement, Channer could see the legs of the police security force, patrolling the grounds. There were also policemen in cars, securing the estate and the roads around it. For an hour this morning, a helicopter had circled Court's Court, until Channer called to complain.

"So you got through to the militia," Koras said.

"Finally. They have a chain of command that would make the ITF look small by comparison."

"What will happen after the semis? Will they scale down the security?"

"Hell, no, mate. They'll scale it *up*."

Koras sat down at the table. "Tell you a secret, Will?"

"Sure."

"Now that we're almost finished here, I'm having second thoughts about voting to play."

"Are you crazy? With the Grand Slam only two matches away?"

"I don't give a shit about the Grand Slam."

"What?"

"We're ruining the game, Will. . . . We play for the love of it. That's why they used to come out to watch us hit. Now they come out to see who's going to die."

Will walked to the sink and ran water into a glass. "Listen to you, for Christ's sake. This is the first time since I've known you that a woman has interfered with your tennis."

"Is it that obvious?"

"I knew it when you ducked out on Wimbledon to see her."

"I remember when I first came on the circuit. I wasn't winning. No one knew me. I'd be out there getting killed, wondering how to hang on for another week. Then I met Athena, and everything changed. And after Athena, there were lots of girls, a whole world full. And now there's just one."

"Put her out of your head. Or you can kiss the Grand Slam goodbye."

Koras said nothing for a moment. Then he stared at Will. "You're right. I'll try to stop thinking about it."

Koras was upstairs when the phone rang. "Laurel!" Koras was excited. "Where are you?"

"I am here," she said and burst out laughing.

"Here?" He felt momentarily confused. "Where?"

"In New York. At John F. Kennedy. You invited me, and here I am!"

"When did you get here? *How* did you get here?"

"I took a charter flight from Luxembourg. We landed an hour ago, but there was the *douane.* How far away are you?"

"Don't worry. Not far." He was frantic with haste now. "I'll come and get you. With the police—"

"The police? But why, Pantakoras?"

"Security," he yelled. "For the matches. Tell me where you will be? Which airline. Give me a landmark."

They made plans to meet at the TWA reservation desk. Koras hung up and ran out of the house without replacing the receiver. He fumbled in his pocket for the keys to the Mercedes, discovered they were not there. A security man with a submachine gun asked if something was wrong.

"Kennedy," Koras said. "We've got to get to JFK."

"Why?"

"To meet someone." Koras ran back into the house, where he encountered Will Channer.

"So she's here."

"Yes. Can you bring my gear to the Tennis Center? I'm going to pick her up—I'll meet you there."

"All right." Channer was smiling. It was not usual for Koras the Surgeon to be so emotional. "You go on ahead."

Koras found the car keys. His hands were shaking. Followed by two escort vehicles, his Mercedes headed west toward JFK.

The policemen posted at the players' entrance to the stadium could not believe their eyes. The convoy escorting Di Rocca was a scene from Walter Hill's *Streets of Fire.*

The lime-yellow Buick convertible, with its chrome rear wings looking like sharks' fins, advanced slowly, flanked by a motorcycle escort, fifty huge bikes driven by gang members wearing black leather. Silver studs glistened on their wristbands. Between the bikes, they carried banners bearing slogans glorifying Di Rocca.

"Holy shit," exclaimed a cop. "Would you like to beat this guy in tennis? Or would you rather lose?"

"Maybe they'll riot, right on the court."

The vintage Buick passed the cordon of policemen and drove inside to park. A group of inspectors in plainclothes met Di Rocca as he got out of the car. Ortega was behind the wheel.

"Have a good night, Jack?" asked one of the security men.

"Terrific. You?"

"We buttoned this place up. Between the police and the regular ushers, we've got six hundred men in the stands, six hundred more watching the entrances."

"What about a kamikaze attack?" Ortega asked, as he came up.

In answer, the security man pointed up, where a helicopter circled lazily.

The policemen surrounded Di Rocca, who looked at his coach and laughed.

At JFK, Koras left the Mercedes in the no-parking zone and hurried inside to find Laure, followed by a red-faced plainclothes security man. His heart was pounding. He didn't really have this kind of time; he was due at the Tennis Center in an hour. Then he saw Laure standing at the TWA counter. In a moment, they were in each other's arms. Her cheek was warm against his. Her face was wet with tears.

"How was Greece?"

"Very warm. And full of tourists."

He was watching the time, so he steered her toward the exit. "I can't believe you're here."

"There is a man following us." She indicated the security guard.

"Oh, that's Johnny Holmes. Frank Fenwick hired him to protect me."

Laure stiffened. "It is my fault."

"I play in an hour. What's your fault?"

"Monsieur Fenwick made the call, about the money. You are in trouble because of it, and because of me."

Koras looked at her and grinned. "And that's why you're here?"

She nodded. Her face was serious. "One of the reasons."

"What's the other?"

"You know, Pantakoras," she said quietly. He could feel his

heart beating wildly, telling him he was in love with the right woman.

Headquarters for the security force was in a large tan RV parked near the main entrance to the Tennis Center. Inside, police personnel wearing headphones were monitoring a bank of TV screens that lined one entire wall. At one end of the room, Chief Ross O'Brien was talking to Lieutenant Lucchesi, while he kept an eye on the television monitors. A dozen cameras routinely swept the entrances and the spectators in the stands. On the desk in front of the two men was a file labeled SABRINA.

"You know anything about this?"

"There was a hooker working the area a year ago, using the name Sabrina. They change names like Di Rocca changes socks."

"We need to check it out."

"I'll send someone over."

"Hanrahan should be in midtown."

"This is dated four days ago, Chief. She could be long gone by now."

"We still need to check it."

O'Brien sat down in a swivel chair and began absorbing the visual information from the television monitors. It was the day of the semifinals and everything was on alert. Lucchesi put in a call to Red Hanrahan.

At the changeover, Koras drank some water, then closed his eyes to concentrate on the deep breathing that would keep him in control. The score was 4–3, in the fourth set, and he was about to draw even after losing the first two sets to Di Rocca. Koras had started off slowly, returning the ball, feeling out his opponent, but Di Rocca had come on with a new ferocity, hitting winners and taking chances. The first set had been Di Rocca, 6–2; the second, Di Rocca, 7–5.

Now Koras was ahead and he could feel the momentum starting to change. He was playing steadily and he could sense Di Rocca's indecision. In the private boxes at courtside, he kept looking at Sally Vicenti, who had offered him $250,000 to lose.

And three boxes away, Laure sat with Athena and Colombier and Saadi.

He could feel the pressures bearing in on him, trying to distract him. On the one hand, there was his honor as a player and a sportsman. Honor had brought him out here today, to play for 20,000 spectators. It had kept him going when he got tired, when he felt sick to his stomach, when he wanted to lose, go home, take a shower, drink a beer.

He thought about Sally and his threat. He thought about Laure and her envelope of money. Koras did not want to die, and he did not think of himself as a hero. But in the end, he knew there would be no reason to keep on tomorrow if he did not do his best today.

As he passed Jack Di Rocca at the umpire's chair, he smiled in a friendly way and said: "You're out, Jack. Kiss the finals goodbye."

And Di Rocca answered: "And you're dead, King."

At the Cherry Hotel in Brooklyn, Sergeant Red Hanrahan took some time to examine the decayed façade before crossing the street. Two youths leaned against a wall, jiving to a ghetto blaster. Down the block, three young girls in bright miniskirts exposed their wares to the pedestrians and cars going by.

Hanrahan went inside. The lobby was filthy and smelled of vomit and forgetfulness. Behind the desk sat a porter who weighed easily four hundred pounds. He was digging into a greasy bag of popcorn as he watched a soap opera on television. The man wore a fluorescent shirt and a soft brown wig.

Hanrahan took a look at the grease-covered counter and decided not to lean on it. He showed his badge. The porter looked over, then swung his eyes back to the television.

"Sabrina," Hanrahan said.

"Who?"

Hanrahan walked around the desk, grabbed the back of the swivel chair, and dumped the porter out of it. The fat man yelled, clawed the air for balance. It was no use. He wound up in a heap on the floor, his feet tangled in the voluminousness of his pants.

"Sabrina. She's a working girl. You want this flea trap to stay in business? Or how about I put in a call to City Health?"

The fat man struggled to his knees. He picked up a phone and pressed three buttons. "There's a cop here, wants to see you. Yeah, I know." Pause. "Tough." He put down the phone and turned to Hanrahan with a pale face that did not mask his anger. "She'll be right down."

"Thanks."

While he waited, Hanrahan leafed briefly through a soiled pornographic magazine that had been left lying on the counter, and then walked to a dilapidated chair at the farthest corner of the room. Before sitting down, he wiped the seat of the chair with his handkerchief, which he did not put back into his pocket.

Sabrina was a magnificent mulatto who could not have been more than twenty years old. Despite the years of drugs and prostitution, she looked fresh, young, almost innocent. Her skin was a soft creamy chocolate. She had a pretty smile that made Hanrahan wonder how she had found her way to this hellhole.

He asked her about the conversation.

"Oh, sure. There were these two guys—I thought maybe they were gay because they come here a lot—in the next room. I'd just finished a trick and was lying there feeling a little sick. Anyway, I overhear this one guy say he wants someone taken out, a hit, like. And the other guy says it will cost fifty grand. And then they talk it over, only I can't hear that much, except I hear this one word, 'flush,' two or three times, and another word, 'player.' "

"What were their names?"

"I only heard one name. Dick."

"Did you get a look at them?"

"I bumped into one. He was coming out. So was I."

"What did he look like?"

"Big, like a football player. He moved like a young guy. And I think he had blond hair. It's hard to tell in here, it's so dark. His hat fell off."

"What kind of hat?"

"It looked, I don't know, too small for his head."

Hanrahan wrote it all down, doublechecked everything, and told Sabrina he would be in touch.

"I like cops," the girl said, touching his sleeve. "Any time you feel like a party, give me a call."

"Thanks."

After Sabrina had left, Hanrahan questioned the fat porter. It took him thirty minutes to pinpoint the night, more than a week ago. The porter had a bad memory and was used to forgetting his clients. With careful prompting, and a promise he would answer the same questions downtown, he did remember a few details.

"Okay, this guy Dick. He was big, with a face that looked carved, like a statue, if you know what I mean."

"Anything else?"

"He wore a hat. Had crazy eyes."

"What color was his hair?"

"Light blond, I guess."

"What about the other one?"

"Him, I've seen around. Goes by the name of Mike."

"What's his line of work?"

"How should I know?"

"What was he wearing, this guy Mike?"

"Leather flight jacket, I think. Sharp. He had on jeans that looked new, and gloves, the kind race-car drivers wear."

"And they were here how many times?"

"Once."

"Who paid for the room?"

"Dick paid. In cash."

Hanrahan kept the questions going, but didn't get much more information. He told the porter he would send around an artist from the department with an Identi-Kit. Then he called Lucchesi at the Tennis Center. Let him figure it out.

After beating Di Rocca in five sets, Koras showered, then put on his lucky warm-up suit and went to look for Laure. A group of six security men went with him, keeping in touch on their walkie-talkies. Laure was sitting with his coach and Fenwick in the cafeteria. Laure hugged Koras, and he introduced her to the swarm of photographers and journalists who were there for the postmatch interview. There were questions about the match and about the Grand Slam. Near the end of the interview, Judson Garwood asked: "What will your strategy be tomorrow against the winner of the Cooper-Laville match?"

"I'll play them the same. Both have big forehands, so I'll play that side first, hoping to open up the backhand for a putaway. I'll go to the net behind everything. And I hope I don't get tired."

Eleanor Stark asked, "How much credence do you put in this hex that Laville has when he plays New York?"

"I haven't seen any evidence of it so far. It looks like Terry's beaten his hex at last."

There was one last question, about money. Frank Fenwick took it.

"When Koras wins the Grand Slam on Sunday, he'll pass the four-million mark. Also, I'm negotiating a contract with a company whose name I cannot divulge for a two-million-dollar endorsement. As you know, that will top Terry Laville's recent contract with Sahara Sports."

There was a clamor to know the name of the company, but Fenwick wouldn't say another word. In the corridor, walking out, Koras took Fenwick aside to ask for more information.

"I didn't know about this new deal, F.F. What's up?"

"Let me handle the deals, Koras. You just get your butt out there and play tomorrow."

"Will it fix my bank loans?"

Fenwick smiled at Laure as he answered. "It will fix everything."

The Laville-Cooper match began five minutes after Koras had finished beating Di Rocca. In the center of the stadium the noise had risen to an unbearable pitch. The tension had mounted during the previous match, and now that Laville was playing and no one had been killed, fans were starting to let off steam by whooping and throwing beer cans. Three times the police flying squads charged into the stands to remove troublemakers. And at the base of the crater, the blows between the players became harder and harder. Cooper pounded a forehand. Laville pounded one back.

At 3–4 in the fourth set, with Cooper leading, Laville threw a tantrum over a line call. He swore at the linesperson, a pretty woman in a blue blazer and official khaki skirt, and then he demanded she be removed. The tournament referee had to be called, and Harrison Cabot himself came down to the court to calm the players.

Davey Cooper, who wanted the point badly, appealed to the stands by grabbing a clipboard and walking around taking votes from the fans in the boxes at courtside.

At last, the umpire brought the match back under control. He removed the linesperson and awarded the point to Davey. Laville's fury seemed to make him play better.

Davey lost the semifinal, 7–6, in the tiebreaker in the last set.

Back at the hotel, Malone called Di Rocca, but there was no answer. He left a message, asking Jackie to get back to him.

Terry Laville was watching a replay of his match against Cooper when the phone rang in his suite at the Meridien. Laville answered. It was Jack Di Rocca.

"Don't talk. Just listen."

"Okay."

"Things have changed. They want you to win tomorrow."

"Terrific. Just like that?"

"Yeah. Forget the hex. Forget the other stuff. Just go out there and win."

"That's an order?"

"From the top," Di Rocca said, and hung up.

Laville tried watching TV again, but kept getting distracted. If he went out, about eleven cops would follow him. He was bored with Nora. He wished Shirley were here. Something kept bothering him, made him want to check with Di Rocca, but when he dialed Di Rocca's house, he could only get the answering service.

TWENTY-THREE

On Sunday, the day of the men's final at Flushing Meadow, Lieutenant Lucchesi and Chief Ross O'Brien left the Mayor's office feeling optimistic. The semifinals were over, and no one had died.

In a brief ceremony, played out with a medium-priced California sherry and some key people from the newspapers, the Mayor had congratulated his police force for their management of the Flushing Meadow affair.

When the Lieutenant and the Chief were comfortably installed in the back seat of O'Brien's command car, O'Brien blew out his breath, a sure sign of anxiety, and asked for an update.

"The Brooklyn hooker, Sabrina. What have you developed on the guy she described?"

"Our only connection was with a rumor floating around," Lucchesi said, "about a contract hit. They were bringing in a shooter from the Coast. We've had men on the airports, and not a single pro has arrived since we heard."

"He could already have been here."

"Yes. But they like to operate from a base, the same way we do."

"Don't lecture me on criminal intelligence, okay?"

"Sorry, Chief." Lucchesi laid out three dossiers on the seat next to O'Brien. "We've narrowed it down this far."

O'Brien flipped open the first dossier. Edmund Schell, a small-time killer wanted in Miami, with two prison terms and a stint in an institution for the criminally insane in Delaware. The photo showed a sweet-faced smiling youth with dreamy eyes. "Pretty boy," he grunted.

The second dossier was fat. Its subject was Rinaldo J. Florentino, who specialized in icepick murders. Florentino had been employed by three families, two in Las Vegas, a third in Pueblo, Colorado. His photo showed a round-faced man with shadowy cheeks. He had relatives in Hoboken.

O'Brien glanced at Lucchesi.

"We've got round-the-clock surveillance on the relatives."

The third dossier was Henry Corelli, alias Michael Mancini, alias Frederick H. Smith, alias Frank Torelli. Corelli/Mancini/Smith/Torelli had served in the Army in Vietnam. He was an expert with pistols and automatic weapons. At the age of twenty-eight, he had competed for a place on the Army's Modern Pentathlon team. The photo showed a blond man with hard eyes and a lean-jowled pockmarked face. Adjectives in the dossier caught O'Brien's attention: "shrewd," "resourceful," "imaginative in the field," "a survivor," "a master of disguise."

O'Brien sighed, closed the dossier. "Let's watch for this guy."

Lucchesi answered with a grin. "We're circulating copies of his mug shot."

O'Brien looked through the car window. His cigarillo was out. A motorcycle zipped past, doing fifteen miles over the limit. The driver wore a red crash helmet, faded blue shorts, sandals. His back and shoulders were sunburned and sweating.

"Hot one today."

"Supposed to hit ninety-two this afternoon."

"Hot."

Leaning over the table, lighting a cigarette from a candle, the Princess smiled seductively at the camera. For this set of pictures, she wore a white skirt and matching jacket with a filmy red blouse. The skirt had a modest slit up one side, perhaps ten inches long. For the occasion, she wore a brassiere. Every brand name would be documented in classy type near the proper photo. The *Elan* layout would be eight full pages, in color. Nora had worked hard, to take her mind off Terry. She was the editor in charge. She would make seven thousand dollars. The Princess would make ten thousand.

"That's it!" the photographer said. "Thank you, ladies."

"Thank you, John."

Nora kissed John Greenwald on the cheek. Until this summer, she hadn't realized how much she missed the old life. When he had packed up his equipment and left with his assistants, Nora and Athena sat down to lunch.

Nora was excited. Doubles was filled with the most beautiful, the most powerful, and the most affluent women in New York.

In the daytime, there were no men, and Doubles was the exclusive province of women. And Nora had selected this upscale domain as part of the background for her fashion layout on Athena. With the session over, the two women could concentrate on their food. Nora wanted to talk to her friend about Terry, but now that the photographer was gone, Athena seemed distraught. She kept looking over Nora's shoulder.

"Are you all right?" Nora asked.

"I'm expecting a phone call."

"Who from? Saadi?"

"No." Athena paused. "Someone else."

"A secret?"

"Yes." Athena speared a bite of lettuce. "How do you think the session went?"

"Just great." Nora was pleased. "I'm a big name at *Elan* now. I owe you."

"I am glad I could help you." She looked past Nora again, distractedly.

"If it's a man, you'll have to wait awhile," Nora said.

"Hmmm." Athena turned back to Nora. "How are things with Terry?"

"Worse. He still wants a divorce. He came back this morning, to get a racket and couple of headbands. There were policemen, so he couldn't hit me. I hated looking at his eyes." Nora paused. "They were so . . ."

"Terry's under a lot of strain."

"Yes. John Greenwald says I might even get back into modeling. They're using older women these days, searching for new markets." Nora bit her lip. "I'm not even thirty, and that hurt!"

Athena patted her hand. "Thirty is a remarkable age. Take it from me. You'll do very well."

A waitress came up to tell Athena there was a phone call for her. Athena excused herself and went to answer. Nora watched the Princess walk off, such a strong woman, so self-possessed. Could she ever be half as strong as the Princess?

When Athena came back, she was smiling.

"Good news, I hope."

"Yes." Athena touched Nora's shoulder. "I'm going away after the tournament. So we won't see each other for a while."

"Going away? Where?"

"I can't tell you right now. But I'll keep in touch."

"Where can I reach you?"

Athena smiled mysteriously. "I shall have to reach you."

"What about Saadi?"

"Saadi is about to receive a huge surprise. Perhaps the biggest one in his life."

The man in Sahara tennis clothes identified himself at the gate as Arthur Smythe. The number on his official USTA pass was 703, and he moved through security with minimum hassle. Smythe was a lean man in his early forties with short blond hair and a pockmarked face. He moved with the precision of a trained athlete. In his right hand was a tennis bag made by Laval Sportif.

Smythe made his way to the USTA locker room, where he opened a padlock on a locker and retrieved a narrow leather suitcase. There were players in here, suiting up, which made it impossible for him to change, so he left the locker room and made his way to the executive offices, where he located a men's room with a large stall designed to accommodate a wheelchair.

Behind the locked stall door, Smythe changed into the uniform of a police officer of the City of New York. When he emerged, he wore shooting glasses and carried a high-powered rifle fitted with a telescopic sight. His name tag read ESTEVEZ. In his right ear was an earplug connected to a radio attached to his belt. With the radio, he could communicate with Sally Vicenti.

By noon on Sunday, Sally Vicenti was tired of calling Jack Di Rocca's house and getting no answer. He told Enrico to find Jackie. Enrico relayed the instructions to Carmine. Then Sally and Enrico took the Mercedes out to Flushing Meadow, for the matches. In the trunk of the Mercedes was a picnic basket containing three bottles of Valpolicella, salami sandwiches, Italian cheese, olives from Italy, and a compact black Sony shortwave radio, rebuilt to copy police tactical frequencies.

Wearing the headphones, Enrico listened to the police talking to each other on the walkies. It took him five minutes to find the band Torelli was using. He talked to Torelli through a tiny boutonniere mike clipped to the lapel of his windbreaker. Enrico was good. He made it look as if he was talking to the boss.

"I got him. Torelli."

"Tell him to stand by." Sally liked the ring of that, stand by.

"Stand by, Torelli."

Sally checked his watch. The men's final was supposed to begin at two sharp. It was ten minutes after, and no players yet. Sally needed this day to be a good one. He had lost $750,000 when Koras beat Di Rocca in the semifinal. The problem was, it wasn't all his money. He owed some people. He also needed to make back the $750,000. That's why he bet on Koras, to win.

After that, he would let Torelli kill him.

At two-seventeen, no players had appeared yet, and Sally could feel the nerves at the side of his head pounding, the sure sign of a headache coming on. Then he saw Terry Laville walk onto the court, with Panties Koras right after him. Laville walked with his usual cocky confidence. Koras looked as usual, cool, easy. Di Rocca had said the Lithuanian did some crazy kind of exercise to chill out before a match. Applause rained down from the packed stadium, a few shouts of "King King Koras!" Sally smiled. It was a beautiful day, sunshine, pretty girls, a good breeze. Made you feel alive.

He told Enrico to open the first bottle of wine.

Muriel was late returning to the hotel, and then she took extra time dressing, so Malone watched the warm-up and the first couple of games on television in the room. There had been a fifteen-minute delay, with no explanation. Now that the players were hitting, Koras looked sharp, but Laville looked like murder on wheels. They were into the fourth game, tied 2–all, when Malone and Muriel got ready to leave their hotel room for the Tennis Center. Malone was just closing the door when the phone rang. He went back in to answer. It was Di Rocca.

"I been trying to get you, Jackie."

In the background, Malone could hear jets taking off, which meant Di Rocca was at an airport. "I got something for you, Malone."

"What?"

"Information."

"What kind of information?"

"Can't say, over the phone. I'm at JFK."

Di Rocca was on the move. "Christ," Malone said.

"Let me meet you, outside Pan Am, twenty minutes. Sooner, if you can make it. If you can't, it's tough."

"Give me a hint, Jackie. It's about you and Laville and the paisan in the tennis shirt?"

"See you at JFK," Di Rocca said and hung up.

"What is it?" Muriel asked.

"I have a feeling it's my bonus, from Archer Bell."

"Bonus?"

"Yeah. It's about to go out the window."

Sunday traffic made the trip to JFK an agony of delay for Malone and Muriel. It took almost an hour to get there from the Meridien, and then when their taxi pulled up in front of Pan Am, there was no sign of Di Rocca. Malone told the driver to wait, meter running, and gave him a twenty.

He and Muriel got out and hurried along the sidewalk. Still no Di Rocca, so Malone headed inside, to the ticket counter, while Muriel stayed to watch the sidewalk. The doors were automatic. As Malone stepped through, a soldier in the dress-green uniform of an Army captain grabbed his arm. It took Malone a very long moment to realize it was Di Rocca, complete with a short military haircut, dark glasses, and no beard.

"Over here. My flight's about to leave."

Malone walked with the heavyset tennis player to the security gate. As they walked, Di Rocca fished in his green flight bag and pulled out a microcassette, which he handed to Malone.

"What's on it?"

"Laville and a Mafia capo named Sally Vicenti. They plan to waste Koras."

"Jesus! How?"

"Hit man named Torelli, one of Sally's. My guess is a rifle, right after the finals."

"How long have you had this?"

Di Rocca handed Malone a diagram, drawn in pencil, of the seating area in the stadium. "Sally's box is here, at courtside."

Malone's mind raced through scenarios as he studied the diagram. "Not much time, Jackie."

"Listen, I know what you're thinking, but I had my own ass to cover. I thought Koras would play ball with Sally. When he didn't, I had to make some decisions." He indicated the uniform, ran his hand over his bare face.

Malone stared at the time. "What does the hitter look like?"

"Never saw him."

"What am I supposed to do?"

Di Rocca jabbed a finger at his rough diagram. "Throw a monkey wrench into Sally's plan." Di Rocca shifted uncomfortably under Malone's stare. "Look, you work for Arch Bell, and his boy Laville. I wasn't going to help any of you. But Koras is okay. I'd hate to see him buy it. See what you can do."

"I ace Sally," Malone said, touching the material of the uniform, "and you get back on the circuit?"

Di Rocca grinned. "I did have that thought."

Malone checked the clock over Di Rocca's right shoulder. It was almost three. The match had been under way forty-five minutes. Hold out, Koras.

Di Rocca tossed his flight bag onto the security conveyor. As he passed through the metal detector, he pushed the dark glasses down on his nose and winked at Malone.

Before Di Rocca was out of sight, Malone went to the nearest pay phone and dialed the hotline number Lieutenant Lucchesi had given out. But all Malone got was a busy signal. Sweating now, he tried three more times. Muriel ran up and he told her briefly what was happening. Using another pay phone, she tried calling. The time ticked away. The lines must be overloaded; they could not get through to the main Tennis Center number, either.

Malone dialed 911. After four rings, a dispatcher answered.

"This is an emergency."

"Go ahead, please."

"I've got information on an attempted hit at the Tennis Center. I need you to alert Lieutenant—"

The dispatcher cut him off. "An attempted hit? Did you say 'hit'?"

"That's right, officer. It's a Mafia hit, a guy with a rifle. He's about six-one, blond, with a pockmarked face . . ."

There was a disinterested, procedural drone to the dispatcher's voice as he interrupted again. "Where are you calling from, sir?"

"Me? I'm at JFK."

"And your name?"

"Malone. Matt Malone. Listen, I'm not kidding. This is—"

"Yes, sir, excuse me a moment. There's a call coming through on another line. Your call will be handled in turn."

Malone heard a crackle and he was standing there sweating, holding the receiver. The dispatcher thought he was a crank. Malone hung up and grabbed Muriel. "Come on."

They ran back outside. The taxi was still waiting, the meter up past $40. Malone told the driver to head for the Tennis Center. The time was 3:25. The match was over an hour old.

At 4–all in the fourth set, Laville threw his third temper tantrum of the afternoon, arguing with the umpire, trying to muddy Koras's timing.

Waiting for the tantrum to subside, Koras walked to the players' box, looked up at Laure, her face a sad smile. She passed a note down. The note said, "I love you," in French.

Je t'aime.

Koras folded it, put it in his pocket, and blew Laure a kiss.

Beside her, Milos started chanting, "King King Koras! King King Koras!"

The crowd took up the chant. Watching Laville, Koras felt his spirits lift. Across the court, Sally Vicenti sat with his number one, who was still plugged in to his baseball game.

Arguing with the umpire about a line call, Laville put his hands on his hips and looked up. He was hearing the umpire's voice, low and controlled, but now he could see the man's face had been replaced with the face of Mikhail Polak. Micky sat in the umpire's chair, his back to the sun, staring down. The sun threw his figure into silhouette, but Laville could sense the lean features, with those sad eyes, staring down at him in judgment.

"Hey?" Laville said, and moved to the side, so he could see better.

"The ball was out, Mr. Laville."

Laville wiped the sweat out of his eyes and looked past the umpire, into the stands, where Nora sat, in Saadi's box. The Princess was with her, looking terrific, her blonde hair blowing a little in the breeze. Saadi was behind the Princess. As Laville watched, Saadi's chauffeur came up to whisper in Saadi's ear. The Arab left the box.

"Let's play, Mr. Laville." It wasn't Micky's voice.

"Yes, sir."

Laville walked back to receive serve from Koras. As he hunkered down in the ready position, he thought of all the photographs taken of himself as the Woodcutter, Lumberjack Laville, awaiting serve, eyes straight ahead, sun glinting off the brass studs in his headband, elbows out.

The ball came, a fluffy floater, making Laville grin at how slow it was. He knew all the shots Koras had, cranking his arm now, winding up for the big kill, sending across a winner for sure.

He was surprised when Koras volleyed it back, deep. Out of position, Laville lobbed. Koras angled his overhead, sucking Laville off court, right into the box where Sally Vicenti sat. Laville slapped at the shot, kept going, climbed the wall of the box, grinned at the wop, who had stood up to get out of the way.

"Sorry, partner."

The crowd applauded. Laville's shot was wild. The point had gone to Koras. Laville fought back, hearing a soft buzz in his ears, the sure sound of failure. Tears came to his eyes when Koras won the game, to lead him for the first time in the match, 5–4.

Then Laville understood. The buzzing was applause. He felt tired now. As he walked to the chair for the changeover, he had a satisfying thought—if he lost, Koras was dead.

In the broadcast booth, tennis commentator Judson Garwood was hoarse with emotion. The final of the men's singles in the U.S. Open was classic, youth versus age, the young wizard against the mature master.

"A cross-court from Koras, dipping, short, pulling Laville wide. Laville hits it down the line, barely in, and now he charges the net. Koras holds the ball on the strings—he's famous for that—until the last minute. We don't know whether it's a lob or a passing shot. It's a lob! Laville goes back, looking tired now himself, all that high living perhaps catching up with him, Jim . . . and he slams an overhead down the sideline. The ball hooks; Koras barely catches it. He's in the forecourt . . . and cagily dumps a drop volley over the net. Laville charges up, but not in time. Not up."

"Not up," echoed the umpire.

"Laville starts to protest, then remembers he's got two penalty points, one warning, one point taken away. The next penalty point awards an entire game to Koras. And that would end the match. So Terry Laville backs off."

At 5–6 in the fifth set, Laville leading, Koras didn't care whether he won or lost. He was too tired. His right knee ached. He wanted to be off the court in a therapy bath. He wanted a beer, some sleep, Laure by his side. But he could tell from the crowd noise—the ooh's and ahhh's on the lobs, the quick machine-gun applause on the put-away volleys, the tightrope tension during the longer exchanges—he could tell that they were enjoying it.

You tried to forget. The world reminded you.

And that was why he and Laville were here—for the crowd, for anonymous tennis fans all over the world, watching on television. They were here for the kids growing up, playing tennis outdoors, under the sun. He wasn't here for himself, for fame and money and applause. Maybe Laville was.

But only because Laville kidded himself.

He and Laville weren't here for Saadi, or for Archer Bell. Or even for Frank Fenwick. No. They were here for the spectators who had paid their hard-earned money to see this match.

That was all. And that was everything in the world. To play your best, no matter what was going to happen to your knee.

"The score in the final set is 6–5," intoned the umpire. "Mr. Laville leads."

* * *

On the walkway between the stadium and the grandstand court, Saadi passed three uniformed policemen, hard-faced men with glinting eyes. The chauffeur was three paces behind him. "Wait here," he said. The chauffeur, an Englishman named Bryce, touched his cap with two fingers. On the stadium court they were playing the finals of the mixed doubles. The western bleachers were in shadow and spectators were scattered about. Everyone with a stadium seat was next door, watching the men's final. A man came up to Saadi. It was Leonardo, the brother of Armando Reyes. He was three inches shorter than Armando, with a flat Indian face and dark eyes. He wore a red player's blazer and tennis shorts.

Saadi started to offer his hand, but Reyes moved toward him menacingly. His eyes looked overheated. "Señor Reyes. What is it?"

On the rim of the court, two policemen stood, watching the match. Reyes came close. "Do not lie to me."

"Lie? About what?"

"You and your man, Laville. I read in the papers you are paying him millions. To you, he is important."

"So?"

"Even in Peru, a man protects his investment."

Reyes's face had a tortured expression. Saadi circled to his left, for a better view of the Peruvian's face. "What is it you want from me?"

"Someone gives the drugs to kill my brother. This someone I am here to determine. Like the tennis, I am conducting my own eliminations."

The man was insane. Saadi's mind raced through several possibilities. "You are mistaken."

"No. I see your woman with Armando. With her, he is El Señor Amor. Also, I hear *historias* of this Laville, King of the Sleeping Pill."

Saadi was sweating now. "Those stories are untrue."

A policeman came into view behind Reyes, and Saadi weighed his chances of calling out. At the same time Reyes opened his hand to reveal a knife with a yellow handle. "Why?

is my question. Why does someone give my brother these thing?"

"It wasn't Laville."

"You lie. I see it in your eye."

Saadi allowed his gaze to slide away, with Reyes watching every move. "He had no reason, you see."

Reyes stepped closer and Saadi smelled sweat and foul breath. "You are a bad liar, señor. He has the reason."

"What?"

"Armando thrashes him in Palm Springs, Atlanta, Tokyo, Hawaii. He flirts with Laville's wife."

Saadi frowned, for effect. "I wasn't aware of—"

But before he finished, Reyes snorted derisively, then turned away from Saadi with a look of triumph and hurried back along the passageway, toward the stadium court. Saadi sat down for a moment to wipe his face with a silk handkerchief. From the stadium he could hear applause and the roar of the crowd. There were twenty thousand spectators packed inside and every one was a potential customer of Sahara Sports.

When Saadi got back to his box, his legs still trembled from the encounter with Leonardo Reyes. Nora Laville had left the Princess alone. Koras had tied Laville 6–games all, and the umpire was announcing the sudden-death tiebreaker.

Traffic held up Malone and Muriel. What should have been a thirty-minute ride turned into more than an hour. Malone was perspiring. Maybe he should have stuck with the telephone. Muriel watched the traffic, her eyes filled with dread.

Before the taxi pulled to a complete stop in front of the security van at the Tennis Center, Malone shoved a hundred at the driver. He and Muriel were out of the cab before it stopped rolling, heading for the gate, where they were searched. Once inside, Malone headed for the security van. He flashed his writer's pass and asked for Lieutenant Lucchesi. Instead, a smooth-faced cop in uniform stepped down out of the van and started asking questions. Lucchesi couldn't be contacted.

Malone knew he was getting the runaround. "What's the score in the final?"

"Almost finished. They're in the middle of a tiebreaker."

"Come on." Malone grabbed Muriel's hand and they started into the stadium.

On the green court, Laville won the point, drawing ahead 5–4 in the tiebreaker, and as the crowd jumped to its feet to applaud, Athena decided it was time. She leaned close, smiling radiantly, and told Saadi she was leaving him. "I'd like an annuity. Let's say a million a year, paid quarterly, for the next ten years."

The Arab started to laugh, but then his face grew pale as he turned away from the tennis to stare at Athena. Despite his European education, his years at an English public school and later at the Sorbonne, Saadi was a suspicious Bedouin at heart. He curled his lip as he snarled at the Princess, "Does this mean you are refusing my offer of marriage?"

"Your mother would never have permitted it. They think me an infidel."

"You don't dare. I took care of your mother's creditors." He grabbed her wrist, but she reached into her bag with her free hand, pulled out a photocopy of a page from *Racquet World*, which she handed to Saadi. The rectangular holes which had once been words showed up clear and black.

"I think you will still take care of them."

"What's this?"

"From your desk."

He stared at it before crumpling it up and thrusting it into his jacket pocket. Today Saadi wore his usual, a white suit from Palm Beach with white shoes and a brilliant red tie. Did he remember carefully slicing the words out of the page, pasting them down on the piece of paper? "What makes you think—"

Athena leaned forward, locked her eyes on Saadi's. "I am not working alone. My partner knows the ins and outs of this. We have your fingerprints on the cover. It was found in your trash basket, in Paris. The subscription was in your name. We have photographs, photocopies."

Saadi looked as if he might faint. "The police will never believe you."

Athena shook her head. "We don't need the police. All we do is leak it to the papers, and to the directors of your companies, and then to the Securities and Exchange Commission. The tennis writers will ruin you. You'll be hooted out of the game."

"What do you want?"

Athena was preparing to leave the box, gathering her possessions. "Koras is about to win. You should have signed him."

The score was 8–7, Koras leading.

Saadi laughed, a dry, mechanical sound. "A half million."

"No. Ten million, paid as indicated. And the loan papers that concern my mother."

Saadi grasped his chair.

To thunderous applause, Laville pulled even. There was dead silence on the next point. After a brilliant exchange, with Laville maneuvering Koras all about the court, Laville won the point, to make it 9–8.

It was now match point. With one ace, Laville could become the American champion. He could prove the hex did not exist. He could stop Koras in his march toward the Grand Slam.

Laville arched his back for the serve. The toss seemed to hang in the air for an interminable moment. He leaped off the ground for maximum leverage as he cracked the ball with a resounding echo that was even louder in the rapt silence of the stadium.

Koras made a courageous dive for it, but it was too late.

Terry Laville was the new U.S. Open champion.

Athena stood with everyone else to applaud the winner, but her tears were for the defeated champion.

"I shall be in touch, Saadi." Feeling terrified and free, Athena left the box, walking proudly.

People were already leaving the stadium as Malone and Muriel started in. He grabbed a man's arm.

"Who won?"

"Laville, the Canadian."

Malone glanced at Muriel and they kept hurrying forward. The jogging made Malone breathe hard, reminding him he wasn't in shape. It was time to give up beer, steak, eggs, Mexican food. People coming out early got in their way. He could see the light coming from the opening, which meant the Stadium Court was just up ahead.

They shoved past two couples, mid-thirties. The women were handsome and well-groomed. The men had corporate haircuts.

"Hey!" one of the men said.

"Sorry! What's going on?"

"Just the presentation."

Malone charged on, through the door, leaving Muriel behind. Down on the court, the presentation was happening. Microphones had been set up. An official was about to hand the trophy over to Terry Laville. Malone could see Archer Bell in his box, and across the court, in his box, was Sally Vicenti. Muriel ran up, red-faced and panting. "There!" He pointed out the Don to Muriel.

Sally Vicenti was having stomach pains, indigestion, pangs shooting up to the center of his chest. He took a heart pill, washed it down with red wine.

Enrico leaned close. "You all right, Sally?"

Sally nodded, coughed. The dizzies came, whirling his head around, and then the flapping of a black window curtain, his mother's house in Borough Park, near the cemetery, the night his father had died. Sally knew he was going to die, soft dark curtains around his face, eyes. The darkness was coming like blinders on a horse, from the dead land.

Then, like magic, the pill worked, a miracle, and Sally opened his eyes to see the crowd, Laville on the court, holding the trophy, Panties Koras standing off to the side, talking to a girl with brown hair, tall and lean, like a college girl. Laville had just made a big mistake and cost Sally a lot of money, winning when he should have lost. And Sally was in trouble.

Two days before, he'd lost a side bet of $500,000 betting on Di Rocca to win the semis. Then he'd been up all night, shifting the pool of $32 million over to Koras to win. Now Laville had overcome his hex and had won his first U.S. Open and there was egg on Sally's face. Losing the money was bad enough. Being out of control was worse. Control was Sally's business, where every act was measured in terms of order and discipline, keeping the ducks in line.

And now in Miami and Chicago and Vegas and Palermo, the capos from the rival families would know Sally had lost his grip. They could take a loss in the millions. They would not take a faulty judgment revealing one of their own out of his depth. There was only one way out—assassinate Koras, right here, as a sign. Use the television to send a message. As he made up his mind and turned to Enrico, Sally had a sickening vision of Koras in front of a hundred microphones, cameras whirring away at the postmatch press conference, confessing to the world about the deal Sally had offered him.

Laville he could take care of afterward, quietly, after Sally found out why Laville had double-crossed him, but Panties Koras was a household word, a big rangy Lithuanian jerk with an honest face. People would believe him. The whole world would believe him.

"Execute it," Sally wheezed.

"Right." Enrico pressed the Talk button on the shortwave, to signal Torelli to proceed.

Police Patrolman "Estevez" was on his feet, like the other twenty thousand spectators, but he was in the shadows at the top of the stadium, right beneath the press box. Everyone else was facing down. He followed the ceremony, and this was what mattered. Terry Laville, the winner, carried the trophy forward. Estevez heard the beep and Enrico telling him to go ahead. He raised the rifle and adjusted the scope until Belynkas appeared in the cross-hairs. At that moment, Terry Laville cut in front, filling the scope. The rifleman swore and more sweat came out on his forehead.

Holding the trophy, Terry Laville walked forward. He was slowly coming out of his trance to hear the ovation from the stadium, underscoring his win over Koras in the finals.

Laville beamed his best smile for the cameras. Now that he had won, Koras would live to fight another day. Playing today, beating Koras, Laville had also beaten the hex. A new day was dawning for Terry Laville. He had won the U.S. Open, fair and square. He had his revenge—he hadn't needed the hit man, after all. By winning, he had actually saved Koras's life. That irony appealed to him. He lifted the cup above his head, offering it symbolically to the public that now shouted his name.

"Laville! Laville! Terry Laville!"

The trophy glinted in the afternoon sun as Laville began a slow circle around the court. The chanting continued. He was halfway around when he spotted Micky Polak coming purposefully toward him. This time Micky wore a shiny red warm-up jacket and seemed to float like a ghost. Laville wanted to run, but his legs wouldn't work. No one else seemed to notice Micky. No, of course they wouldn't—he was a familiar face, with a player's pass. He was closer now, five feet, three feet. He was smiling and speaking Laville's name. Laville. Laville. Or maybe that was the crowd . . .

Laville saw the blade flash in the sun. Funny, because Micky was a gun freak. Everyone knew that. Laville swung the trophy at Micky, who dodged. The knife went in. Then Micky became Armando Reyes; the knife went in again. Laville felt life draining out of him. Armando the Sword. He kicked, landing a good one. Cops were running toward him, jerking guns out. Oh God, if the knife didn't get him, the cops were going to, for using the shotgun in London. As he staggered, Armando stood over him, but it wasn't Armando anymore. It was his brother, the short Peruvian, Leonardo, his face a fallen monument to vengeance and despair.

Laville reached out for the knife that glittered in the sun. He felt a cool breeze, but hardly any pain. The knife flashed again, in slow motion. He heard screams then, and saw the green court coming up to him, and then he was down.

Estevez was about to squeeze off a clean shot into the chest of Pantakoras Belynkas when pandemonium broke out. Officials crowded onto the court as police and paramedics surrounded Laville. Ballboys and ballgirls broke ranks and headed for the entrance. Fans at courtside, unable to move into the aisles, spilled out onto the green deco turf. Two alert-looking security people came up to stand by Koras as a group of four huddled around Laville.

"What's going on?"

"Let's get you to the security area, Mr. Belynkas."

Koras didn't know either of these men. Where had they come from? Where was Rivera? He saw Laure; she had left the box and was racing toward him, with Milo Tigrid behind her.

"Pantakoras!"

"Let her through," Koras said.

Then Laure was in his arms.

Laure went with Pantakoras and the two security men toward the exit leading to the main gate. Spectators jostled them and she could hear Pantakoras talking to Milo. As she glanced up into the stands, she saw a man aiming down at them with a rifle. She screamed just as the man fired. In front of them, one of the bodyguards fell to the ground, clutching his arm. The second security man dropped down by the first, with his gun held in both hands.

"Up there!" she cried, and pointed. There was no one there. Several uniformed officers, their weapons drawn, were working their way toward the spot from which the shot had come.

Milo shoved Pantakoras ahead and grabbed Laure. They headed for the exit, shoving through the crowd.

"Laure! What did he look like?"

"He wore a uniform. Like a flic! Oh, Koras, the police are shooting at you!"

Koras steered them in the opposite direction. "We've got to get out of here." There seemed to be no one they could trust.

Behind them, Milo reached into his equipment bag and brought out a lead-foil wrapper for getting film through a metal detector. Inside was his chrome-plated pistol.

Running through the labyrinth beneath the stadium, Malone knew two things. Number one, Di Rocca had waited too long. Number two, against an experienced mob hitter the only weapon he had was a ball-point pen. Beside him, Muriel was exhausted. "Who are we looking for?"

"The guy Sally hired, the one named Torelli. He's going to kill Koras!"

"But Koras lost."

"Maybe he was supposed to win."

Then, through the crowd, Malone spotted Koras and Tigrid

and the French girl, Laure Puget. They were fifty yards ahead, moving toward the marquee entrance. A cop in an NYPD uniform was behind them, covering their retreat and trying to stay with them.

Koras, Laure, and Milo were passing through a confection area near the Food Village when a vendor with a hand truck loaded with empty Coke bottles lost control. The bottles reeled off the hand truck, shattering as they hit the concrete. Koras pulled Laure out of the way, but the hand truck slammed into Milo.

Milo swore.

"Are you all right?"

Milo stood with difficulty. "You go ahead. I guard your behind."

Koras looked at Laure. "All right. Thanks."

Glass was everywhere. A man with a pushbroom appeared, to start sweeping it up. The Coke vendor got two policemen to detour the crowd around the mess.

Milo looked to be in some pain. He put a hand on his hip, and then took up a position in a vacant hot-dog stand, where he could watch Koras's back.

When he reached ground level, Estevez saw two uniforms coming. Neither one had a rifle, and he knew he would look conspicuous if he kept his. It was a nice weapon. Too bad. He ditched the rifle.

"Who's in charge?" he asked one of the policemen.

"Lucchesi. We're headed for the marquee."

Estevez trotted along with them, his right hand on his holstered pistol.

As Malone and Muriel passed the Food Village, a voice called out. "Ho, you, Malone." Milo stepped away from the shadow.

"Milo, where's Koras?"

The Yugoslav pulled his coat aside to show the butt of his revolver. "I cover their retreat."

Malone moved to him and pointed at the gun. "Can you use that thing?"

"I am trained, I tell you. In the army."

"How long ago?"

"A mere nineteen years."

Malone held out his hand. "Give me the gun, Milo."

With a sheepish look, the Yugoslav handed it over.

Koras and Laure reached the marquee entrance to find a police barrier, sawhorses strung with yellow banners labeled with NYPD in black letters. The crowd had backed up, waiting to be checked by police.

"Damn!" Koras said. They were stuck here.

They shuffled forward with the crowd. Fear was in the air. People kept shoving and pushing, and an officer with a bullhorn was calling for calm.

"Be patient, folks. Just be patient."

When they arrived at the checkpoint, Koras recognized the officer in charge, Lieutenant Lucchesi. Lucchesi looked cool and in control in his three-piece suit. A walkie-talkie crackled in his hand as he beckoned to Koras and Laure.

"When can we get out of here?"

"We're securing the area, Mr. Belynkas. You'll have to wait over there for a minute until we can get a police vehicle in here for you."

Koras began arguing with Lucchesi, who broke off to answer his walkie-talkie. At the same time, he motioned to four uniformed officers, who formed a cordon around Koras and Laure.

Koras was fuming now. He wanted out of here, *now*.

Before they had taken ten steps, Muriel had to stop and rest. Malone was red in the face and breathing hard. Milo grimaced with pain. "Go on," he said. "Go on."

As they stood at the edge of the Food Village, trying to catch their breath, three policemen jogged easily by. One of them, a lean man with a pockmarked face, looked familiar. Where had Malone seen him before?

"How are you feeling?" he asked Muriel.

She nodded but was too winded to speak. Up ahead, people had simply stopped moving.

"What's up there, Milo?"

"The marquee entrance."

Just then, one of the policemen ran through the Food Village, headed back to the stadium. There was something familiar about that one, the way he moved, the efficiency. Malone pulled Milo's chrome-plated pistol from his belt and checked the cylinder to make sure the gun had six bullets.

"Stay with Muriel," he said to Milo.

"Why? What are you—"

Malone was gambling.

Estevez climbed the stairs two at a time. When he reached the rim of the stadium that looked across the tents of the Food Village right onto the marquee entrance, he was breathing deep and easy. Down below, he saw the yellow banners of the police barrier rippling in the breeze, nervous fans backed up a hundred deep and six across at the checkpoint, cops everywhere, a police cruiser stuck in the crowd, nobody able to move. Estevez smiled. He liked panic. By the car, off to the right, he saw his target wearing tennis shorts and a black warm-up jacket. A girl was with him. They were surrounded by four uniforms. One of the uniforms had a rifle. Take him out first. He checked his watch.

Estevez had done shots like this before. He settled into a comfortable shooting position, resting the revolver on the ledge. He took off his cap and aimed at Belynkas.

The last spectators were leaving the stadium as Malone came in. He saw the cop in the uniform high above him, facing out away from the court and toward the parking lot. The sun was hot and Malone was sweating. Sunlight flashed off metal as Malone ran awkwardly up toward the killer atop the wall. His feet felt heavy on the hard concrete steps.

The first bullet hit the policeman with the rifle, the second one slammed into Koras, hitting him in the left arm and shoving him back against the door of the police car. Laure screamed. Koras grabbed her and pulled her to safety behind the car. At the same time, Lucchesi ran over to take command and directed the fire of the policemen to the top of the stadium.

"Okay, now. Keep the shooting steady. No spraying lead."

Two policemen were dragging their downed comrade to safety.

Above them, the shooter fired three fast rounds. Lucchesi swore. It was panic; the crowd shoved against the police barrier and stampeded through the checkpoint. A woman screamed, "Michael!" There were hoarse shouts from the men.

Lucchesi grabbed three officers and pointed up. "Get a squad into the stadium!"

The policemen trotted off, pistols out, muzzles pointed up.

Estevez fired once more, but when they opened up on him from down below, he dropped behind the concrete wall. They hadn't seen anything but his bare head, without the cap, so he figured the uniform might get him out. His gun was still in his hand. Once below the line of sight from the parking lot, he put the policeman's cap back on. Random firing kept up, but passed harmlessly over his head. He hadn't taken two steps before he saw a figure coming up the steps of the stadium.

The man was in his middle forties, with a paunch and a rumpled brown jacket. His face was red from running. His tie was askew. He stood in the shooter's stance, both hands holding a chrome-plated pistol. It was aimed right at him. Estevez knew guns. The piece was a .357 and the man handled himself like he knew a little. Estevez stopped moving, stood there with the police revolver at his side. He only needed a split second. If the man blinked or looked around, he was dead.

Swaying in the hot sun, Malone knew he had never seen eyes colder than these. This was a killer, a reptile. "Put down the piece," he ordered. His voice was harsh from the exhausting chase through the stadium, the climb.

He knew it wouldn't do any good to talk. His man squatted down, at the same time raising his gun and firing. Malone dropped to one knee and fired the .357. The first slug took him in the chest, ramming him backwards. A second shot followed, the killer's gun going off, so Malone, still kneeling, fired again.

The killer dropped the gun, sagged to the metal seats of the bleachers. For a moment, he hung there, the dark wet stain spreading on his chest, and then he toppled over and rolled down three steps onto his back.

For a moment, Malone stood above him with the muzzle of the gun pointed down. He heard shouts below. When he turned, he saw police uniforms entering the stadium. Guns were pointed up at him. Someone with a bullhorn ordered him to throw down his weapon. Malone tossed the gun aside. He was starting to tremble now.

If he had shot the right cop, the tennis killings were over.

TWENTY-FOUR

Milo Tigrid looked at the man in the wheelchair one last time. The chair faced a window that looked out on the world beyond the hospital. Beyond the double panes, the lawns stretched away to the distance in a smooth and silent sheet of immaculate snow, dotted here and there with frozen trees.

Milo left the room.

Behind him, the patient in the wheelchair barely stirred when the door closed. He remembered talking to the "journalist" about a match he had played on a green court somewhere in the past. And then he had gone on to describe, in detail, the match at Flushing Meadow in the waning summer afternoon. The match was over, or was it? He kept meeting his opponent every day, in match after mirrored match, beating him again and again, only to see him rise up, renewed, ready for battle. Then, at last, he would overcome his opponent with heroic effort. His opponent lay beaten. And he himself was lifted up, buoyed by the roar of the crowd, to soar above the stadium.

He shut his eyes, allowed himself to slide into a half sleep, to rest before the next ordeal of a match, only a few hours away. He felt sure of himself, sure of his game, sure of mastery over his opponent. He knew, in his mind, that he would beat Koras once again.

* * *

Milo found Matt Malone talking to a somber young doctor dressed in pea-green hospital clothes, whose name badge read DR. W. SHOUNG.

"It doesn't sound good," Malone said.

Milo thought of the tight bandages around Laville's hands. "What about his hands, doctor?"

"His hands, yes. He used them to shield himself from the knife. Major tendons were severed. In the right hand, he will have partial use. We are hoping for ninety percent in the left."

"And his eyesight?"

"The knife missed his eye while slicing away part of the cheek, so we must assume his eyesight problems are psychologically based. Dr. Shapiro from Psychiatry feels that the patient wishes to construct a world of his own design, and has used this temporary blindness toward those ends."

"He didn't recognize me," Milo said. "He thought I was a journalist."

"He thinks everyone is a journalist," the doctor said, "coming to interview him after his biggest win."

"Jesus," Malone said.

"You mean he'll never recognize anyone again?"

"That is a distinct possibility. His world was evidently distorted before, or he could not have committed those crimes. Now, with the organic brain damage, it may be distorted permanently."

Milo and Malone drove slowly through the park. Malone waited awhile, then said: "Muriel sends regards."

"How is she?"

"Beautiful as ever. She's coming over next week."

Both men were glad to be away from the hospital. "I need a drink, Detective."

"So do I. Point me the way to the nearest watering hole."

They drove through the streets of the small town where the hospital was located until they found the sign: DRINKS, EATS. Malone parked the car and the two men went inside. It was warm, cozy, and almost empty at this time of the day. Malone ordered whiskey, Milo, a martini.

"Did you hear about Di Rocca?" Milo said.

"No. What about Di Rocca?"

"He is in Mexico, they say, with the Princess."

"An unlikely pair."

The drinks came and the two friends toasted. "To Swash, then, a noble animal."

"I shall one day teach him to play tennis," Milo said.

Malone laughed. "Did they ever figure out who sent that threat note?"

Milo shook his head. "I wouldn't know. I think Laville sent it, to throw off the cops, after he killed Polak."

"I put my money on Saadi, to goose the numbers for Sahara."

Milo sipped his drink, made an appreciative face. "And you. Did you ever achieve your money from Mr. Bell?"

"I got the last payment just before I headed out for Paris. He threatened to take me to court, until I told him what was on that tape and showed him the photos of his boy Laville talking to Sally Vicenti."

"I always wanted to be a policeman," Milo confessed. "In order to wield vast power with a just hand. As a boy, I was a fan of Sherlock Holmes, you know."

"You could go into partnership with me. Milo and Malone, intercontinental investigations."

Milo nodded, then looked away. "They say that your American underworld is filled with hordes of beautiful women, waiting to be rescued. Alas, I have this television station to run."

Outside, it was snowing again. They looked through the window as the cars ploughed along, down the street.

"What's your next tournament?" Matt asked.

"The Masters, in New York. But that one, I fear, is my last."

"You said that about the Open. I saw them quote you on TV."

Milo sighed, signaled for two more drinks. "B.J. keeps after me to quit, so that we can snuggle together in her Lear Jet. I think that now I play mostly doubles, with some young tiger who can run down the lobs."

"How is B.J.?"

"Ferocious. She wishes to invite you for dinner."

"Done. If we get back to New York."

Milo settled into the booth. The fresh round of drinks came.

"There is no need to leave when the blizzards rage. Once, in the mountains outside Sarajevo, I was snowed in for a week. My only companion was a girl of twenty, an American student named Drusilla. It was a lovely time."

The two men touched glasses. It was good to be inside, safe from the cold, with a friend.

Mrs. Pantakoras Belynkas was working on her thesis about the Celtic connections to the Grail Legend in the huge library at Court's Court in Westhampton, when the phone rang. It was Athena, who was in Puerto Vallarta with "a friend." Athena was calling to find out the news. As the exiled queen of the tennis groupies, she missed the circuit gossip.

What about Laure and Koras, Athena wanted to know. How was marriage? Where had they been? Where were they going?

"We are just back from Brussels," Laure said. "Koras won the European Champions championship. He beat Davey Cooper in four sets."

"His arm must be better."

"He groans at night, to get my sympathy. But the doctor says he is fit again."

"A stubborn man heals more quickly, they say. How goes the archaeology?"

"My thesis is almost done. Koras has a friend at a university press who is interested in seeing it, perhaps for publication."

"You have it all, my dear. Brains. Attraction. A good man."

"And what about you? What are you up to, with your mysterious lover?"

"We are investing in a hotel in Puerto Vallarta."

"Is it Jack Di Rocca? Everyone thinks so."

"An amazing man," Athena said. "He touches things, they turn to money."

"Oh, Athena, it's you with the Midas touch."

"I try, my dear. Is there news of Saadi?"

"The last we heard he was in Damascus."

"I wish nothing but the best for his mother. Her prejudice saved me from a grisly life in the harem." Athena paused. "When are you inviting me to your house?"

"Oh, please come. Whenever you get to New York."

"Christmas, I spend in Austria. January, in Mexico. April, I think, for New York."

"I'd love to see you."

"You should consult Pantakoras, make certain I won't be intruding, like the Witch of the West. Where is he, anyway?"

"Oh, on the inner court, working out with Will Channer."

"The ageless champion."

"How is the weather in Mexico?" Laure asked.

"It is raining, always raining. And then the sun comes out, there is dust, and one swelters. Ah, well, give my love to Pantakoras."

"I shall. Goodbye, Athena."

"Goodbye, cousin."

Before going back to her writing, Laure poured herself a fresh cup of coffee. She worked another hour. The old Lithuanian cook could be heard in the kitchen, preparing lunch. Pantakoras was punctual and liked to eat at one sharp.

Outside, the security patrol drove by. Hired by Frank Fenwick, they had been on duty ever since the incidents in late summer, at the U.S. Open, when a man shot Pantakoras in the arm.

The police had arrested a gangster named Sally Vicenti. He was still awaiting trial, as was the distraught Leonardo Reyes, for his knife attack on Terry Laville. Everyone on the circuit now knew that it was Terry who had killed poor Mikhail Polak.

There were guests for lunch—Will Channer, looking pink-faced from his workout; Frank Fenwick, who had driven out from his New York office with a new endorsement contract for Pantakoras; Milo Tigrid, in town for the Masters tournament; Muriel Broussard-Gauthier, who had flown over from Paris to confer with her publisher; and Matt Malone, the "writer" who had turned out to be a detective, but whom everyone preferred to think of as the investigator who had saved Koras's life, and Laure's. He would always be welcome in her house.

Most of the talk around the table was of a rising young player named Henrik Heinz, from Switzerland, nicknamed The Hammer for the powerful way he hit the ball. Frank Fenwick wanted to form a corporation to finance him. He wanted Milo and Pantakoras to invest, but he spoke mostly to Laure, who was handling more and more of the finances for her husband.

Laure had to admire Fenwick's financial acumen. He had had the foresight to insure Pantakoras with Lloyds of London against any "unforeseen" event that might hamper his playing career. When the sniper wounded Koras in the arm, Fenwick had made claims, and they had been awarded $750,000 in damages. And the day following the incident, Fenwick had negotiated a book contract for Pantakoras. The advance had been two million dollars, as much as Pantakoras would have made winning his Grand Slam. Finally, Fenwick's lawyers had stymied any claims for repayment of notes held by Sally Vicenti, who had been pressuring her husband about some outstanding construction loans. Thinking back to the money Koras had given her for the Alesia excavations, Laure could only shake her head at the way he handled money.

"We can't lose, folks. It's an investment in the future."

"Bah, F.F.! Here we sit, surrounded by two beautiful women who *have* to be Montenegrin, and you talk only of money." Milo patted Laure on the hand and winked at Muriel. "Where is your romance, my good man?"

"I am not a Montenegrin, Milo," Laure said.

"Nor am I," said Muriel.

"All beautiful women have some Yugoslavian blood, whether they know it or not. If you have the misfortune not to be born in Yugoslavia, we can make you honorary citizens. I, Tigrid, will arrange."

Laughter around the table.

"What percentages are we speaking of, F.F.?" Laure asked. She was a shopkeeper's daughter, with a sharp eye for numbers and investments. Already, she had studied the stock market and had nudged Pantakoras into two different stock buys that had appreciated in value. With the profits, she had bought herself a personal computer—the one she had wanted for years to facilitate her work—and used it to keep track of the investments of Koras, Inc., the new company he had formed.

"See," Fenwick said to Koras. "Laure understands what I'm talking about here."

"In my wife's veins runs the blood of many generations of Celtic accountants."

Laure kissed her husband on the cheek. Later, when lunch was over, she would quietly get together with F.F. and go over the details of the new venture. Pantakoras was an artist, temperamental, creative. He preferred to spend money and let someone else keep tabs on what he had spent. He had no time for planning. In this family, Laure had the head for business.

"Pass me the chicken," Milo roared. "This money talk makes me hungry."

Laure passed the *poulet sauté à la Bercy* to Milo. Over the steaming platter, she saw the eyes of her husband, gazing at her. He smiled, and she smiled back, and as she did so she felt the stirring, deep within herself, of a new life. Pantakoras winked and looked at her with love, making Laure blush. She knew that look. It meant he wanted her. And this afternoon, after they had made love, she would tell him about the child that stirred in her womb, the one they had made together.

And for a while, life would be truly beautiful.